WHITE LAAGER

The Rise of Afrikaner Nationalism

IN THE old days of native wars Voortrekkers drew their
wagons into a circle or *laager*. Within its protection men
defended themselves against the impis of the Zulus or the
Matabele. Today their descendants seek to retreat within a
new *laager* made up of laws and restraints as if they could thereby
be protected against the turmoil of a multi-racial society.

CORNELIS WILLEM DE KIEWIET, *The Anatomy of South African Misery*

WHITE LAAGER

The Rise of Afrikaner Nationalism

William Henry Vatcher Jr.

FREDERICK A. PRAEGER, *Publishers*
New York · Washington · London

The quotation from *Jan Smuts: A Biography,*
by F. S. Crafford (© 1943 Doubleday and Company, Inc.),
is reprinted by permission of the publisher.
Figure 2, 'The man who really won the election',
is reprinted by permission of *Die Burger.*
Figure 7, 'Wind of Change', is reprinted by
permission of the *Johannesburg Sunday Times.*
Figure 12, 'South African Realities' (© Punch 1958),
is reprinted by permission of the proprietors.
Figure 13, 'Brooders', is reprinted by permission
of the *Rand Daily Mail.*

FREDERICK A. PRAEGER, *Publishers*
111 Fourth Avenue, New York 3, N.Y., U.S.A.
77–79 Charlotte Street, London W.1, England

Published in the United States of America in 1965
by Frederick A. Praeger, Inc., Publishers

Library of Congress Catalog Card Number: 65-12064

Printed in the United States of America

Preface

NATIONALISM HAS PLAYED as significant a role in the internal political life of South Africa as it has on the international scene. And understandably so, for South Africa is a world in miniature—a land of sharp human contrasts, whose inhabitants speak various languages and represent many races, religions, and cultures, each of which acts upon and reacts to the others in its own way. Today, the Afrikaners, with their intense national pride and self-consciousness, are the dominant human element in South Africa; they control the government of the country and are conducting human experiments the outcome of which will determine the future of the Afrikaners themselves and of all their compatriots, both black and white.

It is the purpose of this study to examine the forces that have contributed to the development of Afrikaner nationalism and that have dictated the course it has taken. Though some incidental expressions of praise or blame may be found in these pages, the intent of the writer has been to describe, not to endorse or condemn.

The writer is a political scientist and makes no claim to be an historian, although he has found it necessary to draw on history to support his thesis. The first part of this book depends primarily on secondary sources; the rest is based on material obtained in South Africa in 1955–56 and in 1960–61. Sources include the author's own firsthand observations and interviews with persons associated, directly or indirectly, with the Afrikaner nationalist movement, as well as the written record. These observations and interviews were possible only through the co-operation of a host of people, too numerous to list here, who placed their experience and knowledge at the author's disposal. Any merits the book may have are attributable to their patience and generosity.

In the preparation of the manuscript, the writer was assisted by the Hoover Institution on War, Revolution, and Peace at Stanford University, and he especially wishes to express his gratitude to Dr W. Glenn Campbell, the Director of the Hoover Institution, and Dr Peter Duignan, the Curator of the African Collection. He is indebted to Mr Daryle M. Webb of San José State College for his help in the preparation of the illustrations.

William Henry Vatcher, Jr.

Hoover Institution on War, Revolution, and Peace
Stanford University

Contents

Preface		*v*
Introduction		*ix*

PART ONE: THE STRUGGLE FOR INDEPENDENCE

| 1 | Exodus | 3 |
| 2 | Hemmed in a Kraal | 17 |

PART TWO: THE STRUGGLE FOR SUPREMACY

3	They Fall to Rise	33
4	Resurgence	40
5	The Impact of Nazism	58
6	Organizing for Victory: The Afrikaner Broederbond (AB)	76
7	Cultural Offensive	89
8	The Political Offensive: The National Party (NP)	117

PART THREE: ENTRENCHMENT

9	Nationalism Militant	133
10	Apartheid: The Unclosable Gap	148
11	Republic: Climax of a Destiny	169
12	Conclusion	177

Notes	*181*
Bibliography	*193*
Appendices	*243*
Index	*303*

Illustrations

Figure

1   Sir Paul Kruger   22

2   'The man who really won the election'   62

3   Chain of Influence of the Afrikaner Broederbond during the
        second world war   84

4   Organization of the FAK   91

5   Organization of the NGK   113

6   Organization of the National Party   124

7   'Wind of Change'   143

8   Parliamentary Evolution of the National Party   145

9   Native Reserves as established at present   153

10 Consolidation of Native Reserves as envisaged in the Tomlinson
        Commission Report   153

11 The Application of Apartheid in Cities Within Areas Designated White 159

12 'South African Realities'   165

13 'Brooders'   175

Introduction

And He brought forth his people with joy, and His chosen with gladness: and gave them the lands of the heathen: and they inherited the labour of the people.

PSALM 105 : 43–44

AFRIKANER NATIONALISM IS the classic form of all the nationalisms that now flourish on the continent of Africa. It possesses the necessary ingredients: in Afrikaans, a corruption of the Dutch spoken by the early settlers, the Afrikaners have a common language; in Calvinism, of a type little changed by the centuries, a common religion; in their history, a common experience dating back to the seventeenth century. They even have a common ethnic origin—basically Dutch mixed with French, German, and, though it is never admitted, African. Unlike most of the nationalisms of modern Africa, Afrikaner nationalism originated before the twentieth century, and, unlike most nationalists, the Afrikaners have had to share their homeland with a host of highly contrasting ethnic groups.[1] Afrikaner nationalism has had no fatherland that it could in honesty call its very own—a factor that has been a source of embarrassment and annoyance to its leaders. Whereas most nationalisms are nurtured on fear of threats from without, Afrikaner nationalism has developed in response to threats from within the nation. This fact has given it something of an air of impermanence, if not discomfort.

The intermingling of disparate elements generally results in instability and the likelihood of conflict. Throughout the history of South Africa, weaker groups have been held down by stronger ones: Bushmen by Hottentots; Hottentots by Bantu and Europeans; Bantu, Coloureds, and Indians by Afrikaners and Britons (that is, English-speaking South Africans); Afrikaners by Britons, and, for the moment at any rate, all other groups by Afrikaners.

In the long run, intermingling tends to lead to assimilation, the final product of which blends the contributions of the various groups according to the strength of each. How long such a process takes depends on the amount of resistance offered by any of the contributing groups. The presence or absence of resistance in any particular case is determined by the depth of group consciousness and by the seriousness with which the group considers itself threatened. The greater the danger, the more intense the reaction and the greater the resistance to assimilation. Once group consciousness or self-realization is awakened, introversion and ethnocentrism develop among group members and are manifested as loyalty to the group.

ix

There is a rediscovery of the group's past, especially of those aspects that inculcate a pride in belonging to it. Nationalism finds expression in the creation and manipulation of symbols such as flags, statues, monuments, music, and poetry; in the discovery of national heroes; in eulogies of group institutions; and in an almost pathetic attachment to language. Fanatic leaders emerge to fire loyalty and rally members to the cause.

The Afrikaners saw no threat in either the Hottentots, the Bushmen, or the Bantu groups. All of these had a less advanced culture and an inferior technology, especially the Bantu, when the Afrikaners first encountered them. It was only after the advent of the British, with their all-too-evident cultural and technological superiority, that the Afrikaners perceived their institutions and way of life as dangerously threatened, and began to develop a consciousness of belonging to a group and to rally in defense of *ons eie* (our own). As is generally the case, the lead was taken by an extreme wing that was especially sensitive to the threat and that perceived the danger most acutely. From the beginning of the British occupancy in 1795 until the present day, the Afrikaner right wing has been the *primum mobile* of Afrikaner nationalism and has created the pattern that it has followed.

The first hostile responses to the British were made by isolated groups of Afrikaners; they did not become general until the perception of danger spread to Afrikaners everywhere. It was then—as Afrikaners began to seek strength from their past, became aware of the ties of blood, and rallied around their language, their religion, and their way of life—that Afrikaner nationalism became an impressive force in South African politics.

Part One:

THE STRUGGLE
FOR INDEPENDENCE

I   Exodus

Now there arose up a new king over Egypt, which knew not Joseph.

EXODUS I : 8

EUROPEANS BEGAN SETTLING in sub-Saharan Africa in the middle of the seventeenth century; it was only a question of time before they came into conflict with the native Africans, especially after land to which either group could migrate undisturbed was gone and intergroup contacts perforce increased.   Before the arrival of the Europeans, the Bushmen had been able to maintain their own identity in the face of the Hottentots because there was plenty of unoccupied land to which they could retreat.   In their turn, the Hottentots were able to maintain their identity and escape absorption by the Bantu in the same way.   When the Europeans arrived, they upset the direction of population movements and reduced the amount of land available for other groups.   When peoples with cultures at different levels of development come face to face, the less developed culture tends to be absorbed by the more highly developed one, and the people associated with the former are assigned, temporarily at least, an inferior place in the emerging society.

The Hottentots at first remained cautiously aloof from the Dutch. Later, many Hottentots were absorbed by the European community as workers on Dutch farms and in Dutch households.   Some miscegenation naturally took place.   The Bantu were encountered later.   Their more advanced cultural development and their numerical strength and more warlike attitude made them a greater potential threat to the Afrikaners than either the Hottentots or the Bushmen.

But the greatest threat to the Afrikaner, or Boer, did not come from any group native to Africa, but rather from Europe.   The English brought with them a culture that, in relation to that of the Afrikaner, was undeniably superior.   By the time the English arrived in 1795, the culture of the Afrikaners had lagged far behind that of Europe.   Isolation, association with primitive peoples, and their strict Calvinism had caused a cultural retrogression.   This was particularly true in the case of those on the periphery of the settled areas, who depended upon a pastoral subsistence economy.   But, by 1795, the Dutch, now fully at home in South Africa,

3

looked upon the English as intruders who could lay no rightful claim to any share of control of South Africa. Yet the English possessed a superior culture, manifested in a more highly developed and complex pattern of existence. The relationship between English and Dutch paralleled the earlier relationships between the various African groups and between the Dutch and the Africans. The Dutch, with their deteriorated status, might expect to be absorbed by the English community and be given an inferior place in the emerging society equivalent to their cultural and technical contributions to it. Some of the Dutch, however, proudly and stubbornly refused to admit to any inferiority, and rejected any move toward co-operation. Thus the way was paved for an eventual clash. Gandhi once remarked of English-Dutch relationships: 'Their characters and ambitions were similar. Pots from the same pottery are often likely to clash against each other.'[1] In time such clashes drew the Boers closely together, forced them to define their attitudes, and produced a togetherness and sense of belonging and, more especially, a determination to overcome their inferior status. Historically, it is the British who have been the Afrikaners' *bête noire*. The Afrikaners have traditionally regarded the Africans as completely outside the political structure of South African society.

The Rule of the Dutch East India Company.

Until 1795, the Cape was a station of the Dutch East India Company and was administered by officials of the Company. As the number of permanent settlers at the station increased, its territory expanded, to Stellenbosch beyond the Cape Flats, then to the Berg River Valley and beyond. Some of the 15,000 Europeans who were living at the Cape in 1795 were occupying lands hundreds of miles from Cape Town; and, by that time, Company control beyond the immediate area of Cape Town was nominal. By that time, too, most of the Europeans had come to regard South Africa as their only home. Even their language had deviated from the Dutch spoken in the Netherlands and by their Dutch overlords. The Europeans could be classified according to their degree of proximity to Cape Town, the only city of any importance. Those who lived in Cape Town were mostly Company servants. On the periphery of Cape Town were farmers, or *boers*, who either worked for or did business with the Company. Many of them had large numbers of slaves and Hottentots to work their lands. Still further from Cape Town lived the pastoral, seminomadic, farmers, known as the *Trekboers*, who comprised about half the white population. Conditions in and around Cape Town encouraged migration into the hinterland. The Cape Town market was glutted with agricultural goods. Slaves did the work of the colony, reducing opportunities for Europeans. Then, too, land was plentiful, and any free man could acquire a 6,000-acre farm simply by paying the Company a yearly fee. Moreover, it became customary for each of the (frequently numerous) sons of a Trekboer family to acquire his own large farm. Thus, the Trekboer holdings continuously increased. The Trekboers lived in almost complete isolation, and both the Dutch East

India Company and, later, the British administration had the greatest difficulty in controlling them. The development of Afrikaner nationalism was strongly influenced by the attitudes of the Trekboers and their descendants.

The Dutch East India Company did very little for the Trekboers, and as time progressed it could do less and less. Their almost complete isolation and freedom from external control produced an inbred culture, where information could be obtained only from tradition and from hard experience. To the Trekboers, the basis of human knowledge was the Bible, their *Goeie Boek*. In the Bible they found remarkable parallels to their own situation. Like the children of Israel seeking the Promised Land, the seventeenth-century Dutch settlers removed themselves to the promises of the Cape. They were able to liken the Hottentots and slaves, and later the Bushmen and Bantu, to the Amalekites, heathens who could rightfully be 'smitten before the Lord'. In the view of the Dutch settlers, the pagans were pre-destined to serve the white man, to be 'hewers of wood and drawers of water'. They believed these heathens to be descended from Ham: 'cursed by Canaan, a servant of servants shall he be to his brethren'. From Calvinism, the Afrikaners took their belief in predestination and the infallibility of the Bible. Strict Puritans, the early Boers read the Bible daily by the light of heavy tallow candles, and accepted its teachings literally, particularly those of the Old Testament. Felix Gross has said:

> Here were people separated by several days' journey from their nearest neighbour, self-dependent, rulers over their thousands of acres, a law unto themselves, who were happy in their voluntary isolation though deprived of even the simplest amenities of life.[2]

Dr M. H. K. Lichtenstein, who traveled in Southern Africa in the years 1803–6, has given us some indication of the results of such lengthy isolation:

> Without the restoration of some severe civil regulations, and the introduction of some intermediate authority, which could constantly watch over the people, it seemed inevitable that each generation would go backwards in civilization and that they would at last sink nearly as low as . . . the former savage inhabitants.[3]

The characteristics that the Afrikaner first acquired under Dutch East India Company rule proved too durable for either time or the British to erase.

The Great Trek

It was the Napoleonic wars in Europe that brought the Briton to South Africa as ruler and settler, and it was the advent of the British that was to prove a significant source of annoyance to the Afrikaners, especially to the Trekboers, used to living undisturbed by interfering administrators. Between 1795, when the British first occupied the Cape, and the Anglo-Boer War in 1899, the more intransigent Boers regarded the British as increasingly meddlesome interlopers. It was a period of conflicts, in which Afrikaners sought to escape British control, and the British constantly questioned how far, territorially, their authority extended. It was a period in which the Boers established firm contacts with the southward and westward moving stream of migratory Bantu. Such experiences hardened and crystallized Afrikaner attitudes and philosophy, and caused Afrikaners to *laager*, as it were, in defense of their common interests.

The British occupation of the Cape in 1795 was carried out at the request of the Prince of Orange, who had been driven into exile when Napoleon's armies overran the Netherlands. The British maintained a caretaker status for the exiled Prince until 1803, when the Batavian Republic was established, and the Cape was turned over to it. However, when the Batavian Republic allied itself with France in 1806, the British again occupied the Cape; it was formally ceded to them in 1814.

In 1795, there were fewer than fifty British settlers in the Cape. In 1803, there were fewer than a hundred. The Afrikaner population was by this time approaching 60,000.[4]

Thus, except for the years 1803–6, the British were politically dominant in South Africa, to a greater or less extent, from 1795 until May 31, 1961. At first, South Africa was for the British merely a stopping point for ships to and from their Asian possessions. The new British administrators were, however, somewhat more energetic in their efforts to control South Africa than their Dutch predecessors. Along with the British system of government, they introduced organization, respect for law and order, and uncomfortable insistence on law enforcement. These attitudes of their alien overlords were incomprehensible to the Boers.

In 1820, the British Parliament appropriated £50,000 to subsidize the migration of some 5,000 British settlers to South Africa as a means of relieving an acute postwar unemployment problem. The settlers landed in the area where Port Elizabeth now stands and were granted 100-acre plots of land on the western side of the Fish River, in an area known as the Zuurveld, to form a barrier against marauding Bantu tribes. These were the only government-sponsored British settlers ever sent to South Africa and, today, many English-speaking South Africans trace their descent from them. It was not long before most of the 1820 settlers abandoned their farms for the towns, especially Port Elizabeth and Grahamstown, thereby sharpening the distinction already existing between the Afrikaner farmer and the urban Britisher. It was the migratory Afrikaner farmer who opened up the interior and there implanted his institutions, not the urban Britisher.

The emancipation movement influential in Britain in the early nineteenth century soon spread to South Africa. The British Parliament abolished the slave trade in 1807, and slavery itself in 1834. Such actions had a fundamental effect on the Afrikaner attitude to the British, as did the preachments of the London Missionary Society, and especially of one of its most prominent members, Dr John Philip.[5] Sarah Gertrude Millin has written, 'to this day the missionary is to the Boer the fundamental traitor, the white man who stands for black against white'.[6] Missionary zeal and the efforts of the Government to extend its authority over the colony seemed to coincide. The Afrikaners had from the beginning endeavored to maintain a distance between the coloureds (those with mixed blood) and whites and, prior to the so-called Charter of Justice of 1828—the famous Ordinance 50—the Hottentots had to carry passes in moving from one area to another. Slaves were of course treated as personal property. But Ordinance 50 eliminated passes for the Hottentots, and abolished the offence of vagrancy. Thereafter, the Hottentots lost their identity as a group and became a part of a rapidly growing group known as the Cape Coloureds. The complexities of race were beginning to manifest themselves. By 1834, the population of the Cape included whites, Asian and African slaves of various origins, Hottentots, and people of mixed descent; on the periphery of the settled areas, the Trekboers had been in contact with the advancing waves of Bantu tribes since the 1770s. Later, Boer-Bantu relationships were to become as significant in South African history as those of Boer and Briton.

The Dutch East India Company had set the Fish River, some eight hundred miles from Cape Town, as the eastern boundary of Cape Colony. The British accepted the boundary, but the Boers, always looking for richer lands and eyeing the Bantu cattle, and the Bantu, pushed by tribal wars and demanding the same natural resources as the Boers—water, grass, soil— were bound to conflict in the border areas. The Boers, with their superior technology, were bound to win. The competition of the two groups for land led to periodic outbreaks, known as the Kaffir Wars, in which the Boers, equipped with rifles, horses, and wheels, were able to overwhelm the Bantu. Since they could not rely on either the Dutch East India Company or the British for help, the Boers learned how to handle frontier problems in their own way and formed the Commando, a mounted field force that served as their own military arm.

Boer and Bantu had much in common, in that both were pastoral herders. As the Europeans advanced, Boer and Bantu gradually came to occupy the same areas, with Bantu living on Boer farms and continuing to herd cattle. Until the middle of the nineteenth century Boer–Bantu relationships were those of two independent groups. Later, they became more and more those of ruler and ruled. As time went on, the Bantu were more and more absorbed rather than pushed back, living as squatters on land controlled by the Boers or working as laborers for them. As de Kiewiet has observed, the only thing the Bantu lost by absorption (in its early stages) was their independent status.

The British made strenuous efforts to force the Afrikaners to conform to British colonial policy. Under the governorship of Lord Charles Somerset (1814–26) there was a growing insistence on anglicizing the Afrikaners, and on making English the principal medium of communication— a campaign that was certainly disagreeable to the Boers, as were the similar efforts of Lord Milner after the Anglo-Boer War.[7] Such efforts to anglicize them, together with British insistence on law enforcement, the abolition of slavery and the slave trade, Ordinance 50, the humiliation of having to answer in court to charges brought by non-Europeans, the British attempt

7

to establish a fixed boundary to the colony, and the substitution of sale at auction for grants of free land—all produced increasing frustration among the Boers. One of the principal local manifestations of discontent was the Slagtersnek Rebellion of 1815, which resulted from an attempt by a circuit judge to try an Afrikaner for maltreatment of his Hottentot servants. To the Boer, especially the Trekboer, such matters were outside the purview of the law. Anna Steenkamp, a Voortrekker (that is, one who took part in the Great Trek), wrote that racial equality was 'contrary to the laws of God and the natural distinctions of race and religion'. Piet Retief, a Voortrekker leader, demanded that 'proper relations' must be preserved 'between master and servant'.

It was such circumstances that convinced many Afrikaners that they should leave the British-controlled area in favor of a land where they could live unmolested. Certainly, the reasons for the exodus or massive hiving known as the Great Trek were much deeper than the British were able to admit. It was the growing gulf in all religious and political questions that provoked the Afrikaners to leave: the liberal tendencies of the British toward the Africans and Coloureds, the exclusion of the Afrikaners from participation in government, and basic differences between Boer and British culture. Stubborn British contempt for anything non-British, coupled with British liberalism and power politics, contrasted with the Afrikaner's urge for individual freedom.

The Great Trek greatly influenced the development of Afrikaner nationalism. It became a symbol of defense of everything the Voortrekkers believed to be right. The Voortrekkers became the spearhead of Afrikaner resistance. The Great Trek was a traumatic experience, and reflected the determination of the Boers to live according to their own belief.[8] Their resolve was expressed by Piet Retief, one of the ablest Voortrekker leaders. 'We quit this colony,' he declared, 'under the full assurance that the English government will allow us to govern ourselves without its interference.'[9] One Afrikaner well-wisher not participating in the Trek expressed the hope that 'although parted by distance, they should ever remain united in heart'.[10]

Between 1835 and 1843, some 12,000 Afrikaners, about one-fourth of those living in Cape Colony, inspanned their oxen to their covered wagons and, with their wives, children, servants, cattle, and sheep, 'quit' British control. One group moved around territory that the British had demarcated as African to Natal, establishing in 1839 the Republic of Natalia with its capital at Pietermaritzburg. Another wave crossed the Orange and Vaal rivers and eventually founded the Orange Free State between the Orange and the Vaal and the South African Republic (Transvaal) beyond the Vaal.

Until 1899, British-Voortrekker relations reflected vacillation on the part of the British and a determination to remain free of British control on the part of the Boers. The Afrikaner Voortrekkers had moved beyond the British-controlled and British-established boundaries, and the British were unsure of the legitimacy of their continued authority over them. They were baffled and perplexed. Should they attempt to control these defected subjects, or ignore them? Until the Anglo-Boer War, the question remained unanswered. In accordance with their philosophy of the rule of law, the British manifested an obvious concern for correctness in their dealings with the Voortrekkers; however, they were also swayed by the 'imperial factor', which played a prominent role during the latter part of the nineteenth century, by the zeal of missionary organizations bent on bringing salvation to the heathen, by the discovery of diamonds and gold, and, in the latter part of the century, by apprehension as to the territorial ambitions of the Germans who loomed threateningly in the background.

The Zulus in Natal and the Matabele in the high veld constituted a threat to the Boer emigrants. On February 6, 1838, Piet Retief and his party were massacred by the Zulu chief Dingaan. On February 16, another Afrikaner party was wiped out at Bloukrans. On December 16, 1838, Andries Pretorius led 460 Afrikaners against 11,000 of Dingaan's warriors to inflict a devastating revenge that broke the Zulu power. The river where the battle took place was renamed Blood River, and it has become a symbol of determined Afrikaner resistance in the face of overwhelming odds.[11]

After Blood River, the Voortrekkers were free to stake out claims in Natal. They remained there until the British, after a period of indecision, used an attack by a Boer Commando on the Pondo, who were in a treaty relationship with the British, as an excuse to intervene. There was some fighting between the Boers and British, but most of the former finally rejoined their fellow Voortrekkers north of the Vaal river. The British annexed Natal in 1843, and the Voortrekkers lost their sea outlet.

In the 1840s, the territory between the Orange and Vaal rivers was occupied by Afrikaners, Africans led by Moshesh,* and a people of mixed white and Hottentot descent known as Griquas. The Griquas were divided into the West Griquas, whose chief was Andries Waterboer, and East Griquas, whose chief was Adam Kok III. The British made treaties with Waterboer, Kok, and Moshesh in order to keep peace along the Orange river. In 1846, the British became involved in a war with the Bantu on the eastern frontier of Cape Colony—a war that erupted as a result of drought and colonial demands for land. Sir Harry Smith, who became governor of the Cape in 1847, decided to carve up Kaffirland, as the area beyond the eastern frontier was called, into Victoria East, a new district for Cape Colony, and British Kaffraria, a new crown colony, thus eliminating the old eastern frontier altogether. In 1848, Smith made the bold decision to annex the territory between the Orange and the Vaal rivers and constitute it as the Orange River Sovereignty, an action displeasing to Boers on both sides of the Vaal. Sir Harry Smith reflected British attitudes in a letter to a Voortrekker, Andries Hendrik Potgieter, dated June 2, 1848, in which he referred to his proclamations, and noted that these were published 'for the benefit of all

* Various groups who had survived the Matabele massacres of the early nineteenth century were unified by Moshesh to form the Basuto.

who have become emigrants—for no subject of any country can divest himself of the allegiance he owes his country. You are all, and must for ever be, British subjects'. Sir Harry was answering a manifesto signed by 1,050 Voortrekkers that entreated the governor 'to leave us at peace and without further interference upon lands we have honestly procured from the lawful proprietors'.[12]

The British Colonial Secretary, who was concerned about expense, accepted the acquisitions regretfully. However, the move had the effect of capturing another portion of the land occupied by the Trekkers, and the draft constitution of the Orange River Sovereignty looked forward hopefully to a united South Africa under one flag. These hopes were shattered, however, when a new British governor agreed to the Sand River Convention of 1852, which recognized the independence of the Boers beyond the Vaal river, and to the Bloemfontein Convention of 1854, by which the British sovereignty beyond the Orange river was abandoned.

Insulated from outside opinion, the Orange Free State and the South African Republic developed along their own lines. Calvinist dogma and Boer biblical interpretations flourished. There were no succeeding waves of emigrants to bring new blood and new ideas to invigorate the stock as there were in the American westward movement; and inbreeding of philosophy, religion, and outlook resulted in the stereotyping of ideas. The extremest forms of the Boer philosophy and way of life predominated in the interior, only to flow back at a later date to the areas from which the Voortrekkers had come.

Until the mid-nineteenth century, the economy of South Africa was based primarily on trade, farming, and livestock. The colonies of the Cape and Natal were somewhat more prosperous than the Boer republics because of their maritime outlets and traffic. Cape Town, and later East London, Port Elizabeth, and Durban, still derived benefit from the East Indian trade. Wool and hides were the only moneymakers. The grain and wine industries were faring poorly. The climate of Natal was favorable for sugar cultivation, and after 1860 the English imported Indians to work the cane fields.

The Indians worked as indentured laborers for five years, after which they could renew their contracts, return to India, or remain in Natal as free men and receive crown lands or cash equivalent to the price of passage to India. Most elected to remain, and by 1874 there were some 30,000 free Indians in Natal. The indentured Indians were low caste, illiterate Hindus. They were followed by free Muslim traders, who created a source of intraracial strife. By 1960, the number of Indians in South Africa was nearly half a million. Their effect on Afrikaner nationalism was negligible until they began to compete with the Afrikaner economically and, more recently, politically. Most of the Indian population remains in Natal, which traditionally has had a pronounced pro-British orientation. The Indians have never been permitted to take up residence in the Orange Free State; a few entered the Transvaal during the gold scramble and their descendants remain there, but no newcomers are now allowed to become permanent residents.

Until the latter part of the nineteenth century immigration from Europe was a mere trickle, save for the 5,000 British settlers of 1820, 4,300 laborers who arrived in the period 1844–47, and some 12,000 British and German settlers who came during the governorship of Sir George Grey (1857–62), a staunch advocate of large-scale white immigration. Conditions in South Africa did not attract immigrants: the abundance of cheap African labor all but eliminated any demand for unskilled European laborers, and soil and climate precluded intensive agriculture. Thus, in the nineteenth century as in the 1960s, employment opportunities for the unskilled immigrant to South Africa were relatively few, and the waves of European emigrants seeking new homes passed South Africa by in favor of Australia, New Zealand, and the Americas. In recent years, moreover, a highly selective immigration policy has kept out non-Europeans and indeed Europeans from southern and eastern Europe.

Meanwhile, relations between the European population and the Bantu were becoming fixed into the pattern familiar today. The Kaffir Wars resulted in a gradual loss of Bantu independence, and the release of a vast reservoir of cheap labor. The whites came to rely on this Bantu labor, at first tapped for the Trekboer farms, then for the diamond fields, later for the gold mines, then to supply domestics; today, in addition, Africans are engaged in factory work.

The Growth of the Republics

The events of the latter half of the nineteenth century intensified the mutual hostility between Boer and Briton, and eventually led to a war that ignited a fiery Afrikaner nationalism which has still to run its course. Until 1888, the Orange Free State displayed a much less intransigent attitude toward the British than its fellow-republic north of the Vaal; and indeed the Transvaal Afrikaners proved to be the most determined early leaders of resistance to any form of British control. Thus, it would seem that the degree of resistance was proportionate to the distance from Cape Colony. The die-hards were those who did not mind being wrenched from accustomed surroundings, and whose convictions were sufficiently strong to take them farthest from the British. The majority of Afrikaners who remained behind in Cape Colony gradually accepted the British system of law, order, and equality before the law, and in time established a somewhat more liberal tradition than those in the republics.

At the time of the Sand River and Bloemfontein conventions, some 15,000 Afrikaners resided in the Orange Free State (OFS) and another 22,000 in the Transvaal. The OFS was quick to set up a government under a written constitution with an elected *Volksraad*, or assembly, and president. In 1858, the South African Republic was established in the Transvaal and its constitution closely resembled that of the OFS. It contained a clause relating to non-Europeans: 'The people desire to permit no equality between coloured people and the white inhabitants, either in church or state.' The life of the Transvaal *Volksraad* was turbulent, and it tended to ignore the finer interpretations of the constitution, a noisy contrast to the more orderly government of the Free State, which Sir James Bryce was later to term a model of its kind.[13]

The presence of the Basuto and, later, the dispute with the British over the sovereignty of the diamond fields, together with the leadership of President J. H. Brand were unifying factors for the Orange Free State, and patriotism early developed there. In sharp contrast, there was little evidence of patriotism in the Transvaal, which was divided in politics and religion. Even the Dutch Reformed Church was split into three groups. Several republics had arisen in the area and sound political leadership was lacking.[14] In the Transvaal, only Africans and Afrikaners struggled for land, a struggle in which the latter were the winners. In the Orange Free State, the existence of the half-caste Griquas, as well as Afrikaners and Africans, made the situation more complex. The East Griqua problem was settled when Adam Kok sold his land rights to the OFS and moved out of the republic with his people.

For well over a decade, the British maintained a policy of noninterference toward the republics, and the interior ruled itself. In 1864, not for the first time, fighting broke out between the Boers and the Basuto, after which the former were able to dictate terms to Moshesh. Moshesh asked for British protection, which was granted in 1868 in order to prevent further breaking up of Basuto territory. In 1869, the British annexed Basutoland and established a fixed boundary line between Basutoland and the OFS that gave the Basutos more land than the treaty with the Boers had left to them. The British intervention was considered an unfriendly act by the Free Staters.

Diamonds and Discord

The discovery of diamonds and gold changed drastically and dramatically South Africa's economy and the course of its history. Before the discovery of diamonds in 1866, the economy of South Africa was based on what the soil could produce and on cattle and sheep. Wool was the primary export. Before the discovery of diamonds, the territory beyond the Orange river was largely uninhabited save for scattered Voortrekker families, groups of Africans, and itinerant missionaries. The discovery of diamonds occasioned the rapid opening up of the interior—roads and railroads were built to carry food, equipment, and diamond-seekers to the diamond fields and to take out the workings.* The discovery marked a turning point in European-African relations, for now African labor was required for industry. The diamond fields were South Africa's first industrial community, and between 1871 and 1895 some 100,000 Africans were employed as 'mine boys'.[15] For the Africans, the discovery of diamonds and, later, gold contributed to their detribalization and urbanization, emphatically demonstrated

* A year after diamonds were discovered Kimberley was the second largest city in South Africa.

white dependence on African labor, and helped to emphasize the servile relationship of blacks to whites.

Diamonds were found in the area of what is now Kimberley, located near the juncture of the Vaal and Orange rivers. At first, the Boers were merely disturbed and spiteful spectators of what was going on at Kimberley, an operation that has been described as 'an insane asylum turned loose on a beach'[16]. The Afrikaners traditionally maintained a detached view of industry, mining, and commerce; it is only in very recent years that they have seen the important relationship between business and government, and have made a determined effort to participate in the former, the better to secure their position in the latter. The Afrikaner was content to remain, for the time being, what he was commonly called—a Boer or farmer. By contrast, the British, long an industrial people, eagerly sought diamonds and gold— a contrast that emphasized the differences between the practical-minded Briton and the Calvinist Boer. As Felix Gross has said:

> The *Uitlanders* [new-comers or outlanders, the outgroup, a name given to the British in Afrikaner territory] worshipped their idols in the temple of the Stock Exchange, whereas the Boers were still adhering to the laws of Moses. The new-comers were building up their future on bank credit while the Boers saw security only in the possession of land and stock.[17]

The question of sovereignty over the diamond fields did much to unite the Boers of the Orange Free State and to provoke a sympathetic response from their brethren in the South African Republic. Nicholas Waterboer, successor to Andries as the leader of the West Griquas, insisted that the diamond fields were within his jurisdiction. The Boers contested his claim. Both the Transvaal and the Orange Free State claimed a portion of the fields, but the Orange Free State appeared to have the better right. The British High Commissioner induced the President of the South African Republic to let the governor of Natal arbitrate the case. The governor decided against the Transvaal, and the High Commissioner dismissed the claim of the OFS and annexed all of Waterboer's territory to the British Crown on October 27, 1871.[18] Thus, what appeared to the Boer republics as a vicious scheme of encirclement was carried a step further. Later, it was discovered that Waterboer's claims were false and President Brand of the Orange Free State was able to extract £90,000 from the British Government in compensation for the OFS claim. In 1880, Griqualand West was included in Cape Colony.

Annexation and Revolt

British hesitation and indecision in dealing with the Voortrekkers and their descendants armed them with a strong claim to independence. At first, the British questioned exactly how far their authority extended over their 'defected subjects' and wavered in imposing it. After the Boer republics became established, suggestions that some type of union or federation should

13

be created between the two British colonies* and the republics interspersed British demands for control.

Culturally and politically, the colonies were very different from the republics. For Cape Colony, responsible government was slow in coming. The British government was more eager to grant it than the people of Cape Colony were willing to accept it. Cape Colony was not wealthy, and there were costly frontier problems that involved the British government in considerable expense that it would just as soon have relinquished. In 1865, Cape Colony still had only 181,000 whites, although it had a non-European population of half a million.[19] The Cape has always been the most liberal part of South Africa with respect to non-Europeans. When it received representative government in 1854, voting was not restricted by color. There were qualifications of property and sex, but these were equally applied to all. The Cape received responsible government in 1872, when Lord Kimberley was Britain's Secretary of State for the Colonies.

Natal, in which the white population was predominantly of British origin, received representative government in 1856 and responsible government in 1893. By that time there were nearly 50,000 Europeans living in Natal and 500,000 Africans. Theophilus Shepstone, son of a missionary who had arrived with the British settlers of 1820, placed the Africans of Natal on semi-autonomous reservations.[20] Because they retained their tribal customs and laws, Africans were not entitled to vote in Natal. Africans who asked to be excused from tribal law could, in theory, qualify for the vote, but only if they fulfilled conditions so rigorous as in practice to exclude nearly all applicants.

Lord Carnarvon, Kimberley's successor as Colonial Secretary, looked forward to a confederated South Africa under the British flag, British-sponsored and British-controlled. As a first step, he ordered Shepstone to undertake a provisional annexation of the Transvaal.† John Charles Molteno, the Cape's first Prime Minister, was also a strong advocate of federation of all South Africa. In 1871, the Cape Assembly passed a resolution favoring union in some form, and in 1875 the two Boer republics and the two colonial legislatures approved confederation in principle. In 1877, the British Parliament passed the South Africa Act 'for the union under one Government of such of the South African colonies and states as may agree thereto'.[21] This Permissive Federation Act had little support in South Africa, and Shepstone offered the Act for the approval of the Transvaal *Volksraad*, but it was rejected, while several hundred armed Boers stood outside. On April 12, 1877, Shepstone peremptorily ran up the British flag in Pretoria, thus fulfilling part of Carnarvon's scheme. In the words of Sir James Percy FitzPatrick: 'He plucked the fruit that would have

---

* British Kaffraria was incorporated in Cape Colony in 1865.

† Later Carnarvon sent Sir Bartle Frere to South Africa as High Commissioner, with orders to bring about a federation of which he was to be Governor-General. In this Frere was unsuccessful. He was censured by Carnarvon's successor for his Zulu policy.

fallen.'[22] There was little opposition to annexation at this time. Anti-British feeling was waning and the Transvaal was divided and economically weak; gold had not yet been discovered. The presidency of Thomas Francois Burgers (1872–77), formerly a minister of the Dutch Reformed Church, was torn by internal strife, and some three hundred families sought to escape his autocratic rule by trekking beyond the Kalahari. Bickering between Burgers and the *Volksraad* seems to have been more the rule than the exception.

The annexation of the Transvaal disturbed the Orange Free State, which feared the loss of its independence, and it rejected any thought of confederation. One Orange Free Stater expressed the growing sentiments in his country in a letter to a newspaper:

> Brother Transvaal, keep good courage and fight for your independence; the Cape Colony and the Free State are your friends, we are one blood. Do the English not know that if you chop a tree, the shavings fly off?[23]

The annexation even stirred up the Afrikaners in the Western Cape and injected a good deal of enthusiasm into an Afrikaans-speaking campaign begun by the Reverend Stephanus du Toit. The Zulu War of 1877–78, fought mainly by British troops, did much to disquiet the Transvaalers, and even caused British-oriented Natal to speak of neutrality. In 1880, the Basuto War, a result largely of the efforts of the Cape Government to disarm the Basuto, ended in embarrassment for the British.*

The hostility to the British in the Transvaal was the result of conflicting philosophies and ways of life—both intractable. Shepstone did little to improve Boer-British relations. Nor did it help matters to remind the Transvalers, as did the Anglican Bishop of Pretoria, that the Transvaal was now British territory.[25] Cecil Rhodes attributed all subsequent difficulties with the Transvaal to the 'shocking misgovernment by the Imperial Commission who conducted business on lines of a second-rate line regiment'.[26] The British, as in the Cape prior to the Great Trek, were impatient with Boer intransigence. They demanded a rigid adherence to law and a strict accounting of all taxes and outlays by local officials who were hardly accustomed to such discipline. Vice President Paul Kruger of the Transvaal traveled twice to London to seek an annulment of the annexation—to restore what had been lost. Carnarvon declined, but promised that Dutch could be considered as one of the official languages. Carnarvon's successor, Sir Michael Hicks Beach, was, however, more favorable to self-government. Meanwhile, in January, 1879, the Transvalers swore to regain independence, while the Disraeli government in Britain remained intent on confederation. The aggressiveness of the British government brought the Afrikaners of the Cape, the OFS, and the Transvaal closer together. As Petris Jacobus Joubert, one of the Transvaal leaders, put it: 'We are, after all, one nation, one blood,

---

* The result of the Basuto War has been described as 'the first political victory of an African people against an oppressive law . . . and they won their victory by armed revolt'.[24]

one bone, and one flesh. Our interests are your interests, even as the Bible says: "Our God is your God and our people are your people." '[27]

The OFS *Volksraad* sympathized with the Transvalers. Jan Hofmeyr in the Cape loudly protested against the annexation, and the Reverend Stephanus du Toit suggested the formation of an Afrikaner Bond on lines that were clearly anti-British. In September, 1879, some 6,000 Afrikaners gathered at Wonderfontein in the Transvaal in one of the mass gatherings that have been characteristic of Afrikaner nationalism, raised the *Vierkleur*, the four-coloured flag of the South African Republic, and demanded the summoning of the *Volksraad*. In November, 1880, the *Volksraad* met and named the triumvirate, S. J. P. Kruger, Joubert, and Marthinus Wessel Pretorius (son of Andries Pretorius, the Republic's first President), to take control. In April, 1880, Gladstone and his Liberals assumed office in London, and he appeared—judging from his campaign speeches—eager to find a solution to the increasingly serious situation in South Africa.

The British failed to crush the ensuing revolt of the Transvalers, known to the Afrikaners as the First War of Freedom (*Eerste Vryheidsoorlog*) and to the British as the First Boer War; after being defeated by the Boers in the Battle of Majuba Hill in February, 1881—a victory that has been used as an important symbol of Afrikaner nationalism—the British decided to evacuate the Transvaal. A convention was signed at Pretoria that assured the South African Republic 'complete self-government, subject to the suzerainty of Her Majesty'. The attempt at confederation and the failure to subdue the Basuto had weakened the British position, and the scarcity of British troops in South Africa and the reluctance of the British government to become involved in further expenditure and responsibility did nothing to improve it. The terms of the convention were, however, harsh: the Transvaal had to accept equal civil rights for all, prohibition of slavery, a share of the Transvaal debt, which had been growing since annexation, and fixed boundaries. There was no mention of the franchise. The *Volksraad* at first refused to have any part of the document, but on the advice of Kruger, who warned that rejection would lead to a renewal of the war, it reluctantly accepted.[28]

2   Hemmed in a Kraal

Ye are my brethren, ye are my bones and my flesh.

II SAMUEL 19 : 12

KRUGER ONCE COMPLAINED that the South African Republic was being
'hemmed in a kraal', that is, encircled by the British, the Portuguese, and
the Germans.   From the end of the First Boer War until the outbreak of
the Second Boer War in 1899, relations between the British and the Transvalers became increasingly tense.

When the British relinquished their control of the Transvaal, they
could not foresee the problems that were to arise with the discovery of gold
in the heart of its territory.   British dealings with the Transvaal had been
inept, and they contributed greatly to the eventual outbreak of full-scale war.
They certainly damaged British imperial prestige, and produced the worst
relations between Boers and Britons since the arrival of the latter in 1795.
The Transvalers were alerted to British scheming, and a unity of spirit
among Afrikaners everywhere was provoked.   From this point, Afrikaner
nationalism, spearheaded by the Transvalers, becomes definitely militant.
Conscious efforts to invoke pride in Afrikanerdom began, varying in intensity
with the irritations inflicted by the British.   One Afrikaner suggested: 'Let
us bear ourselves as one nation; for how wonderful it will be, if God wills,
when our United flag flies over South Africa.'[1]

Up to 1883, the dynamic political factors in South Africa were
differing attitudes of Boers and Britons, the Bantu, and diamonds.   From
1883, the imperial ambitions of Germany and renewed emphasis by Portugal
on her claims to territory in southern Africa presented a new threat.   In
the 1880s, the major European powers competed with each other for the
possession of territories in Africa.   Before the mid-1880s, many British
officials appeared unwilling to add more territories to the British Empire;
indeed, in some cases, they seemed eager to scuttle responsibilities already
assumed.   In 1879, the British had decided against the annexation of
Zululand; they abandoned the Transvaal soon after.   They dawdled over
deciding whether the Cape or the Imperial government should control
Southwest Africa.   On the other hand, the discovery of diamonds brought

17

South Africa into the international limelight, and considerably increased British interest in the area. Moreover, the British were compelled to maintain troops in South Africa to protect the African tribal territories from encroachment.

The people of the Transvaal, smarting under the annexation of the South African Republic in 1877, rejoiced when the British left in 1881. The episode made a significant contribution to the growth of Afrikaner nationalism, and was certainly a major setback for the British plan for a confederation. In 1884, a new convention, signed in London, restored to the South African Republic 'her complete independence. There was, however, one article which curtailed her rights, namely, the well-known Article 4. But the hateful suzerainty was repealed. The assertion made by Mr Chamberlain at a later date that the British suzerainty was still in force is false'.[2] The arrival of German representatives in southern Africa gave the Afrikaners an opportunity to frustrate the British further by flirting with a rival power.

It was in the 1880s, too, that Cecil John Rhodes, a man of unlimited ambition and determination, became a major figure on the South African political and economic scene. He envisaged bringing territory from the Cape to Cairo under the British Crown and linking the two ends of the continent by rail. He moved speedily, at times frantically, to implement his dream. He made a vast fortune from diamonds, gold, and other interests, and, having entered politics, eventually rose to become Prime Minister of the Cape. He was responsible for the occupation of the lands north of the Transvaal—the later Rhodesias—by British settlers, a move that further advanced the encirclement of the Boer republics by potentially hostile elements.

Seldom have two men more strikingly summed up the opposing trends of their times in their own personalities than Rhodes, the great imperialist and business magnate, and Stephanus Johannes Paulus Kruger, that rugged symbol of Boer intransigence, president of the South African Republic from May 6, 1883, until May 31, 1902. Kruger, who was in Disraeli's view an 'ugly customer', was *Oom* (Uncle) Paul to his own people. He was an example of the pious Boer, uneducated save for biblical teachings —he even maintained a steady attachment to the belief that the earth was flat. The following message, which he sent to his troops during the Boer War, was characteristic of him:

> Brothers! I exhort you to act with all promptness and with zeal. . . .
> Read Psalm 33, from verse 7 to the end. . . . The enemy have fixed their
> faith in Psalm 83. . . . Read also Psalm 89, the 13th and 14th
> verses. . . . I need not draw your attention to the destructive-
> ness of the enemy's works, for you know it, and I point again to the
> attacks of the Devil on Christ and His Church. This has been the
> attack from the beginning. . . . I am still searching the entire Bible,
> and I discover no other way which can be followed by us, and we must
> continue to fight in the Name of the Lord.[3]

Both Rhodes and Kruger were stubborn and intractable. If Kruger was a 'stubborn Dutchman', he was not more stubborn than Rhodes. A conversation between them, as reported by Kruger, reveals the total and irreconcilable conflict of their philosophies:

Rhodes: We must work together. I know the Republic wants a seaport. You must have Delagoa Bay.

Kruger: How can we work together there? The harbour belongs to the Portuguese, and they won't hand it over.

Rhodes: Then we must simply take it.

Kruger: I can't take away other people's property. If the Portuguese won't sell the harbour, I wouldn't take it even if you gave it to me, for ill-gotten gains are accursed.[4]

F. S. Crafford offers an interesting description of the simplicity of Kruger's manner of life, in striking contrast to the formality of British and colonial government circles:

The old Boer patriarch . . . ruled his people like a feudal lord. His autocratic habits had antagonized many of his colleagues in the *Volksraad* . . . as well as numerous of his associates, but he was strongly entrenched in his presidential position . . . by virtue of his many undeniably great qualities, that none had dared to question his authority or dispute his will. . . .

The President and his second wife . . . lived in a very simple iron-roofed house in Church Street near the Dopper (strict Calvinist) Church, where they worshipped regularly. They had spent together a long life beset with many hardships and trials, which had greatly strengthened the bonds between them. Tante Siena had born Oom Paul seven daughters and nine sons, and almost always children and grandchildren were to be found in and about the house.

Paul Kruger lived as his forebears had lived—a quiet, unpretentious, religious life. It was his habit to rise in the early hours of the morning, take his Bible from a shelf and pore over it for a long time. Then came the family prayers; '*Zonder God vermag ik niets* (Without God I attempt nothing),' he used to say. After devotions he would go to the front step, where he would sit down, a few yards from the street. Here he would consume numerous cups of strong coffee and puff for hours at his pipe, which rarely left his mouth during the day. As the people passed by he would hail them with a gruff 'good morning', and then exchange a few words with them, for in Pretoria he knew them all.

In the course of the day many callers would turn up on business, official or otherwise, or merely to converse with the President. All were equally welcome. As soon as visitors came, coffee would be poured and handed round and then Oom Paul and his friends would discuss the weather, the crops, the *Uitlander* question, or anything else of interest. His people had great belief in the wisdom of Paul Kruger, and young and old, rich and poor, town dwellers and rustics from the backveld—all used to come, singly or in groups, to seek advice. And the President was always ready and even eager to receive them, no matter how pressing official business might be.

When deputations visited him, he would light his pipe and draw at it thoughtfully for a minute or two before saying: 'Now Oom Paul is with you. Tell him what you will—or ask what you will—speak!' And then, regardless of time, he would converse with them until they were ready to take their leave. . . .

In a fairly large room in his house the President used to preside over meetings of his executive council. Here and in a couple of smaller rooms, used as offices, he conducted his official business, which . . . was carried on in a casual, unsystematic way and was subject to frequent interruptions from children and visitors.[5]

By 1886, gold had been discovered in the Transvaal. The Witwatersrand, or Rand, as the gold-bearing formation is called, is an enormous reef of generally low-grade ore extending to great depths. Gold meant the advent of diggers and traders, bringing with them the myriad problems of a money-based society, in contrast to the land and cattle economy of the Afrikaner. It meant, too, the direct contact of Boer and Briton, with President Kruger, who was not interested in gold, seeking always to resist British incursions. The burgeoning population of Johannesburg, as Bryce discovered during his visit in 1895, was largely English-speaking.[6] In time, these new arrivals, or *Uitlanders* (Outlanders), as the Boers labeled them, came to demand certain rights, especially freedom of passage in and out of the Transvaal for themselves, the minerals they dug, and their equipment, and, finally, the right to vote. Kruger recoiled at what he considered the insolent demands of intruders, and, indeed, did everything he could to hamper their scramble for gold. His obstinate refusal to extend the franchise to them was one of the major issues leading to the outbreak of the Boer War.

Milner regarded Kruger's treatment of the *Uitlanders* in the Transvaal as the 'permanent subjection of the British to Dutch'. J. X. Merriman, in a letter to President Steyn,* insisted that 'the greatest danger lies in the attitude of President Kruger and his vain hope of building up a state on a foundation of a narrow unenlightened minority'. Moreover, Kruger taxed the *Uitlanders* heavily, his police intimidated them, and he did all he could to discourage their entrance by rail. He even tried to destroy rail traffic to and from the Cape by imposing prohibitive rates on the Transvaal stretch of line, and then closed the drifts across the Vaal river when the traders attempted to circumvent such a move by transshipping to ox wagons at the border.† In all his efforts, Kruger was supported by his own people, especially the *back-velders*, or country people. Kruger reasoned: '*Ons Voortrekkers het die land skoongemaak; ons is geregtig tot die vet van die land*' ('Our pioneers cleared the land; we are entitled to the fat of the land').[7]

* March 11, 1898.

† Kruger reversed this latter action, however, under threats from the British government.

As de Kiewiet has said: 'Because the Boers had little art, less architecture, and no literature, they depended on their farms, their Bibles, and their blood to set them off sharply against native and outlander.'[8] The question posed by the *Uitlanders* required patient understanding, a quality neither Rhodes nor Kruger possessed. Kruger realized only too well that extending the vote to the *Uitlanders,* with their swelling numbers, would be tantamount to turning control of the machinery of government over to non-Afrikaners. It was a situation in some ways prophetic of the refusal of the present government of South Africa to enfranchise its African subjects. Kruger, like his modern successors, naturally had no intention of committing political suicide. Not only did he balk at any talk of giving the franchise to non-Afrikaners, but he steadily increased the requirements for voting. It was a dilemma that was to be solved only by the Boer War, for neither side could concede. But the mere presence of *Uitlanders* proved a catalyst in the development of Afrikaner nationalism. It brought the Afrikaners in the Transvaal closely together, and in time developed a sense of unity among those in the OFS, the Cape, and Natal as well.

Within six years of the discovery of gold, the gold field holdings were consolidated, and, whether Kruger liked it or not, gold brought prosperity and, indeed, the industrial revolution to the Transvaal. By 1895, the Transvaal had a railroad to Delagoa Bay and no longer depended on British-controlled ports. Kruger could then strike back at the British and counter tariffs with tariffs with impunity.

There were other forces at work to frustrate Kruger, forces that seemed destined to propel all South Africa into war. In 1887, Kruger approached the Orange Free State with the suggestion of a federation of the two republics as a means of strengthening the Afrikaners' bargaining position with the British in Cape Colony and Natal. At that time, Jan Hendrik Brand was President of the Free State, and though he wished to maintain an independent status, he was not unfriendly to the British. He declined Kruger's suggestion, and instead proposed that Kruger make friends of the *Uitlanders.* He then proceeded to negotiate with the Cape and Natal for a common customs union, thus snubbing Kruger, who was not invited to the negotiations.

The Transvaal was becoming the heart of right-wing Afrikanerdom and Kruger the personal embodiment of all that Afrikanerdom stood for. The Transvaal, unlike the Free State, was not in the least eager to co-operate with the British on British terms. Yet, various forces were persistently converging on the Transvaal to bring it into line. In the east, it could obtain possession of no outlet to the sea. The British had annexed Natal in 1843. Later, the Republic tried to obtain Kosi Bay as a sea outlet, and to obtain access to it through Swaziland. Although the Transvaalers acquired almost complete control of Swaziland by 1894, they were unsuccessful as regards Kosi Bay. (Swaziland became a British protectorate in 1906.) Meanwhile, however, the Transvaal had been linked by rail with the Portuguese port of Delagoa Bay in Mozambique, much to the annoyance of the British and the South African colonial governments.

FIGURE 1: Sir Paul Kruger

(Drawing by Denis de Roubille in *Feuille des Caricatures Politiques*, 1899)

West of the Transvaal lay the land of the Bechuana. In 1874, the British missionary, David Livingstone, had appealed to the British government to intervene to prevent tribal wars and to keep the Voortrekkers out. The British declined to do anything until 1878, when they occupied southern Bechuanaland, only to withdraw three years later. In 1884, the Transvalers tried to make part of Bechuanaland into a Transvaal protectorate. The British government replied by formally annexing the entire area as far as the newly established German Southwest Africa. The British action had been urged by Khama, the Christian chief of the Bamangwato tribe, by missionaries, and by Rhodes, who conceived of Bechuanaland as a vital part of his planned Cape-to-Cairo corridor.

In 1889, Rhodes was granted a royal charter authorizing the occupation of the land to the north of the Transvaal by his British South Africa Company. It was hoped that the territories of the chartered Company would prove as rich in minerals as the Transvaal.

The isolation of the Boers and their insulation from new ideas was intensified by these, in their view, intentional efforts to hem them in. Not only were the British enveloping the republics, but they were causing contention in their very midst. Gold in Johannesburg brought primary benefits only to the *Uitlanders*, whom the Boers regarded with miserly contempt. Moreover, the British were not the only threat. The Germans and the Portuguese were also consolidating their claims in southern Africa. Worst of all was the existence of Rhodes with his warlike admonitions to Kruger: 'If you do not take care you will have the whole of South Africa against you.'[9]

The Growth of National Sentiment

The diamond fields controversy, Carnarvon's confederation scheme, the annexation of the Transvaal and Griqualand West, and, particularly, the infelicitous British handling of the Transvaal 'shocked Afrikaner national sentiment into being';[10] the grant of self-government to the Cape in 1872 gave the Cape Afrikaners the means for individual and group expression. Up to that time, resistance to the British had come from the Voortrekker element. Now the spirit of the Voortrekkers was beginning to flow back to the colonies, and cries of 'Africa for the Afrikanders' (Afrikander was the earlier term for Afrikaner) were beginning to be heard. The Cape Dutch had come to accept British paramountcy, and a good deal of integration had taken place. It required a serious threat to the Boers of the republics to revive in the Cape Afrikaners a sense of identity with them and to arouse them to the defense of a group of which they felt themselves a part. Once aroused, however, they resented any attack on the republics as also threatening themselves. Antagonism against the British increased. The stimulus was sufficiently forceful to arouse latent sentiment and to provoke it to overt action. The Boers generally were impelled to *laager* together in defence of common ideals. Even in the Cape Parliament, the Dutch members would sit by themselves, away from the British, whom they were beginning to suspect.

23

Up to this time, high Dutch was the formal language of the Afrikaner used in schools, churches, and among the better-educated families; Afrikaans was only a colloquial language. But as British-Boer relations deteriorated, Afrikaner national sentiment increased, as did the demand for the recognition of Afrikaans as an official, formal language to replace high Dutch. This demand indicated the stage to which Afrikaner nationalism had advanced. A national language is a fundamental ingredient of nationalism. The emergence of Afrikaans as a formal language heightened the Afrikaner's sense of belonging to a unique group, while the development of a language different from any other marked the group with a singular identity.

The inspiration for the new role of Afrikaans came from the Cape. In 1875, the Reverend Stephanus Johannes du Toit, a minister of the Dutch Reformed Church from Paarl, not far from Cape Town, and Arnoldus Pannevis, a school teacher, encouraged by the stir caused by the Carnarvon confederation scheme, organized *Di Genootskap van Regte Afrikaners* (The Society of True Afrikaners), whose purpose was 'to stand up for our language, our nation and our people'. The Society encountered a good deal of opposition from those who adhered to high Dutch, opposition that was particularly sharp when it was suggested that the Bible should be translated into Afrikaans. That the suggestion was made at all is a good indication of the intensity of nationalism at that time.

One of the strongest opponents of du Toit's efforts was Jan Hendrik Hofmeyr. In 1878, Hofmeyr founded the *Boeren Beschermings Vereniging* (Farmers Defence Society) to fight an excise tax that was hurting the wine producers.[11] With the support of the society, Hofmeyr entered Parliament the following year. Du Toit condemned the Farmers Defence Society as too narrow and local, and recommended, in an article in the issue of *Di Afrikaanse Patriot*, the first newspaper in Afrikaans and the organ of *Di Genootskap van Regte Afrikaners*,* the establishment of an

> Africander Bond in which all Africanders can feel themselves at home, and work together for the good of a United South Africa: in which no question of nationality will divide us, but in which all who recognize Africa as their fatherland can live together and work as brothers of a single house, though they be of English, Dutch, French or German descent, with the exclusion of all who talk of England as their home or of Holland or Germany as their fatherland, and who only want to fill their pockets here with Africander prosperity and then go and spend it in Europe; which will consequently promote the true interests of our land and all parties, and prevent the sacrifice of the interests of Africa to England or of the farmer to the merchant. . . . Such a Bond is necessary, and the need of such a Bond is felt each day more and more; such a Bond will be welcomed by thousands and tens of thousands, and is indispensable to the future of Africa.

In the issue of July 4, 1879, he elaborated his ideas.[12] The principles of the

* June 20, 1879.

24

Afrikaner Bond were similar to those of the National Party of today, though not so precisely spelled out. The Bond was to encompass all of South Africa, not just the Cape. It was pointedly anti-British, though membership was not exclusive, and anyone who claimed South Africa as his only home could join. It advocated greater use of Afrikaans, and sought to develop a loyalty to South Africa as opposed to the British Crown; and, like the modern National Party, it objected strongly to newspaper publication of 'harmful' information.[13]

One can grasp the true significance of the Bond in perusing *Di Patriot*, edited by Stephanus du Toit's brother, Daniel François. What the paper had to say about confederation, for example, differed but little from later nationalist thinking on that topic. In one issue we find this statement:

> We have often said it, there is just one hindrance to Confederation, and that is the English flag. Let them take that away, and within a year the Confederation under the free Afrikander flag would be established. But so long as the English flag remains here, the Afrikander Bond must be our Confederation.[14]

The article then suggested the British restrict their interests to the naval base of Simonstown on the Cape Peninsula.

The growth of the Bond was not spectacular until 1881, when the First Boer War provided a stimulus to attract interest to it. Branches of the Bond were then formed in the republics, although most of its strength lay in the Cape.

In 1880, another confederation scheme was introduced into the Cape Parliament. Kruger journeyed to the Cape to argue against it. The trip in itself had a unifying effect. Kruger visited Afrikaner communities and stirred up considerable excitement for his cause. Hofmeyr, who had been a strong advocate of union, now argued against it until the British granted the Transvaal complete independence. Meanwhile, Hofmeyr was losing many of the members of his Farmers Defence Society to the Afrikaner Bond.

In 1881, du Toit moved to the Transvaal to become its Superintendent of Education; in that position he insisted on the use of Dutch as the only medium of instruction contrary to the bilingual policy of President Burgers. He advocated a united South Africa, independent of the British and with its own flag, and strongly criticized President Brand and J. H. Hofmeyr as pro-British. But the Cape remained the stronghold of the Bond, and with du Toit out of the way Hofmeyr moved to assume control. As a member of the Cape Cabinet, Hofmeyr had been influential in having Dutch accepted on an equal basis with English in Parliament; an Education Commission had recommended the use of Dutch in the lower schools if the school committees so advised. By 1883, Hofmeyr succeeded in effecting an amalgamation of his Farmers Defence Society with the Afrikaner Bond, and he became its president. Hofmeyr's moderation was reflected in the subsequent growth and policy of the Bond. In 1883, it adopted a constitution of fifteen articles.[15] The object of the Bond was clear: 'The formation of a

South African nationality by the fostering of true patriotism, as preparation for its final destiny: a United South Africa.'

In 1889, the Bond became the Africander National Party of the Cape. It promulgated a 'Programme of Principles' somewhat more detailed than the Bond's constitution;[16] Article 3 stated the Party's purposes:

(a) That a firm Union of the different European nationalities in British South Africa be brought about; and
(b) That the self-dependence of South Africa be promoted.

This was very like the later Botha-Smuts one-stream co-operative policy of Boer and Briton under the British flag, but with an unmistakable South African sentiment. Du Toit was more demanding than Hofmeyr in his insistence on separation from the British; he was indeed the forerunner of Dr Hendrik F. Verwoerd who in 1961 finally made the historic decision to break with the Commonwealth and establish an independent republic.

Hofmeyr was, as Sarah Gertrude Millin has observed, 'one of the ablest of South African statesmen'.[17] He was a quiet man, and preferred to operate behind the scenes; yet for nearly thirty years he led his party in Parliament, and its members voted as he told them. Hofmeyr perceived wisdom in the co-operation of Briton and Boer to form a union of all South Africa and a united party of the two groups. He even supported Rhodes, though he never joined his ministry. Thus, Hofmeyr was the forerunner of Botha, Smuts, Strauss, and Graaff. Unhappily, the realization of his hopes was bitterly hampered by the intransigence of Rhodes and Kruger. The latter lives on in the National Party. He was the forerunner of Hertzog, Malan, Strijdom, and Verwoerd. He was the personification of Afrikaner ideals, and in a very real sense he is the leader of Afrikanerdom's right-wing extremists today, dictating policy from the grave. Kruger's stubbornness eventually paid off.

Into the Vortex of War

In July, 1888, President Brand of the Orange Free State, a moderate of the Hofmeyr type, died, and with him went his temperance. He was succeeded by Francis William Reitz,[18] who believed all Boers should unite together against the paramountcy of the British—a belief in which he had the warm support of Kruger. It is possible that had Brand lived, the Boer War could have been averted. His successor played into Kruger's hands.

In 1889, the first indications of a shift in the policy of the Orange Free State occurred. In that year, the Orange Free State entered into a defensive alliance with the Transvaal. In the years following 1889, the British colonies and the Transvaal were engaged in bitter rivalry over railroads and tariffs. Railroad lines through the Cape and Natal were constructed to compete with the Delagoa Bay line for the traffic of the Transvaal gold fields. Meanwhile, *Uitlander* grievances, which included policy mistreatment, discrimination, and denial of the franchise, and which were expressed through the medium of the South African League, 'established at the undoubted instigation of Cecil

Rhodes',[19] provided another source of friction. In 1895, Rhodes' friend, Dr Leander Starr Jameson, led an abortive raid on the Transvaal and, finally, in 1899, the Anglo-Boer War broke out. It is not necessary here to describe the events surrounding the Jameson Raid nor the immediate factors that resulted in the war. It is only necessary to point to the effects.

The purpose of the Jameson Raid was to give the discontented *Uitlanders* on the Rand an opportunity to rise and demand satisfaction. Although it failed, it left in its wake a trail of suspicion that for the time being ended any hope of South African union—certainly of any union within the British orbit—and nullified any efforts by the moderate Cape Boers under Hofmeyr's leadership to persuade their *broers* in the Free State and Transvaal of the advantages of union with the British. It hardened Kruger's recalcitrance and exposed Rhodes' precipitance. (Rhodes was obliged to resign as Prime Minister of the Cape after the Raid.) It seemed that passion was now to rule reason, and that war was inevitable.

In 1897, Sir Alfred (later Lord) Milner was appointed Governor of Cape Colony and High Commissioner for South Africa. Milner was as much mistrusted as Rhodes; he was looked upon as the mouthpiece of Joseph Chamberlain, the intensely imperialistic British Colonial Secretary. Kruger insisted that 'there is no doubt that Mr Chamberlain appointed Sir Alfred Milner only with a view of driving matters in South Africa to extremes', and characterized Milner as the 'typical jingo, autocratic beyond endurance and filled with contempt for all that is non-English'.[20]

In 1898, William P. Schreiner became Prime Minister of Cape Colony. He was a moderate and was supported by the Afrikaner Bond. Reitz was succeeded in the Free State by Marthinus Steyn, who immediately formed a military alliance with Kruger. In 1898, Kruger was returned to the Transvaal presidency by a large majority.* Matters were quickly coming to a head. The *Volksraad* appeared willing to grant President Kruger great authority. How much authority was well illustrated by his dealings with his chief justice. When, in 1897, Chief Justice J. G. Kotze declared a number of laws of the Transvaal to be unconstitutional and invalid, the *Volksraad* deprived the courts of the power to test their constitutionality and empowered the President to dismiss any judge who disagreed.

In October, 1899, the storm burst, and open conflict broke out. Ever since the arrival of the British, some of the Boers had resisted the way of life that the British had sought to thrust upon them. The nineteenth century was a period of sparring, of jockeying for position, of give and take. Relations became more intense as the century advanced and remonstrations more frequent. And, as de Kiewiet has remarked, 'in the end only a great crisis could break the resistance which events of the century had built up'.[21] At last the Boers embarked on a war that they could not hope to win.[22] Despite the close alliance and determined struggle of the two Afrikaner republics, the Anglo-Boer War resulted in defeat by the superior forces of the 'hated' British—a defeat, moreover, that took place in plain view of the African

* The *Uitlanders*, it must be remembered, could not vote.

27

peoples whom the Boers looked upon as inferior. Kruger's insistence that the 'black man had to be taught that he came second, that he belonged to the inferior class which must obey and learn' and that 'severity was essential'[23] in dealing with Africans was an attitude that thereafter became more than ever peculiarly characteristic of the Boers.

The Boer War was the ultimate frustration for the Afrikaners. In the nineteenth century, they had abandoned the Cape to British control with hardly a struggle. Now they had been chastised on their own home soil, and they could see nowhere else to go. But their anxieties and grievances remained. The Afrikaner could no longer maintain the isolation he desired. Up to this time, his religion and philosophy had remained pretty much immune from foreign 'contamination'. Now he was forced at gunpoint to accept assimilation. The xenophobic Boer was convinced he was right and could not accept defeat at the hands of those he was positive were wrong. The recollections of the past were too deeply ingrained. The war triggered a fiery Afrikaner nationalism bent on avenging the humiliations of defeat—a nationalism that took some sixty years to reach the triumph of an Afrikaner-dominated South African Republic. The war developed a singleness of purpose in Afrikaner thinking. If it had not taken place, there would have been no Boer unity, without which the Boer could never have come to power in South Africa. But Boer unity also meant the deepening of the divisions between Briton and Afrikaner and, eventually, the dominance of Afrikaner views on race, society, and politics throughout South Africa.

Before the arrival of the British, the rural Afrikaners had occasional grievances against the authorities of the Dutch East India Company, but, for the most part, they were content to be left alone, isolated on their vast land holdings. Men of the soil, traditionally unrestricted in their movements, they learned to rebel at efforts to control them, whether by officials of the Dutch East India Company or, later, by officials of the British Crown. The establishment of British authority gave the Boer cause to complain; unable to express their grievances through representative means or force, the right-wing extremists set out on the Great Trek, the first major expression of Boer discontent. The Trek played a significant role in the development of group consciousness among the Afrikaners, and in fostering the idea, which survived for many years, that it was the British rather than the Africans who offered the principal threat to the Afrikaner way of life.

The gradual, if apparently indecisive, extension of British control in the direction of the Voortrekkers, intensified the concern of the Afrikaners for their own future. Slowly, and by fits and starts, British territory increased in extent. Each of the various annexations and withdrawals by the British increased the group consciousness of the Boers. By the 1880s, sufficient unifying factors existed for the development of a strong national sentiment that only required further incidents to propel it forward. From that point, Afrikaner nationalism became militant. It changed from localized manifestations of discontent into genuine national sentiment encompassing the whole of Afrikanerdom. The efforts made by du Toit and others in the Cape to induce pride in and official use of the *taal* or language of the Afrikaner were a sympathetic response to what was transpiring in the Transvaal. The establishment of the Afrikaner Bond, a political organization, reflected the emergence of a general political consciousness. At first, such manifestations received only tepid support, but Lord Carnarvon's confederation scheme and the annexation of the Transvaal injected greater purpose. The discovery of gold in the very heart of the Transvaal and the frantic rush of *Uitlanders*, most of whom were British, to retrieve it, heightened Afrikaner self-consciousness and provided the immediate causes of the Anglo-Boer War. Meanwhile, Africa was attracting international interest, and such interest forced the British to be more demanding.

The war itself united the Boers as nothing else could have done. Like the Great Trek, it was a form of political protest. In 1899, force was the only means of protest left to the Boers. They had been 'hemmed in a kraal', in the interests of the 'imperial factor' and British 'paramountcy'. The Boer War demonstrated how intense Afrikaner group consciousness could be and how determined the Afrikaners were to maintain their way of life against the British threat. The bitterness of the Boer extremists was seen in their utter contempt for fellow-Boers who surrendered to the British or who enlisted in the British-organized National Scouts. They designated these persons 'hands-uppers', as opposed to the 'bitter-enders' who fought to the last. The personality and position of the President of the Transvaal contributed to the growth of group consciousness. Kruger provided the force about whom the Boers could collect. Moreover, the absence of class distinctions among the Boers meant there was one thing less to divide them among themselves.

In a sense, the Boers did not surrender at Vereeniging; they merely laid down their arms. It was a negotiated peace, for which both sides made concessions. Certainly, the British were impressed by the dogged determination of the Boers, and after spending three years seeking to ferret out all Boer commandos, the British ordained peace at a price. The Boers lost their independence, and British sovereignty was finally extended over the whole of South Africa. The British had vacillated for decades over the extent of their authority, and the question was now settled. South Africa was united under the British flag. Ultimately, however, the fact of union facilitated the Afrikaner takeover of the government of the whole of South Africa.

Despite the growth of group consciousness, differences existed among the Boers. There were the moderates, represented by Hofmeyr and Brand. Hofmeyr pressed for the recognition of the Afrikaans language, but was not anti-British. Instead, he advocated co-operation among all the Europeans in South Africa. Even at the peace negotiations at Vereeniging, the moderates and the right wingers competed. Smuts and Botha were amenable to the final terms. Presidents Steyn and Kruger were not. Smuts, Botha, and Hofmeyr continued into the twentieth century as the representatives of Boer conservatism, but not extremism. But from the early days of Afrikaner nationalism to the present, one tendency has been repeatedly in evidence—an extremist right wing periodically splits, or hives, from the conservative main body, and eventually has its own way.

Part Two

THE STRUGGLE FOR SUPREMACY

3   They Fall To Rise

They stagger . . . and are at their wit's end.   Then they cry unto the
Lord in their trouble, and he bringeth them out of their distresses.
                                            PSALM 107: 27, 28

THE SHAME OF DEFEAT and the ordeals of the British concentration camps the
Boers could not forget nor would they permit themselves to forget them.
Milner opined in April, 1903, that 'the South African struggle continues.   It
has changed in character, it is no longer with bullets, but it is war still'.[1]   The
violent nationalism provoked by the Boer War grew and flourished; it was
further stimulated during the first and second world wars and by world
opposition to Afrikaner policy after the second world war.   Its most intense
development has taken place in the period since 1948, when the Afrikaner
extremists finally came into power.

During the period between May 31, 1902, when the Anglo-Boer War
ended, and May 31, 1910, when the Union was proclaimed, the Boers were
stunned by defeat.   For Afrikaner nationalism, it was a low-water period, a
time for reflection.   The war had brought the Boers of both the Cape and
the republics close together; it was certain that the strong group identity they
had developed would prove a disadvantage to the British (who were, in any
case, outnumbered by the Afrikaners) in any type of government established
in South Africa.

After the war, Milner, whom the Boers looked upon as 'the man who
made the war', was appointed High Commissioner of the new British crown
colonies of the Transvaal and Orange River.   He was already High Commissioner for South Africa and Governor-General of the self-governing Cape
Colony.   In accepting his new responsibilities he resigned as governor of
Cape Colony.

The first task was war reconstruction and repatriation of some of the
numerous Afrikaners in civilian concentration camps (where many died) and
in prisoner-of-war camps.   In accordance with the terms of the peace treaty,
the British government contributed impressive sums for rehabilitation.

One of the major postwar problems was the Chinese labor question.
When the war ended, the mine owners were eager to resume large-scale
operations.   Workers were needed to reinforce the native laborers.   This

33

raised the question of white dependence on African labor. F. H. P. Creswell, a former mine manager who became the leader of the South African Labour Party, believed that white labor could and should be used in South Africa and that it was a false economy to depend on cheap nonwhite labor. Milner held the same view because he was interested in attracting British immigrants to South Africa. However, he felt that mines were not the place for white labor since in his opinion they had only a short life. What the mines needed was cheap labor. At any rate the mine owners imported low-paid Chinese indentured laborers to re-establish the mining industry, much to the chagrin of the Afrikaners, who were hostile to the introduction of any new racial group. By December, 1908, 150,000 Chinese were working in the mines. Opposition to the use of indentured labor in Great Britain and Afrikaner hostility to Asians in South Africa led to their repatriation by 1910. But the stigma remained.

The steps toward union of the four colonies were gradual and hampered by hatred and suspicion. The peace treaty had looked forward to eventual self-government for the ex-republics. Milner helped pave the way by creating a customs union and by bringing the railways of the Transvaal and the Orange River colonies under joint control. The peace treaty had assured the Boers that the Dutch language would be taught in the public schools on parental request and that its use would be permitted in courts of law. But Milner, steeped in British traditions, was eager to bring the blessings of his own culture to the Afrikaner through the introduction of English teachers in the schools. Milner's attitudes reflected the opinions of many of the British, including a number of those who had made South Africa their home. A memorandum prepared by the government of Natal at the close of the Anglo-Boer War emphasized pride in British institutions. After observing that the Afrikaner had 'neither a literature nor a grammar', the memorandum suggested that

> The general good of the new colonies and of South Africa requires the predominance of the English language. . . . English should be the official and predominant language in the higher courts and in the public service—combined with such concessions in favour of Dutch as justice, convenience and circumstances require. . . . English should be the medium of instruction in all secondary schools, and in all standards in primary schools in English districts, and in the higher standards in all other primary schools.

Such attitudes had their counterpart in the Draft Republican Constitution produced by Boer extremists in 1942, which demanded 'Afrikaans . . . as the first official language'.

In 1905, Milner was replaced as High Commissioner and Governor by Lord Selborne, while in Britain Sir Henry Campbell-Bannerman became the Prime Minister of the Liberal government that replaced Balfour's Conservative administration. Campbell-Bannerman proceeded to give the Transvaal and Orange River colonies self-government, fulfilling the promises of Vereeniging. In 1906, the Transvaal received a constitution similar to that of the

Cape; and Louis Botha, the last Commandant-General of the Boer forces in the war, became the Prime Minister of the Transvaal with Jan Christian Smuts, another Boer general, as one of the leading members of his cabinet. Botha had already established his *Het Volk* (the People's) Party in May, 1904. Its platform included demands for religious and mother-tongue instruction in schools and for general acceptance of both Dutch and English as the languages of South Africa. It opposed the importation of Chinese laborers.

The Orange River Colony obtained self-government in 1907, and its constitution, too, followed the pattern of that of the Cape. The party that acceded to power was the *Orangia Unie* (Orange Union), which had been formed in 1905, with J. B. M. Hertzog, who, like Botha and Smuts, had been a Boer general during the war, as one of its leaders. Impetus for political organization in the Orange River Colony, as in the Transvaal, was provided by the educational system imposed by Milner and the latter's efforts to anglicize the Boers. The emphasis of the Orangia Unie was cultural protection *ons eie* (our own).

The Afrikaner organizations attracted a number of English-speaking persons. However, the more consciously 'British' elements set up their own groups. In the Orange River Colony, establishment of the Constitutional Party, headed by Sir John Fraser, was announced in January, 1907. Its purpose was to oppose responsible government for the Orange River Colony. It had little support and a short life. In the Transvaal in 1904, ex-*Uitlanders* and former opponents of Kruger representing the large mining interests, organized the Transvaal Progressive Association; its leaders were Sir Percy FitzPatrick, Sir George Farrar, and Sir Abe Bailey. In the same year, E. P. Solomon and Harry Solomon organized the Responsible Government Party, which favored responsible government for the Transvaal. The Independent Labour Party, headed by H. W. Sampson, was formed a few years later: in January, 1910, it joined with other small parties to establish the South African Labour Party, headed by F. H. P. Creswell.

The Cape Boers had a longer tradition of party political organization than their brothers in the former republics. The Afrikaner Bond had been formed in 1879, and, after du Toit was out of the picture, Hofmeyr's moderation predominated in its thinking. Hofmeyr had long been an advocate of union. He was a pragmatist who knew that Briton and Boer had to work together; under his influence, the Bond's constitution of 1883 used the term 'Afrikaner' to encompass all South Africans of European descent who acknowledged South Africa as their only home. To him, union was an ideal to be aimed at, and he encouraged his own people to participate in government with this end in view. The Bond remained loyal to the British Crown. During the Boer War, however, the members of the Afrikaner Bond felt sentimentally closer to their northern kin; doubts were raised in many of them as to the wisdom of maintaining their traditional views. The war had banished the hopes of Afrikaner extremists for an independent South Africa, and the Bond's broader concepts of nationhood were looked upon favourably by many Boers in the former republics. In 1907, Hofmeyr expressed his hope of an indivisible Dutch-English union whose people would have a strong sense of pride in being British South Africans; in this he reflected the opinion of Botha, that 'we have to live together long after the war is ended'.[2]

In the Cape, many English-speaking people joined the Progressive Party, led by Dr L. S. Jameson, the friend of Rhodes and organizer of the Jameson Raid, who was Prime Minister of the Cape until 1908. The Progressive Party had favored the suspension of the Cape constitution at the end of the Boer War, and had thus incurred the hostility of the Afrikaner Bond. Meanwhile, in the former republics, the sentiments of the followers of Botha and Hertzog toward the ex-*Uitlanders* were unchanged. The Cape Bondsmen and the members of *Orangia Unie* and *Het Volk* were drawing together. John X. Merriman succeeded Hofmeyr as leader of the Africander National Party, renamed the South Africa Party; the SAP ousted the Progressives in the Cape in February, 1908. The way was becoming clear for the union of the four colonies and for the amalgamation of the three mainly Afrikaner parties—Botha's *Het Volk*, Hertzog's *Orangia Unie*, and Merriman's South Africa Party (SAP)—events that were shortly to take place.

Thus, by 1908, conditions were more favorable for political union than they had ever been. Milner, to whom the Boers attributed responsibility for the war, who had much to do with the arrival of the Chinese, who had supported Jameson when the latter proposed the suspension of the Cape constitution in 1902, who had imposed the English educational system in the former republics, had left office and a new government in England wished to make amends in South Africa. The former republics had acquired self-government. John X. Merriman and his South Africa Party had captured control of the Cape Colony from Jameson's Progressives. Even in Natal, traditionally British in orientation, feeling in favor of union, which was then viewed as a measure of protection for the whites, grew after the Zulu rebellion of 1906.

Economically, it was reasoned, South Africa would fare much better united. In 1903, the Transvaal joined the customs union that had been formed in 1889 by the Orange Free State, the Cape, and Natal, but had hitherto functioned clumsily. Certainly, a centralized administration would be more efficient, and many believed that union would reduce British interference in South Africa. Business and mining interests favored union. Organizations were formed throughout South Africa to marshal public opinion behind the cause of union.

In July, 1907, the British High Commissioner and Governor, Lord Selborne, published a memorandum, entitled 'Review of the Present Mutual Relations of the British South African Colonies', in which he argued strongly for Union. He observed in words portentous of today:

> Where two nationalities . . . are so generally mixed together throughout the sub-continent as are the British and the Dutch . . . the fusion between them is merely a matter of time, as it was with the Saxons and Normans, who were related to one another in a similar degree of kinship.

The three Afrikaner parties in office favored union, and in this they had the

support of the opposition parties. In 1908, a customs and railways conference held by the four colonies passed a resolution requesting the colonial
legislatures to appoint delegates to a national convention to draft a union
constitution.

The National Convention opened on October 12, 1908, in Durban,
Natal. Like the gathering that met at Philadelphia in 1787, the South
African Constitutional Convention lasted three months. It was, however,
somewhat smaller in size, consisting of twelve from Cape Colony, eight from
the Transvaal, five from the Orange River Colony, five from Natal, and three
from Rhodesia, which was toying with the possibility of joining the Union,
but which, then as later, hesitated to take the final step. Sir Henry de
Villiers, the Chief Justice of Cape Colony, chaired the proceedings. One-
third of the members were farmers, a fact that had much to do with loading
of the rural vote in the Act of Union as finally drawn up. Another third
were lawyers. Two-thirds had fought in the Anglo-Boer War. The
Convention of 1908 envisaged a unitary rather than a federal state. Sitting
as observer at the first annual Congress of the Progressive Party in November,
1960, in Johannesburg the writer detected among the delegates, in this case
mostly university people, a belief in the advantages of federation, and the
hope that perhaps it might still be a possible solution to the national race
problem. But Smuts represented the views of the majority at the 1908
convention when he pressed for a unitary state, rather than a federation like
the United States where, as he said, 'the sovereign power was so dispersed as
to be ineffective for the essential purpose of civilized government'.[3]

The convention resolved its differences through compromise. There
were questions of parliamentary representation. The small white population of Natal was, like that of the Eastern Province of the Cape, mainly of
English origin, with English traditions. It feared being overwhelmed by a
predominantly Afrikaner government. The other small state, Orange River
Colony, with a population that was mostly Afrikaner, wanted assurance of
equal representation in Parliament. The Cape, with its Dutch and English
traditions, wanted the existing franchise rights of its Africans and Coloureds
guaranteed. The Transvaal, much the most prosperous of the four, feared
it might have to share the wealth brought by gold with the other three. Such
fears formed the basis of a compromise. Each colony was to become a
province of the Union. For the first ten years of union each province was to
send ten members to the Senate; in the Assembly, each province was guaranteed a minimum number of seats, together with a certain number of additional seats, to be allocated on various premises. The effect would be to give
the rural areas greater representation than urban areas; moreover, Natal and
the Orange River colonies would have more seats than they would have been
entitled to under a system strictly proportionate to population.

The Cape delegates had wanted an open franchise, subject only to
property qualifications, as well as open representation for the new Union.
The delegates from Orange River and Transvaal, where only Europeans
could vote, opposed this. In Natal, the franchise was theoretically open to
non-Europeans, but the qualifications required were such as to restrict all but

two hundred non-Europeans from voting in 1910. Cape Colony was the most liberal. Property and wage qualifications were applied to all alike, and 22,784 non-Europeans (one-third of them Africans and two-thirds Coloureds) had the vote in a total electorate of 152,221. A compromise was reached by which the franchise qualifications for each province were retained, and those of the Cape were especially protected. It was agreed that any changes would require a two-thirds vote of Senators and Representatives sitting jointly in Parliament. This was the price of union. As Smuts reminded Parliament on January 26, 1949, 'the Cape . . . never would have gone into union unless this . . . agreement had been come to'.

The Afrikaners insisted that Dutch be granted equal status with English, and bilingualism, like the Cape franchise, was entrenched in the constitution; that is, an amendment affecting these two matters would require a two-thirds vote of both houses of Parliament sitting jointly.

The constitution left room for the admission of Rhodesia, on terms to be approved by the Privy Council, and of Swaziland, Basutoland, and Bechuanaland, with the consent of the British government in consultation with the inhabitants.

Another compromise concerned the location of the national capital. Cape Town, capital of Cape Colony, was to be the legislative capital; Bloemfontein, the capital of the Orange River Colony, the judicial capital; and Pretoria, the capital of the Transvaal, the administrative capital—an arrangement intended to placate any jealousies that might arise.

Government was to be centralized, with provincial administrations responsible only for such matters as elementary and secondary education—not university or African education—local roads, and hospitals. Each province was to have an Administrator, appointed by the central government, and a Provincial Council. Thus, the national Parliament was to be supreme; in Parliament, bills would be passed by a simple majority vote, save on matters pertaining to the two entrenched clauses. Theoretical sovereignty resided in the Crown, acting through a Governor-General appointed by the British monarch. The Prime Minister was to be appointed by the Governor-General.

In August, 1909, the British Parliament approved the South Africa Act embodying the above provisions, and the Union came into being on May 31, 1910, eight years after Vereeniging and fifty-one years before the establishment of the South African Republic. Viscount Gladstone, son of the former British Prime Minister, was the first Governor-General of the Union. He selected Louis Botha, the Prime Minister of the Transvaal and leader of Het Volk, as the first Prime Minister of the Union, thus establishing a precedent. All subsequent Prime Ministers of South Africa have been Afrikaners: Smuts, Hertzog, Malan, Strijdom, and Verwoerd.

The first general election was held in September, 1910, and Botha was confirmed in his post with a majority of sixty-eight seats. Before the election, Jameson's Progressive Party amalgamated with Fraser's Constitutional Party to form the Unionist Party, with Jameson as its leader. The Unionists represented industrial interests and outspokenly favored British supremacy, and had thirty-seven members in the first Parliament. Subsequently, in 1921, they merged with the SAP.

Natal had not experienced the turmoils of the other provinces, and it was not surprising that Natalians selected independents as their first representatives to Parliament.

As the British Secretary of State for Colonies explained to the House of Lords on July 27, 1909, the constitution represented 'a delicately balanced compromise'. It represented the utmost that the various elements would accept, even though the machinery set up might have provided better means for expressions of the differing local interests characteristic of a nonhomogeneous society. In the fervor of their enthusiasm, the South African constitution makers were not so farsighted as the gentlemen at Philadelphia in 1787. Certainly, Smuts wrongly assessed the American experience. One result of the imposition of unitary government on such a diversified society as that of South Africa has been the confusion of citizenship. In America, all persons are citizens of the United States and of the state in which they reside. The duality has helped to ease the differences that exist among the states. In South Africa, there is only one citizenship, a fact that has contributed to the attitude expressed in the saying 'there are no South Africans'. The experience of the United States has shown that a federal system, as the delegates to the Progressive Party conference of 1960 seemed to grasp, can be a means for compromising differences in a country with a heterogeneous population.

As de Kiewiet has noted, the Union constitution represented a triumph for the frontier Boer. The British lost the Boer War by winning it and in effect capitulated South Africa to the Boers. Yet, curiously enough, they had no alternative. It is probable that the Boers would not have signed a peace treaty in 1902 had not certain provisions favorable to them been included, and they would not have agreed to union in 1908-9, without certain guarantees in the constitution, especially with respect to language rights and the franchise.

In the postwar period, the Afrikaner nationalists were groping for an answer to the dilemma of defeat. Save for the common stigma borne by all who could be termed 'Afrikaner' or 'Boer', there were few factors that contributed to the growth of national consciousness; defeat had a sobering effect and was cause for a good deal of serious introspection; it also prompted yet further introversion. At the same time, the formation of Afrikaner political organizations and the establishment of 'Christian-National' Afrikaner schools—developments that took place largely as a response to Milner's efforts at anglicization—were to have a lasting influence on Afrikaner nationalism.

4   Resurgence

*And the Lord said, I have surely seen the affliction of my people
. . ., and have heard their cry by reason of their taskmasters; for
I know their sorrows.*

EXODUS 3 : 8

WITH THE ESTABLISHMENT of the Union, the way was open for the eventual
supremacy of the Afrikaner. As already remarked, all Union Prime Ministers
have been Afrikaners; but not all of them have represented extreme Afrikanerdom. The first, General Botha, was a moderate, whose policies produced
opposition from more extremist elements that led to the political hiving of
Hertzog in 1912, the establishment of the National Party in 1914, and its
accession to power, in a coalition government, in 1924. Hertzog's co-
operation with Creswell in 1924 and with Smuts in 1933, led in turn to the
hiving of a yet more extreme group, the 'purified' Nationalists of Dr Daniel
Malan, in 1934. It was the last-named group that finally gained complete
ascendancy in 1948. Each of the hivings listed above represented the defection of an extreme right wing from a conservative main body.

Afrikaner nationalism has its roots in the Dutch East India Company
period, but its greatest growth has been since the Boer War. In the twentieth
century, Afrikaner nationalism has been a slow-moving but aggressive and
persistent force in South Africa. Its leaders have been those Afrikaners with
the strongest sense of grievance, including military men, ministers of the
gospel, farmers, lawyers, scholars, and journalists. These individuals have
given form to present-day Afrikaner nationalism. They have incited a
strong sense of group consciousness among Afrikaners, and they have
propelled nationalism on its path by constant reminders of past periods of
crisis: the Boer War, a British imperialist war with all its hardships and concentration camps; the Union constitution, claimed to be the result of a
British conspiracy; and the humiliating efforts of Milner to anglicize South
Africa after the war.

The events following the Union certainly helped to intensify Afrikaner
nationalism: the first world war and the suppression of the Afrikaner Rebellion; the strikes of 1913, 1914, and 1922; the postwar depression; the establishment of the Afrikaner Broederbond in 1918, and the later influence on it

of the rise of national socialism in Germany; the second world war and its aftermath, the decline of Britain as a world power and the rise of nationalism in Asia and Africa—all were factors in the continued growth of extreme Afrikaner nationalism. Extremist Afrikaner leaders feared a loss of group identity from the co-operative spirit manifested by Botha, Smuts, and Hofmeyr; they resented the decision to go to war on two occasions, 1914 and 1939, against a people who, in their view, were less dangerous than the British. A climate favorable to nationalist extremism was produced by the economic distresses of the 1920s and 1930s, which threatened the Afrikaner in particular; by the rise of nazi Germany, and the sympathetic *Herrenvolk* ideas the nazis espoused; by the threat of the growing self-consciousness of the non-European community; and, finally, by the urbanization of the Afrikaner, which, being accompanied by the diminution of group identity, inspired efforts to restore that identity. The press, largely British-oriented and strongly critical of Afrikaner extremism, unwittingly fostered a greater sense of belonging among Afrikaners. All these forces nurtured the nationalism that exists today. Each has intensified group consciousness and contributed further to the growth of fanatical determination.

It was not until 1948 that the extreme Afrikaner nationalists in the Kruger tradition finally achieved sole power without having to form part of a coalition. The difficulties they had experienced in achieving such control presaged that they would exert their best efforts to preserve what they had won and to create a society in which the identity of their people would not again be threatened. Group consciousness is fed by threats to the group, growing more intense in proportion to the degree of seriousness that the members attach to the threat, the degree of class homogeneity in the group, the number of factors common to the group, and the geographical closeness of the membership.

Until recently, Afrikaners generally reflected a feeling of inferiority toward the British, which of itself strengthened a sense of togetherness among them. On the other hand, Afrikaners have had a long association with the Africans to whom they feel superior. These two relationships set them apart as a distinct group. And there has been in late years a deliberate attempt to conquer any vestiges of a feeling of inferiority toward the British. Afrikaners have a common history dating back to van Riebeeck, which they do not permit themselves to forget. The very concern about the survival of the Afrikaner way of life that the British have in the past given the Afrikaners has further strengthened their sense of belonging to a particular group.

This has been particularly true in the field of education. After the Boer War, many teachers from England were employed in South Africa, especially in the Transvaal and Orange Free State; the Afrikaners refer to their presence as part of Milner's efforts to anglicize South Africa. As late as 1960, the Reverend W. J. du Toit, a minister of the Dutch Reformed Church, stated:

Following the peace treaty of Vereeniging in 1902, Sir Alfred Milner was determined to anglicize the Boer population of the conquered republics. With this in view, he imported teachers straight from England and decreed that only one official language should be used in every school, 'and damn the consequences' (his well-known words).[1]

Most instruction was given in English, with Dutch as a secondary language. This state of affairs provided the incentive to establish Afrikaans-medium schools in the ex-republics, and was a primary cause for early Afrikaner efforts to organize politically after the Boer War. The ministers of the Dutch Reformed churches urged the establishment of church schools such as had existed in the republics to be subsidized by the state. In them, Afrikaans would be the medium and Calvinist tenets would form the basis of instruction. These suggestions were provoked by the existence of Roman Catholic and Anglican church schools to which many Afrikaner parents sent their children. The extremists claimed that the type of Afrikaans-medium schools they had in mind would provide 'Christian-National Education' (*Christelike Nasionale Onderwys*), and the struggle for CNE has persisted since that time. Afrikaner leaders have recognized the importance of the school in inculcating a pride in the *Boerenasie.* They also have recognized that without separate Afrikaner schools the Afrikaner tradition and culture would be submerged by the English.

The struggle was twofold: for recognition of Afrikaans and for the establishment of Afrikaans schools. In the post-Boer War period, the Afrikaans movement revived the Afrikaner spirit. The treaty of Vereeniging had guaranteed the teaching of the Dutch language in the schools on parental request, and in the Union constitution Dutch was given equality with English. Milner had decreed that in government schools in the Transvaal Dutch should be used as a medium of instruction for only two subjects, five hours a week, and only with the express permission of parents. Dr E. G. Malherbe of the University of Natal comments that 'the power of the State was used to bring about the denationalization of a people through the medium of the schools'. In opposition to such efforts, Christian-National Education (CNE) schools were established, especially in the Transvaal. After self-government was granted to the former republics, conditions changed. In 1907, the Transvaal provided for education in the mother tongue to Standard III; after Standard III, English was to be the medium for all but two subjects, and a knowledge of English was a prerequisite for promotion. In the Orange Free State, the so-called Hertzog Act of 1908 authorized instruction in the mother tongue up to Standard IV and its use in three subjects thereafter. Hertzog, as the Orange Free State's Minister of Education, came to be associated with resistance to the use of English by Afrikaners in schools; eventually he espoused the 'two-stream' policy for the Union, a policy defined as 'two nationalities, each flowing in separate channels'. Thus Milner's policy contributed to the growth rather than the decay of Afrikaner nationalism. Hertzog insisted on equal language rights because he feared that without equality of language Afrikaans and the

Afrikaner would be overwhelmed by the more advanced and dominant British culture.

The Split between Botha and Hertzog

In 1910, the various Afrikaner parties of the former colonies merged in the South Africa Party (SAP), and it was as leader of the SAP that General Botha became Prime Minister. Hertzog, who had been Minister of Education in the Orange River Colony, accepted the position of Minister of Justice in Botha's cabinet. Hertzog remained firm, however, in his conviction that the 'twin-stream' policy was the only way to prevent the total anglicization of South Africa. In a speech at Germiston, on December 5, 1911, he made his feelings clear. He insisted that the old Dutch-speaking South Africans represented the true South Africa, and for them there had been no other country. But, unlike Malan at a later date, he interpreted the term 'Afrikaner' broadly enough to include both Afrikaans- and English-speaking persons whose roots were in South Africa and who placed South Africa's interests above those of any other country. The English, he observed, were of two types: those who had lived long in South Africa and had accepted it as home and those who still maintained allegiance to Britain. In other words, 'the two streams still flow, though a good deal of the one has been diverted into the other'.[2] In a speech at Nylstroom, on October 5, 1912, he remarked: 'In 1910 the people might have assimilated the opposition just as a farmer might put a bastard sheep among his "mofschapen," but once the separation had been made complete by such things as the "Vote British" cry, reunion became increasingly difficult.'[3] As Oswald Pirow, Hertzog's Minister of Justice and, in the 1930s, founder of the New Order, has said: 'General Hertzog . . . saw only Afrikaners and a handful of Afrikanerised English as against the balance of the population who were prepared to perpetuate the injustice of the treaty of Vereeniging.'[4]

Botha's insistence on Boer-British co-operation was diametrically opposed to Hertzog's belief in the twin streams, and after Botha's reaffirmation of co-operation during a trip to England in 1911 to attend an Imperial Conference, the breach widened. In 1913, Botha described his policy as 'the building up of a united nation on nonparty lines'. He strove to merge Boer and Briton into one united South African community. It should be noted that both Botha and Hertzog conceived of a united nation, differing only in how unity should be achieved. Apparently, Hertzog wanted unity under the Afrikaner standard while Botha envisaged amalgamation of Boer and Briton, the final product to be worked out by time. Hertzog feared that time would result in British dominance, and he saw Botha's co-operation with the British as a confirmation of this. He believed Botha was placing South Africa in a position of subservience as part of the British Empire, even though Botha had insisted he 'would never tolerate anything which affected South African autonomy'. In addition Hertzog had championed the cause of the Afrikaner in the Free State, which led to his being attacked in the British press as rabidly anti-British. Moreover, Hertzog disagreed with

Botha on the constitutional issue, and the two interpreted self-determination somewhat differently. Hertzog believed that South Africa must have absolute independence in all matters, including liberty to decide whether or not to go to war or even to secede from the Empire. On one occasion he declared: 'We are . . . a brother state with full control of our own affairs and responsible to ourselves alone. South Africa must work out its own salvation.' At De Wildt in December, 1912, he insisted that 'imperialism suits me only when it is of use to South Africa. Where it clashes with the interests of South Africa, I am its inveterate opponent'.[5] He worked for complete independence, and was influential in the preparation of the Balfour Declaration of 1926, which led to the Statute of Westminster of 1931. Hertzog was a man of great determination, tempered by a respect for the law. His motto was that of the prophet: *Nie deur Krag of Geweld nie, maar deur My Gees sal dit Geskied* ('Not by force or violence, but by My spirit will it be done'). He had sided with the judges against President Kruger; in 1913, he opposed the deportation of labor agitators without trial; and, in 1914, he did his best to stop the Boer Rebellion. Hertzog's respect for law and relative moderation were sources of misgiving to the more demanding Boers. Later, in 1934, he was to join in a coalition government with Smuts. In 1935, he openly attacked the Broederbond, the influential Afrikaner nationalist secret society. However, he opposed South Africa's entry into the second world war, and thus returned to the extremist fold, only to leave it again when he discovered he could not accept all the principles of the Nationalists of the 1940s.

Efforts to reconcile the opposing points of view of Botha and Hertzog proved abortive, and, in 1912, Botha resigned as Prime Minister in order to be able to reconstitute his cabinet without Hertzog, since, as he said, 'General Hertzog proved to be not prepared to resign'. Hertzog then formed the National Party, the beginnings of the National Party of Malan, Strijdom, and Verwoerd. Hertzog pleaded for a South African nationalism unobstructed by British imperialism. For his part, Botha found it impossible to head a government that 'spoke with two voices'.

The controversy, freely reported in the newspapers, fanned the flame of nationalism. The National Party was conceived in despair and nurtured on frustration. On December 28, 1912, General de Wet, a critic of Botha, speaking from a huge compost heap which served as a platform, expressed the feelings of Hertzog and his followers when he declared that 'I would rather be on a dung heap with my people than in the palaces of the Empire'. In November, 1913, the Union Congress of the South Africa Party met and gave Botha a vote of confidence by 131 to 90, thus serving to complete the split. Early in January, 1914, members of the South Africa Party of the Orange Free State held a special congress at Bloemfontein to organize the National Party. Hertzog had the support of former President Steyn, of the OFS, and of General de Wet, as well as the group known as the Afrikaner Young Turks. The 'Programme of Principles' of the new National Party declared:

> The National Party represents the national conviction and aspirations of the South African people within the Union . . . acknowledges the

guidance of God in the destinies of countries and peoples and seeks to develop the people's life along Christian national lines . . . recognizes the necessity of fostering a strong sense of national autonomy and expressly declares that the interests of the Union and its people should be put before those of any other country or people.[6]

Hertzog had a strong hand in the composition of this document, and he spent his remaining years seeking to implement its provisions; but it was the 'purified' Nationalists of Dr Daniel Malan who were to give it fuller voice.

The newly organized National Party was slow in getting started. It faced a great deal of opposition. The whole of the press, both English and Afrikaans, was against it, supporting largely either Botha and the party in power or Sir Thomas Smartt's Unionists in opposition. The South Africa Party, from which the Nationalists had split, not only was in office, but also had funds and organization to maintain its position. Generals C. F. Beyers and J. H. de la Rey, who sympathized with Hertzog on the language issue, decided to support Botha and preserve party unity. Hertzog had meager organized support: former President Steyn was a sick man; only the Young Turks provided some local basis for the party by the establishment of 'vigilance committees' in various provinces. In Parliament, Hertzog had only five members, although he had a potential ally in the Labour Party. The possibility of such an alliance first became apparent on April 29, 1913, when Labour sided with the Nationalists in a no-confidence vote. The views of F. H. P. Creswell, the leader of the Labour Party, in some ways coincided with those of Hertzog; certainly, as regarded the Rand magnates. Hertzog and Creswell combined against the government on various occasions, and in 1924 they joined forces to oust the SAP and set up the coalition Pact government.

The government's decision actively to support the British in the first world war was the first major event to encourage the growth of the new National Party, for it caused many to question the government's aims. The Boer War had ended only twelve years before, and the wound was far from healed. These had been years of uncertainty, when much had depended on the determination of Botha and Smuts to defend their position, as well as their personal courage and stamina.

Rebellion

The government's decision to declare war against Germany in September produced an immediate reaction. To the 'rock-hard' Boer, the primary enemy was Britain, not Germany—a fact demonstrated by the Afrikaner Rebellion of 1914. General C. F. Beyers, the Commandant-General of the Union's Defence Forces, resigned on September 15, 1914, because, as he wrote to Botha: 'It is said that the war is being waged against the "barbarity" of the Germans. We have forgiven, but not forgotten, all the barbarities perpetrated in our country during the Boer War.'[7]

That same evening, Generals Beyers and de la Rey left Pretoria for

Potchefstroom, in the Western Transvaal, apparently to meet General Jan Kemp, Smuts' comrade in the Boer War, who headed four mounted regiments, and arrange with him to march on Pretoria under the *Vierkleur* (the four-colored Transvaal flag) and overthrow the Union government. The coup was to be led by General de la Rey, whose dissatisfactions with Botha had been growing for some time. He had been patient at first, but, as Crafford has noted, 'at Vereeniging Botha had induced him to agree to the treaty by telling him that a favorable opportunity for regaining Boer independence would come later on when Britain was in trouble'.[8] To de la Rey that opportunity had now come and the assistance extended to Britain by Botha could scarcely be construed as advancing the cause of Boer independence. The extent of the bitterness of the extremists can be discerned in the epithets that they piled on Botha during this period: 'Judas,' 'traitor,' 'bloodhound,' 'murderer'. Like Hertzog, Malan, Strijdom, and Verwoerd, de la Rey favored an independent South African republic, with no association with Great Britain. Unlike Hertzog, he apparently believed force should be used to attain it.

General de la Rey was accidentally killed by a policeman while passing through Langlaate in the Johannesburg suburbs, and the planned *coup d'état* was abandoned. Meanwhile, Generals Kemp, de Wet, and Beyers continued as the foci of Afrikaner discontent. General Maritz, the commander of South African forces in the Northwestern Cape, defected to the Germans in Southwest Africa, and, despite the moderating efforts of Hertzog and Steyn, a clash between the Boer intransigents and the government became inevitable.

The Rebellion of 1914 failed miserably because the rebels, though a significant force, were poorly armed and greatly outnumbered, and apparently disliked attacking fellow-Boers. The rising was suppressed by the Botha-Smuts government, after more than three hundred persons had been killed. General Beyers had died (of drowning), but General Kemp, later a cabinet minister, and General de Wet were incarcerated. The execution of Commandant 'Japie' Fourie as 'an example' (to quote Pirow) caused agitation against Smuts, who refused the reprieve sought by the Nationalists. The Fourie execution has become a symbol for the Nationalists. In the outer office of the National Party in Pretoria, hangs the picture and last will and testament of 'Japie' Fourie, prominently attesting to the importance attached to his death.

The rebellion taught the Afrikaner extremists the wisdom of careful planning—that one should not reap before the corn is ripe. Meanwhile, they learned the importance of proper organization. The rebellion reconfirmed what the Boer War had taught, that force was not the answer, that battle must be pitched in the political arena. Thus, in a real sense, modern Afrikaner nationalism, conceived in the Boer War, was born in the 1914 rebellion. If the first world war had not taken place, the Boers might have been better able to adjust to the conciliatory policy of Botha and Smuts. The war forced on them the decision to organize, first covertly in the form of the Afrikaner Broederbond, later openly in the form of the 'purified' National Party.

When the rebellion had been suppressed, the government was able to launch a military campaign against the German colony of Southwest Africa. General Botha took personal command of the South African forces and achieved victory with a small loss of life. The government then decided to hold a general election in June, 1915. The results were not encouraging. The rebels had been disenfranchised; yet the Nationalists were able to win nearly a third of the votes.

Smuts went to London in 1917 to join the Imperial War Cabinet. In 1918, Botha travelled to Paris to sign the Treaty of Versailles to which his partner, Smuts, had made such an important contribution, particularly as regards the mandate system and the organization of the League of Nations. Shortly after his return to South Africa in 1919, Botha died, and Smuts inherited the position of Prime Minister, supported by the British, by Afrikaner war veterans, and by the Rand magnates.

The Hertzog-Creswell Coalition

In the development of the National Party, the period 1913–24, which culminated in the party's first advent to office, was highly important. It saw the height of Hertzog's power and the rise of Roos and Malan, and the organization of the Afrikaner Broederbond. Steyn's death in 1916 seems to have impressed Hertzog with his responsibilities to the Steyn-Kruger tradition.

On July 26, 1915, the Cape Town daily paper *Die Burger* commenced publication to give voice to Afrikaner sympathies. Dr Daniel Malan, a minister of the Dutch Reformed Church, was its first editor. In October, 1915, the National Party position was consolidated in the Cape by Dr Malan, and the young lawyer Tielman Johannes de Villiers Roos took charge in the Transvaal, Botha's home ground. The Nationalists attacked Botha and Britain where it hurt the most. They continually referred to British ambivalence—British statesmen were now, at the end of the first world war, preaching the Wilsonian concepts of the rights of small states and self-determination, but had not hesitated to terminate the independent existence of the South African Republic and Orange Free State in 1902. The Federal Council of the National Party at Bloemfontein went so far as to pass a resolution asking the Central Committee of the National Party to take steps to demand of Britain the 'restoration of our independence'. A deputation was accordingly sent to Paris in 1919 where its members saw Lloyd George, but returned empty-handed, save for the conviction that the reasoning of the party council at Bloemfontein had been correct. Even Hertzog, far less volatile than his lieutenant in the Transvaal, Tielman Roos, was now convinced that Vereeniging should be avenged and a republic established outside the British Empire.

After Smuts succeeded Botha in 1919, he decided on an election early the following year. The results were bad for Smuts and reflected growing popular dissensions. The persistence of Malan, Roos, and Hertzog paid off. The Nationalists won the largest number of seats (forty-four), followed by the SAP (forty-one), the Unionists (twenty-five), Labour (twenty-one), and Independents (three). Hertzog had attacked Smuts for his war policy, pointed to his association with Britain, and declared: 'It is the sole object of General Smuts to form a great British Empire. South Africa is too small for him. He wants to stand on a mountain instead of an antheap and to have his feet in two continents.'

A coalition was Smuts' only hope, but there were difficulties in its way. Creswell would not take part in it and, in any case, Labour was discredited because of its praise of Russian communism. Hertzog would not join with the Unionists under any circumstances, but would ally his party with the SAP on condition that the Prime Minister be elected by the MPs in coalition. Because of the Nationalist majority, this would, of course, make him Prime Minister, which Smuts could not accept. The Unionists at the time were willing to amalgamate with the SAP, but Smuts felt the time was not ripe. In September, 1920, Afrikaners of both the SAP and the National Party met at Bloemfontein to try to work out a reunion of the two groups that had split in 1914. All the meeting did was to emphasize to both the SAP and the National Party the impracticability of such a move, since Hertzog insisted on sticking to his demands for a republic. Finally, Smuts convinced his party and the Unionists of 'the Nationalist danger to South Africa and the Empire', and the SAP and the Unionists joined forces after all. One result was to increase the British element in the SAP, where it was eventually to predominate. Another election was held in 1921, and this time Smuts and his new party won a clear majority of seventy-nine seats, while Labour obtained only nine; the Nationalists gained one seat and had a total of forty-five. In the election of 1924, however, Smuts was ousted by a coalition of Hertzog and Creswell.

Friendly relations between the Nationalists and Labour had been developing since April, 1913, when Hertzog and Creswell voted together on a no-confidence motion against the government. In 1913, there was a strike of miners on the Rand. Government troops were called in to put down the strike, and a number of persons were killed. The shootings aroused the miners, and Botha and Smuts assumed great personal risk in negotiating with them; as a result, the belief grew that Smuts and Botha, the leaders of the SAP, represented the interests of the mine owners, while Hertzog, along with Creswell and his party, were the friends of the working man. In January, 1914, there was a general strike involving railway workers and miners. Again the government intervened, this time taking the extreme step of deporting the strike leaders, much to the shock of Creswell and his party. Hertzog criticized the government for the use of martial law and deportation without trial. Thus, the bond between Hertzog and Creswell was strengthened as when both attacked Botha and Smuts.

The first world war rallied all English-speaking South Africans behind the SAP, and the two strikes had already confirmed SAP support of the mainly English-speaking mine owners. These were the experiences that brought the Unionists, largely representing the English element, and the SAP together—an alliance that was, in the opinion of many, a fatal mistake for Smuts. Certainly, Botha had always opposed it.[9] The industrial upheaval produced by the general strike of 1922 was the climax of growing discontent, and proved to be Smuts' *coup de grâce*. The immediate cause of the strike was the attempt of the mining companies to implement the recommendation of the Low Grade Mines Commission of 1920, and remove the legal color bar imposed in 1911 (by the Mines and Works Act, which protected white labor in certain mine jobs), in order to permit the hiring of more cheap African labor. Smuts was determined to suppress the 'Rand Revolution' by force to 'prove an object lesson to the people of this country forever'.[10] Both Hertzog and Creswell, from their different standpoints, opposed the large financial interests and wished to protect the white workers. The government's actions against the strikers brought them together, and enabled them to join in ousting Smuts from office in 1924. The alliance of Nationalists and Labour was a strange marriage of convenience; essentially, it was a white man's front against the Africans created for the purpose of raising white wages and ensuring jobs for the 'poor whites', the overwhelming majority of whom were Afrikaners. The 'poor white' problem is, indeed, the key to much of South African history during the 1920s.

In the early twentieth century, large numbers of whites and non-whites alike left the South African countryside and flocked to the towns. The reasons for the depopulation of the rural areas were many: they included periodic droughts, the upheaval caused by the Boer War, the collapse of the ostrich feather industry at the beginning of the first world war, and farm inefficiency and bankruptcy;[11] at the same time, the growth of industry, which was exceptionally rapid during the first world war, greatly increased the demand for labor in the urban areas. In 1870, South Africa was almost entirely rural. By 1904, the white rural population had dropped to 47 per cent; by 1931, to 39 per cent; and by 1961, only 16 per cent of the whites were on farms.[12] Urbanization exposed the Boers to a culture and technology clearly superior to their own, and has thus had a disturbing influence—a denationalizing or detribalizing effect. This has presented even more compelling reasons for the subsequent efforts of Afrikaner extremists to organize and retribalize their people.

The rural whites have always been, and still are, predominantly Afrikaner. Many of the English settlers of 1820 did not remain long on their farms in the Eastern Province of the Cape, and later English immigrants have generally elected to live in the cities. The Afrikaner was a farm dweller from the beginning, living a simple existence on his vast land holdings. There, he developed a particular distaste for efforts to control him, whether by the Dutch East India Company officials or British administrators. He rebelled at paying taxes and disliked the discipline associated with efforts to earn profits. He recoiled at British efforts to educate him. The Bible, especially the Old Testament, comprised the basis of his knowledge. There was only slight social distinction between the poorest and the wealthiest *burgers* (citizens). The use of a gun and a horse determined the worth of a man, and the possession of land and sheep and cattle determined his wealth. Land was plentiful, and each of many sons could have as large a holding as his father.[13] By the beginning of the eighteenth century, it was not uncommon to find white squatters (who became known as *bywoners*) settled on farms in the outlying areas, at first mainly for safety. During the nineteenth century the practice was common. Landless men, the *bywoners* farmed on a share system. Very early, however, manual labor came to be regarded as the province of non-Europeans—at first, Hottentots and slaves; later, in Natal, Indians; and finally Bantu (the very word commonly used for unskilled labor in Afrikaans is *Kafferwerk*). Gradually, farm labor was turned over to non-Europeans. The Africans lost control of the land, but they continued to work it, and to derive a living from it as tenants, herdsmen, laborers, and renters. In time, the two groups, Afrikaners and Africans, began to fuse. According to some authorities, a high percentage of Afrikaners have some non-European ancestry, a factor profoundly disturbing to the official values of Afrikanerdom; the fact of widespread miscegenation has in itself contributed to Afrikaner nationalism and its effort to maintain the identity of Afrikanerdom as a white group.[14]

When the Afrikaner began moving to the towns, he took with him the attitudes he had inherited from the farm. He was unskilled, but being white, he could not engage in unskilled labor. This was *Kafferwerk*.[15] In the Boer republics, privilege had depended on the color of one's skin. The Transvaal constitution had insisted that there should be 'no racial equality in church and state'. But as growing numbers of Afrikaners moved to town, the problem of how they were to gain a livelihood and maintain their privileged status as whites became acute. Africans and poor whites competed for the available jobs. The poor whites closely resembled the poor blacks. Both were landless and both were unskilled. But black labor was cheaper than white, and the poor whites in any case considered themselves above manual labor. As a result, unemployment and ever greater depths of poverty and degradation were the lot of many whites. Meanwhile, the Africans, more and more of whom were being forced by circumstances into the ranks of a depressed black proletariat, labored for wages too low to do more than barely support life.

The Afrikaner Nationalist leaders grew increasingly concerned with the problem of the poor whites. The presence of this group, with nothing but their sense of racial superiority to set them off from the African masses, was a significant factor in the development of Afrikaner nationalism during the 1920s. Efforts to improve the position of the poor whites, to develop in them a heightened sense of their identity as part of the Afrikaner people, and to prevent their absorption into an undifferentiated proletariat, occupied much of the attention of the Afrikaner leadership during that period. The Labour Party was equally concerned to protect the interests of white labor —until 1946, it represented only white workers. In that year, it opened its doors to all workers, regardless of color, a step that was followed by a drastic decline in power. In 1958, for the first time since Union, no Labour members were returned to Parliament.

This was the background against which the results of the 1924 election reflected growing dissatisfaction with the government. Hertzog's National Party captured sixty-three seats, Smuts' SAP, fifty-three, and Labour, eighteen. In addition, there was one Independent. With the National and

Labour parties joined in a 'pact', Hertzog had a sizable majority, and became Prime Minister.

Once in power, Hertzog set to work to translate into action some of the principles he had in common with Creswell. Coalition, however, limited Hertzog's freedom to act, at least to the extent that the Labour Party insisted on retaining the British connection. The limitations on Nationalist action were set forth in the Creswell Memorandum, published immediately after the election. The Labour Party was mainly British in its leadership (though not in membership), a fact that was a bone of contention to the most ardent Afrikaner extremists. Like the Nationalists, the members of the Labour Party felt the economic threat of the Africans, with their lower wage rates. The Nationalists, like Labour, took a strong stand in favor of the subordination of the Africans to the whites. In a sense, the parties were beginning in the 1920s to assume a philosophic basis. The SAP now combined the membership of the British Unionists and the old South Africa Party, and it represented big business and a policy of conciliation between the various groups in South Africa. On the other hand, the Nationalists, most of whose members were hard-core Afrikaner extremists, had joined forces with the British-led Labour Party on common ideological grounds. To make the coalition possible, both parties made concessions: Labour agreed to drop its demands for socialism, while the Nationalists agreed to shelve national independence. Such toying with principles was difficult for the most intransigent Boers to understand. At the National Party Congress of 1922, Dr Malan, representing the extreme element, had made it quite clear that coalition would mean a departure from principle. Dislike of compromise was one of the reasons why Malan eventually broke away from the National Party—as Hertzog had broken away from the SAP—and formed the 'purified' National Party. In 1922, he declared that coalition

> means the continuous trafficking in principles; it means the violation of conscience; it means double heartedness, and dishonesty on the part of the political leaders, who have to try all the time to placate the most widely differing elements among its supporters. It means the raising of opportunism to the level of statesmanship, and the dethronement of principle in order to make way for political lack of character. Under a coalition no problems can be tackled or solved in a manly way.[16]

'Fusion'—The Alliance of Hertzog and Smuts

It had long been the aim of Hertzog and his Nationalists to take South Africa out of the British Empire and establish a republic; by 1926, however, following the Balfour Declaration, Hertzog could rightfully say: 'The old British Empire as it existed in the past now exists no longer.'

The Balfour Declaration grew out of an Imperial Conference that took place in London in October, 1926. The Declaration stated that the self-governing communities of the Empire, consisting of the United Kingdom and the Dominions, 'are autonomous communities within the British

Empire, equal in status, in no way subordinate one to another in any aspect of their domestic or external affairs, though united by a common allegiance to the Crown, and freely associated as members of the British Commonwealth of Nations'. The Declaration added that in certain areas any act of a Dominion repugnant to the Imperial (British) Parliament was invalid. This Declaration was the first formal step in the constitutional development of the Commonwealth.

As a result of the Balfour Declaration, a South African Ministry of External Affairs was set up in 1927, and by 1929 South Africa was sending ministers plenipotentiary to Washington, Rome, and The Hague. It was beginning to appear to the anglophiles as though Hertzog was up to his old tricks, and that it would only be a matter of time before he would take South Africa out of the Commonwealth. To counter such fears, Hertzog declared:

> I am in favour of the British connection being maintained. The Nationalists do not look upon secession as a matter of practical politics. A Government is in power which considers itself the trustee of the people and no longer the agent of any other country. Though I hold it in common with a great many of the most distinguished English statesmen that any Dominion has the right to secede, such a decision, so far as the Union is concerned, would be a flagrant mistake and a national disaster.

Hertzog added: 'I hold further that only in the gravest national consideration could such a step be taken without the concurrence as a whole of the two great sections of the people.'

The next step in the development of the Commonwealth was the Statute of Westminster of 1931, which gave the Dominion parliaments complete legislative sovereignty; henceforth, acts of the Imperial Parliament were to be valid in a Dominion only if approved by the parliament of that Dominion. The Statute of Westminster freed the Union government from any formal control by the British government; the King of England was still sovereign in South Africa, but in South African affairs he could now act only on the advice of his South African ministers.

The Status of the Union Act, passed by the South African Parliament in 1934, gave final confirmation to the independent status of South Africa within the Commonwealth. It proclaimed the Union Parliament to be a sovereign legislative body; in conformity with the Statute of Westminster, no British legislation was to apply to South Africa unless also enacted by the Union Parliament. The only remaining limitation on South African sovereignty was the continuation of the Privy Council in Great Britain as the highest court of appeal for the Commonwealth. After the passage of the Statute of Westminster and the Status of the Union Act, the posts of Governor-General of South Africa and High Commissioner for the territories of Bechuanaland, Basutoland, and Swaziland were no longer held by the same person. Since the Statute of Westminster, the British High Commissioner in South Africa has also held the office of High Commissioner, and in 1937 Sir Patrick Duncan became the first South African to hold the post of

Governor-General. Despite all this, the mere fact that government was carried on in the name of the British monarch was enough to disturb die-hard Boers.

Further to emphasize its independence, the South African Parliament had passed the Union Flag Bill in 1927, after a heated debate lasting three sessions (1925–27); the bill gave South Africa its own national flag to be flown alongside the Union Jack. Malan, then Minister of the Interior, in introducing the Flag Bill told Parliament:

> A flag is not a mere cloth; a flag symbolizes national existence, a flag is a living thing; it is a repository of national sentiment. A flag is able to move fears; a flag can stir the deepest springs of action and it can inspire to the nobler efforts. For a flag a nation can live; for it, it can fight and it can die.[17]

The flag finally agreed upon represented a compromise—not a very inspiring national symbol, but Natal talked of secession, her traditional defense, and the compromise calmed her. The Boer die-hards wanted the old Transvaler *Vierkleur* as the national flag; the British elements wanted to retain the Union Jack. The result was a red, white, and blue flag with small replicas of the flags of the Orange Free State, Transvaal, and the Union Jack arranged along the centre.*

In 1929, Hertzog resigned in order to reconstitute his government. As a result of the election that followed the Nationalists had a clear majority of seventy-eight seats, to only five for Creswell's Labour Party and three for the National Council Labour Party which had split from Creswell's group. However, Hertzog included two Labour leaders in his new cabinet as he had done in his first ministry.

The major issue facing Hertzog's second ministry was economic depression, which was to be the cause of his downfall, as it had been that of Smuts in 1924. The question of the gold standard became a critical issue. Hertzog refused to leave it as Britain had done. This decision caused Labour to withdraw from the Pact government in 1931. Hertzog's Economic Minister, Havenga, vowed to 'use all the resources of the state' to maintain the gold standard, but events would not permit it; the ensuing crisis paved the way for the re-entry into politics of Tielman Roos, who had become a member of the Supreme Court. Roos dramatically resigned his position in order to emphasize the seriousness of the problem; and he seemed bent on leading South Africa out of the crisis by uniting the Nationalists and SAP in a national government under his leadership.[18] Smuts countered by suggesting that the gold standard should be abandoned and a coalition government formed under Hertzog's leadership. Hertzog agreed, and after some persuasion from his old friends Deneys Reitz, Sir Patrick Duncan, and Jan Hofmeyr, Smuts accepted the post of Deputy Prime Minister. In other

* As Mr. Arthur Barlow pointed out to the author in 1961, the Union Jack was finally abolished as an official emblem by Parliament in 1957 with little debate, thus demonstrating how far the idea of independence had progressed in thirty years.

words, 'Roos had thrown the generals into each other's arms and in doing so, had brought disaster on himself'.[19]   Had there been no economic depression, and had Hertzog been able to remain on gold, Roos might have come to some kind of terms with Smuts against Hertzog.

In 1934, the coalition was made permanent, when the Nationalist and South Africa parties 'fused' into what became known as the United South Africa National Party.   Fusion was essentially the child of the depression. The extremists of both parties splintered to form the British-oriented Dominion Party under Colonel Stallard, and the *'gesuiwerde' Nasionale Party* ('purified' National Party) under Dr Daniel F. Malan.   A republic had been the wish of many Afrikaners ever since the British first took control of South Africa in 1795.   Hertzog had temporarily conceded the issue in 1924 as the price of getting Labour support; with the announcement of the Balfour Declaration in 1926, the passage of the Union Flag Bill in 1927, and the Statute of Westminster in 1931, Hertzog felt that all reasonable demands had been satisfied and that he could afford to enter into fusion with Smuts.   He made his satisfaction clear to the Orange Free State National Party Congress in 1930: 'After the decisions of the Imperial Conferences of 1926 and 1930 there is today not a single reason why on constitutional and political issues Dutch- and English-speaking South Africa should not feel and act in a spirit of a consolidated South African nation.'   Thinking ahead, he added: 'This is bound to happen and that it shall come about is the task to which the National Party is now called. . . .'   Hertzog went on to say: 'English- and Dutch-speaking South Africa stand ready today—as never before—ready to shake hands in mutual sincerity as equal.'   He added, 'and as equal Afrikaners'.[20] The statement shows how close the thinking of Hertzog and Botha and Smuts had become, now that some assurance of independence had been attained.   Hertzog still believed that, ideally, a republic was best for South Africa, but he was willing to wait until the English-speaking section of the population had accepted the idea.   Smuts and Botha maintained a steady belief in co-operation of the two European groups within the framework of the Commonwealth.   As Marquard has observed: 'Hertzog always looked over his shoulder to see if the Afrikaners were following him; Smuts looked to see if the English-speaking South Africans were following him.'[21]   The result was that the English distrusted Hertzog and the Afrikaners Smuts—as was later to become apparent on the war issue.   However, the two were both in favor of reconciliation of Boer and Briton, though they had travelled along different paths.   As far as the republican issue was concerned, Hertzog was essentially a gradualist; it was his gradualism that caused his split with Malan.   Thus, by 1934 the differences between Hertzog and Smuts were minor—in sharp contrast to 1912, when Hertzog defected from the SAP. The Smuts-Hertzog coalition, agreed to on February 21, 1933, was based on seven points, which included such tender issues as equal language rights for Afrikaans- and English-speaking persons, national autonomy as confirmed by the Statute of Westminster and symbolized by the national flag, maintenance of a sound rural population and continuance of the white labor policy, economic guarantees, and an effort to solve the 'native question' on the basis of separate political development of whites and Africans that would emphasize the requirements of white civilization without depriving the African of his right to develop.[22]

On March 15, 1933, the Cape Nationalists met in a special congress and accepted the seven points of the coalition, although Malan declined an invitation to join the cabinet. As Pirow has noted: 'By his refusal to join the coalition cabinet he handed over the future of the old Nationalist Party to General Smuts; but by becoming the leader of the Nationalist extremists he paved his way for a future Premiership.'[23]

On May 17, a general election was held. The Nationalists obtained seventy-five seats and the SAP sixty-one. Nationalist seats were distributed as follows: in Cape Province, twenty-seven; in the OFS, fifteen; in the Transvaal, thirty-two; and one in Natal.

Fusion was not accomplished easily, however. Both Hertzog and Smuts favored it. For Hertzog one of the most difficult obstacles was Malan. Malan had been the leader of the Cape Nationalists for years and had been in Hertzog's cabinet as Minister of Interior. He had made his views on coalition clear when Hertzog had joined with Labour in 1924. To Malan, coalition was bound to limit the freedom of action of any group. By 1933, however, he recognized that the National and South Africa parties had a good deal in common. Apparently, too, he was, at any rate at first, personally sympathetic to Hertzog, but the more extreme elements, such as the Afrikaans press and the Young Turks, and certainly the Cape Nationalists, influenced him to act otherwise.[24] Malan had expressed his objections to fusion in 1922, when the Labour-Nationalist coalition was being contemplated. In 1933, however, given certain assurances by Hertzog, he appeared agreeable to union. At the same time, he indicated that he personally would accept union, but that forces behind him stubbornly balked at the idea. In the issue of Die Vaderland of February 27, 1934, Malan was quoted in these words, which, according to Pirow, were approved by Malan in advance. 'Dr Malan declares himself enthusiastically in favour of a united Afrikanerdom by which is meant an Afrikanerdom of English- as well as Afrikaans-speaking members on the basis of South African nationhood.' He was simply parroting Hertzog's words of 1912.

Hertzog, for his part, was insistent on fusion. As early as 1920, he had declared that 'there is today not a single reason why on constitutional and political issues Dutch- and English-speaking South Africa should not feel and act in a spirit of a consolidated South African nation'. And Hertzog was fully aware that fusion would result in the hiving of extremists of both parties. Malan, meanwhile, was insisting he wanted 'reunion' and not 'fusion'. By reunion, he apparently meant reunion with only those in the SAP who were sympathetic to the National Party program. He said in a letter to Hertzog, dated September 16, 1933:

I am concerned with the preservation and propagation of Nationalism. I therefore feel that the National Party, which so far has been the best embodiment of that principle, may be surrendered for something else only if Nationalism is completely safe within such a new party and can maintain its fullest evolution.

By 'fullest evolution' he meant, of course, an independent republic, and what he would consider a proper solution to the 'native question'. As immediate steps toward such an end, he demanded that the new party should guarantee the abolition of appeal to the Privy Council, the right to openly advocate a republic, the appointment of a South African as Governor-General, the right to be neutral, the right of secession, and the use of the South African flag and *Die Stem van Suid Afrika* as the only national emblems.

Hertzog could not agree to include in any constitution the right to be neutral, since South Africa was already a member of the League of Nations and a signatory of the Kellogg-Briand Pact. As for the right of secession, he insisted that, in South Africa's interpretation, the Balfour Declaration and the Statute of Westminster already contained it, and it was unnecessary to put such a statement in the constitution. And Malan had praised the Balfour Declaration when it was made. Millin, in her two-volume biography of Smuts, quotes Malan's earlier acceptance of the Balfour Declaration:

Republican Independence is dead. (December 14, 1926)

Instead of looking upon Great Britain as the conqueror, we look upon her now as the mother of our freedom. (December 15, 1926)

The independence which the Nationalist Party has always lived for is now attained, and cannot well be more complete. (September 30, 1927).

The Status Act Bill of 1934, which had been introduced to appease the Malanites, apparently pleased Malan, but it failed to keep him from defecting. He apparently had already decided to leave the party to oppose fusion. He remarked: 'The independence which the Statute [of Westminster] gave us has now been assumed by us. Before we accepted the independence which was offered to us we did not have sovereign independence. . . . There is no longer a British Empire and it is misleading to speak of such an Empire.'

However, as Millin has observed, the Act really pleased no one. For the British it spelled defeat, and for the Boers only one more step toward an eventual republic.

It is strange that only a few weeks before Malan spoke so warmly of the Statute Act, his followers had accused Hertzog of betraying Afrikaner-dom. Perhaps, as Pirow has suggested, the answer lies in the fact Malan had not yet fully emerged as a leader.[25] He preferred to listen to others, in what he called 'leadership in council'. This seems to have placed him at the mercy of even more extreme Nationalists. The National Party's Federal Council met on October 13, 1933, after the National Party Provincial Congresses had met, and with the exception of the Cape Congress, had all backed Hertzog. Malan addressed the Federal Council at length. In essence, he declared the Cape Nationalists were completely unable to accept fusion. The other three representatives of the provinces then asked Hertzog to submit terms of reference for a new united party. By December,

Hertzog had a draft ready that he hoped would satisfy both parties, and he sent Smuts a copy.

At the National Party's Federal Council meeting in Pretoria on June 20, 1934, Malan and six others met together and agreed to oppose fusion. In July, the Cape National Congress met at Somerset West and voted 164 to 18 against fusion. Thus, the split was complete and the *'gesuiwerde' Nasionale Party*, commonly known as the Malanites, became the official opposition party.[26]

The fusion of the SAP and the National Party was completed in December, 1934, and the United South African National Party came into being.[27] 'The Programme of Principles and Constitution' of the fused United South African National Party was based on a series of compromises between Smuts and Hertzog, and influenced by Malan, although he finally decided against acceptance. The divisibility of the Crown and the right of secession and neutrality were not included in the party constitution. It emphasized 'developing a strong feeling of South African national unity'; that 'the government of the country shall be carried on on a basis of South African national principles and in a spirit of South African independence in harmony with our sovereign independent status, confirmed by the Statute of Westminster and the Status of the Union Act, 1934'; the maintenance of the existing relationship with the British Commonwealth of Nations, together with the guarantee that 'no one will be denied the right to express his individual opinion about or advocate his honest convictions in connection with any change of our form of government'. In other words, republican propaganda was to be allowed. Bilingualism was affirmed; and the national flag was to be the symbol of authority.

When Parliament met in January, 1935, the number of National Party members had dropped from seventy-five to nineteen. The OFS had four, including Charles Robbert Swart who later became Minister of Justice under Strijdom and subsequently Governor-General of the Union and President of the Republic. J. G. Strijdom, later Prime Minister, was the only Nationalist member from the Transvaal. The remainder were from the Cape.

Fusion, the product of the economic crisis, helped to crystallize the thinking of die-hard Afrikaners. Yet for the time being, it seemed to be Smuts who came out ahead. Hertzog was Prime Minister, and Smuts only his deputy, but Hertzog lost many of the Cape Nationalists who stuck by their leader, Malan. Nineteen Nationalist MPs defected, but Smuts lost only five of his followers to Colonel Stallard's Dominion Party. Stallard's party later disbanded. In the long run, however, the picture was very different. By 1948, the Malanite strength in Parliament had increased to seventy, sufficient to enable the Malanites to form a government. As a result of the war issue in 1939, the remainder of Hertzog's group defected, so that by 1948 the United Party was simply what the SAP had been prior to fusion—a party representing mainly English-speaking South Africans, but headed, as had become traditional, by an Afrikaner. Thus, the United Party of today can trace its history back to du Toit and Hofmeyr. In it, the moderate Hofmeyr tradition has always prevailed over extreme deviationist threats.

5 The Impact of Nazism

*Let them shout for joy, and be glad, that favour my righteous
cause.*

PSALM 35 : 27

BETWEEN 1933 AND 1945, events outside South Africa played a conspicuous
part in the development of Afrikaner nationalism.

The rise of national socialism in Germany and the rapid spread of its
philosophy found many admirers of the nazis among hard-core Afrikaners.
Neither Smuts nor Hertzog was, of course, in any way influenced by nazism.
Smuts was a friend of Britain, acknowledging South Africa's membership in
the Commonwealth and the responsibilities it entailed. He was acclaimed in
Britain, and was awarded many honors. He had been a member of the
Imperial War Cabinet in the first world war and had played a significant role
in the formation of the League of Nations.

Hertzog, on the other hand, was less favorable to the British connection. He was an Afrikaner nationalist, seeking the development of a truly
South African polity. Yet, as already noted, his definition of 'Afrikaner'
included anyone of European descent who placed South Africa first. While
he thought a republican form of government desirable, though no longer
essential, since effective independence had been achieved, he certainly
believed a republic should only be created legally and by the expressed will of
the people. He did not feel any of the need for violent change that impelled
sympathy with nazism.

Malan and the extreme right-wing Afrikaners were in a different
position. They wanted a republic, a single national flag and national
anthem, the right to be neutral, the right to secede, and more especially, the
ascendancy to power of the Afrikaner. At the time of fusion, the Malanites
were few in number (they were concentrated mainly in Cape Province) and
seemed to have little likelihood of acceding to political power. They became
oriented toward the German nazis, in whose philosophy and methods they
found something that conformed to their own pattern of thinking.

When the second world war broke out in September, 1939, South
Africa was divided, as it had been in 1914. Hertzog insisted on neutrality;
Smuts on joining with Britain. A cabinet split was inevitable. It was no

surprise when Hertzog announced the split to the Parliament on September
4, and asked for approval of his policy of 'qualified' neutrality.   He told
Parliament: 'I do not think I deserve to be left in the lurch at the last moment.
I said that South Africa would not be drawn into any war unless our interests
were threatened and I shall stand by that to the end.'[1]   Smuts then spoke for
active support of Britain, pointing to all the dangers of Hitlerism.

Hertzog's motion was defeated by eighty votes to sixty-seven.   He
therefore resigned, and asked the Governor-General, Sir Patrick Duncan, to
dissolve Parliament.   This Sir Patrick refused to do.   Instead, he asked
Smuts to form a cabinet.   The new government immediately declared war
on Germany.[2]

Hertzog then rejoined the National Party in Parliament, in opposition
to Smuts.   The party was renamed the Reunited National or People's Party
(*Die Herenigde Nasionale of Volksparty*, popularly referred to as the HNP),
with Hertzog as its head and Malan as his deputy.   Both agreed that republi-
canism 'is best suited to the traditions and aspirations of the South African
people and is the only effective guarantee that South Africa will not again be
drawn into the wars of Great Britain'.   The second world war, like the first,
brought the extremist Afrikaners together in opposition to participation in
the war on the side of Britain.   Sentiment against the war was strong
throughout South Africa, and the climate favorable for the growth of all
kinds of organizations to exploit such feelings.   But at the same time the
war caused a split in the Nationalist ranks that contributed to the strength of
the government.   Hertzog did not remain long with Malan, and eventually
he was read out of the party for being too sympathetic with Smuts and the
British cause, a poor tribute to a man who had done so much for Afrikaner
nationalism.

At the critical National Party Congress held in Bloemfontein in 1940,
the fundamental differences between the 'rock hards' and 'softs' became
clearer.   Hertzog introduced a resolution that read: 'The party aims at the
development of a strong sense of South African unity, based on the equal
rights of the Afrikaans- and English-speaking sections of the population
together with the recognition and appreciation of the cultural inheritance of
each.'

Swart, a protégé of Hertzog who was destined to become the first
President of the Republic, then moved a restatement of Hertzog's resolution
on behalf of the Federal Council.   The restatement, which was accepted by
the Congress, read as follows:

> The Party aims . . . at the cultivation of a strong sense of national inde-
> pendence as well as a strong feeling of national unity based on a common
> and undivided devotion to South Africa and its interests, and the recog-
> nition of equal language and cultural rights of both sections of the white
> population.

Hertzog retorted that 'he had made it clear in September, 1939, that
he would not be a member of a party which did not guarantee absolute
equality to the English- and Afrikaans-speaking people.   The "equal

language and cultural rights" clause in practice meant that no English-speaking person could be a leader in the party'.   Hertzog left the stormy meeting and the party with these words: 'I shall go.   Havenga and Brebner will come with me and, later, Malan will follow.'³   Swart, the Nationalist leader of the OFS, expressed regret that General Hertzog should retire 'on what amounted to the rights of the English-speaking people'.

On January 24, 1941, a small group of Hertzog's friends formed the Afrikaner Party, and, when Hertzog died in 1942, 'Klassie' Havenga became its head.

Thus it was that the outbreak of war in Europe destroyed the 'Fusion Government', and caused a realignment of South African political parties. Hostility to Britain brought the Afrikaners back together and caused the two major parties to divide along linguistic lines.   Without the war, the United (Fusion) Party would probably not have split.   Malan's Nationalists had gained only a few seats in the 1938 elections, and the UP was well in control of the government.

Thus, the rise of nazi Germany, by causing the outbreak of war, was indirectly responsible for the stimulation of Afrikaner nationalism and the split in the South African government.   Shortly after war had been declared, Hertzog told a large audience that Smuts, by his actions, had done more to bring about a complete break with Britain than anyone since Lord North. He blamed Smuts for destroying the United Party, and said that by that action he had brought back nationalist Afrikanerdom.

The nazis also made a more direct contribution to the development of Afrikaner nationalism.   Nazi ideas undoubtedly influenced the conception of the proposed *apartheid* policy that helped Malan into power in 1948.   The *Herrenvolk* (master race) philosophy of Hitler justified control by the European (*baasskaap*) and more especially by the Afrikaner, since, in the Afrikaner view, English-speaking South Africans could not be trusted to carry out such a scheme.   Hitler's philosophy certainly stiffened Afrikaner pride of race, and the nazi ideas of nationalism corresponded amazingly to the Afrikaners' own unorganized thinking.

Moreover, Hitler's attacks on the Jews found a sympathetic response among Afrikaners, the most impoverished ethnic group among the European population of South Africa.[4]   Many Jewish businessmen and financiers had prospered in the gold and diamond industries.   The South African Jewish community was swelled by refugees from Hitler's Germany during the 1930s. Since most Jews, whether South African born or recent arrivals from Europe, were better educated and had more business and professional motivations and experience than most Afrikaners, they were generally also more prosperous.   Comparisons provoked savage attacks on the Jewish community. Dr Theophilus Ebenhaezer Dönges offered a clue to such attacks during the Voortrekker celebrations in December, 1938, when he noted that 400,000 Afrikaners were living below the breadline through no fault of their own.[5] By perusing South African newspapers for the period immediately before the second world war, one can grasp the intensity of Afrikaner attacks on the Jewish community.   The Jews were blamed for many Afrikaner ills, no matter how trivial. Even the Dutch Reformed Church (DRC) of South Africa joined in the hue and cry. In the April 21, 1937, issue of *Patria*, for example, the DRC Synod raised its cudgels against the Jew; and a special committee of the OFS Synod discovered after careful study of the Bible that 'the Jews were not the chosen people'—although this conclusion was voted down (by sixty-four votes to sixty-one) by the whole Synod because of its nature as an 'intricate theological question'. Malan pressed for legislation to prohibit the immigration of Jews, and Eric Louw, later to be Foreign Minister, prepared such a bill for submission to Parliament. In this regard, said Louw, the National Party was ready to co-operate with every Christian Afrikaner whose only fatherland was South Africa and who desired only one national anthem and one flag.

In May, 1938, the Afrikaner extremists put up posters throughout South Africa warning against inter-racial marriages, an action that evoked a flood of criticism. The Afrikaners laid the responsibility for the criticism on the Jewish doorstep. The poster itself reflected the 'pure race' concepts of the nazis, and opposition to such ideas was quite naturally attributed to the Jews.

Smuts, whom Crafford describes as the great compromiser, attempted to pour oil on troubled waters and thus himself became the target of Nationalist attacks. The Nationalists pilloried him as the associate of capitalists, mine owners, and Jews. On May 23, 1938, the Malanite paper *Die Burger* of Cape Town published a cartoon by Boonzaier entitled 'The Victor'. It depicted Smuts and Hertzog carrying on their shoulders a heavy figure of a caricatured Jewish capitalist, and being led by the 'Imperialist Press'. The caption read: 'The man who really won the election.'

Malan's attitudes toward the Jews were summarized in a speech he made on July 10, 1939. He referred to the Jewish question 'which hangs like a dark cloud over South Africa. Behind the organized South African Jewry stands organized world Jewry.... They have robbed the population of its heritage so that the Afrikaner lives in the land of his father but no longer possesses it.'[6] In 1937, Dr Hendrik F. Verwoerd, professor of psychology at Stellenbosch University, was picked by Strijdom, then Nationalist leader in the Transvaal, to be the first editor of *Die Transvaler*, the official organ of the Transvaal National Party. Verwoerd's first editorial was an attack on the Jews. In referring to members of the Jewish community the Afrikaner used the expression '*hy is van die nasie*', that is, 'he is one of the chosen race'.

Afrikaner attacks on the Jews can be explained by Afrikaner fear of the threat of Jewish economic competition. After the nazis had given them the idea, the Afrikaners began to compare their lot in South Africa with that of the Jew. This was the period when the Afrikaner was moving from the farms to the cities, where he found himself at the bottom of the economic ladder—uneducated, untrained, bewildered. The Jews, in contrast, were accustomed to city life. They were better educated, economically more aggressive, and consequently considerably more prosperous. Numbered among the Jews were prominent financiers, merchants, scholars, bankers, industrialists and politicians. In the cities the Afrikaner could compare his

FIGURE 2: The man who really won the election
(Cartoon by Boonzaier from *Die Burger*, May 23, 1938)

lowly lot with that of the Jew, and he could easily be persuaded that the Jew
was the cause of his unfortunate state. At the same time that the Jew was
caricatured as a bloated capitalist, his enemies, without any sense of incon-
sistency, also portrayed him as a communist revolutionary, bent on arousing
the black population to revolt. Note, for example, the text of a notice of
the South African National Peoples Movement, dated November 13, 1937:

> Fellow South Africans. If you are satisfied with the Jewish tactics of
> protecting Kaffirs and Asiatics, it is not necessary for you to attend this
> meeting. . . . We say: Down with the Jewish Communism! Down
> with the exploiters of Democracy! Down with the exploiters of the
> Trade Unions! Down with the Bolshevik agitators who want to make
> South Africa a second Spain, in order to satisfy their hatred of a people
> of half-awakened Christian Afrikaners! . . . Down with Judaism, the
> enemy of the whole world!

To Hitler's own treatment of the Jews, the Afrikaner was sympathetic, and Afrikaner leaders found Jewry an exploitable issue.

The intensity of the attacks on the Jews during the Hitler period was such that anti-semitism still persists in South Africa, albeit to a diminishing degree. But in areas where there are relatively large Jewish communities, such as Johannesburg which is the home of some 50,000 of the republic's total Jewish population of 150,000, invidious comparisons are still made. Malan was apparently of the belief that the proportion of Jews in any community should never be more than five per cent, an idea that is still echoed.

Nazism inspired the establishment of a number of right-wing organizations that influenced the course and policy of the National Party. The most significant were the Grey Shirts, the Brown Shirts, the Black Shirts, the Ossewa-Brandwag, and the New Order. These organizations sprouted at a time when Hitler was running high, wide and handsome in Europe, and they were nurtured by the belief that nazism would triumph. Likewise, to the serious Afrikaner, Britain, not Germany, posed the more dangerous threat. *Die Burger* asked: 'Why should we fight for Britain, the only country which has ever attacked us? At this rate, no matter where, when and why Britain chooses to fight, we shall *ipso facto* be embroiled too.' Hard-core Afrikanerdom not only could not see the necessity of fighting Germany on the side of Britain, but often did what it could to disrupt the war effort. After war had been declared in 1939, the government was forced to take action against the extremists, as it had done during the first world war. Dr J. F. J. van Rensburg, leader of the Ossewa-Brandwag, was provoked to declare on January 1, 1941,

> that Afrikanerdom finds itself in a position of need and crisis as never before since October 1899 must be perfectly clear even to a blind man; that dangers, external as well as internal, threaten our whole existence is equally unmistakable. . . . Its sentinels are now being threatened with imprisonment, with prohibition regulations, internment, spying, house searching, assault and all the methods of intimidation which the enemies of Afrikanerdom have at their command in the Afrikaner's one and only fatherland.[7]

The Reverend J. D. Vorster, a minister of the Dutch Reformed Church, who was later brought to trial because of his political beliefs, told the members of the *Afrikaanse Nasionale Studentebond* (the Afrikaner university students' organization), at a meeting at Groot Schuur on September 15, 1940: 'Hitler's *Mein Kampf* shows the way to greatness—the path of South Africa. Hitler gave the Germans a calling. He gave them a fanaticism which causes them to stand back for no one. We must follow his example because only by such holy fanaticism can the Afrikaner nation achieve its calling.' He insisted that the Afrikaner must destroy capitalism and establish a pure republic: 'The basis of this republic will be that the Afrikaner will no longer co-operate with the Englishman. He will make the conditions, and the Englishman will be compelled to submit to these regulations.' He added that there would be a Great Trek, but this time it would consist not of Afrikaners, but of Jingos and Jews.[8]

Of the 'Shirt' movements, the Grey Shirts were the most forceful and long lasting. The South African Grey Shirt Party, professedly nonpolitical, was openly pro-Hitler and anti-Jewish.[9] It was headed by L. T. Weichardt, a South African of German descent. The Grey Shirts were absorbed by the National Party in March, 1939. In November, 1940, Weichardt revived the organization, under the new title of the South African National Socialist Bond, much to the displeasure of Malan.[10] Malan was of the opinion that separate groups outside the National Party would inevitably cause its disruption.[11] Later, Weichardt was interned by the government. The *Cape Times* (October 22, 1937) published an editorial giving some indication of the effects of Weichardt's organization on Malan as leader of the Nationalists:[12]

> Shortly after fusion, the professional politicians in the ranks of the schismatic Nationalists were impressed with the vote-catching possibilities of the Grey Shirt creed. Under the disapproving eye of their leader they flirted with anti-Semitism. Dr Malan at that time was still parading his high principles and frequently proclaimed 'I will not take action against the Jew as Jew, and I will have no part in raising yet another racial issue in this country'. But the de Waals, Strijdoms and Erasmuses simply ignored him, and he followed reluctantly in their footsteps.

Dr Verwoerd, editor of *Die Transvaler*, apparently found a great deal in common with the nazis, and used his paper to give expression to his feelings. In 1943, he was brought to trial in the case *Verwoerd vs. Paver and others* before Mr Justice J. Millin (husband of Sarah Gertrude Millin). Justice Millin declared that Verwoerd 'did support nazi propaganda, he did make his paper a tool of the nazis in South Africa, and he knew it'.

The formation in Southwest Africa (a South African mandate) of the Hitler Youth and other nazi organizations compelled Smuts in April, 1939, to send police reinforcements to Windhoek, the capital. The Nationalists insisted that this move was merely an excuse by Smuts to embroil South Africa in war, as he had done in 1914. Later, of course, impressively successful nazi organizations were founded elsewhere in Southwest Africa and, more significantly, in the Union. The Robey Leibbrandt case is illustrative of Afrikaner flirtations with the nazis during the war. Leibbrandt, a former policeman, was convicted of collusion with Germany. He was caught sending information to the nazis with German equipment, and he had apparently been to Germany, and returned by submarine. Mr Justice Steyn gave him a life sentence. When 'Blackie' Swart became Minister of Justice in 1948, Leibbrandt was released.

The Star published an exposé of overt nazi activities in the Union on January 27 and 28, 1938. It noted, *inter alia*, the existence in major centers in South Africa of such German organizations as the National Socialist Party (*Nationalsozialistische Deutsche Arbeiter Partie*), the Hitler Youth (*Hitler Jugend*), the Labor Front (*Arbeitsfront*), Strength through Joy (*Kraft Durch*

Freude), and the charity organization Winter Help (*Winterhilfe*). It observed that these groups, whose members were mainly German, held occasional public demonstrations, as well as private meetings addressed by high German officials, extensively disseminated propaganda, and granted rewards for good work on behalf of the Reich—all of which helped to weld the Germans in South Africa into a tightly knit organization.

The nazis also provoked the rise or contributed organizationally to a number of non-German groups in South Africa, secret, semisecret, and open. Of these, the Grey Shirts, Brown Shirts, Black Shirts, and the Ossewa-Brandwag (literally, 'Oxwagon Fire Guard') have already been mentioned. The Ossewa-Brandwag (OB) seems to have had the greatest following and longest existence of any of the nazi-influenced groups. By November, 1940, it claimed a membership of 200,000.[13] It was professedly a nonpolitical cultural association. In fact, its political influence was considerable. The OB came under attack by the government after war was declared against Germany because of its anti-government and pro-nazi sympathies and its terrorist tactics, including bombings; and because of its militant organization and ability to arouse the Afrikaners against the government. The OB forbade its members to trade with Jews, 'the man with a crooked nose, the danger to the country'.[14] Harry G. Lawrence, Minister of the Interior, exposed the OB in a speech on November 11, 1940, noting that not all its members were subversive, but that only a few were in the movement for cultural reasons, and that most of those arrested for dynamite outrages on the Rand were OB members.[15] While the OB did not openly enter candidates in political races, its influence on elections was important. Malan knew it, and therefore for a time curried favor with the OB. Later, however, 'Malan proved his strength and his tenacity of purpose when he smashed van Rensburg's Ossewa-Brandwag movement on the wheel'.[16]

The OB competed with Malan's HNP for power over Afrikanerdom, and Malan early sought to destroy or at the least control it. On October 13, 1940, Malan addressed the OB at a mass gathering in Pretoria, where he was carried shoulder-high to the platform. He told the OB at that time that it represented a nation that, during the centenary celebrations of 1938, had taken an oath 'to tread the path of South Africa'.[17] In November, 1940, Malan addressed the Cape HNP Congress at Cradock and offered full support to the OB. He declared he had come to an understanding with the OB's *Grootraad* (Chief Council), and that it had been agreed the OB and the HNP would co-operate in 'the highest interests of the Afrikaner nation' without either body interfering in the affairs of the other.[18] Malan, however, sought to make his position clear. On one occasion he declared: 'I am the only link between the Ossewa-Brandwag and the Herenigde Nasionale Party. . . . The OB is a mighty organization which wishes to discipline our people and make it easier for us to attain our national ideals. We need the OB on the one side and the political party on the other.'

The Ossewa-Brandwag grew out of the celebrations of December, 1938, the centenary of the Voortrekker movement. It was founded by Colonel J. C. C. Laas in February, 1939, as a cultural organization. It soon became semi-militant, and less cultural and more political. Laas resigned on October 3, 1940. On January 15, 1941, Dr (Hans) J. F. J. van Rensburg, a former administrator of the OFS, replaced Laas as Commandant-General of the OB. Van Rensburg looked upon the OB as Afrikanerdom mobilized—economically, culturally, and for mutual protection.[19] The Reverend J. D. Vorster revealed that OB members were carefully selected because the Ossewa-Brandwag was the movement that would rule the country in the future as the only purely South African movement—the movement that would make chiefs, leaders, and rulers of the Boer nation 'which at present is being crushed, despised, humiliated, and abused by foreigners and intruders'.[20]

In September, 1940, the *Cape Times* disclosed that the OB planned to set up a Christian-National dictatorship 'when the opportune time comes'. It noted that the OB had members in critical posts in the public service, the railways, the police, the banks, the mines, and in all important industries in the Union and these men would, at a given signal, seize key positions, paralyze communications, and take over the government. It was, according to the *Cape Times'* informant, the OB's intention, following such a *coup*, to make Afrikaans the official language of South Africa and to expel the Jews. The British would be permitted to remain as long as they subscribed to Afrikaner ideals.

The nazi leanings of the OB could be seen in the official titles of the organization, its uniforms, *Stormjaers* (Storm Troopers), and its anti-semitism. There are even indications that the OB used the swastika emblem.[21] Perusal of the OB's constitution makes the nazi association unmistakably clear.[22] The title is printed in German gothic type. The group emblem, an eagle like that of the nazi Reichstag, is centered on the cover. The document includes an oath that members took and a pledge to accept the orders of the leaders. The OB went to the extent of drawing up a constitution for a Boer republic. *Die Suiderstem* (September 28, 1940) published a reproduction of it, and it aroused a great deal of controversy. Commenting on the 'Constitution for a Christian-National Republic' on September 24, 1940, *Die Suiderstem* declared that the OB proposed nothing less than a nazi state. Under it, citizenship was to be restricted, Afrikaans was to be the official language, and the president was to have unlimited powers. *Die Suiderstem* observed that the only differences from the nazi state were that 'president' was to be substituted for 'Fuehrer', 'Burgerraad' for 'Reichstag', 'Raadslede' for 'Gauleiters', 'republiek' for 'Reich' and 'Christian-National' for 'National-Socialist'. Oswald Pirow, former Minister of Justice and leader of the right-wing parliamentary group called the New Order, regarded the OB as the 'storm troops of Afrikanerdom'.[23]

In the address he gave when he was sworn in as leader of the OB, van Rensburg exposed his nazi inclinations:

With democracy in its academic sense I have no special quarrel. In any case, one should not speak evil of the dead. But I wish to add that a democracy or any other -cracy is not an end in itself but merely a means to the end. The end is the nation. If I can serve my nation better by

democratic action, I will do so, but if I have to choose between **Afri-**
kanerdom and democracy, then there is no choice. Then I am not the
least concerned about the system.[24]

The *Sunday Express* (January 19, 1941) described the OB as:

based on Hitler's National Socialism. The whole structure of the local
organization, with special emphasis laid on discipline, is Germanic in its
conception. Dr van Rensburg must have got his ideas from his political
foster-father, Pirow, and to suggest that they are in reality rowing down
two different streams is nonsense.

The Ossewa-Brandwag was dramatic in its appeal, and attracted the
attention of Afrikaners generally, and especially of young Afrikaners. 'At
one stage,' wrote Oswald Pirow, 'the OB completely eclipsed all the party
leaders and had a greater personal following than Dr Malan.'[25] The massive
interest in the organization was not unlike that aroused by the Torch
Commando, which emerged in the postwar period in response to Nationalist
actions, and which, like the OB, appeared—swept on by the tide of passing
sentiments—and was gone.

From 1939 until 1946, when it became associated with Havenga's
Afrikaner Party, the OB had a continuing influence on South Africa and the
National Party. It forced the HNP to do some serious thinking about its
own position, and, more important, to define its philosophy in specific
terms. In a sense, it was the divergence of opinions between Hertzog and
Malan as to the desirability of such ideas as those expressed by the OB that
led to the final break between these two leaders and the establishment of the
Afrikaner Party, which was considerably less extreme than the HNP.
Hertzog manifested these differences in his speech accepting honorary
membership of the Afrikaner Party:

We cannot leave Afrikanerdom in the lurch just because a wave of
insanity has swept over a portion of our people.... I want to warn you,
in spite of the strong forces which are forcing us off our balance, we
must not allow an unhealthy spirit to develop. We feel that the present
leaders are not on the right road. Our people must come back to sanity.
Our resignations are intended as a warning.... I want to warn our
Afrikaners not to expect that Germany will work out their salvation for
them. Germany is fighting her own battles. I am not one of those
persons who say: 'Let the Germans come to South Africa and all will be
well.'

Another group that emerged among Afrikaners during the period of
nazi ascendancy was the New Order, a group of seventeen members of
Parliament led by Oswald Pirow, who was a close friend of van Rensburg.
Pirow, along with Havenga, supported Hertzog's desire for neutrality in the
second world war. Pirow was a great admirer of Hertzog, and later became
his biographer. The New Order, like the OB, was nazi-inclined; the
members remained within the National Party, however, until January, 1942,
when they resigned.[26]

All these organizations had the same ultimate goal, namely, the establishment of a 'Christian national' state, in which the Afrikaner, traditionally the low man among the whites in South Africa, would be in control, and would impose his way of life on the whole state—or, at the very least, be able to guarantee it for himself. Van Rensburg made this clear on one occasion when he said that the Voortrekkers and the Huguenots were 'as two rocks on which our nation has been built. We regard our children not merely as object of experiment for theories of pedagogy, but as essential and valuable links in an historical organic chain—the chain of the Afrikaner nation'.[27]

The rise of Hitler gave direction to Afrikaner ambitions. It offered them hope when their position appeared hopeless. Hitler's aims and policies in several areas coincided with theirs. Hitler was anti-semitic, and the Afrikaner discovered he could be too. Hitler was anti-communist, and so was the Afrikaner. Both even succeeded in believing in a link between communism and the 'Jewish plot'. Hitler was professedly anti-capitalist, and the economically unsuccessful Afrikaner—typically a poor farmer or a member of the urban proletariat—had long been anti-capitalist. Hitler was an ardent German nationalist, and espoused the theory of the master race. The Afrikaner was sympathetic, and perhaps Hitler's greatest influence in South Africa was in precisely the area of nationalist and racist philosophy. The conditions for an upsurge of violently racist nationalism already existed: Hitler's example gave it purpose and direction. But the Afrikaner nationalists could not believe that their program could be carried out under the existing form of government, and various schemes for an alternative were produced—which also reflected nazi thinking. Pirow expressed the hope that the National Party would not attain power too soon, because in that case it would be only a new government and not a new form of government: 'If we come into power within a few years and must take over the existing form of government, then I had rather that we did not come into power at all. The time has arrived for a radical change in the nature of our form of government.'[28]

Four publications produced by the National Party during the second world war represent the thinking of the Nationalists at the time. What is perhaps more significant is that they illustrate the influence of nazism on the Nationalists, whether exerted directly or indirectly through pressures from nazi-oriented organizations such as the OB and New Order.[29]

The first, *The New South Africa—The Revolution of the Twentieth Century* (*Die Nuwe Suid Afrika—Die Revolusie van die Twintigste Eeu*), was written in 1940 when totalitarianism was in the ascendancy. The author was Dr Otto du Plessis, 'Enlightenment Secretary' of the National Party and editor of *Die Volksblad*.[30] Malan declared that most of the ideas of the New Order had been embodied in the National Party program, and would be carried out when the Nationalists came into power. Du Plessis' work gave an account of that program and the philosophy behind it. He stated that democracy, as Oswald Spengler foretold in 1914 in *Der Untergang des Abendlandes*, would be superseded by a new order. He noted that in the democracy which emanated from England 'the freedom of the individual was emphasized to such an extent that the indispensable discipline in national life was pushed more and more into the background. Just as every person should discipline himself, so should every nation'. He then proceeded to show how the new order, 'with Hitler and Mussolini in the foreground', had overcome the old order.

> The philosophy at the basis of the new order in every state is undiluted and unequivocal nationalism. . . . The state and the nation are all powerful. Every citizen and every corporation and organization and every group functions as a subdivision of the state, and in the interest of the nation as a whole. . . .
>
> Nationalist Afrikanerdom longs for the death of that system [democracy] which will also mean the death of '*Uitlanderism*' and Unionist domination of South Africa.
>
> Afrikanerdom, the only real nation in the Union, has, under the imported British system, not known full political, economic, and social freedom. It consequently pines for the new system of a new order, which would bring with it true national freedom in all spheres of life. No matter what the result [of the war] may be, Afrikanerdom is fully determined that South Africa will be completely torn away from the British connection.
>
> In the economic sphere the new South Africa will have to employ the great resources of the fatherland, especially the gold resources, for the benefit of the whole population. The capital must be placed at the service of the whole population and especially the older-established population group.

He likened the state of affairs in the New Order to that expressed in the German battle cry: 'Every German must be small so that Germany can be great.' Thus, the New Order would 'hit the hardest' the 'big capitalists; the rich people or plutocrats; the unnational press; the unestablished and unassimilable elements, e.g., the Jews; national groups who place their own interests above those of the national community; international organizations like the Freemasons'.

According to du Plessis, the republic would be symbolized by a South African flag, and would have one national anthem, one citizenship, one head of state, who would not be the representative of a foreign head of state, but the chosen leader of the people. South Africa would be governed by 'the state president with his executive council and a parliament'.

He concluded that such a system could come about only by a 'social revolution'. British parliamentarianism with all its ceremonies and procedural niceties would be supplanted by harsh discipline. It is possible he even believed that political parties should be eliminated. That opinion was certainly held by the OB.

Du Plessis' thesis was accepted as expressing the ideology of the OB, and the *Draft Constitution* and the *Social and Economic Policy* were patterned after it.

The du Plessis work was soon followed by *The Republican Order* (*Die Republikeinse Orde*), published in 1941 by the Federal Council of the National Party in Bloemfontein with the subtitle, *Future Policy as Set Out by Dr Malan* (*Party se Toekomsbeleid soos deur dr Malan uiteengesit*). In addition to statements by Malan, the publication provides a commentary on his thinking and includes a declaration by the Federal Council of the National Party. It discusses the determination to bring into being a republic and the New Order, which has 'already either openly or by implication been included in our party's programme of principles and of action'. Anti-British sentiments are expressed: 'Whatever may be said in favour of the British parliamentary system . . . it has always been a failure in South Africa when viewed from the nation's point of view.' *The Republican Order* stated that the one-party system of Germany would not necessarily 'fit in equally with every other nation', although it condoned dictatorship. Evidently, what was wanted was the political system of the old Boer republics: 'The Boer nation, which is the creator and protector of our own South African nationality, brought about a system in the Boer republics which is our own and differs from the British parliamentary system.' At the time *The Republican Order* was written, Germany was making its greatest advances, and appeared to be winning the war. The Council patterned its program accordingly. 'That a victorious Germany . . . would want to see the British connection broken is obvious,' and it would also want to 'conclude peace with a friendly government'.

The third of these publications is Malan's *Draft for a Republic* published in January, 1942, soon after his introduction in Parliament of a proposal for the establishment of a Christian-National Republic.[31] The Republic, he told Parliament, was to be independent of the British Empire and of any other foreign power, based on the old South African republics, but adapted to modern conditions. It should eliminate 'all that is harmful in the present British liberal democracy'. It should maintain equal language and cultural rights for both sections of the European population, and give protection against 'capitalists and parasitic exploitation . . . and against hostile and unnational elements'.[32] The *Rand Daily Mail* believed that by this motion Malan wanted to prove that the National Party was the real spearhead of the drive for a republic, in order to get the extremists of the New Order to subscribe to his modified form of nazism and thus regain the support of the OB. The *Draft for a Republic* outlined the constitution Malan would introduce in the new state. The *Sunday Times* suggested that the Draft Constitution had been prepared by members of the Afrikaner Broederbond, who submitted it to Malan, and who also had given a copy to the OB who made 'improper use' of it through the widely discussed circular of January, 1941 (which Malan objected to because it exposed the republican movement).[33] After Malan introduced his proposal for a republic to Parliament, he then felt 'the time for publication is ripe'. *Die Transvaler* in its introduction to the Draft Constitution said:

It is published with the permission and on the authority of Dr D. F. Malan, leader of the Herenigde Nasionale of Volksparty. . . . It will be

the last vestiges of the British yoke was natural, and nothing new. Because of the traditional conflict with the British, it was only to be expected that anything associated with Britain had an unpleasant connotation for the Afrikaners. The obvious alternative to British-style parliamentary democracy was the system developed in the old Boer republics—revised in the light of national socialism. When the tide of war turned against Hitler, and thousands of South African troops finally returned home after fighting the nazis, nazism became unpopular and there was almost a reaction against it. Then, of course, all references to Germany and the organs and documents that so clearly showed nazi influence were carefully avoided. But the change did not go very deep; in the election of 1948, the Nationalists finally achieved office by playing on racial fears and prejudices, particularly that of being overwhelmed by the Africans. The Nationalists promised a solution, *apartheid*, not very different from Hertzog's 'separation' scheme of the 1920s. Had Hitler won the war, the provisions of the draft constitution would probably have been implemented along with those in du Plessis' essay. In the actual postwar world, however, the development of internationalism has had a profound influence on the course of events in South Africa; more especially, it has caused the Afrikaners to *laager* more tightly, while at the same time forcing them to play a part on the world scene, which they can now scarcely ignore.

Although Malan's quarrels with such groups as the New Order and Ossewa-Brandwag were in some respects personal, they were mainly based on his belief that Afrikaner efforts should not be split, but should be channeled through the National Party, of which he was the head. In February, 1942, Malan labeled the OB a 'gangster organization' that, instead of seeking the unity of Afrikanerdom, tried to create confusion within it.[35] And when Pirow's New Order broke with the National Party, the latter began to lose members to the former. Such splits can only weaken an organization, and Malan knew it. By 1948, however, all Afrikaner groups had joined together to oust the Smuts' régime, and Havenga's Afrikaner Party coalesced with Malan's Nationalists to enable them to take over the government.

6 Organizing for Victory:
The Afrikaner Broederbond (AB)

By the hand of my servant David I will save my people . . . out of the hand of their enemies.

2 SAMUEL 3 : 18

TRADITIONALLY, THE AFRIKANER has chosen farming in contrast to the city-dwelling Briton who has engaged in the professions, business or mining.   In the first part of the twentieth century, Afrikaners who abandoned their farms for the cities were at a disadvantage compared with the more experienced British.   There was, indeed, a period when the race-conscious Boer and the African competed for the available unskilled jobs.   Thus, urbanization and industrialization introduced a new element in Boer-British rivalry—and stiffened the determination of the Afrikaner extremists to alter the situation. Meanwhile, the Boer War was lost to the British and the 1914 rebellion was put down by Smuts and Botha, whom the Boer die-hards regarded as traitors to Afrikanerdom.   Military and economic inferiority stimulated the development of Afrikaner nationalism.

A major factor in the Nationalist accession to political power in 1948 was the Afrikaner Broederbond (AB).   As late as 1925, Afrikaners were ashamed to use their own language in town, for fear it would mark them as what T. C. Visser called 'the beggars'.[1]   The AB helped the Afrikaner to throw off his inferior status.   It gave purpose, organization, and expression to his grievances and aspirations.   English-speaking South Africans have generally regarded the organization as menacing and sinister.   The English press in South Africa has always been quick to disclose information about the AB, and any release about the AB can be a sensation.   But for the mass of Afrikaners, the organization has been of vital assistance in improving their formerly dismal situation and helping them to cease being ashamed of their origin, their language, and their culture.   Achievement of those ends, however, necessitated infringement on the entrenched positions of non-Afrikaners and, hence, the displeasure of the latter.

After the 1914 rising had been crushed with the aid of two of their own generals, open opposition to the *status quo* by the Afrikaners was no longer feasible. The only alternative was secret organization. In 1918, the Afrikaner extremists went underground and organized the Afrikaner Broederbond, or 'band of Afrikaner brothers'. The Broederbond has been one of the main sources of Afrikaner strength. Among South African whites, the Afrikaners for many years formed a depressed group. Economically, educationally, politically, they were at a disadvantage compared to the English-speaking community. Afrikaner reactions to this state of affairs were as might be expected. As long as the Afrikaners were physically and culturally isolated from the British, they were not conscious of the differences. But as the British enveloped, infiltrated, and finally overthrew the Boer republics, comparisons became inescapable. And as the Afrikaner left the countryside and migrated to the cities, distinctions were accentuated, for in the cities the two groups came into direct competition.

The Afrikaner Broederbond is a secret society, and this limits the availability of information about it. There have been a number of writings on the AB, but they vary greatly in the weight that can be attached to their statements. AB members are permitted to reveal their identity with the organization, but not that of fellow members; nor are they allowed to give information about the organization.* The only detailed information about the AB that is public knowledge refers to the period between 1918 and 1922, when the organization was not secret; the AB was, however, then considerably less important than it later became. Information has also been brought to light by defectors. Hertzog's attack on the Broederbond in one of his annual addresses to his constituents at Smithfield (November 7, 1935), when he was Prime Minister, was based on evidence supplied by its defected Secretary.[2] In a similar denunciation delivered at Bloemfontein in December, 1944, Smuts made use of a report prepared by his military intelligence department.[3] It was based on information given by defectors, as well as other documentary evidence. It was submitted to General Smuts on March 29, 1944, and, although classified as secret, has been quietly yet widely circulated in South Africa. It contains an excellent account of many aspects of the AB.[4] In addition, the defector Louis J. du Plessis wrote a series of letters to newspapers about the AB; a collection of them was later published as a pamphlet.[5] He claims to have been associated with the AB during its inception, and gives a good deal of interesting information about its formative years. *Die Transvaler* published four articles[6] in reply to General Smuts' attack by the self-admitted Secretary of the AB, Mr Ivanhoe Makepeace Lombard, on December 14, 20, and 30, 1944, and January 3, 1945. These offer some clues as to the purpose and organization of the AB and attempt to explain its secret nature. At the same time the House of Assembly debated the ban that Smuts had placed on membership of the AB by civil servants, and these debates contain much useful material. In 1949, the Council of the Dutch Reformed Church decided to investigate the AB, because of the general accusations being made against it. Its report was issued in 1951.[7] Leo Marquard notes, however, that since 'some ministers

* A number of people have openly admitted membership.

of the Afrikaans churches are members of the Bond . . . the committee of inquiry can, therefore, not be regarded as impartial'.[8]

The AB makes good copy for newspapers, and the English-language press in South Africa periodically runs stories about AB activities.[9] On February 1, 1952, the Canadian publication, *Maclean's Magazine*, ran a feature story by Albert Fick on the AB, entitled 'South Africa's Ku Klux Klan'. In 1954, Alex Hepple, for years parliamentary leader of the Labour Party, wrote a pamphlet, *Trade Unions in Travail, The Story of the Broederbond-Nationalist Plan to Control South African Trade Unions,* that presents an interesting account of the Broederbond's relationships with labor. Useful summaries of the Broederbond have been given by Leo Marquard in *The Peoples and Policies of South Africa,* and Gwendolen M. Carter, in *The Politics of Inequality: South Africa Since 1948.* The periodical *Africa Special Report* (now entitled *Africa Report*) published an article on the AB in October, 1947, and Anthony Delius has described it in an article in *The Reporter,* January 9, 1958.

There can be no question as to the magnitude of the influence of the Afrikaner Broederbond. The stress laid on the exclusive nature of the Afrikaner's rights to South Africa by the Bond was the major contribution to the growth of South African nationalism—and a major reason for Hertzog's opposition to it. It is to be recalled that Hertzog was of the opinion that the term 'Afrikaner' should include all English- and Afrikaans-speaking South Africans who considered South Africa their only home. It has been recorded that Hertzog much resented newspaper reporters who interpreted his references to 'Afrikaners' as 'Afrikaans-speaking persons'.[10] For the AB, the term included only Afrikaans-speaking persons. Hertzog, in his 1935 speech exposing the AB, observed that it was a

> secret political association only to and consisting only of Afrikaans-speaking members, the leading political spirits of whom are determined to rule South Africa over the heads of the English-speaking among us; and who are striving to raise Dutch-speaking Afrikanerdom to domination in South Africa, with the neglect of the rights and claims of the English-speaking portion of our population.

L. J. du Plessis, who defected from the AB, concluded from this aspect of AB policy 'that it is not only colour *apartheid* but also race *apartheid* that is the ultimate aim of the Bond'.* Hertzog's concern over the AB's exclusive interpretation of Afrikaner was revealed in a letter to his son Dr Albert Hertzog, later Minister of Posts and Telegraphs in Verwoerd's cabinet and allegedly one of the AB's so-called Twelve Apostles. The elder Hertzog wrote:

> It is clear that the Afrikaans-speaking section of Afrikanerdom must be the only section of the South African people to be taken into account [by the AB] and the English-speaking section must not be considered.

* He was using the term 'race' to distinguish different groups of European origin.

Not only must the English-speaking section of Afrikanerdom, with other non-Afrikaans-speaking sections of our nation, be regarded as inferior sections of the South African nation, but the Government must not adopt any measure in co-operation with, or to the advantage of, the non-Afrikaans-speaking section, unless the so-called Afrikaner nation are unanimous in approving it. . . .

I desire no less heartily than you the unity of Afrikaans-speaking people, but I am not prepared to buy that unity at a price which must of necessity doom the whole of Afrikanerdom, both Afrikaans- and English-speaking, to endless division and strife, with self-destruction as the ultimate outcome.[11]

In his speech exposing the Bond, Hertzog quoted a circular letter to all Bond members from the organization's chairman and highest authority, Professor J. C. van Rooy of Potchefstroom University, and its Secretary, I. M. Lombard of Johannesburg. It concluded with these words:

Let us keep the eye fixed on this, that the main object is . . . that Afrikanerdom shall reach its ultimate destiny of domination in South Africa. . . . Brothers, our solution for South Africa's troubles is not that this or that party shall gain the upper hand, but that the Afrikaner Broederbond shall rule South Africa.

The Bond intended to ensure that Afrikaners should never again be forced to undergo the humiliations they had experienced in the past. In Hertzog's words, it was striving 'after the ideal of the everlasting existence of a separate Afrikaan's nation with its own culture', and sought 'to let the Dutch-speaking Afrikanerdom gain domination in South Africa, and to bring about that the Dutch-speaking Broederbond shall rule South Africa'.[12] Much later, L. J. du Plessis was to write that the AB aimed at 'segregating all Afrikaans-speaking persons from the rest of the population and making them the exclusive and privileged element in South Africa'.[13]

Hertzog, of course, had no objection to the AB's original purpose of caring for the cultural needs of Dutch-speaking Afrikanerdom; its constitution clearly stipulated that party politics are excluded from the Bond. However, as he was to discover, 'party politics could not for always be kept out of it; and according to the measure that the influence and political views of a certain section in our public life increased in the Bond, the Bond recreated from a cultural to a party-political association'.

The AB has evolved gradually into a large-scale undertaking, quite different in scope from the announced intentions of its founders. From being a cultural organization, it passed gradually into the economic and later into the political sphere. The defenders of the AB liken it to the Freemasons and Sons of England, which, they maintain, are secret organizations, but its opponents point out that the difference lies in the field of interest of the AB. The military intelligence report of 1944 on the organization insisted that the AB had, 'octopus-like, spread its tentacles into the economic, as well as the educational and cultural fields in South Africa. In addition, it has representatives in key positions throughout the Civil Service'.

Until the middle of the 1930s, the activities of the AB were in fact largely confined to cultural fields and its growth was slow. The organization came into being on May 24, 1918, in Johannesburg, under the label *Jong Suid Afrika*. At first it had only fourteen members, including H. W. van der Merwe, H. J. Klopper, the Reverend Bertie Naude (the first president), and D. A. C. du Plessis. On June 18, 1918, the name was changed to Afrikaner Broederbond. L. J. du Plessis has described its beginnings:

> Preliminary talks on the formation of an Afrikaans organization to propagate the Afrikaans language and bring together serious-minded young Afrikaners in Johannesburg and along the Reef were held in my family home in 1918. It was finally called the Afrikaner Broederbond and every member was expected to carry a button in his coat with the letters AB on it. It was nothing more than a semireligious organization, meetings being held in the parsonages of the Jeppe and Irene congregations as well as in the Irene church hall, where the Reverend William Nicol was minister. The idea originated in the mind of Mr H. J. Klopper, present MP for Vredefort. Like other movements, this one flourished for a while and then appeared to die. It was during one of these low-tide periods that I was for a time its secretary. I think I am correct in saying that the Bond really progressed when large numbers of teachers joined it, including Mr I. Lombard and Mr Greybe. . . . The last meeting I attended was round about 1922 in the Carlton Hotel when it was decided, by majority vote, that the Bond would go underground.[14]

The decision to 'go underground' tended to weed out the moderates, leaving those who sought a *Boere Republiek* with fanatical determination.

On December 9, 1919, the AB members decided that members should swear an oath of affirmation to the organization's principles, and, according to the report issued by the DRC (referred to above), the AB therefore really traces its origin to that date. On September 21, 1920, the AB adopted a constitution. In 1921, the AB decided to struggle for the establishment of Afrikaans medium schools, and AB instructions were 'to fight secretly but with all your might for unilingual medium schools'. It was also decided to carry secrecy to the extent of avoiding postal communications between members.

According to the military intelligence report, the AB faced various crises prior to 1944. The first came in 1924, when the Labour-Nationalist pact government took office. The Bond members came to realize, however, that the pact would give Afrikanerdom greater parliamentary expression. In 1927, the AB decided on active participation in community affairs 'leaving no avenue neglected'. As a result the *Federasie van Afrikaanse Kultuurvereniginge* (Federation of Afrikaner Cultural Organizations) was established in 1929 to co-ordinate and develop Afrikaner cultural activities; in 1939, the FAK invaded the economic field by arranging for the establishment of the *Reddingsdaadbond* (Rescue Action Association).

Another crisis resulted over the creation of the Fusion Government of Hertzog and Smuts in 1933, and the subsequent hiving of the Malanites to form the Herenigde Nasionale Party. The HNP was to become closely identified with the AB, and, in effect, to become the front organization and political arm of the AB, leading Hertzog, himself a former AB member, to declare in 1935: 'There can be no doubt that the secret Broederbond is nothing else but a purified Nationalist Party busy underground, and the purified Nationalist Party is nothing but a secret Afrikaner Broederbond continuing its activities above ground.'[15]   This was a significant development.   From 1933, the AB and the HNP worked hand in hand.   About that time, Dr Malan, the leader of the Cape Nationalists, became an AB member, which helps to explain his ambivalence as regards fusion after 1933. As Hertzog observed:

It is quite clear at present to everyone why Dr Malan changed so suddenly from a supporter to an opponent of Afrikaner unity.   His joining of this secret anti-English-Afrikaner movement must have obliged him inevitably to discard the policy of national unity with the inclusion of the English-speaking Afrikaner; and he was also further obliged by his connection with the Broederbond to enter the road of national disunity and disagreement.

Also in 1933, as a result of the Smuts-Hertzog coalition, the Afrikaner members of the National Union of South African Students (NUSAS) broke away to set up their own organization, the *Afrikaanse Studentebond*; at its first annual congress, Dr N. Diederichs, an AB *broer*, was named chairman and Dr Hans van Rensburg, honorary president.

Another crisis arose in 1935 with the attack on the Broederbond by Hertzog, who was then Prime Minister.   By that time the AB had over 2,000 members.   As a result of Hertzog's exposure a number of his followers resigned from the AB.   However, it was the AB that was responsible for the censures on Hertzog at the Bloemfontein National Party congress in 1941. After that Hertzog went into retirement and died the following year.   In the election of 1948, Smuts was defeated, and he died a short time later.   One can only conjecture what part the AB played in his defeat.

The rise of Hitler in Germany gave greater purpose, direction, and organization to the AB.   It even borrowed nazi titles for some of its organizational apparatus.   In 1938, the AB was influential in ensuring that the *Ossewa Trek* (Voortrekker Centenary) was directed by the *Afrikaanse Taal in Kultuurvereniging* (ATKV), headed by H. J. Klopper, one of the original AB members.   The *Ossewa-Brandwag* was an outgrowth of the *Ossewa Trek*. In its early days, as a purely cultural association under its founder Colonel Laas, it competed with the AB-sponsored FAK.   Following a skilful whispering campaign to the effect that he was a Freemason, Laas resigned; he was replaced by Dr van Rensburg, a member of the AB.   Both Dr van Rensburg and Dr N. Diederichs, later Minister of Economic Affairs, visited nazi Germany and appeared impressed by national socialism.

The second world war produced the fourth crisis and a great incentive for action. It caused Malan and Hertzog temporarily to reconcile their differences; but eventually Hertzog felt compelled to resign, leaving the leadership of the Nationalists to Malan. In 1940, Hertzog was not elected chairman at the HNP congress at Bloemfontein. Significantly, the dissension occurred over the question of equal language rights for English- and Afrikaans-speaking South Africans. Hertzog walked out of the congress and out of the HNP with a few followers, including Havenga. They set up the Afrikaner Party in protest.

In 1941, there was yet another crisis, when a split occurred between Malan and Pirow that led to a rupture with the OB as well. The effects extended to the *Uitvoerende Raad*, the highest council of the AB, some of its members siding with Malan, and others with Pirow and van Rensburg. Another split occurred when van Rensburg prematurely published the *Konsep-grondwet* for the republic. An attempt was made to create a united front (*Eenheidefront*) in an effort to breach the split. The united front was headed by Professor L. J. du Plessis of Potchefstroom University, who was, at one and the same time, a member of the *Uitvoerende Raad* of the AB and policy planning chief (*Beleidstudiehoof*) of the OB.

During the war years the Smuts government was fighting on two fronts: against the Germans in North Africa and Europe, and against the Afrikaner extremists at home. The government's view of the dangerous nature of the Broederbond was confirmed by the report of its military intelligence department. In December, 1944, at the United Party congress at Bloemfontein, Smuts made this report the basis of an attack on the AB for its disruptive activities, 'a sort of Gestapo . . . a dangerous, cunning, political Fascist organization of which no civil servant, if he is to retain his loyalty to the State and the Administration, can be allowed to be a member'.

On December 15, 1944, the government gave public servants, including teachers, the choice of resigning from the AB or the government service. One government official, Wentzel C. du Plessis, said he would resign from the AB if Smuts would impose the same demands on members of other secret organizations, such as the Sons of England, the Masons, and the Truth Legion. Smuts replied that no such action was necessary since those organizations were not political in nature.[16] Du Plessis left the government; in 1948, he stood for Parliament in opposition to Smuts, and beat him.*

Thus the AB moved from being a purely cultural body, expressed and implemented through the FAK, to the economic and political field. Meanwhile, its membership had grown to well over 3,000 by 1961, a significant increase, since the AB does not set out to be a mass organization.

The structure of the Afrikaner Broederbond is monolithic, and is set up on a cellular or nest basis. A cell has between five and ten members, and a division not more than forty. Whether classed as a cell or division, each group is independent, and is directly responsible to the ruling *Uitvoerende Raad*. Each cell or division has its own directorate and its own by-laws.

* Du Plessis later became Ambassador to the United States, subsequently Director of the Africa Institute in Pretoria and in 1963 Administrator of Southwest Africa.

most interest in the matter and had most knowledge of it'.[30] Essentially, the AB is a policy- and program-formulating body; it is not an operational group. Those who translate a plan into action do so as though on their own initiative. Lombard has cited the establishment of the *Volkskas* (the Afrikaner bank) and the FAK as examples. Both were founded as apparently independent institutions, but were in reality sponsored by the AB. He has also noted that the AB has given economic help to certain organizations or causes it has sponsored, such as the Reddingsdaadbond, the FAK, the Afrikaner Engineering Faculty at Stellenbosch University, the Afrikaner Medical Faculty at Pretoria University, and the repatriation of Boers from Argentina.[31]

The AB has acted mainly by sponsoring organizations and placing members in key positions within them, and by extending economic help of various kinds to Afrikaners.

To implement such schemes, the AB has stressed the use of Afrikaans and has demanded the establishment of single language medium schools; it has set up a variety of exclusive Afrikaner organizations; it has undertaken financial schemes for the improvement of Afrikaners; and has entered the political arena, understanding that the only way to achieve paramountcy is to control the government. The chairman of the executive council of the AB, Professor J. C. van Rooy, stated:

> After the cultural and economic needs, the AB will have to dedicate its attention to the political needs of our people. And with this the aim must be a completely independent real Afrikaans Government for South Africa. A government which by its embodiment in our own personal Head of State, bone of our bone, and flesh of our flesh, who will inspire us and bind us together to irresistible unity and power.[32]

Hertzog declared that 'since 1932 the Bond has been more and more placed at the disposal of the purified Nationalist Party and its purposes', and 'fallen almost exclusively into the hands of the Purified Nationalists, with the pushing aside as far as possible of all Brothers who do not belong to the Purified Party'. In 1948, when the extreme Afrikaner Nationalists finally came into power, the AB at last had the means for full implementation of its policy at hand. Since 1948, the main function of the AB has been supervisory and getting the right people into the right jobs. Contrary to the belief of many, the AB is unquestionably just as influential now as it has ever been in the past. The only change is that the aim of getting the political party that represented its views into power has been achieved.

The investigations made by the military intelligence arm of the Smuts government in 1944 were the last official inquiries into the Broederbond. Since that date, however, there have been periodic exposures of AB activities in the English-language press. It is now generally assumed that most of the cabinet ministers in the present government of South Africa are members of the AB. According to information in the English-language press, Dr H. B. Thom, Rector of Stellenbosch University and head of the FAK, was formerly head of the AB. It is believed that he was replaced in

December, 1960, by P. J. Meyer, who, among other offices, holds the position of head of the South African Broadcasting Corporation (SABC). According to the *Sunday Times* of September 18, 1960, Hendrik Verwoerd, the present Prime Minister, Albert Hertzog, son of the late Prime Minister and Minister of Posts and Telegraphs in the Verwoerd cabinet, and J. J. Kruger, formerly editor of *Die Transvaler* and subsequently 'cultural expert' for the SABC, are all members of the AB.

In July, 1959, the *Rand Daily Mail* revealed the existence of 'the junior wing' of the Broederbond, which was known as the *Ruiterwag*. The ceremony of initiation to the Ruiterwag and copies of membership application forms for the AB and Ruiterwag were published in full, together with the names of the seven members of the presidential council, 'the supreme body of the Ruiterwag'. The name of the organizing secretary of the FAK was among the seven. The exposure apparently caused the members of the Ruiterwag to decide to dissolve.[33]

7   Cultural Offensive

He giveth power to the faint; and to them that have no might he increaseth strength.

ISAIAH 40 : 29

THE FIRST MAJOR ACTION of the AB was the establishment of the *Federasie van Afrikaanse Kultuurvereniginge* (FAK or Federation of Afrikaner Cultural Organizations) on December 18, 1929, to undertake various Afrikaner cultural programs and co-ordinate and stimulate others.[1] According to Lombard, the FAK received financial help from the AB.[2] Dr N. J. van der Merwe, a writer and prominent Nationalist, observed that the 'FAK is born of strife, and is even a product of a conflict of soul, in which the Afrikaner is searching for a united front against hostile forces which divide him, and smother his soul'.[3] The FAK has done a great deal for Afrikaans and the Afrikaner. It has attempted to make the Afrikaner conscious of his ethnic identity, and, more especially, develop pride in *ons eie*.

It has succeeded in engendering a sense of belonging, of mission. It has brought unity out of a diversity of undertakings, and has concentrated attention on the problems and needs of the people it represents. As might be expected, its ambitious undertakings have provoked criticism from the political opponents of Afrikaner Nationalist extremism. In the United Party's *Information Guide and Speakers' Notes,* prepared for its election candidates, is the following statement:*

> The young people of South Africa have been subjected to a ruthless campaign of 'indoctrination' in our Afrikaans-medium schools, normal colleges and universities—a campaign carried out with the unswerving object of leaving the indelible impression in the minds of the young people of today that 'they must get their own back'. What is 'their own' and what meaning has this 'revenge' after so many years of living together, working together, of mutual dependence and joint responsibility for making South Africa what she is today?

The FAK has been influential in arranging Afrikaans festivals and in organizing economic associations and groups of railway and other workers.

* Volume II, page 271.

It has given great stress to the preservation and encouragement of *volk* music and literature, historic monuments—anything to advance the cause of the Afrikaner. Dr Dönges, Minister of Interior under Strijdom and Minister of Finance under Verwoerd, told the FAK congress in July, 1937: 'Culture is to the nation what character is to the individual. . . . It is the ideology of a nation as expressed in every sphere of national life and embraces literature, art, religion and customs, social, economic, and national aspects of life.'[4] And the FAK has developed in accordance with this very broad definition.

A visitor to the relatively modest FAK offices in the TO Building in Johannesburg is not likely to be impressed with the powerful nature of the organization, but it must be remembered that the main function of the FAK is co-ordination. The FAK is made up of individual members, affiliated groups, and co-operating bodies. Political parties, under the terms of the FAK constitution, are excluded from affiliating or associating with the FAK. In 1960, the FAK had some 5,100 individual members, each of whom donated between 2s and 10s a year to the organization. In return for their interest, members receive a quarterly newsletter, booklets that are published from time to time, and a yearly report.

The co-operating bodies originally numbered about twenty. By 1937, there were about three hundred of them, consisting of cultural organizations, church councils, youth and student associations, and charitable, scientific, and educational groups. By 1960, their number had grown to about five hundred. The FAK classifies them as churches, women's organizations, teachers' organizations, and youth organizations. The provincial executive committee of each of the three divisions of the DRC pays dues. This does not prevent individual Dutch Reformed churches from contributing, and a number do. The youth organizations co-operating with the FAK include such groups as the Voortrekkers, the Afrikaner equivalent of the Boy Scouts, and the Afrikaanse Studentebond (ASB). The affiliated bodies, which are organizations similar to the FAK, but limited to special interests, pay dues to the FAK and receive its publications, but the FAK does not instruct them as it does local FAK branches. Among the affiliates are national cultural organizations, such as the Afrikaanse Taal en Kultuurvereniging (ATKV), an organization for railway employees; the Afrikaanse Taal en Kultuurbond (ATKB) for postal employees; the Afrikaanse Kultuurvereniging Volk en Verdediging (AKVV) for members of the defense forces; the Afrikaanse Kultuurvereniging van die Suid Afrikaanse Polisie (AKPOL) for the police; and the Afrikaanse Verpleebond (AVB), for nurses. There is also a national association for Afrikaner folk music and dance.

The organization of the FAK is not complicated. At the top is a seven-man FAK executive committee (*Uitvoerende Komitee*). The members of the executive committee receive no pay. The committee meets regularly and 'from time to time as required'. In 1956, for example, it met four times. There is a smaller group, the *Dagbestuur*, made up of three members of the executive committee, including the chairman and vice chairman. In 1956, the Dagbestuur met only twice. In addition to the executive committee, there is a paid staff with offices in Johannesburg. The staff is headed by a secretary, a position formerly held at different times by Lombard and Meyer.[5]

Four of the members of the executive committee are elected by the FAK congress and three by the *Afrikaans Nasionale Kultuurraad* (ANK). The congress is composed of all affiliated associations and of individual donor members. The ANK is composed of representatives of the executive committees of the various co-operating bodies. The FAK congress meets in alternate years. The congress first met in 1930 and the ANK in 1936. The membership of the executive committee, elected by the congress, and the ANK reflects the interlocking nature of all Afrikaner organizations.[6]

Federasie van Afrikaanse Kultuurvereniginge

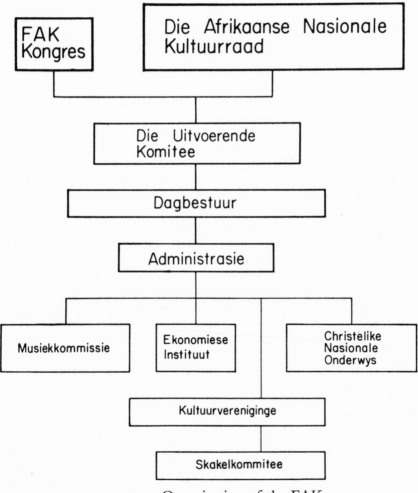

FIGURE 4: Organization of the FAK

The FAK has branches throughout South Africa; they are responsible for implementing the policy and directives of the parent organization. There are *Skakelkomitees* (binding or liaison committees) in towns and cities, and their function is to bring the various Afrikaner cultural organizations together. In some areas even town councils are members of the local *Skakelkomitee*. Another type of local organization is the *Kultuurvereniging* (cultural organization), which arranges for performances of music, dance, plays, and so on. Local *Skakelkomitees* and *Kultuurverenigings* are responsible to the FAK in Johannesburg. The type of influence they wield can be deduced from the 1952 annual report of the Johannesburg *Skakelkomitee*, which advised the Afrikaner 'to attend his Afrikaner church, speak Afrikaans everywhere, read Afrikaans books and papers, send his children to Afrikaans medium schools, go to Afrikaner *volk* celebrations, buy Afrikaner products, support Afrikaner businesses, and make use of the services of Afrikaner welfare organizations'.[7]

The Economic Institute and the Reddingsdaadbond (RDB)

The Economic Institute and the associated *Reddingsdaadbond* have done much to improve the economic position of the Afrikaner; their activities have included raising money and investing it in different types of businesses. English-speaking South Africans look upon such schemes with suspicion, and even contempt. Yet, without assistance of this nature, there would have been little opportunity for the Afrikaner to establish himself in the urban areas on even the level of the Indian population, traditionally a community that included many merchants. For an individual, advancement was difficult and painfully slow. The alternative was group effort. *Volkskas*, the Afrikaner bank, was established in 1934 with financial help from the AB, and has made impressive advances despite competition from the London-dominated Barclays Bank and the Standard Bank, which had been the principal South African banking institutions for a number of years.[8] English-speaking South Africans insist that its rapid rise has been the result of devious methods—and that political pressure has been put on churches and even municipalities to transfer funds to Volkskas.

Until the die-hard Afrikaners captured political control in 1948, however, Volkskas' growth was relatively slow. Its original capital was only £600. In 1949, its assets were £16 million. Since that date its growth has been even more impressive; its assets were £53 million in 1955, and well over £60 million by 1958. It was still a midget beside Barclays, with assets of £224 million, and Standard with assets of £206 million in 1958,[9] but, as the Minister of Finance Dr van Rhyn said in 1955, Volkskas is a 'genuinely South African financial institution, which had its origin in this country and is of the people—owned and directed by South Africans—the only bank of its kind in South Africa'.

The Reddingsdaadbond (literally, Rescue Action Association) has endeavored to inject economic vitality into the dismal squalor of Afrikaner urban existence. Fritz Steyn, in a pamphlet published in 1943, *Die Bron van*

Ons Ellende (The Source of Our Misery), described the plight of the Afrikaners in the cities. He observed that 'the Afrikaner nation is the poorest element in the white population of our country, and is even poorer than Indians'. He estimated that the Afrikaners controlled less than five per cent of capital investments in industry, and that Indians, five times outnumbered by the Afrikaners, had 5,000 more dealer's licences.[10] Dr Diederichs, head of the RDB until 1948, showed in his pamphlet, *Volksverbondenheid van die RDB*, that urban Afrikaners were workers rather than entrepreneurs—railway and factory workers, bus conductors, miners and clerks. Professor L. J. du Plessis, a member of the executive council of the Broederbond, revealed that in 1945 only one Afrikaner company had a capitalization of £1 million in contrast to 116 non-Afrikaner companies quoted by the Johannesburg Stock Exchange as having at least that amount.[11]

The reasons for the dilemma of the urban Afrikaners were, of course, in part those already referred to—their relatively recent arrival in the cities and sudden exposure to capitalism, their general lack of interest in business, their rural outlook, their lack of education and of any urban tradition. A more important factor has been the lack of capital and the inability to attract capital from abroad.

The FAK saw the need for mobilizing the resources of the Afrikaner, and it also realized that to keep the *volk* united required collective effort. Dr T. E. Dönges has insisted: 'The foreign influences must be removed from our trade unions, and they must take their place foursquare on a national basis. . . . It is the task of the RDB to keep the Afrikaner worker, in the midst of foreign elements, in his church, language, and *volks* environment.'[12]

The creation of the RDB was prompted by the Trek Festival in December, 1938, celebrating the 'second trek'—this one to the cities. At that time, the Reverend J. D. Kestell, a minister of the DRC, was concerned about the unhappy status of many Afrikaners, and he used the occasion of the Voortrekker Centenary to issue an appeal for help for the 'sunken' descendants of the Voortrekkers.[13] As a result of his speech at Bloukrans, *Reddingsdaad* committees were formed throughout the Union to raise at least half a million pounds. The FAK then arranged for an Economic Conference to be held at Bloemfontein in October, 1939, to decide how the money (£150,000 was in fact subscribed) should be spent. According to Alex Hepple: 'At this conference the entire complexion of the original idea of the *Reddingsdaad* was changed. The conference was dominated by prominent Nationalist politicians, including Dr H. F. Verwoerd, Dr T. E. Dönges, and Dr A. J. van Rhyn . . . Dr Albert Hertzog and Dr N. Diederichs.'[14]

The Conference of 1939 established the Economic Institute to help improve the condition of Afrikaners.[15] The Economic Institute, which is headed by an executive committee, has sought to alleviate and improve the backward status of the urbanized Afrikaner—the Carnegie Commission in 1931 judged that fifteen per cent of Europeans, mainly Afrikaners, could be classed as 'poor whites'—and has fought to gain for him a share of industry and commerce. Today, the Institute is administratively controlled by the

FAK, and, since 1956, when the RDB ceased to function, the Institute has assumed some of the responsibilities of that body.

The Economic Institute has operated in four major areas: setting up *volksorganisasies,* administering the *Reddingsdaadbond,,* carrying out the resolutions of the Economic Congress of 1939, and studying ways for improving the lot of the Afrikaner. Dr M. S. Louw, managing director of Sanlam, an Afrikaner-owned corporation, suggested the importance of Afrikaner involvement in business: 'If we want to achieve success we must use the technique of capitalism, as it is applied in the most important industry in this country—the gold-mining industry. We must establish something like the finance houses of Johannesburg.'[16]

In 1939, the Institute sponsored the establishment of the *Federale Volksbeleggings Beperk,* a finance group that in turn has assisted Afrikaner organizations such as banks and mining companies. The Institute lent this corporation £36,050 for such purposes. Other groups it has helped to establish are *Sasbank Beperk, Sonop Beperk, Uniewinkels Beperk*—anyone who visits Pretoria is impressed with the beauty and size of their building, *Saambou Permanente Bouvereniging* (building company), *Voortrekkerpers Beperk* (a publishing house). Sanlam, an insurance agency, was established before the Institute came into existence, and was apparently helped by the AB. In 1954, its assets were nearly £20,000,000.

Also at the 1939 Economic Conference, the *Reddingsdaadbond* (RDB) was established under the chairmanship of Dr Diederichs, a Nationalist MP, an economist, and as already noted, a director at various times of a number of Afrikaner-owned companies including the Rembrandt Tobacco Corporation; later, he became Minister of Economic Affairs in the Verwoerd cabinet. His philosophy can be summed up in his own words: 'We are not concerned here purely with a fight between two ordinary political parties. ... No. ... What is at issue is two outlooks of life, fundamentally so divergent that a compromise is unthinkable.'[17]

The RDB has tackled the job of assisting Afrikaners in adjusting psychologically to the conditions of urban life, acting as a sort of employment agency, granting loans for commercial and technical training, advising on business management, and even financing business. Throughout South Africa, it has persuaded farmers to pool their money and invest it, with the result that a considerable amount of business has been transferred to Afrikaner control. In 1940, business interests in small South African towns were almost entirely in the hands of Jewish or English-speaking South Africans; ten years later a substantial part of them were controlled by Afrikaners.

The organization of the RDB was similar to that of the FAK, with which it was closely associated. At the head of the RDB was a national executive committee, with offices in Johannesburg. The executive committee was assisted by a paid staff. RDB branches were established throughout the Union, Southwest Africa, and other areas where there were Afrikaners to implement the organization's program. In 1946, there were 381 branches, each of which was affiliated with the FAK. Every two years the RDB held a national congress of branch representatives. The executive

committee of the FAK elected the members of the RDB's executive committee; the FAK committee also selected a full-time director for the RDB on
the recommendation of the FAK's Economic Institute. The RDB's
economic council worked closely with the Economic Institute. Until 1946,
the RDB collected money for the *Reddingsdaadbond* established in 1939 by
the National Economic Conference and administered by the Economic
Institute to 'rescue' poor whites. After 1946, the RDB retained the sums
collected for its own purposes. Members of the RDB paid a fee that entitled
them to funeral and accident insurance, use of recreational facilities, and
entry to consumer co-operatives. In 1946, the organization's peak year,
there were 17,000 paid-up members. But by 1950 the number had dwindled
to 9,000 paid members, and there were only twenty-six branches.

Finally, at the RDB Congress held in October, 1956, it was resolved
that, after a life of seventeen years, the RDB should cease to exist. It was
remarked, however, that the 'battle was not fought in vain. The fire is
lighted which cannot be extinguished. It is going to spread like a brush
fire'. By 1956, Afrikaner industrial capital investments had increased to
eleven per cent of the national total. Yet, for the supporters of the RDB,
this was only a beginning. More than sixty per cent of the white population
of South Africa is Afrikaans-speaking, and an eleven per cent share in industrial capital investments still fell far short of the ambitions of the RDB. And
the argument still persists: *'Ons eie is minderwaardig'* ('Our own is inferior')—
and must be assisted.

The RDB also sought to separate Afrikaners from non-Afrikaner
influences. One object was 'to make the Afrikaans labourer part and parcel
of the national life and to prevent the Afrikaans workers developing as a
class distinct from other classes in the Afrikaans national life'.[18] To accom-
plish this, the White Workers Protection Association (*Blankewerkers Besker-
mingsbond*) was established, 'founded on Christian-National traditions of the
people of South Africa'.[19] Membership was restricted to 'white persons
only, who are members of the Protestant Church'. The association, a study
and advisory group, was closely associated with the National Party and the
RDB. Active members have included such prominent Afrikaners as Jan de
Klerk, secretary of the National Party, B. J. Schoeman, Minister of Labor in
the Strijdom government and Minister of Transport in the Verwoerd
government, and Dr N. Diederichs, chairman of the RDB.

Die Mynwerkersunie (The Mineworkers Union) was another effort to
segregate the Afrikaner from 'the evil materialistic influences of the Witwatersrand'. Dr Albert Hertzog played the leading role in the attempt to
develop trade unionism along Christian-National lines. Hertzog, it may be
added, is one of the most controversial figures of modern South Africa. His
many positions, some of which have already been mentioned, have also
included directorships of *Afrikaner Pers Beperk*, publishers of his father's
paper *Die Vaderland*, and of *Volkskas*; he is also a member of Parliament and
at the time of writing, Minister of Posts and Telegraphs. Alex Hepple, for
many years a Labour MP, has presented an informative account (*Trade
Unions in Travail*) of Hertzog's associations with the Mine Workers Union and

of the efforts of other hard-core Afrikaners to gain control of the Garment Workers Union, the Building Workers, the Leatherworkers Union, and others. The Afrikaners have worked vigorously to develop Christian-Nationalism in the trade union field.

Cultural Activities of the FAK

The FAK has been singularly aware of the value of music, opera, plays, literature, monuments, and language, in inculcating and maintaining a strong nationalism, and a feeling of unity within a group. From time to time, the FAK sponsors massive rallies and festivals, which have the effect of infusing and renewing pride in *ons eie*. In 1960, Anton Hartman, director of the musical section of SABC, was the chairman of *Die Musiekkommissie* (Music Committee), of the FAK. He was also an advisory member of the executive committee. The ubiquitous Lombard was also a member of the Music Committee. This committee has emphasized the importance of music in providing inspiration for Afrikaner nationalism. It has encouraged the writing of new Afrikaner music, and extolled the singing and playing of the traditional Afrikaner songs. In 1960 the FAK sold over 70,000 copies of a song book prepared by the Music Committee. The Music Committee also publishes church music and recordings of Afrikaner music.

The committee sponsors operatic productions in co-operation with the *Opera-Vereniging van Suid Afrika* (Opera Organization of South Africa) and periodically holds congresses of Afrikaner folk music and folk singing, such as that at Stellenbosch on October 3, 1957. It has established an *Instituut vir Volksmusiek* (Folk Music Institute), and offers scholarships to study music to promising students.

The FAK has also sponsored a National Theater Organization (NTO), which presents plays in Afrikaans to Afrikaner audiences throughout the country.

The FAK lays emphasis on encouraging the development and continued use of Afrikaans. In 1959, the FAK sponsored a language festival that began in Cape Town on April 6 and ended in Pretoria on May 30. It closed with a massive rally, attended by about 60,000 people, at the Voortrekker Monument. During the festival, the FAK sold 72,000 lapel buttons with the inscription *Die Wonder van Afrikaans* (The Miracle of Afrikaans) below a picture of an eternal flame—the light of Majúba Hill.*

In 1960, the FAK made a feature length film entitled *Doodkry is Min* (*Impossible to Kill*). It depicts fruitless efforts, by the British in particular, to abolish the Afrikaans language, and aims at building up pride in its use. The FAK held a giant fund-raising premier of the film in the Pretoria amphitheater in 1961.

The FAK has helped to establish Afrikaner publishing houses, to produce literature in Afrikaans about Afrikaners. It also presents awards for literary and other contributions to Afrikaans. It sponsors youth hostels,

* A monument bearing the same insignia was erected in the new industrial city of Welkom in 1960.

encourages church and social affairs. It has donated funds to the van Riebeeck School for Afrikaners in Kenya, reflecting the emergence of a pan-Afrikaner emphasis.

The FAK was one of the sponsors of the 1938 Ossewa Trek, celebrating the centenary of the Voortrekker Movement. Over 100,000 persons attended, and the Ossewa-Brandwag, the Economic Institute, and the Reddingsdaadbond were conceived during the celebrations. In 1952, the FAK sponsored the celebrations of the tercentenary of the arrival of van Riebeeck. On both occasions many Afrikaners dressed in Voortrekker costumes; and the various feasts, rallies, talks all helped to focus public attention on the Afrikaner, his contributions to South Africa, and, in particular, his pre-eminent right to live and rule there.

In October, 1960, shortly after the vote to establish a republic, the FAK sponsored a *Republikeinse Dankfees* (Republican Thanksgiving Feast) to celebrate the occasion. It was a highly emotional affair, and the solemnity with which it was endowed is clearly evident in the commemoration booklet prepared by the FAK. This, along with the celebrations that accompanied the actual proclamation of the republic on May 31, 1961, was the climax of FAK efforts.

The FAK recognizes the importance of monuments and statues as cornerstones of nationalism, and it has been responsible for their erection throughout South Africa. One of the most imposing is the massive Voortrekker Monument, situated on a hill overlooking Pretoria—a lasting tribute to the pioneers of the 1830s. Inside the monument are statements about the pioneers and pictures of incidents from their history. At noon each day, the sun streams through a small opening in the dome on to the center of a sarcophagus of a pioneer with the inscription *Ons vir jou Suid Afrika* (We for you, South Africa). At each corner of the base of the monument is a statue of one of the Voortrekker heroes. Beneath the monument is the Voortrekker amphitheater, where giant rallies are held. When the Voortrekker Monument was dedicated in 1949, over 100,000 persons attended the ceremonies.

At Blood River in Natal is a monument commemorating the defeat of the Zulus by a band of Voortrekkers bent on avenging the massacre of Piet Retief and his followers. The inscription reads *Die Gelofte* (The Solemn Vow). The most famous nationalist statue is, however, probably the one of Paul Kruger, which now stands in the center of Church Square in Pretoria. One person has described it as symbolizing 'man's ability to tolerate ugliness'. Paul Kruger was not a handsome man, yet the huge hulk of his frame and his long-bearded square face topped with a stovepipe hat epitomize in every detail the stubborn naïveté, the pious self-righteousness of the Afrikaner —a constant reminder of his people's determination to resist all godless incursions. In a sense, Paul Kruger has been the foundation stone upon which Afrikaner nationalism has been built. The house in which he died at Clarens, Switzerland—he refused to die on British territory—has been purchased by the FAK as a national monument, and the Kruger *Sterfhuiskomitee* (literally, Death House Committee) was established to supervise and maintain it. In 1960, Lombard was its chairman. (The FAK even conducts annual pilgrimages to the place in South Africa where Kruger is buried.)

The national heroes eulogized by the FAK are the hard-core resisters —Kruger, Retief, Malan, Strijdom, Verwoerd, and to a lesser extent, Hertzog. Distinguished Afrikaners such as Hofmeyr, Smuts, and Botha, who co-operated with the British and did not insist on die-hard Afrikaner nationalism and ultimate Afrikaner supremacy, are ignored in the FAK's program.

Thus, the FAK stresses all things Afrikaner: language, music, song, literature, dress, customs, experiences. For example, the concentration camps established by the British in the Boer War are constantly recalled to bolster nationalistic feelings. The FAK has even purchased one of these camps to serve as physical evidence of Afrikaner grievances. The Voortrekkers, who represented die-hard resistance to British suzerainty, are brandished before *die volk* like a cloth before a bull. Van Riebeeck has been all but deified. His statue at Cape Town greets the visitor to South Africa and reminds the Briton that the Dutch were there first. All these manifestations have, it is needless to say, incurred the displeasure of English-speaking South Africans.

The Press

The press has played an important role in the development of Afrikaner nationalism, and has been a medium for welding the Afrikaners into a united nation.

The South African press is divided along racial, ethnic, and linguistic lines and tends to reflect the views of the various ethnic groups that make up the population. The English-language newspapers are by far the largest in circulation, and they form the most impressive organ of opposition to the Nationalists. Of the nineteen daily newspapers published in the republic, only five are in Afrikaans; there are four English and two Afrikaans Sunday newspapers, and nine English and nine Afrikaans weekly or fortnightly magazines. Six of the English dailies have been published for more than a hundred years. The English-language press is largely group owned and generally represents big business; by South African standards, it is quite liberal in racial matters. These characteristics are the basis of Afrikaner complaint and the reason for the Nationalist desire to muzzle the press. The situation as regards the press has hampered efforts to inculcate a strong Afrikaner nationalism. The total circulation of English newspapers and periodicals is nearly two million, and of Afrikaans one and a half million. In 1961, however, total pro-Afrikaner daily newspaper circulation was 165,600, as opposed to 731,000 for English-language papers. As W. S. J. Grobler, the organizing secretary of the FAK, told the writer, for every hundred Afrikaners, nine Afrikaans newspapers are sold; but for every hundred English in South Africa, sixty-one English newspapers are sold. There are five Afrikaans dailies: *Die Transvaler* and *Die Vaderland*, published in Johannesburg; *Die Burger*, Cape Town; *Die Volksblad*, Bloemfontein; and

Die Oosterlig, Port Elizabeth. The circulation of *Die Transvaler* is about 50,000, and the readership is about four times the circulation. *Die Vaderland*, long influenced by Hertzog, has about the same circulation as *Die Transvaler*. In contrast, the *Sunday Times*, an English language newspaper, has a circulation of 360,000, and it is estimated that one and a quarter million Europeans read it.

Thus, the Afrikaner press is considerably outnumbered when it comes to newspapers, but fares somewhat better in periodicals and magazines. The reason for this is perhaps presentation and habit. Afrikaner newspapers tend to be somewhat duller, quite biased, and much more recently established than the English press. Moreover, Afrikaners generally have been urbanized for only a brief period, while English-speaking South Africans have a long, sophisticated tradition of newspaper reading. The English element, more prosperous, more literate, and with more curiosity about international and business affairs, has had more reason for buying newspapers. Nor is the readership of English-language newspapers entirely confined to South Africans of British origin. The younger Afrikaner associates things British with modern living and tends to read English-language newspapers. Until recently, Afrikaans was looked down on, and Afrikaners shied away from using it.

Since, as has been indicated, South African political parties are generally organized along language lines, the leading Afrikaans papers are pro-government. The three dailies owned by Nasionale Pers—*Die Burger*, *Die Oosterlig*, and *Die Volksblad*—tend to be less emotional, less fanatical than *Die Transvaler* and *Die Vaderland*. *Die Vaderland* is published by a company created on July 1, 1962, by the merger of *Afrikaans Pers Beperk* and *Dagbreek Pers Beperk*. The same company also published a Sunday paper called *Dagbreek*, which has incorporated *Sondagblad*, formerly the Sunday edition of *Die Vaderland*. Dr Verwoerd, previously chairman of *Dagbreek Pers Beperk*, is now chairman of the merged company. He is also chairman of *Voortrekkers Beperk*, which publishes *Die Transvaler*. The new company also publishes the magazines *Brandwag*, *Rooi Rose*, and *Zonk*, the last for Africans. Of the Afrikaans dailies, *Die Burger* has the best news and comment. *Die Transvaler* is more important, however, for the understanding of government policy because it represents more closely the views of the Prime Minister. Its editor, Dr G. D. Scholtz, informed the writer that the government does not lay down a particular line for the paper to follow. But the board of directors includes a number of cabinet ministers—its chairman is the Prime Minister—and the board names the editor; it would hardly be surprising, therefore, if the views of the editor reflected the thinking of the Nationalist government.

Indeed, Dr Scholtz explained to the writer (November, 1960) that *Die Burger* was the unofficial organ of the Nationalist Party in Cape Town, *Die Volksblad* in Bloemfontein, *Die Transvaler* in Johannesburg, and *Die Nataler* in Durban. He stated that they were 'unofficial' because they derived their support from the Nationalists, and the directors were all widely known Nationalists, but they were not owned by the Party as such.

None of the Afrikaans dailies is much more than fifty years old. The oldest is *Die Volksblad*, which was started in 1910 by General Hertzog. *Die Burger* was first published in 1915, with D. F. Malan as editor. *Die Vaderland* dates from 1935, and *Die Transvaler* from 1937. *Die Transvaler* was founded by Strijdom on a stock-share basis. In 1960, there were approximately 25,000 shareholders. Strijdom picked Dr Verwoerd as its first editor, a post which he retained until 1948, when he became a senator. Strijdom himself was the first chairman of the board of directors. The Transvaal has traditionally been the home of extremist Afrikanerdom, and it is natural that *Die Transvaler* should be one of the most reactionary of Afrikaans publications on that score alone.

Christelik-Nasionale Onderwys (Christian-National Education)

A highly controversial issue in South Africa today is Christian-National Education (CNE).[20] A particularly anxiously debated question is whether the Nationalist government is now attempting or will attempt to apply the principles of this system devised by Afrikaner extremists to non-Afrikaners. The opposition insists that that is exactly what is being done. Those who oppose CNE suggest that it is misnamed, that, in fact, it is not Christian, for its beliefs 'breed hypocrisy, cowardice, dishonesty'.[21] Father Trevor Huddleston, the Anglican priest who wrote the well-known *Naught for Your Comfort*, expressed the attitudes of many when he said: 'We are told that we must love our own—at the expense of our neighbour. This is a denial of everything that we mean by the word civilization and a denial of everything that we mean by the word love.'

In July, 1939, the FAK sponsored a Christian-National Education Conference in Bloemfontein. This conference reaffirmed Christian-National principles and called for the establishment of an institute to spell out such principles and direct their implementation. The FAK then proceeded to organize the *Nasionale Instituut vir Christelik Onderwys en Opvoeding* (National Institute for Christian Teaching and Education).[22]

In 1948, the Institute made public the basic policy it had formulated. Professor J. C. van Rooy, Broederbond leader and chairman of the FAK, prefaced the declaration of policy with the statement that 'the whole of Afrikanerdom insofar as it is represented by its organized branches in the FAK' had approved the document. 'Let everyone, therefore, accept this policy, every parent, every teacher, and pupil . . . to the Glory of God, and to the salvation and blessing of our people and the fatherland.'[23]

After the Boer War, as a reaction to Milner's insistence that English be the medium of instruction in all public schools in the OFS and Transvaal 'and damn the consequences', Dutch leaders set up private Afrikaans schools to revive Afrikaner morale and teach the tenets of Calvinism. The Dutch Reformed Church took the lead in agitating for the establishment of such 'Christian-National' schools, and DRC predikants were active in school committees. After self-government was granted to the OFS and Transvaal, the Boer schools were dissolved and amalgamated with the government schools. Thereafter, agitation for CNE schools waned, but it never quite died. The Anglican and Roman Catholic Churches sponsored a number of schools, which attracted many Afrikaner children. Afrikaner leaders became concerned and, when the language issue sharpened during the 1940s, the DRC again began intensive agitation for CNE. The result was the preparation of the CNE policy document of 1948 by a group of university professors and Nationalist leaders, the inspiration emanating from Potchefstroom University.[24]

In a sense the struggle for CNE is a defensive effort. It is a reaction to forces that have threatened to drown Calvinist influence. It is another attempt to *laager* and to inculcate pride in *ons eie*. Repelling forces tend to equal propelling forces, and CNE's fundamentalist extremism is a product of the intensity of the pressures against the Afrikaner. As far as CNE is concerned, 'Christian' means 'Calvinist' and 'Nationalist' means 'Afrikaner'.

There are two aspects of CNE that should be considered: firstly, the nature of the educational policies that it advocates, and secondly, its position with regard to the question of educational segregation. But first it is necessary to outline the structure of educational administration in South Africa. European primary and secondary education and teacher training, other than that given in the universities, is administered by the provincial authorities; university education and the education of non-Europeans is in the hands of the national government—European higher education is the responsibility of the Minister of Education, Coloured education of the Minister of Coloured Affairs, and African education of the Minister of Bantu Education. When the National Party came to power in 1948, it was in a position to implement the CNE program nationally in those areas of education controlled by the National government, but it encountered considerable difficulty when it attempted to do so at the provincial level. By 1960, through a united effort, it had put CNE into practice in every province save Natal, the least nationalistic and most pro-British area of South Africa.

What, then, does CNE advocate? Basically, CNE teaches a respect for *ons eie*, our own. 'We want no mixing of languages, no mixing of cultures, no mixing of religions and no mixing of races.' In theory, each racial or ethnic group is to be permitted to develop to the limits of its capabilities in the context of its own culture, language, and traditions under the guidance of the Afrikaner as 'the senior partner'. The philosophy underlying CNE, according to Article 5 of the 1948 CNE Report, is that: 'The highest aim of all instruction and education is the moulding of people in God's image so that they become fully equipped for every good work.' Article 5 also notes that it is God's will that man should master the earth and rule over it. Furthermore, it declares that God has given each nation its own particular national task in bringing about His will. Education is the means for passing along to future generations a nation's cultural heritage. If this end is carried out, the will of God will be realized; and this can only be accomplished through CNE.

Article 6 deals with the content of education. The theory of evolution is denied. Religious knowledge, the mother tongue, civics, geography, history—all must be taught with reference to National and Christian principles. History should be seen as the fulfilment of God's plan for humanity. As Leo Marquard describes it: 'God had given to each people a country and a task, and it was the Afrikaner task to rule South Africa, and no one had the right to question what was divinely ordained.'[24]

According to CNE policy, teachers must accept CNE doctrine before appointment. 'The spirit of all teaching must be Christian-Nationalist; in no subject may anti-Christian or non-Christian or anti-Nationalist or non-Nationalist propaganda be made.'

Article 7 discusses method and discipline, and states that 'all authority in the school is God-given authority'.

Article 8 takes up the question of the control of instruction—the proper relationship of home, church, state, and school in the educational process.

Article 1 insists that all white children should be educated according to 'their parents' attitude to life and to the world', and Article 8 states that there should be at least two kinds of primary and secondary schools: one for those whose home language is Afrikaans, in which Afrikaans should be the medium of instruction; and the other for those whose home language is English, in which instruction should be in English. 'We believe that the mother language is the most important secular subject taught at school' and 'that alongside of the mother language national history is the chief means of fostering love of one's own'.

The Nationalists' struggle for single-medium schools had been long, bitter, and exacting. It has provoked heated controversy. The National Party, along with the FAK and the CNE Institute, has advocated single-medium instruction in the language of one's parents. Article 137 of the Act of Union gave equal status to English and Dutch, and, by an act of 1925, Afrikaans replaced Dutch. Milner had insisted on English as the medium of instruction despite opposition, so that the British may be said to have been the first in this century to insist on single-medium instruction. Later, single-medium Afrikaans schools were provided to counteract the attraction of Anglican and Catholic church schools for many Afrikaners. So long as attendance at the single-medium, mother-tongue schools was voluntary, however, many Afrikaner parents sent their children to the English-speaking schools. English has always been the more important language in business, in international affairs, and, until 1948, even in politics. The Afrikaner learned that in the business world and in international relations Afrikaans has very limited use, while English is a *lingua franca*. Moreover, the difficulty of obtaining an adequate supply of Afrikaans-speaking teachers hampered the implementation of the single-medium policy at first, as did the financial strain on the provinces of supporting two sets of teachers. But to strict Afrikanerdom, *moedertaal* (mother-tongue) instruction is vital if Afrikaner nationalism is to be kept alive. CNE accepts bilingualism, but, in the CNE view, the second language should be taught as a 'foreign language'.

Since voluntary mother-tongue, single-medium instruction had proved ineffective, the Nationalists have taken steps to make it mandatory. Instruction in the mother tongue is now compulsory in all public and private schools in the Transvaal, and the Transvaal Administrator has the authority to decide the language medium of any school; in the OFS and the Cape, mother-tongue instruction is compulsory to Standard VIII, and the provincial officials—not the parents—decide what the mother tongue is. In Natal, the Nationalists have agitated a long time to strip the parents of the right to decide the language in which they wished their children to be instructed, so far without success. But Natal is now the only province where parental option exists.

In 1960, the government introduced into Parliament the Union Education Advisory Council Bill to bring about a uniform system of education. The function of the council, appointed by the Minister of Education, Arts, and Science, would be 'to advise the Minister generally in regard to the policy to be adopted in connection with the education of White persons'. The opposition insisted that the bill was a 'wooden horse concealing Christian-National Education'.[26] The bill was, however, passed.

As regards teachers, Article 9 of the CNE document states explicitly:

> The highest demand we make of the teacher . . . is that he must be a man with a Christian attitude to life and to the world without which he for us is nothing less than a most terrible danger. . . . We, therefore, wish to see the institutions for the training of our teachers functioning as Christian and National institutions.

In all provinces there are teachers' organizations, and in all but the OFS there are separate English-speaking and Afrikaans-speaking associations. In addition, African, Indian, and Coloured teachers have their own associations.

Article 14 of the CNE policy statement deals with Coloured education, and this apparently includes both Cape Coloureds and Asians. It declares that the education of Coloureds is part of the Afrikaners' task of christianizing non-white races.

> We accept the principle of trusteeship of the non-European by the European, and particularly by the Afrikaners. This trusteeship imposes on the Afrikaner the solemn duty of seeing that the Coloured people are educated in accordance with Christian and National principles. . . . We believe that the Coloured man can only be truly happy when he has been Christianized. . . . We believe that welfare and happiness of the Coloured man rests upon his realizing that he belongs to a separate racial group. . . . The financing of Coloured education must be placed on such a basis that it is not provided at the cost of European education.

In all provinces, there are separate Afrikaner and English schools, as well as separate non-European school systems. There has been a move to place all Coloured and Asian education under the control of the Department of Coloured Affairs; the Coloureds, however, maintain that they should be grouped with the Europeans, since their language and culture is associated with that of the Europeans.

Article 15 deals with African education:

We believe that the education of white South Africa with respect to the native is to Christianize him and to help him on culturally, and this vocation and task has found its immediate application and task in the principles of trusteeship, no placing of the native on the level of the white, and in segregation . . . that instruction and education for natives must lead to the development of the native community on Christian-National lines which is self-supporting and provides for itself in all ways.

Article 15 further declares that the aim of African education should be to inculcate the European view of life, especially that of the Boer nation, which is to be regarded as the 'senior trustee' of the Bantu. The African's mother tongue should be the medium of instruction, but Afrikaans and English should also be studied since they 'constitute for the native the keys for the adoption of culture which is necessary for his own cultural advancement'. Thus, trilingualism is made mandatory for the African.

The Bantu Education Act of 1953 placed the supervision of all Bantu education under the Department of Native Affairs; in 1958 a new Department of Bantu Education was established. Before the Bantu Education Act, most educational facilities for the Bantu were provided by state-supported mission schools. The act provided for the takeover of these schools by the state. Those that refused to be taken over would have to continue without subsidy. The Roman Catholic and Seventh Day Adventist churches refused to turn over their schools, and launched a fund-raising campaign to make continued operation possible. CNE, as applied in the government's Bantu schools, tends to educate the African for a permanently subservient role. A different curriculum leads to a different leaving certificate examination from that of other schools. Higher education is the responsibility of the national government, and is handled by the Department of Education. The universities have been established by act of Parliament and are financed by the state, as well as by student fees, and donations. The Minister of Education is responsible for all university appointments; in the Afrikaans-language universities, the DRC plays an important part through its strong influence on the government.

Until the passage of the Extension of University Education Bill in 1959, the universities of Cape Town and the Witwatersrand were open to Europeans and non-Europeans alike. The 1959 bill ended further enrolment by non-Europeans in those universities. The Nationalists also provided for the establishment of three non-European universities: one in Natal for Zulus, one in the Transvaal for Sothos, and one in the Cape for Coloureds. The University College of Fort Hare, which had been attended by Africans, Coloureds, and Asians, was placed under the Minister of Bantu Education and made a school for the Xhosas.

The European universities of Cape Town, Witwatersrand, Rhodes, and Natal are English-speaking, while those of Stellenbosch, Pretoria, Potchefstroom, and the Orange Free State are Afrikaans-speaking. Thus, single-medium universities, as well as single-medium schools, help to perpetuate the breach between the Afrikaans- and English-speaking persons.

The University of South Africa is an examining institution and an extension university for those who cannot attend regular classes. The European university heads include among them such prominent Broederbonders as Dr Thom of Stellenbosch, former head of the AB and, in 1960, head of the FAK; Dr Chris Coetzee, Rector of Potchefstroom University; and Dr Samuel Pauw, Rector of the University of South Africa.

CNE theories about higher education are discussed in Article 11 of the 1948 policy document. This is the article in which the fundamentalist Calvinist doctrines of CNE are perhaps most clearly revealed. 'We believe that the content of higher education must be scientific, but that it must be established on the basis of Christian faith.' The article insists on the teaching of Christian doctrine and philosophy.

> The teaching and practice of the secular sciences must start from the Christian attitude to life and to the world; the light of God's truth must not be absent from any single science. We believe that above all our university teaching should be thetic rather than anti-thetic; never purely eclectic. Nor must any attempt at reconciliation be made. Christian institutions must expound Christian science positively, contrast it with non-Christian science, but never give unco-ordinated instruction, merely choosing here and there, and they are not entitled to try to reconcile the fundamental opposites, or indeed to neutralize them; Creator and creation; man and animal; individual and society; authority and freedom remain in principle insoluble in one another.

In other words, all theories of evolution are false and as *Blackout* comments: 'Creation took place in six calendar days and fossils must be explained—presumably, as Professor Chris Coetzee explains them, as "examples of degeneration since the flood".'

Such is the content of Christian-National Education. 'Christian' is defined in Article 1 of the policy document as 'based on the Holy Scripture and expressed in the Articles of Faith of our three Afrikaans Churches'—in other words, fundamentalist. 'National' is interpreted in these words: 'We love everything that is our own, with special reference to our country, our language, our history, and our culture.' And, as Dr A. H. Jonker has observed: 'When they talk about *nasionale* education they mean education in accordance with the spirit, the outlook and the doctrines of the reunited Nationalist Party—nothing more and nothing less.' The aim of CNE is stated to be 'the propagation, protection, and development of the essentially Christian and National character of our nation'. 'Our' here refers solely to the Afrikaners.

Naturally, the promulgation of the concepts of CNE aroused hostility among the non-Afrikaner population of South Africa, hostility that has intensified as it has become apparent that the Nationalist government intends to make it the basis of the entire South African public educational system. Non-Afrikaners resent the imposition of Afrikaner ideas, and the way in which Afrikanerdom has taken it upon itself to act as the spokesman and formulator of principles for all other groups. The latter believe that something is being foisted on them that is peculiarly Afrikaner. Public debate has turned on whether the Nationalist government will implement the full CNE program. The Nationalists continue to deny it, while putting one part of it after another into force.

Another continuing controversy stemming from CNE has been the dispute about the 'conscience clause'. This clause, which has been included in the statutes of all the universities, reads:

> No test of religious belief shall be imposed on any person as a condition of his becoming or continuing to be a professor, lecturer, teacher, or student of a university college, or of holding any office or receiving any emolument, or exercising any privilege therein, nor shall any preference be given to or advantage be withheld from any person on the ground of his religious belief.

Afrikaner extremists have made a number of attempts to render it ineffective. In 1949, when Potchefstroom sought parliamentary approval for status as a full university, a modification of the clause was approved; the University of the OFS was unsuccessful in an attempt to delete the clause from its statute, but that document contains a clause which appears to nullify the conscience clause. As Prime Minister, Strijdom maintained that the clause was 'an anomaly in South African legislation because the constitution recognizes the sovereignty of God'. The Extension of University Education Act establishing separate non-European universities omitted the conscience clause because, as Verwoerd said, 'inasmuch as all Bantu education arose from religious instruction and is still and should be coupled with it, there will be no insertion of a conscience clause in their statutes'.

The opponents of CNE have organized to fight it, but with relatively little success. The Education League was formed to prevent the Nationalists from applying CNE to non-Afrikaners and to ensure the continuance of the conscience clause. English-speaking teachers have opposed CNE, while Afrikaans-speaking teachers have openly favored it. Few Afrikaners have opposed it. The men who had prepared the CNE policy had considerable standing in the Afrikaner community, two becoming cabinet ministers and one the Cape superintendent of education. By 1961, CNE was official policy in the OFS and the Transvaal; in the Cape, although not official policy, it was applied in practice. Only in Natal had the provincial council refused to accept it. Mother-tongue instruction in primary schools has been generally accepted, but its importance has been overstressed by Afrikaner nationalists, since most white South Africans are, in fact, bilingual. Its principal advantage for Afrikanerdom is that it enables the education of Afrikaners to be carefully controlled so that strong group pride and loyalty can be inculcated. When the Afrikaners were permitted to go to the school of their choice, many chose English-language institutions, thus diluting their sense of belonging to a particular group. In the absence of political and nationalistic factors, English would undoubtedly be the official language of South Africa. Thus, for the purposes of hard-core Afrikaner leaders, single-medium, mother-tongue schools are a necessity.

Finally, mention should be made of the two student organizations: the National Union of South African Students (NUSAS) and the *Afrikaanse Studentebond*.[27] The former was founded in 1924 by Leo Marquard as an organ for university students. In 1932 NUSAS split; in October, 1933, representatives of the Afrikaans universities met in Bloemfontein to consider establishing a separate Afrikaans university student organization in view of Dr Malan's split with the Coalition Party. The chairman of the meeting was P. J. Meyer, subsequently head of the SABC and the Broederbond and Secretary of the Economic Institute and a member of the FAK's Executive Committee. Dr Malan addressed the delegates on 'Nationalism as an Outlook on Life'. The *Afrikaanse-Nasionale Studentebond* (ANSB) was organized and became associated with the FAK. The first annual congress of the ANSB was held in 1934 under the chairmanship of Dr N. Diederichs and approved the constitution. The constitution specified its aims: 'The Bond rests on a Protestant-Christian and cultural nationalism basis and acknowledges the leadership of God in the sphere of culture as in every other sphere of life concerning the Afrikaans peoples' traditions as embodied in history.'[27]

During the war years the ANSB formulated a political policy and issued a 'Freedom Manifesto' (July 1, 1940) that enunciated the republican ideal. Four points of the manifesto are of particular note because of the stress on what have been consistent demands of the hard-core Afrikaner extremists:

> The Union of South Africa is to be changed into a republican state in which the President, chosen by the people for a fixed period and responsible to God alone, will conduct an authoritarian government, with the assistance of an executive council and regional and vocational representatives.
>
> Within a Christian-National education system, teaching will be thoroughly adjusted to the requirements of our commercial life through the establishment of technical, professional and effective academic educational facilities.
>
> The state will employ the press, radio, film and library media, as well as other means, for a healthy people's education.
>
> Afrikaans will be the official language of the country and English will enjoy full rights as the second language.[28]

During the war years, the ANSB was openly pro-nazi, along with other die-hard Afrikaner organizations; it co-operated closely with the Ossewa-Brandwag and even appointed Dr van Rensburg as its leader. The defeat of nazism spelled the decline of the ANSB.

In 1948, a new student organization for Afrikaners was formed, the Afrikaanse Studentebond (ASB). The ASB constitution declares that 'the Bond rests on a Christian-National basis as embodied in the Afrikaans peoples' tradition'. NUSAS rejects such Christian-National concepts. ASB membership is open to 'all white registered students and institutions of higher education'. NUSAS makes no distinction as to race. The ASB constitution describes the purpose of the organization as 'the furtherance of the common interests of Afrikaans students'. NUSAS encompasses the broader scope of all South African culture. Another declared purpose of the ASB is 'the maintenance and expansion of white Christian civilization in opposition to communism'. One of the factors that clearly differentiates the ASB from NUSAS relates to language. The ASB constitution declares that 'the official language of the Bond is Afrikaans'.

The ASB is associated with the FAK, and, in 1961, C. Kuhn, the organizing secretary of the ASB, was also the Assistant Secretary of the FAK. ASB members include students of the Afrikaans-speaking universities (Stellenbosch, OFS, Pretoria) and teacher-training colleges (Pretoria, Heidelberg, Potchefstroom, Wellington, and Paarl). Mr Kuhn told the writer that some 16,000 students belonged to the ASB in 1961. He explained that a yearly fee of approximately thirty-five cents per student is included in the university fees; the university pays it to the Student Representative Council, and the Council sends a part of it to the ASB office in Pretoria. The ASB issues a bimonthly news-sheet, *Voorlaaier*, and holds an annual congress in July at a different member university.[29] Presidents of the various student bodies attend the congress, and each university is entitled to representation in proportion to its size.[30] There is an executive council of nine elected by the ASB congress which includes the president of the ASB. In addition, there is a small paid staff. Mr Kuhn indicated to the writer that the ASB conceives that in future there will be student organizations for Coloureds, Africans, and Asians, as well as the present English (NUSAS) and Afrikaner (ASB) groups, and he expressed the hope that eventually a confederation of all these groups might be formed. NUSAS opposes this idea, insisting on a single organization representing all groups regardless of race, language, or creed.

The philosophy of the ASB is summarized in an article by Professor Coetzee of Potchefstroom University, in the *ASB Gedenkblad, 1948–1958*, entitled '*Die Grondslag van die ASB.*' Professor Coetzee has been one of the leading exponents of Christian-National Education. In the article, he noted:

> The ASB avows that independent nations arose in the course of time through God's farsighted estimate. All people are of the same blood, but God has grouped people, historically, as separate nations. The Afrikaner believes that God also created the nations. He did not want thereby to imply that one nation is better or worse than another, no more than he believes this by avowing that God creates every man.
>
> And just as God bestows His various gifts on each person, just so does He bestow on each person his nationality, his language, his culture, his history. Yet the believing Afrikaner regards this too as ordained by God. It is God that orders that there should be separate nations. It is He who at the Tower of Babel disarranged the language of the people which had until then been the same language with the same words, so that one could not understand the language of the other—so that they

could not be one people any longer. Since this mixing-up of the languages, the Lord has spread man all over the world. Each people with its own language has received its own culture and history. And the Lord planted in the heart of each nation the love of its own, so that in Psalm 78 the Psalmist could point to 'my people' and tell the lessons of their history to his people and their descendants.

In the long history of the chosen people of Israel there appears at the end one of the glorious lessons of history: the amalgamation of religion and nationality. The Lord God was the God of the people of Israel: 'This is My people and I am their God!' The educational system is old. Israel was then also built on a solid religious national basis. The history of the Afrikaner people throughout the centuries teaches us the same thing: The Afrikaans tradition is a Christian-National tradition. Therefore it should surprise no one that the youth of South Africa—the Afrikaans youth—should place in its Constitution the scientific development of the youth consonant with the traditional Afrikaans peoples' character or the Christian-National basis according to the traditions of the Afrikaans people.

The creation of a separate association for Afrikaner students was paralleled by similar Nationalist hivings in other fields during the 1930s. That was the period in which the two-stream policy became a reality in all aspects of national life—economic, political, social, and cultural. In the 1930s, the 'purified' Herenigde Nasionale Party (HNP) broke away when the old National Party fused with the SAP. Afrikaner trade unionists grouped themselves in the *Blankewerkersbeskermingsbond*; Afrikaner boy scouts hived to form the Voortrekkers; Afrikaners left the Red Cross for the *Noodhulpliga*, and the established women's organizations for the new *Afrikaanse Christelike Vrouevereniging*; even separate commercial institutes, such as the *Afrikaanse Handelsinstituut*, were set up. Much of this activity was guided by the Broederbond, through the FAK, which had been organized to co-ordinate, assist, and even direct schemes designed to bring about a genuine Afrikaner consciousness—a pride in belonging to Afrikanerdom.

A good deal of the enthusiasm for separatism was the product of the alliance between Smuts and Hertzog. Fusion was more than the hard core of the Afrikaners could take. Prior to 1933, for example, membership in the AB was not limited by party affiliation; after that date only members of the HNP were invited to join.

At first, the nationalism of the 1930s was mainly defensive, and had as its object the preservation of group identity. Later, stiffened by the influence of nazi ideas and organization, its policy changed and hardened. The late Dr T. B. Davie, principal of Cape Town University from 1948 until 1955, told the writer, it has 'quite unnaturally assumed a rapacious, dominating urge to enforce its ideals on others'. In September, 1940, the Reverend J. D. Vorster told the ANSB rally at the University of Cape Town that it was their sense of mission that enabled the nazis 'to triumph over all other peoples'.

The Dutch Reformed Church (DRC)

No discussion of Afrikaner nationalism is complete without some reference to the Dutch Reformed Church. Just as the National Party has represented the political interests, the FAK the cultural interests, and the Reddingsdaad-bond and the Economic Institute the economic interests of the Afrikaner extremists, so the DRC has been the vehicle of their ideas in the field of religion. Nearly ninety per cent of Afrikaners, and, according to the 1951 census, over fifty-three per cent of all Europeans in South Africa are members of the Dutch Reformed Church. Among Europeans, the DRC has more than twice as many members as the other Protestant churches combined, and almost twice as many as all other religious denominations, including the Roman Catholic Church. Evidently, the DRC and Afrikanerdom are almost synonymous, and the importance of the DRC to Afrikanerdom is considerable. In contrast, English-speaking South Africans are not united by a common religion; among the major Christian denominations they are divided as follows: Anglican fifteen per cent, Methodist eight per cent, Roman Catholic five per cent, and Presbyterian three per cent.

All the National Party leaders are stanch Calvinists. Sir de Villiers Graaff told the writer that when he visited Dr Verwoerd after the attempt on his life in 1960, the Prime Minister referred to God over a dozen times in the course of a two-hour conversation, and insisted that the fact of his survival was proof of divine acceptance of Nationalist policy. A prominent DRC minister in Pretoria told the writer that members of the government frequently consulted with him on matters of state. Moreover, many church leaders are important members of the National Party. Many church officials have actively entered politics, among them the late Dr D. F. Malan. He stepped down from the pulpit in 1915 to become the first editor of *Die Burger*; later he became leader of the Cape Nationalists and, finally, Prime Minister. In racial matters, the DRC has long practiced what has now become government policy. It believes that the separation and distinction of different racial groups was ordained by God at the time of creation and should be respected. It considers that the different racial groups should attend separate churches, and that non-Europeans should not be permitted to have membership in or control of the parent church. This view is diametrically opposed to the beliefs (if not always the practice) of other Christian churches; in 1960, the government was unsuccessful in an attempt to enforce the establishment of racially separate churches in all denominations. The DRC seeks to help non-Europeans to set up their own separate churches. Because of the relatively small amount of DRC missionary activity, it is widely believed that the DRC disapproves of the proselytizing of non-Europeans. This is not the case. The DRC, unlike most other South African churches, derives its sole financial support from internal sources; and in the past its resources have been dismally meager and certainly not equal to supporting lavish missionary efforts comparable to those of the Roman Catholic Church, the London Missionary Society, or the American Missionary Society. Only since a large number of Afrikaners established themselves in the cities has their ability to contribute to DRC missionary activities improved. The improvement has paralleled the relatively great increase in prosperity of many urban Afrikaners since the 1920s. The magnificent modern DRC churches being built throughout South Africa today are an interesting contrast to the humble, almost pathetic, structures of just a few years ago.

It is hardly surprising that the DRC has given active support to the National Party, since the membership of the two institutions is to all intents and purposes the same. The United Party, on the other hand, is a heterogeneous group. Among its members are about 125,000 Afrikaners, who have remained with the party from the days of Smuts and Botha, as well as the English-speaking South Africans, including members of the Jewish community, that predominate in it. It is not a single cultural-religious group like the National Party. The DRC is the only religious body in South Africa that offers its support as a group to the National Party. In this sense, the National Party is the political front organ of the DRC.

The annual meetings of the federal councils of the DRC, as well as the various official organs, usually deliver a good deal of political comment. Perhaps the best illustration of this is a document published by the NGK, one of the three divisions of the DRC, following its twenty-second annual meeting in 1951. At the meeting, the general question of church-state relations was discussed. The discussion was published under the title *Fundamental Principles of Calvinist Christian Political Science*. Leo Marquard has summarized this important document, and it is not necessary to do so again here.[31] The entire document should, however, be read for an understanding of the political philosophy of the DRC.

Its primary element is the belief that the state is divinely ordained and created. It is considered to exist quite independently of its citizens, since it is a manifestation of the will of God. The state, therefore, has exclusive powers over the citizenry. The overriding sovereignty of God in all political matters has, of course, been spelled out in the various National Party constitutions and in the constitution of the republic of 1961. From that doctrine, it follows that the rulers are responsible to God alone. They, in effect, are God's earthly agents, acting in His name. Given this belief, the frequency with which government leaders seek the guidance of DRC ministers is readily understandable. The doctrine strongly rejects the concepts of popular sovereignty, the equality of all men, and the origin of sovereignty in the mass of the people—concepts that receive at least lip service in most of the rest of the world, and date back at least to Rousseau. For the theologians of the DRC and the National Party, the vote is merely the symbol of divine authority, for use only by the Christian and by those who are 'politically mature'. But possession of the vote, in any case, conveys no authority to make laws. Laws are God-given. If a government does not act in accordance with God's will, it loses the mandate of heaven and can legitimately be replaced.

The issue of the Afrikaans journal *Woord en Daad* for February 2, 1961, contained an article that brought out even more clearly the contrast between Afrikaner views and those of the English-speaking community. The writer,

C. N. Venter, observed that the Calvinist lived first and last for the kingdom of God—in contrast to the English conception of religion, that is, 'deism, the so-called natural, rational religion' in which 'God stands outside the world'. To the Calvinist, republican citizenship is a 'foreshadowing of, and transition to, on the pilgrimage to the heavenly mountain; of citizenship of the Celestial Kingdom and of the ultimate eternal Kingdom of God'. The author regretted that non-Afrikaners

> mock us whenever we mention the will of God—as regards the result of the referendum as well—not to speak of our belief that it was God who spared Dr Verwoerd's life by a miracle after the attack on his life. Thus two theological conceptions stand in contrast to each other—theism and deism. . . . A great task lies ahead of us to incorporate the English-speaking people by genuine organic assimilation in our spiritual attitude and idea of citizenship.

Another article in the same issue declared:

> The average Afrikaner is a Calvinist who believes that God rules every-thing to the finest details; the average Englishman is a Liberalist who does believe in God but as a God who leaves the decisions to mankind and allows the human being to determine his road. . . . As long as this gulf between the ideas regarding God exists, the levels of contact will be few.

The DRC is the backbone and heart of Afrikanerdom. The *kerk* is the center of every Afrikaner community, and church activities dominate the Afrikaner's social calendar. The DRC pastor is, as the word implies, the shepherd of his flock. He is the interpreter of the Lord. The church provides numerous social functions—barbecues, folk dancing, folk and religious singing—all of which make the individual feel conscious that he is part of the group. On Sunday, the Afrikaner attends church and spends the remainder of the day in quiet reflection. For the strict Calvinist, no work is permitted on the Lord's Day—not even simple household chores. Sunday 'blue laws' are rigidly applied. For an outsider, Sunday in South Africa is dull indeed. All bars, motion pictures, stores, and most restaurants are closed. It has even been suggested that all popular music be forbidden on the radio. Instances of farmers who have beaten African laborers for offending the Lord by working on the Sabbath are not uncommon.

In effect, the DRC maintains strict seventeenth-century Puritanism similar to that practised by the early settlers in New England. In America, however, Puritanism has been greatly diluted with the passage of time. Among the Afrikaners, with their long history of isolation from external influences, it has remained generally pure, even in the face of the changing circumstances of the late nineteenth and the twentieth century. Calvinism in South Africa has changed little over the years.

Since the days of van Riebeeck, the DRC has split into three segments, but fundamentally there is little disagreement among them.

The *Nederduits Gereformeerde Kerk* (NGK) is the parent church of the

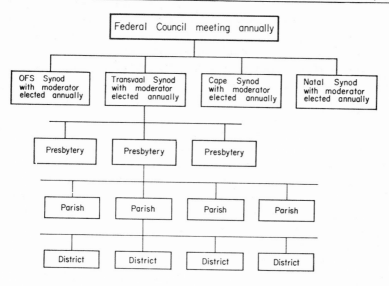

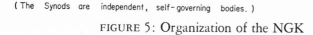

(The Synods are independent, self-governing bodies.)

FIGURE 5: Organization of the NGK

three, the body originating in the Netherlands and established in the Cape in the seventeenth century. In 1951, it had 1,108,000 European and over 600,000 non-European members. Most of the members were in the Transvaal and the Cape, which had about half a million each; there were also 160,602 in the OFS, and 46,052 in Natal. The NGK is the largest and most influential of the three groups, and is usually the body meant in references to the Dutch Reformed Church. It is well organized and maintains strong control over its members. Like the National Party, the NGK is federally constructed. Each province has a synod, headed by a moderator, who is elected at the annual synod meeting. The Federal Council, composed of representatives of each independent synod, meets once a year to discuss matters of mutual concern. At the bottom of the organizational hierarchy is the congregation, or parish, ruled by a council composed of elders and deacons and chaired by the minister, or *predikant*. As Marquard notes, ministers are 'called' by the council by vote. Where two persons receive an equal number of votes lots are cast. Between the congregations and the synods are the presbyteries, each comprising several congregations. Each parish has its own *kerk*. Parishes are subdivided into districts, which, in large cities, can be as small as a few blocks. Each such subdivision is headed by an enthusiastic layman who, according to the Reverend J. Reyneke, pastor of *Die Grootkerk* in Pretoria, visits each member of his district at least once a week. He is the link between the church and its membership. The NGK publishes *Die Kerkbode* as its official organ. European ministers of the NGK receive their training at the University of Stellenbosch and the University of Pretoria. NGK organization has its practical aspects. It evokes a strong sense of membership and helps to develop totality of church influence and in turn a strong sense of belonging to a particular group.

Both the other Dutch Reformed churches broke away from the NGK in the mid-nineteenth century. The *Nederduitsch Hervormde Kerk* (NHK) was established in the Transvaal in 1858. Today it has fewer than 200,000 European members, over eighty per cent of them in the Transvaal, and about 30,000 non-European members.

In 1859, *Gereformeerde Kerk van Suid Afrika* (GK) was established in the Orange Free State. Its headquarters today are at Potchefstroom, and its ministers are trained at Potchefstroom University. It is much more strictly Calvinist than the mother church, a fact that helps to explain many of the fundamentalist concepts emanating from Potchefstroom University. The GK has no rigid organization, no moderator, and, unlike the NGK, no permanent administration; and authority lies on the whole with individual churches. According to the 1951 census, the GK had 112,000 European members scattered throughout the Union, with more than half of them in the Transvaal and a quarter in the Cape. In addition, it had more than 30,000 non-European members.

The DRC has always played an important part in Afrikaner life. During the nineteenth century, the church was responsible for building churches and schools. During the Boer War, DRC pastors ministered to the Boer Commandos and some of them even fought—as did General Roux, who later returned to his congregation. After the war, the DRC participated in the work of rehabilitation, and rebuilt schools and churches. These endeavors were a significant contribution to the development of Afrikaner nationalism, for they focused attention, although not directly designed to do so, on *die volk*. The first world war and the rebellion of 1914 'split the Afrikaner and his church, and a new generation of ministers, strongly imbued with nationalism, partly followed and partly led the new political movement'.[32] Between the two world wars, a number of DRC ministers, such as the Reverend J. D. Vorster, openly expressed admiration for the nazi movement. Most DRC ministers gave strong support to the National Party of Dr Malan and backed it in its opposition to participation in the second world war. The Church was involved in the movement after the first world war for the use of Afrikaans, which in turn played an important role in the further development of Afrikaner nationalism.

In South Africa, the DRC is the only body that rivals the National Party in influence. However, as Edwin S. Munger, American Field Services representative in Africa, said: 'The Dutch Reformed churches are in no position to oppose the National Party—and the National Party is in no position to oppose the *kerk*.'[33] The Church supports the party, and the party accepts religious guidance from the Church. However, the Church would be unwise to tangle politically with the National Party for, as one DRC leader has pointed out, 'one of the first casualties would be the present unity of the Dutch Reformed churches'.[34] The Church's influence is essentially passive. The Church has the loyalty of the Afrikaner, and the Afrikaner controls the government, through the medium of the National Party. In this sense, the influence of the DRC on the South African government might be said to parallel the influence of the Catholic Church on the government of Ireland. Most government leaders are Afrikaners, and since 1948 the vast majority of cabinet ministers have been members of the DRC. As already remarked, government leaders do not hestitate to consult DRC pastors and treat their opinions with filial respect.

Aside from its influence on government policy, the principal importance of the DRC for Afrikaner nationalism is the fact that it is largely responsible for the closeness of the Afrikaner community. It has certainly been a rallying force behind nationalism. As the common denominator of Afrikaner unity, it helps to keep the group together spiritually. The writer recalls an ocean voyage from Mombasa to Trieste in which a large portion of the passengers were Afrikaner. They exhibited many of the easy-going, relaxed characteristics of Americans who have, in a sense, suffered some similar historical experiences.* Each night they would gather on deck to sing hymns and Afrikaner folk music and read from the Bible. They would ask a blessing before each meal, and on Sundays would attend divine service. Among themselves and even in the presence of English-speaking persons they would speak Afrikaans, even though they were equally at home in English—much to the annoyance of those passengers who did not speak Afrikaans.

Having been a minority group throughout most of their history, Afrikaners have learned the value of the *laager*, that is of the united front. Internal differences seldom leave the Afrikaner 'family'. Unlike the members of the English-speaking community, they try to avoid carrying their differences to the public arena. Now that they control the government of South Africa, they appear to recognize even more acutely the need for keeping differences at home. The case of Havenga is an example: he was the leader of the Afrikaner Party at the time it joined with the Nationalists to defeat the United Party, and was the logical heir of Malan. However, he was outwitted by Strijdom, a younger man, and the latter became Prime Minister. Havenga must have resented this strongly, but he refrained from airing his bitterness in public.

But the DRC, like most other human institutions, has not been immune to internal disputes. When the World Council of Churches, of which the three Dutch Reformed churches were at one time all members, met in Johannesburg in December, 1960, it forced a serious reassessment of attitudes toward Church doctrine by many Afrikaners. The consultation of the meeting discussed the whole question of race relations, and concluded that 'we are united in rejecting all unjust discrimination' but within a wide range of 'divergent convictions . . . on the basic issues of *apartheid*'. The delegation of the NHK headed by A. J. G. Oosthuizen, chairman of the Pretoria Synod, issued a separate statement in which it rejected 'integration

* Although, as one Afrikaner opined, 'America won its war of independence from the British!'

in any form. The agreement that has been reached contains such far-reaching declarations that we cannot subscribe to it'. It made known its 'gratefulness' to the government for having taken positive steps to solve the racial problem, and pledged itself to continue 'to witness to the government and people in accordance with the Word of God'. The NGK of the Cape and Transvaal wanted it made clear that the statement of the consultation was not incompatible with the racial policy of the government. The other DRC delegates accepted the consultation's statement. The World Council meeting provoked vigorous discussion in the press, particularly in the English-language papers which, no doubt, sensed a situation that might be turned to the disadvantage of the Afrikaners. Sharp differences of opinion were expressed on the racial question. The public discussion finally prompted the decision of the three Dutch Reformed churches unanimously to withdraw from the World Council of Churches.[35]

A more serious manifestation of disunity within the DRC was brought to public attention in November, 1960, when eleven Dutch Reformed Church leaders denounced the government's racial policy in a book, *Vertraagde Aksie* (*Delayed Action*). It was to be expected that such manifestation of disunity would make headlines in the English press. A more significant aspect of the affair was that it reflected discontent among prominent leaders within the DRC. One of the writers insisted that 'the Church should long ago have warned the government of our country—and must still'. Another observed: 'It is well known that our Afrikaans-speaking churches are in favour of total *apartheid*, if, through the division, all groups are given the fullest rights. The fact is, however, that such division is not possible at this period in our history.' Still another opined: 'We [whites and other races] can never live without each other. We can never live as though the other were not there.'

At the General Assembly of the NHK in March, 1961, there was perceptible tension when Professor A. S. Geyser, one of the authors of *Delayed Action*, questioned some of the Church's scriptural interpretations. Geyser declared that for the two centuries following the arrival of Jan van Riebeeck there was no *apartheid,* and in that period racial mixing was commonplace. He noted that even Simon van der Stel, one of the early governors of the Cape, was colored.

It must be assumed that factionalism will continue to develop in the DRC. Probably the existence of different points of view within the DRC itself will further harden the opinions of the Afrikaner extremists. Whether the government will pay any attention to any changes in the views of the churches is quite another matter.

8 The Political Offensive: The National Party (NP)

And I will clothe him with thy robe, and strengthen him with thy girdle, and I will commit thy government into his hand: and he shall be a father to the inhabitants of Jerusalem, and to the house of Judah.
ISAIAH 22 : 21

THE NASIONALE PARTY is the political organ of hard-core Afrikanerdom, and it is through the medium of the party that the hard-core Afrikaners control the government. Fully to understand Afrikaner nationalism, it is necessary to take into account the nature of the National Party—how it is organized, how it exercises control, its leadership, and its ideology.

The current views of the National Party are the result of a long evolutionary process. The NP is of, by, and for the Afrikaner—it is not comparable with the major political parties in America which represent a relatively broad spectrum of society and accept a degree of change more readily. The NP is the party of Kruger, of du Toit, of Hertzog, of Malan, and of Strijdom and Verwoerd. In its earlier more moderate days, it was the party of Jan Hofmeyr, Botha, and Smuts. With the passage of time, its principles have become inflexible, its prescriptions more specific. Today, modern technology and internationalism no longer permit the luxury of the rugged isolationism that was still possible in Kruger's time. True, the NP looks back to the days of Kruger with longing, but forces both within and without South Africa have made it impossible to turn back the clock. Kruger could apply his policy with impunity, save for *Uitlander* complaints and demands. Verwoerd can advocate a policy, but finds it increasingly difficult to apply what he advocates. Thus, the political party of Afrikaner nationalism has passed from the rigorous and unflinching policy of du Toit and Kruger, through a period of co-operation with the British under the leadership of Botha and Smuts and the SAP, to the hiving under Hertzog, to the Hertzog-Creswell Pact, to the Fusion Government of Smuts and Hertzog, and finally to the hiving of the 'purified' party of Daniel Malan. The party's development has been tempered by the Afrikaner's strong feelings of inferiority and persecution caused by the British acquisition of the Cape and British efforts to impose an alien philosophy, culture and language, by defeat in the Boer War, and by the generally more advanced state of British culture. Other factors affecting its growth were the first world war and the rebellion, the Great Depression, the rise of Hitler, and, finally, the second world war. The National Party has been guided by the Afrikaner Broederbond, which was from an early date determined to achieve political power. During the 1930s the party was attracted by nazi successes, and strong forces, manifested in the Ossewa-Brandwag and New Order, forced it into a more militant and radical programme; but the defeat of Hitler had a sobering effect, as did the NP's accession to power in 1948, and postwar criticism of South Africa from abroad.

The structure of the National Party of South Africa is a loose federal system. The parties in each province and in Southwest Africa are completely independent, but, as with the FAK organs, the Afrikaner press and the DRC, there is the invisible control of an interlocking directorate that keeps the reins pretty firmly in its hands and thus provides unity. And, too, the intense consciousness of belonging and loyalty to group found among party members further contributes to unity. At first glance, it might appear paradoxical that Afrikaner organizations should be so loosely organized when the NP is making the government more and more unitary. Among Afrikaners, however, differences of principle seldom arise, whereas in the country as a whole, with its diversity of peoples, wide divergences of principle are present. The Nationalist extremists can count on Afrikaners; not non-Afrikaners. A highly regimented system is required to enforce Nationalist policies in the country at large.

Nationally, the organization of the NP is loose, but provincially it is tight. A close study of the party's provincial organization is necessary to appreciate the strength of the NP and its contribution to Afrikaner nationalism. Since the NP in each province is set up independently (although the variations in organization are only minor), the example used here is that of the Transvaal.

To be a member of the National Party in the Transvaal, one must be classified as white, be domiciled in one of the provinces or SWA, be at least eighteen years of age, be a member of a NP branch, and renounce membership in any other political party—the Constitution of the National Party of the Transvaal declares: 'In the political field the Party demands the undivided loyalty of all its members'—and sign a membership card with the following pledge:

> I the undersigned hereby solemnly declare that I accept the principles of the National Party and that I will to the best of my ability adhere thereto, and that I of my own free will and sincerely bind myself to fulfil faithfully the obligations attaching to membership of the National Party, in accordance with the Constitution, and to submit to the authority and discipline of the Party. I do further declare that I am not a member of any other political party or organization having a political aim.

Every member of the party is a member of a branch and, since branches are divided into groups, also a member of a group. In this sense, the group is the basic unit of the party, and is equivalent to the cell of the Ossewa-Brandwag. Groups were first established in 1951, at the suggestion of Malan. Each group consists of about ten people and is headed by a committee member, who is elected annually at a meeting of the branch, or by the group itself, or by the members of a branch. The group is where party control and influence originates, a situation that is reflected in the functions of the chairman:

1. He maintains a register of the members of his group (the register is regularly inspected by the branch secretary).
2. At least once in every three months, he gets in touch with every member of his group or holds a group meeting.
3. He ensures that all members of his group are on the voters' roll.
4. He channels party information to all members of his group and distributes party literature.
5. He recruits new members.
6. He encourages the maximum turnout of voters on election day.

In country districts, where a local branch may have only a few members, there are no groups, and the branch is the basic party unit. Branches vary greatly in size. The constitution of the Transvaal NP specifies ten as the minimum branch membership: the Cape, twenty-five; some branches may have as many as two hundred or more members. According to the Transvaal Party constitution, 'branches shall be established in every electoral division' and 'in each polling district', as far as possible.

Each branch is governed by an annually elected Branch Committee. In the Transvaal, these committees comprise between five and fifteen people of whom about one-third are women. The Branch Committee includes a chairman, vice-chairman, secretary, and treasurer (in some instances these two positions are combined), and as many additional members as the branch may determine. The Branch Committee appoints an Executive Committee to 'exercise the full power and authority of the Branch Committee when the latter is not in session'. The Branch Committee's officers do not necessarily include the group leaders, but it is certain the latter have a good deal of say in branch activities.

The functions of the Branch Committee include:

1. Keeping a register of the branch members. This is regularly examined by the ward secretary, or division secretary where there is no ward.
2. Recruiting new members and trying 'to enlighten others who are not likeminded'.
3. Ensuring branch members are registered on the voters' roll.
4. Supporting the party and its candidates during elections.
5. Holding an annual branch meeting.
6. Raising money.
7. Collecting membership fees and forwarding these to the ward or division.

As far as possible, each Branch Committee meets every three months; the meetings are called by the branch secretary on the request of the chairman.

In many cases (especially in urban areas), the branches are grouped into wards, which in turn are grouped into (electoral) divisions. Each ward, where they exist, has its Ward Committee which is composed of the chairmen and secretaries of the branches, with one additional member of every branch within the ward and the leader of the National Youth League in the area. Branches with more than 200 members are entitled to an additional representative. The Ward Committee annually elects from among its members an Executive Committee composed of a chairman, secretary, and three additional members to act for the Executive Committee when it is not in session. Like the group committees, which are subordinate and responsible to the branch, the ward committees are generally subordinate and responsible to the Division Committee; if there is no Division Committee, the ward committees are responsible to the Head Council of the Province. The Division Committee may delegate its authority, with the exception of certain exclusive powers, to the ward committees. The powers that the Division Committee is not entitled to delegate are: approval of branches, terminating party membership of individual members, dissolution of branches, and deciding such matters relating to elections. The functions of the Ward Committee are those of an intermediate body: overseeing the proper organization, operation, and membership of subordinate bodies, ensuring the calling of annual meetings of all branches within the ward, reporting periodically to the Division Committee the names of all party officers within the ward, making a statement of disbursements and receipts, and acting as a channel of communications between the Division Committee and the lower echelons.

The National Party finds the electoral division a convenient organizational unit. The Division Committee (called District Committee in the Cape) is responsible for a single electoral area. Where there are no wards, the Division Committee is directly linked to the branches. Otherwise, it is above the ward committees in the party organizational hierarchy. The Division Committee is composed of the chairmen and secretaries of all ward committees within the division, together with three additional representatives for each ward. Where there are no wards, the Division Committee consists of the chairman and secretary and one additional member of each branch. In such cases, branches with more than 200 members are entitled to an additional representative. If there is only one branch in an electoral division, the Branch Committee acts as the Division Committee. The National Youth League within the division is also entitled to two representatives on the Division Committee. Each Division Committee meets at least once a year; every year, it elects a chairman, vice-chairman, secretary and treasurer (at times the offices of secretary and treasurer are combined in one person), and a Head Council member and his alternate. These individuals, along with the leader of the Youth League Branch in the Division and as many additional members as may be desired by the Division Committee, form the Executive Committee of the Division Committee, and, as such, act for the latter when it is not in session. Wherever practicable, at least one-third of the members of the Executive Committee of the Division Committee are women.

The Division Committee is responsible for the general supervision of its area, a particularly important task, since the area is an electoral unit. The Division Committee can terminate membership of any branch member, subject only to his right of appeal to the Head Council. It likewise has the power to dissolve any branch, also subject to appeal. An interesting feature of the duties of the Division Committee is the stress laid on fund raising. Each Division Committee must pay a membership fee to the Head Office equal of one shilling for each of half the number of votes received by the National Party candidate in the electoral division. If no candidate is nominated, the Head Council levies whatever amount it considers suitable. The levy is, in effect, a fine. The fees that the Division Committee remits to the Head Office are collected from party members. Every year, the Division Committee holds a republican rally, and turns over two-thirds of the proceeds to the Head Office. For failure to hold such a rally, the Head Council imposes a fine. The Division Committee also acts as a collecting agency for the Head Office, receiving moneys destined for the Head Office from the branches. The Division Committee determines the amounts to be paid annually by each branch to its account, and supervises branch and ward levies. It audits the financial books of each branch annually, and controls the finances of the branch and ward committees.

The special function of the Division Committee is responsibility for party electoral procedure and activities. Section 69 (f) of the Constitution of the Transvaal NP states: 'Every Division Committee shall manage all matters in connection with the nomination of candidates for Parliament or the Provincial Council as provided for in the Regulation Governing Elections.' All nominations are subject to approval by the Head Council, and the Head Council 'shall not be obliged to make known its reasons for rejection'. Candidates must have been registered members of the NP for at least twelve months before nomination and must comply with national, provincial, or local election requirements. Only branches take part in the actual nomination of candidates for local, provincial and parliamentary offices, and only registered party members participate in nomination. Nomination dates are set by the Head Office, and written nominations are submitted through the branches to the Division Committee together with a written approval of the candidate. The Division Committee forwards these documents to the Head Council for approval. If the Head Council receives several nominations for the same candidacy, all but one are eliminated by a special Division Committee meeting or 'in the case of a local authority election, a meeting of only the usual delegates from each branch within the area or ward on the Division Committee'. Nominees become official party candidates.

Once nominations are made, the division committees 'do everything in their power to win elections for the Party and to assist the Party candidates in every possible way'. They 'assist branch committees and ward committees with the registration of voters'. The division committees have another significant responsibility that reflects their hierarchical authority: 'Every Division Committee shall approve of the agenda items of branches.' This demonstrates further the pyramidal structure of the National Party.

On the Witwatersrand and in Pretoria, the principal urban areas of the Transvaal, two bodies have been formed to link the division committees with the Head Office: the National Party Council of the Witwatersrand and the National Party Council of Pretoria. These two bodies are semi-autonomous. In the rural areas of the Transvaal, there is no additional organ between the Division and Head Office.

The heart of NP power lies at the provincial level. Section 98 of the Transvaal National Party Constitution declares that 'the Provincial Congress shall be the highest authority of the National Party of the Transvaal'. The Congress meets once a year; it is made up of the members of the Head Council, one delegate from each branch (two if the branch has more than two hundred members), two delegates from each Regional Committee of the National Youth League, the province's Nationalist members of Parliament and of the Provincial Council, and representatives of the Federal Council. These last-named are non-voting members. The Congress determines party policy. It elects the Provincial Leader and representatives to the Federal Council, and it debates the financial report of the Head Council. Each session of the Congress is opened and closed with prayer. Section 85 (a) states: 'Whenever the Congress is not in session, its powers shall *ipso facto* be delegated to the Head Council, who may take action in regard to all matters.'

The Head Council is composed in the Transvaal of one representative of each electoral division elected by the Division Committee, fourteen members appointed by the Head Council itself, four elected by the Head Council of the National Youth League, the Chairman of the Rand Conference and the Chairman of the National Party Council of Pretoria, the Provincial Leader, Provincial Council Leader, all Nationalist ministers from the Transvaal, and members of the Executive Committee in the Transvaal. The Head Council has power to dissolve any committee or body of the Party in the province 'without reason' and reconstitute it as it sees fit, fix dates for nominations of candidates, decide appeals from the decisions of lower echelons in the hierarchy, approve or reject all party nominees for public office (and it 'is not obliged to make known its reasons for rejection'). Furthermore, the Head Council convenes the annual party congress, reports to it on party activities, and prepares its agenda; the Head Council also appoints special committees from time to time to study particular problems, supervises subordinate bodies, keeps a watchful eye on the press, supervises the Head Office, and does 'everything necessary to promote the interests and organization of the Party'. The Head Council meets at least twice a year, and when the Head Council is not in session its powers are delegated to its Executive Committee. The chairman and secretary of the Head Council hold the same offices in the Executive Committee. In addition, the Executive Committee includes the Provincial Leader of the Party, the Vice Chairman of the Head Council, the Chairman of the National Party Council of the Witwatersrand, the Chairman of the National Party Council of Pretoria, the National Party Provincial Council Leader, the Provincial Leader of the National Youth League, and such other members as the Head Council may elect. The Executive Committee meets as often as is necessary.

All NP provincial head offices maintain a small headquarters: that of the OFS is in Bloemfontein, that of the Transvaal in Johannesburg, that of the Cape in Cape Town, and that of Natal in Durban; the head office of the NP in Southwest Africa is located in Windhoek. In each province, the National Party publishes a periodical giving news of party affairs.

A provision of the constitution of the Transvaal NP (Section 110) states that 'the Congress may from time to time decide to authorize the Leader-in-Chief, as well as the Provincial Leader . . . to act with full power and authority of Congress whenever the Congress is not in session'. Thus, in certain circumstances all authority might be placed in the hands of the Provincial Leader or Leader-in-Chief, and the effective distribution of power in the federal system reduced.

In terms of power relationships, all the provincial systems are similar; in each instance the higher organ controls the lower ones. The Branch Committee controls the group and membership, and it can terminate the membership of an individual or group without reason. Its decision to do so is, however, subject to appeal in all cases to the Head Council. Ward committees, division committees, the Witwatersrand Division of the National Party of the Transvaal, the National Party Council of Pretoria, the Head Council, and the Congress—all have similar powers over lower echelons in the hierarchy. Each oversees the finances, fund-raising activities, and electioneering of lower units.

The National Youth League (*Die Nasionale Jeugbond*), founded in 1938, is an adjunct of the party, and it performs important functions, especially during elections. Like the parent party, the Jeugbond is federally constructed, and its activities are carefully co-ordinated with those of the Party. In 1960, the leader (*hoofleier*) of the Transvaal Jeugbond was W. S. J. Grobler, who was at the same time the Organizing Secretary of the FAK. The Jeugbond publishes *Jeugbonder*, a monthly news sheet, as its official organ. The national Leader-in-Chief of the party is the Union Leader of the Jeugbond.

As we have noted, each provincial National Party organization 'is and shall be an independent body but shall join a Federal Union with the organizations of the National Party in the other provinces in accordance with the Constitution of the Federal Council'. The Federal Council includes the Leader of the Parliamentary caucus of the National Party, seven representatives named by each Provincial Congress and Southwest Africa, and one representative appointed by the Federal Council of the National Youth League as well as the provincial leaders and half a dozen members of Parliament. The Leader of the Parliamentary caucus is chairman of the Federal Council; that is, Leader-in-Chief of the National Party. When the party is in power, as it has been since 1948, the Leader-in-Chief is Prime Minister.

The Federal Council must meet at least once a year; any council member may attend any provincial congress and participate in its discussions, but may not vote unless, of course, he is a member of the Congress. The purpose of the Council is to co-ordinate party policy and activities, much as do the Republican and Democratic National Committees in the United States. The Council is empowered to convene republican congresses to consider matters of national importance, but such congresses are advisory only. None have met since 1942. The Federal Council is responsible for its own rules and organization. It uses the committee system, and two of its committees are of especial importance: the Information Committee issues pamphlets and other publications and produces the official party newspaper, *Die Kruithoring*; the Steering Committee, which is composed of the provincial leaders, is the real seat of power in the party. The latter committee meets more frequently than the Council, usually monthly. It is concerned with party policy, which must be approved by the provincial congresses, but, since the committee itself includes all the provincial leaders, such approval is usually a matter of routine. In South Africa, the members

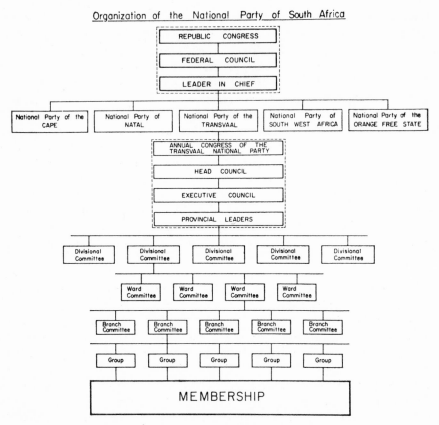

FIGURE 6: Organization of the National Party

of the Steering Committee are also key persons in the cabinet; thus there is a close relationship between party and government. (In the United States, the chairman of the National Committee of the party in power is not the President, although the President is recognized as titular head of his party.) Since National Party leadership and government leadership are the same, party principle becomes government principle. In essence, when the party controls the government as closely as it does in South Africa, the two become fused as one. In 1963 the provincial leaders were H. F. Verwoerd for the Transvaal, J. J. Serfontein for the OFS, W. Maree for Natal, T. E. Dönges for the Cape, and J. G. van der Wath for Southwest Africa.

The Federal Council maintains a small office in Bloemfontein, headed in 1962 by Senator M. P. A. Malan, Chief Information Officer (*Hoofinligtingsbeampte*) of the party. He also acted as the Secretary to the Federal Council. The office sends out press information and party propaganda. In July, 1960, it commenced publication of *Inligtingsdiens van die Nasionale Party van S.A.,* which contains National Party views on items of current interest.

The struggle to achieve the leadership of the National Party and, hence, when the party is in power, the position of Prime Minister has on two occasions produced crises. In 1954 Dr Daniel Malan decided to retire in order to avoid a situation similar to the unfortunate bickering in the United Party that followed the death of Smuts. As his successor, Malan had picked Nicolaas Christiaan ('Klassie') Havenga, the head of the former Afrikaner Party, which in 1948 had joined with the Nationalists to defeat Smuts. However, the Transvaal nominated its Provincial Leader, J. G. Strijdom, and succeeded in electing him. Strijdom pushed further the die-hard Nationalist program.

In 1958, Strijdom became ill, and he appointed his Minister of Justice, Charles Robbert Swart, as acting Prime Minister. Swart had at one time been Hertzog's secretary, and had had a good deal to do with his expulsion from the party in 1941. He later became Governor-General and, in 1961, first President of the Republic of South Africa. When Strijdom died, in September, 1958, it was assumed Swart would be elected as the new party leader. Strijdom had selected 'Blackie' Swart as his successor in a spirit of compromise. His personal choice was the Transvaler, H. F. Verwoerd. However, he knew the Cape wanted Dr Theophilus Ebenhaezer Dönges, and he feared that his choice would cause a split in the party. The Transvaal Party leaders rejected Strijdom's suggestion, and the Cape leaders, who had been prepared to accept the compromise, immediately pushed their own candidate. A crisis ensued. Swart was eliminated on the first ballot and Dönges on the second; finally, Verwoerd was chosen. As in 1954, the more extreme nationalist won, thus refining hard-core policy still further. Verwoerd had hesitated before deciding to be a candidate for the position of Party Leader because Swart was older, but his view was that no one should withdraw in these circumstances, since he believed that the will of God was revealed in the voting.[1]

One professor of the University of the Orange Free State expressed to the writer the opinion that the election of Verwoerd was a victory for what William James referred to as the 'tough-minded', as opposed to the 'tender-minded'. He cited cabinet appointments to illustrate his point. Dr Albert Hertzog and Dr N. Diederichs can be considered as genuine and extreme die hards. Neither Malan nor Strijdom would have them in their cabinets. Both Hertzog and Diederichs have expressed admiration for Hitler and have been influential leaders of the Broederbond. The writer's informant added: 'Malan was the Christian, Strijdom the patriot, but Verwoerd is the intellect and schemer.' During the voting for the new leader in September, 1958, the vote was split and Verwoerd was the minority choice. Verwoerd was therefore obliged to accept the support of Hertzog and Diederichs (which was probably not difficult for him, since he himself had been openly pro-nazi during the second world war) and give them places in his cabinet.

The National Party is, then, a hierarchy, with control always emanating from the echelon above. The party stresses strict discipline, obedience, loyalty, and organization. Certainly, this is reflected in the terse, harsh pledge to which every official and office holder must subscribe:

> I hereby solemnly and sincerely declare that I acknowledge the sovereignty and guidance of Almighty God in the destiny of countries and peoples; and that I will in a spirit of brotherhood together with my fellow party members, seek the development of South Africa's national life along Christian-National lines;
>
> And that I will with undivided loyalty uphold the declared principles of the National Party as the national political front of Afrikanerdom;
>
> And that I of my own free will bind myself in declaring my undivided loyalty to my Party and to fulfil faithfully the obligations attaching to my membership of the Party;
>
> And that I am not a member of any other political party or political organization;
>
> And that I will submit to the organization of the Party according to the Constitution.
>
> May Almighty God help me herein on the Road of South Africa to Unity, Freedom and Justice for my People and my Country.

The principles of the National Party are spelled out in its 'Programme of Principles' prepared by the Federal Council and subject to periodic reappraisal. The document acknowledges the 'sovereignty and guidance of Almighty God' and 'seeks the development of our country along Christian-National lines'. It declares the party to favor developing 'a strong sense of national self-reliance and independence' as well as 'a strong sense of national unity' under the motto 'South Africa First', but protecting 'the rights of every section of the population'. Eyeing South Africa's relations with Britain, the program insists that 'South Africa is a sovereign independent state' and 'the party undertakes faithfully to maintain this independence . . . and to remove anything which may be inconsistent with the fullest realization of this independence'. Portentous is the section which states: 'The unity basis of South Africa shall be maintained' but 'for the time being' the party 'declares itself in favour of the retention of the provincial system'. The party also recognizes the right to 'change, in a constitutional manner, its constitution or its form of government' and 'believes that the republican form of government, independent of the British Crown', is best suited to South Africa, and is 'in fact the only effective guarantee that South Africa will not again be involved in the wars of Great Britain'. The document discusses the national flag 'as the one and only symbol of our own South African nationhood', immigration of 'desirable persons . . . who can be easily assimilated', equal language rights for English and Afrikaans, the recognition of both the Bantu and the Coloureds as 'permanent sections' of the country's population under the 'fundamental principle' of 'Christian trusteeship'. But, 'the Party . . . declares itself in favour of the territorial and political segregation . . . and separation . . . generally and residentially and, insofar as it may be practicable, also in industry'. It seeks to protect 'all classes of the population against the immigration and competition of the Asiatics, *inter alia,* by prohibiting further encroachment into their sphere of living, as well as by means of any effective scheme of segregation and repatriation'. Economically the party is 'emphatically against' the promotion of 'class strife, or the sacrifice of any national interests for the benefit of organized capitalism'. The program also declares that 'the rural population will be subject of particular endeavour and concern'. As for education, 'the Party regards it as the duty of the State to supervise education and to ensure that every child shall, according to his aptitude and available opportunities, receive education based on sound educational and national principles', and 'regard shall be had both to the Christian-National basis of the state as well as the right of the parent to determine on what lines this education shall be in regard to the moral and religious training of his child'.

Unlike the United Party, which receives much support from a relatively few large business concerns, the National Party relies on small contributions from many people. Financially, the various National Party units are self-supporting. Branches collect an annual membership fee which differs from province to province. In addition, there are special appeals and efforts called *strydkas* or 'fighting funds'. Like political parties everywhere, the NP also raises funds through such functions as teas, sales of work, and so on. It has very few large individual sources of support to draw on. Today, however, the party is well off financially, as the editor of *Die Transvaler* indicated to the writer. He noted that in 1940 the party was nearly bankrupt; in 1961, on the other hand, the Transvaal NP alone had an annual income of about £150,000, or nearly half a million dollars.

The National Party, like all Afrikaner organizations, is well organized and exudes an unusual amount of enthusiasm and a sense of purpose or mission quite similar to that found in labor parties. Members of the National Party are a homogeneous group, with a common language, culture, religion, race; many of them even have a similar economic position. There exists a oneness, a common denominator of interest; the principles of the party, basic and longstanding, are generally acceptable to and advocated by the entire membership. Thus, the National Party and Afrikanerdom are, by and large, one and the same.

There are Afrikaner organizations covering every field of human activity. The Broederbond has endeavored to provide the unifying force to weld them into a single whole. But, as Malan discovered, to achieve unity is not easy. In the 1930s it must have seemed that it had been almost attained. The National Party was the political arm of Afrikanerdom, the FAK the cultural arm; the Reddingsdaadbond was the economic arm, and the Ossewa-Brandwag the military arm. The DRC provided for the things of the spirit. But the structure that had been created was soon disrupted by elements of personal ambition. Van Rensburg, the leader of the OB, developed an air of independence, and eventually broke with the NP. Perhaps the idea that a victorious Hitler might approach him with a request to rule South Africa was too much for him. The aims of the OB, the New Order, and the Nationalist Party were similar; when they fell out, the issue was always one of leadership and authority.

The AB obviously struggled with this problem of intragroup bickering, and an attempt to establish a united Afrikaner front was made in 1941, as has been noted. A Provisional Committee of National Unity (*Voorlopige Volkseenheidskomitee*) was set up with Professor L. J. du Plessis, Chairman of the Economic Institute, as its head. The committee included representatives of the three Dutch Reformed churches, the Ossewa-Brandwag, the FAK, and the Reddingsdaadbond. It drew up a constitution and program based on Christian and National lines in preparation for political action through the National Party. The creation of the Afrikaner Front was made public on June 13, 1941, in a document entitled 'Declaration of the Peoples Organizations' ('*Verklaring namens Volksorganisasies*').[2] The aim of the Front was 'a free, independent, republican, Christian-National state, based upon the word of God, eschewing all foreign models . . . with a Christian-National educational system . . . and the strongest emphasis on the disciplining of the people'. The signatories included three DRC ministers (the Reverend J. P. van der Spuy, Chairman of the Church Council, the Reverend I. D. Kruger, Chairman of the Inter-Church Commission of the Dutch Reformed churches, and the Reverend D. F. Erasmus, Vice Chairman of the Calvinist Association), I. M. Lombard, Chairman of the FAK, J. F. J. van Rensburg, Commandant-General of the OB, L. J. du Plessis, Chairman of the Provisional Committee and Chairman of the FAK's Economic Institute, and N. Diederichs, organizational leader of the RDB.

Die Transvaler printed Dr Malan's acceptance of the Declaration.

I can give you the assurance that my acceptance of your Declaration and your offer includes also the sincere and enthusiastic acceptance of my whole party and its leaders in all four provinces, especially as the decisions at our recent Union Congress, which were unanimous and without a single dissentient, are in full accord with everything expected of us in your Declaration.

Of course, Malan had every reason to be pleased with the Declaration. In reviewing the second world war period one gets the impression of Malan as a man struggling to control a giant—especially as regards his relations with the OB and the New Order—and that he welcomed any offer of co-operation. Malan himself was an ambitious man, otherwise he could not have accomplished what he did. And he was deeply chagrined by any person or group who attempted to challenge his ambitions or his view of correct policy. He eventually won, mainly because his challengers became unpopular with the defeat of nazism; in 1946, the OB associated itself with Havenga's Afrikaner Party, and the Afrikaner Party later merged (1951) with the National Party, thus finally completing the Afrikaner Front.

After the Declaration was announced, an Afrikaner Unity Committee (*Afrikanereenheidskomitee*), consisting of representatives of the FAK, RDB, OB, and the National Party was organized to work out a common policy, but squabbles over leadership developed, and subsequent relationships between the groups continued to be delicate.

Part Three:

ENTRENCHMENT

9   Nationalism Militant

WHEN THE SECOND WORLD WAR ended in 1945, the South Africans who had
fought the Axis returned home and were warmly acclaimed. Nazism had
been discredited, and any association with it had become unpopular. As in the
first world war, Smuts was on the winning side, and he personified victory,
the 'brave new world'. In the second world war, as in the first, Smuts not
only participated in winning the war, but also, and more importantly, in the
attempt to guarantee the peace. He figured prominently in the establishment
of the United Nations, as he had in that of the League of Nations before it.
It seemed as though he had reached a pinnacle from which he could not be
toppled. In 1947, King George VI and Queen Elizabeth and their two
daughters visited the Union and were well received; Smuts, obviously deligh-
ted with the visit, could assure South Africa that Britain provided a 'guarantee
of universal peace'. Nationalist progress appeared to have been halted.
Certainly, the political climate did not bode well for the extremists of the
National Party. In 1948, even Charles Robbert Swart, one of Afrikanerdom's stanchest leaders, saw no hope for political victory that year, and
advised his colleagues to work for victory in 1953. To defeat the United

---

* These verses can be roughly translated as follows:
> But the thorn tree slowly recovered as it poured
> its own sap into its wounds. Now the passage of time
> has healed the wounds so that only one scar remains
> to mar the tree's beauty. The wounds have healed well
> with the years, but the scar has grown bigger and is
> still growing.

Totius was the pseudonym used by Jakob Daniel du Toit, a son of the Rev. S. J.
du Toit.

Party, thirty additional Nationalist seats in the House of Assembly needed to be won.

Yet, behind the flush of victory disturbing forces were at work that combined to turn out the United Party and Smuts himself and hand South Africa over to the 'frontier'. Financially, South Africa had fared well during the war. At the end of the conflagration her external debt was all but retired; she had accumulated impressive dollar and sterling balances; and, due to comparatively free trade and America's willingness to buy her gold output, she had been able to make large purchases without touching her sterling reserves. Moreover, the supply of money in South African banks had nearly quadrupled since the outbreak of the war. But postwar economic readjustments were inevitable. Contributions to the United Nations Relief and Rehabilitation Administration, the World Bank and the International Monetary Fund drained nearly £60,000,000 from South Africa. Meanwhile, extravagant imports continued, and the economic status of the gold mines, the source of South Africa's primary export, was deteriorating as the price of gold was not keeping pace with the costs of production. Then there were necessary outlays for helping drought-stricken farmers. In addition, Parliament had been induced to grant the United Kingdom a three-year gold loan of £80,000,000—half of which was to be spent on South African foodstuffs, much to the delight of rural Afrikaners. Despite such temporary setbacks, however, South African reserves continued to mount, and the prospects of developing South Africa's uranium deposits were encouraging.

But as a result of the war the English had been discredited in Asia. By the late 1940s, they had been forced to grant independence to India, Pakistan, Ceylon, and Burma, and it appeared that a similar course would have to be followed in other parts of the Empire. For the Nationalists, this was a significant argument in their long battle for a republic. Nationalism was on the move in Asia, and cautious whispers indicated it would shortly burst out on a large scale in Africa. Such a trend was disquieting to the Afrikaners, but it offered them further ammunition to support their own efforts.

Along with nationalism, came a sweeping tide of internationalism, which South Africa could scarcely escape. International criticism was focused on South Africa: newly independent India complained of the Union's treatment of its Indian community; other states questioned its administration of Southwest Africa, the former German colony that South Africa had received as a League of Nations mandate after the first world war, and that Smuts refused to transfer to the newly established United Nations. South Africans began to feel they were being attacked from every side.

Smuts and the United Party had become identified with the English-speaking South Africans as well as with Britain and the Commonwealth. The Nationalists, on the other hand, continued to symbolize hard-core resistance to British influence, and they were as determined as ever to seize political power. Smuts' decision to follow Britain in declaring war against the Axis powers had caused a deep split in the Afrikaner ranks. During the war, Smuts had formed a National Government consisting of a coalition of the United Party, the Dominion Party, and the Labour Party, as well as the native representatives in Parliament. The National Government had the support of 85 out of the 153 members of the House of Assembly, and its strength increased to 110 following the election of July, 1943. When Parliament voted for war, Hertzog left the United Party and Smuts, and rejoined the Malanites to establish the 'reunited' National or People's Party. However, as has been mentioned, the National Party Congress held at Bloemfontein in November, 1940, led to the resignation of Hertzog and Havenga. In the following year, they founded the Afrikaner Party, taking ten MPs with them. The Afrikaner Party advocated equal civil, religious, and cultural rights for both European groups, and opposed South Africa's entry into the war. In 1942, seventeen more Nationalist MPs hived off under the leadership of Oswald Pirow, former Minister of Defense and Commerce and Industries in the Fusion Government, to form the New Order group. The New Order group had already existed for some time within the NP. Its members never considered themselves a separate political party, and they voted with the Nationalists. They merely objected to Malan as head of the party. In a sense, too, the New Order tended to act as the parliamentary voice of the Ossewa-Brandwag, which likewise never considered itself a political party. In the election of 1943, neither the Afrikaner Party nor the New Order won any seats, while the United Party gained twenty-five seats.

By 1948, Afrikanerdom was well organized politically. Havenga joined with Malan in an electoral pact 'for the rejection of the Smuts-Hofmeyr administration', although at that time Havenga refused to amalgamate his group with the National Party. Havenga and the Afrikaner Party Congress declared their intention of co-operating with the NP in order to achieve national unity, but stated that, for the moment, they believed they could best serve the country by maintaining their separate identity. Smuts' wartime coalition ended in the autumn of 1945, with the withdrawal of the South African Labour Party and of the Dominion Party (later renamed the South African Party). W. B. Madely and C. F. Stallard, leaders respectively of the Labour Party and the Dominion Party, resigned from the cabinet. The Ossewa-Brandwag became associated with Havenga's party in 1946, while the New Order, along with the various 'shirt' movements, dissolved peacefully. Culturally, the FAK and its associated bodies had infused purpose into Afrikanerdom and given it direction; the Economic Institute and the Reddingsdaadbond had taken the Afrikaner a long way toward financial independence, and the DRC provided moral uplift. All these various activities were apparently co-ordinated behind the scenes by the Afrikaner Broederbond and the entire effort had one goal: to capture political power. Thus, the election of May, 1948, took place in the midst of an unfinished revolution. The Nationalists exhibited a contagious enthusiasm; they knew what they wanted, and were determined to get it— undoubtedly such psychological factors are important ingredients of success. Moreover, the country could now afford the luxury of change, and the war no longer provided an automatic justification of the *status quo*. In 1948, though Swart, Malan, and Havenga may have found it difficult to believe during the campaign, the advantage was surely on their side.

A study of the 1948 election campaign is interesting for the clarity with which it points up the differences between the major South African political parties. The United Party's program was defensive, relying on the record of its administration during the war and in the immediate post-war period, a record that, as Eric A. Walker has observed, was 'not wholly defensible'.[1] The Nationalists, after carefully assessing the situation, decided that a program that was challenging, controversial, and unique was called for if they were to win the necessary seats. The republican issue was not used as part of the Nationalist platform during this campaign and the NP generally omitted anti-British and anti-Jewish references from its campaign material. They therefore selected an issue that proved to be most profitable to them—that of race relations. In 1947, they issued an election manifesto entitled *Race Relations Policy of the National Party*. The manifesto exploited what the Nationalists considered weaknesses in the United Party.[2] The most important issue, the Nationalists insisted, was the failure of the government to deal effectively with the threat that the Bantu posed to white civilization. Malan asked whether the European should maintain his own purity of race or eventually be submerged 'in the black sea of South Africa's non-European population'. To counter such a possibility, the Nationalists presented a program for separate development, or *apartheid*, not dissimilar to that espoused by Hertzog in 1912; it was presented as a means of assuring the continued existence of 'white civilization' in a country in which non-Europeans outnumbered Europeans by four to one. The Nationalist election manifesto laid down certain principles:

> In general terms our policy envisages segregating the most important ethnic groups and subgroups in their own areas where every group will be enabled to develop into a self-sufficient unit.
>
> We endorse the general principle of the territorial segregation of the Bantu and the Whites. . . .
>
> The Bantu in the urban areas should be regarded as migratory citizens not entitled to political or social rights equal to those of the Whites. The process of detribalization should be arrested.
>
> The interests and employment prospects of the White workers in White areas will be protected.

'The choice before us', the manifesto declared, 'is one of two divergent courses: either that of integration, which in the long run amounts to national suicide on the part of the whites, or that of *apartheid*. . . .'

The Afrikaner Victory and the Role of Delimitation

The victory of the Nationalist-Afrikaner Party coalition in May, 1948, was a surprise even to the Afrikaners; it was certainly one to the United Party leaders, many of whom were forced to ask the new government for a few days' respite for packing. There were cries of electoral misconduct—a natural reaction. The National Party won seventy seats, and the United Party won sixty-five. In addition, the Afrikaner Party won nine, thus giving the National-Afrikaner coalition seventy-nine seats in all—a noteworthy majority, when one considers the pre-election pessimism of Afrikaner politicians. Moreover, although the presence of uncontested seats lends a note of conjecture to such calculations, it seems that the Nationalist-Afrikaner coalition had only a minority of the total vote. It has been estimated that the National Party received 401,834 votes, and the Afrikaner Party 41,885, a total coalition vote of 443,719; whereas the United Party is estimated to have received 524,230. According to this calculation, the Nationalists received 36.4 per cent of the popular vote and the Afrikaner Party 3.6 per cent, a combined total of 40 per cent, and the United Party 50.4 per cent. The NP victory therefore depended on the fact that the Act of Union, as has been noted above, permitted proportionately greater representation to rural constituencies, the stronghold of the Afrikaners, than to the cities. According to the Act of Union, each province was entitled to that portion of 150 seats in Parliament proportionate to the number of Europeans on the voters' list of that province in relation to the total number of white voters in the Union (Section 32). Section 40 provided that 'each province shall be divided into electoral divisions and shall . . . contain a number of voters, as nearly as may be, equal to the quota of the province'. It added, however, a clause that entitled the Delimitation Commission entrusted with the responsibility of electoral apportionment to employ considerable discretion:

> The Commissioners shall give due consideration to—(a) community or diversity of interest; (b) means of communication; (c) physical features; (d) existing electoral boundaries; (e) sparsity or density of population, in such manner that, while taking the quota of voters as the basis of division, the Commissioners may, whenever they deem it necessary, depart therefrom, but in no case to any greater extent than 15 percentum more or 15 percentum less than the quota.

The First Delimitation Commission of 1910 established the tradition, favorable to the Afrikaners, of loading the urban constituencies and unloading the rural ones. In the early days of the Union when party lines did not follow linguistic groupings so closely, this was not as politically important as it later became. By 1948, however, the United Party had become strictly the party of English-speaking South Africans, and the National and Afrikaner parties those of Afrikaans-speaking South Africans. According to a memorandum prepared by the Johannesburg advocate Arthur Suzman for the Torch Commando and submitted to the Tenth Delimitation Commission (1952):

> By reason of loading and unloading, the rural constituencies under the 1948 Delimitation in effect gained six seats at the expense of the urban constituencies. In other words, had there been no loading, there would

have been six more urban seats and six fewer rural seats, i.e., a difference of twelve in all.[3]

Certainly, like some overconfident American Republicans in the same year, a number of United Party members failed to vote in 1948. On the other hand, few Afrikaners failed to appear at the polls on election day. For them, the ballot was their best weapon for beating the British (and, after 1948, for maintaining control).

Thus, on May 26, 1948, Afrikanerdom, led by 'tough-minded rock-hards', finally achieved political control of South Africa, thereby completing its primary objective.

It was a memorable day—a day on which the frustrations of centuries were repaid. At last, the Afrikaners had become masters of their own house, a position they now have no intention of yielding. 'Today,' Dr Malan exclaimed, 'South Africa belongs to us once more. . . . May God grant that it will always remain our own.'[4]

Consolidation

By the time the South African Republic was proclaimed in 1961, the Nationalists had already moved a long way towards consolidating their position. Unlike Hertzog who had founded the National Party in 1914 and who had been able to hold office only in coalitions, Malan, Strijdom, and Verwoerd had no need to share their power or make annoying compromises. In the Pact Government of 1924 to 1929, Hertzog was compelled to defer a great deal to the British-dominated Labour Party; in the 1930s, when the National Party was amalgamated with Smuts' SAP as the United South African National Party, Hertzog was again joined with English-speaking South Africans, and limited in his actions as an Afrikaner Nationalist. However, Hertzog was considerably less rabid a nationalist than his successors. In 1914, he was considered a radical, but by 1934, when Malan broke with him to set up the 'purified' Nationalists, the extremists considered Hertzog had 'softened'. But perhaps it is not incorrect to say that Malan himself softened when he achieved office. During the election campaign of 1948 he had set aside the republican issue, he had avoided all anti-British and anti-Jewish references, and immediately after election he quickly reassured the English-speaking community of his good intentions, promising equal rights to all whites. However, Malan depended on the Afrikaner Party of Havenga for his majority, and Havenga was certainly a moderate compared to the hard core. Havenga himself became Minister of Finance and Deputy Prime Minister in the Malan government. To some extent, Havenga's presence acted as a drag on Malan, and there were times when Havenga refused to agree to extreme courses. For example, in December, 1948, he strongly opposed the proposal to abolish the native vote in Natal and to place the Cape Coloureds on a separate voters' roll until there was a sufficient majority in Parliament accepting it. But Havenga's resistance was minimal compared to the opposition Hertzog had experienced from members of his governments, and Malan and his successors had the wholehearted sympathy of Afrikanerdom. Indeed, as the opposition has often declared, the postwar Nationalist rule has been a government of the Afrikaner, by the Afrikaner, and for the Afrikaner.

One of the early objectives of the Government was to improve its parliamentary strength. In 1949, a bill was passed giving Southwest Africa (still not officially part of Union) representation in the Union Parliament; it was granted six seats, even though it had only 24,000 electors. In its first parliamentary elections, which took place the following year, Southwest Africa returned six National Party representatives, thereby increasing Malan's strength to the point where he was no longer dependent on Havenga. However, Havenga continued to refuse to support Malan in his effort to place the Cape Coloureds on a separate voters' roll.

Undoubtedly Havenga had personal ambitions for power, and, prior to 1950, he was in a splendid position to manoeuvre. Rumors circulated that Havenga had made overtures to the United Party, and the suggestion was even made that he might succeed Smuts as its leader. It was supposed that he hoped to align the moderates of both parties behind him and establish a new party.[5] But after the parliamentary strength of the Nationalists had been increased by the arrival of the Southwest African contingent and the Afrikaner Party had lost its former position of power, Havenga turned more to the idea of fusion with the Nationalists. The Nationalists welcomed this prospect, for they realized how consolidation would embellish their own strength.

Malan and Strijdom publicly acclaimed the idea of a merger in October, 1948. In the following month, the National Party's Federal Council passed a resolution that looked forward to union. But Havenga retorted a week later that the 'necessary good faith and feeling obviously do not yet exist'.

The Afrikaner Party had accepted candidates who were at the same time members of the Ossewa-Brandwag. The party had opened its ranks to the OB in 1946, and it was undoubtedly as a result of that action that it won nine parliamentary seats in the 1948 election. In December, 1948, van Rensburg addressed the Afrikaner Party Congress, and was warmly received. Yet, Havenga assured Malan that 'I have never been a member of the Ossewa-Brandwag and we have no relations with them, and never associated ourselves with their ideals or objectives'. The OB had long since fallen from Malan's favor, and, indeed, members of the National Party were compelled to forswear allegiance to any other political organization including the OB. The provincial elections of 1949 demonstrated the massive strength of the Nationalists, and showed equally clearly that Havenga's strength lay only in his nine parliamentary seats.

The OB was opposed to a merger of the NP and the Afrikaner Party, and the Nationalists themselves were split over the question of its terms. Here again, the extremists prevailed. Malan and Havenga, along with most of their parliamentary supporters, favored opening a unified party to non-Nationalists. However, the rock hards—Strijdom, Verwoerd, Swart and Louw—would not accept the idea. They insisted that the party remain pure,

retaining its Christian-National and republican principles. Any new adherents must accept these principles undiluted.

Eventually, on June 25, 1951, the idea of a merger was agreed to after
both sides had conceded certain points (the differences between them were
never great). The Transvaal Nationalists agreed to strike a clause excluding
Jews from the party from their Constitution, and the Afrikaner Party agreed
that its members should forswear membership in any other political association, including the Ossewa-Brandwag. The official name for the merged
party, combining *Die Afrikanerparty* and *Die Herenigde Nasionale of
Volksparty*, was *Die Nasionale Party*—a name that 'formerly described the
political home of both our co-operating parties, and also included all nationally minded Afrikaners from both white language groups'. The *Rand Daily
Mail* (June 25, 1951) observed that through co-operation 'Afrikanerdom has
risen out of the condition of disunity, impotence, and mortification in which
it found itself . . . regained its self-respect and has reached a climax of unity
and power'.

On August 23, 1951, the merging parties issued a statement of
principles that reflected minor concessions on the part of the die-hards. The
statement included among the party's aims:

1. Furthering the welfare of South Africa and its people.
2. Development of an effective sense of national self-sufficiency based on
   undivided loyalty to South Africa.
3. Acknowledgement of equal language rights of Afrikaans- and
   English-speaking South Africans.

The statement declared that the National Party favored *apartheid* and the
creation of a republic separated from the British Crown; but the latter should
be brought into being only by the broad will of the people (that is, by a
special election referendum); it also supported immigration of 'desirable'
white people with 'due regard' to the established population; the establishment and extension of Christian-National education; and the protection of
'the civilized worker' and his living standard from 'displacement by uncivil-
ized labour'. On October 22, 1951, the two parties formally merged, at last
bringing a united political front to Afrikanerdom.

Havenga retained the post of Finance Minister until 1954, when he
followed Malan into retirement, disappointed that the party had not dubbed
him Malan's successor. Thus ended a moderating influence, and the course
of the party was set even more firmly and narrowly.

Malan's successors, Strijdom and Verwoerd, have had the freest rein
of any of the hard-core Nationalists. They have been more extremist than
Hertzog and Malan, although, as is commonly the case with politicians, the
responsibilities of office have somewhat tempered their aspirations.

With the amalgamation of the Afrikaner and Nationalist parties, the
political split in Afrikanerdom that had occurred during the second world
war was finally healed. Yet in recent years the hard-core Nationalist leaders,
aware of their tenuous position among Europeans and their minority position
with respect to non-Europeans, more than ever recognized the necessity of

maintaining a solid front among Afrikaners. To the Afrikaner extremist the two-stream policy is not only desirable, it is essential. Politically, the Nationalists welcome the support of English-speaking South Africans. On the other hand, they recognize the importance of keeping Afrikanerdom together as a single force. Every Afrikaner who defects from the National Party represents a tactical defeat, and makes the position of the party less certain. And there have been a number of defections from and controversies within the NP since 1948. In 1959, Japie Basson, Nationalist MP from Windhoek, defected to form the National Union Party. In 1960, a group of DRC leaders questioned the government's policy in the book *Delayed Action*, as was described above. In the controversy over the Cape Coloured vote, some Nationalist leaders expressed the opinion that the Cape Coloureds should be accepted by the whites and given the vote as whites, and even be permitted to stand for Parliament. Such differences are exploited by the opposition in the hope of creating doubts in the minds of Afrikaners as to the wisdom of Nationalist policy, and thereby enhancing its own chances of ousting the government.

Thus far, however, manifestations of Afrikaner discontent with the NP leadership have been insignificant, and they have been more than compensated for by the splitting of the opposition. In 1953, no fewer than three new parties were established by former United Party members—the Union Federal Party, the Liberal Party, and the National Conservative Party. In 1959, the Progressive Party was organized by other former United Party members and joined by eleven United Party MPs. The Nationalist Government, of course, gained in strength with each split in the opposition. Moreover, sentiment since the establishment of the Republic indicates that the popularity of the Nationalists is growing among English-speaking persons.

Strengthening Parliamentary Control

The Nationalist Government has done a great deal to increase its parliamentary strength. First, there was the grant of seats to Southwest Africa. (Save for the defection of Basson, the Southwest African members have been consistently pro-Government.) In the two new delimitations of constituencies made since 1948, the Nationalists have taken advantage of their position to increase their electoral strength. In the 1958 election campaign the Nationalists advocated reducing the voting age from twenty-one to eighteen, and they interpreted their re-election as a mandate to carry out that measure. Their confidence that more of the eighteen to twenty-one age group would favor them than the opposition has been justified by events. (In this sense, CNE has proved its effectiveness.)

The removal of the Coloureds from the common voting roll in the Cape, finally achieved in 1956, also strengthened the Nationalists, since constituencies with numerous Coloured voters generally favored the opposition. The lengths to which the Nationalists went to overcome difficulties in the way of removing the Coloureds from the common roll illustrate their determination to get what they want, and the methods they are willing to employ to achieve their ends.

In 1950, Parliament passed the Separate Representation of Voters Bill to remove the Cape Coloureds from the common voting list and to give them their own European representatives in Parliament. This Act was contested on the ground that it had been passed by a simple majority only; it was argued that since it affected one of the entrenched clauses of the Act of Union, it required a two-thirds vote of both houses of Parliament. When the matter was brought before the South African Supreme Court, it declared the Act unconstitutional, and therefore invalid. Malan, then Prime Minister, rejected the decision of the Court; the High Court of Parliament Act of 1952 was passed, which set up a High Court of Parliament with precedence over the Supreme Court on constitutional matters. The High Court of Parliament consisted of Nationalist members of Parliament and Nationalist senators, and was, in effect, a Nationalist parliamentary caucus. The High Court then reviewed the question of the Separate Representation of Voters Act, and reversed the decision of the Supreme Court. But the High Court of Parliament Act was declared invalid by the Court of Appeals, South Africa's court of last resort.* To avoid further juridical skirmishes, the government then proceeded to pack the Supreme Court. In 1955, Parliament passed the Appellate Division Quorum Act which increased the number of Appeal Court judges from five to eleven, and specified that in cases involving the validity of Acts of Parliament all eleven must sit. The six vacancies thus created were filled by government supporters. Parliament, dominated by the Nationalists, was now supreme. But in 1956, to make doubly sure, the government put through the Supremacy of Parliament Bill; this removed the testing rights of the courts, except as regards Clause 137 of the South Africa Act as amended in 1925—the Clause that provided for the use of both English and Afrikaans as official languages.

The election of 1953 had considerably improved Nationalist strength in Parliament, but the party still did not control the two-thirds majority of both houses necessary to change an entrenched clause of the Act of Union. To obtain it, the Senate Bill was passed in 1955; it increased the membership in the upper house from forty-eight to eighty-nine, and changed the method of electing senators. Under the new law, the government was assured of the support of a larger number of senators. As a result, Nationalist parliamentary strength in the two houses combined rose to 171, and the NP had a clear two-thirds majority. Finally, in February, 1956, Parliament in joint session passed the Separate Representation of Voters Amendment Bill which removed the Coloured voters in the Cape from the common roll and placed them on a separate roll for the election of European representatives in Parliament. Parliament also passed the South Africa Act Amendment Bill,

* In 1950, Parliament had abolished appeals to the Privy Council in London as the final arbiter. At that time C. R. Swart, then Minister of Justice, declared: 'Our appellate division is the most competent court in the whole world to adjudicate on South African law.'

which excised the entrenchment of voting rights from the South Africa Act. In May, the Supreme Court (in Cape Town) ruled unanimously that the Senate Act was valid, and in November the Appeal Court (in Bloemfontein) dismissed an appeal. Thus, the long struggle to remove the Coloureds from the common roll was ended. The Cape Coloureds now elect four whites to represent them in the House of Assembly. In the first election under the new Act, they returned four members of the United Party.

In 1960, the Nationalists put through another bill to reduce the Senate to fifty-four members, thus completing the cycle. In the re-established Senate, the Nationalists had a comfortable majority of thirty-nine seats.

WIND OF CHANGE

FIGURE 7: Wind of Change
(Cartoon from the *Sunday Times* (Johannesburg), February 28, 1960)

In 1960, the Nationalists strengthened their position still further by abolishing native representatives in the Parliament. In 1936, Parliament had voted to remove Africans from the common voting roll in Cape Province; African voters were placed on a separate roll and given three white representatives in the House, four in the Senate, and two in the Cape Provincial Council. At the time native representation was abolished, the four members in the Senate consisted of two Liberal Party members and two Independents; the three in the House were two Liberals and one Independent. These members constituted the Liberal Party's only parliamentary representation.

Thus, by 1961, Nationalist strength in Parliament had improved considerably since the uncertain days of 1948. In April, the National Party had 102 members in the House of Assembly and thirty-nine in the newly constituted Senate, or two-thirds of the total membership of Parliament, an impressive increase over 1948. Moreover, the Nationalists have polled an increasing percentage of the total votes cast in each election since 1948. In 1953, they received forty-nine per cent of the total vote and in 1958, over fifty-five per cent. In the vote on the Republic held on October 5, 1960, the Nationalists polled over fifty-two per cent, if one assumes the 'yes' votes represented the Nationalists and the 'no' the opposition. Republican elections indicate a continuing rise in Nationalist support. The parliamentary election of October 18, 1961, increased Nationalist strength in the House of Assembly by three members, while the Progressive Party lost ten seats and the United Party gained eight. It would appear the Nationalists continue to move from strength to strength.

Contrasting Political Concepts of English- and Afrikaans-speaking South Africans

Nationalist toying with the processes of government has been loudly criticized by the English-oriented opposition. The system of government that the Nationalists inherited in 1948 was not of their own creation; it was certainly very different from that of Paul Kruger. It was British in structure, and demanded traditional British attitudes and conditions to operate smoothly. The Afrikaners, however, have understandably failed to acquire much appreciation of the British system. Successful responsible cabinet government assumes the existence of a relatively homogeneous population sharing similar values, a situation not found in South Africa. Moreover, the British system of government assumes that those who participate in it understand and accept its rules.

The system of government in the old Boer republics was quite different, and much more authoritarian. Before Union, the British system worked well in Natal and the Cape under such stalwarts as Rhodes, Schreiner, and Merriman because they understood and accepted its rules. The same might be said of the Union under Botha, Smuts, and the coalitions of Hertzog, although the system was perhaps less satisfactory. But the British type of parliamentary government has always been repugnant to extremists such as Malan, Strijdom, and Verwoerd, both because it was British and because it was not in harmony with their aims or their philosophy of government. In

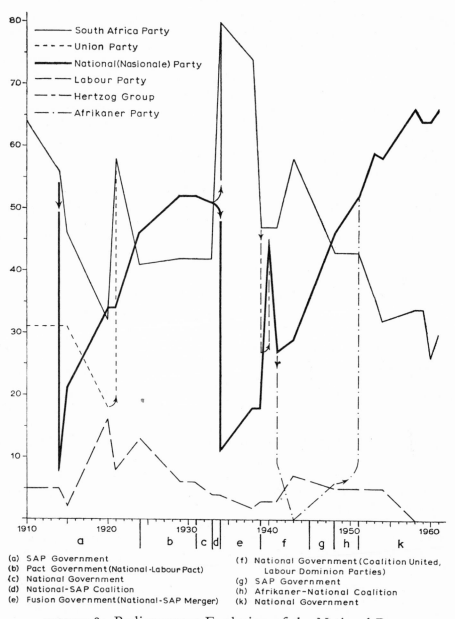

Legend:
——— South Africa Party
− − − − Union Party
━━━ National(Nasionale) Party
─ ─ ─ Labour Party
─ ─ · ─ Hertzog Group
─ · ─ Afrikaner Party

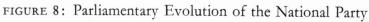

(a) SAP Government
(b) Pact Government (National-Labour Pact)
(c) National Government
(d) National-SAP Coalition
(e) Fusion Government (National-SAP Merger)

(f) National Government (Coalition United, Labour Dominion Parties)
(g) SAP Government
(h) Afrikaner-National Coalition
(k) National Government

FIGURE 8: Parliamentary Evolution of the National Party

the British system each political party accepts the structure, but differs in terms of conduct and ideology within the structure.   In South Africa, parties tend to reflect racial, religious, and cultural differences rather than philosophical ones, and are the more keenly felt.

Under the British system the party in office rules within accepted limits, while the party out of office is the official opposition and has a recognized responsibility to criticize the government; give-and-take in negotiating and debating bills is assumed.   The Nationalists have shown little willingness to accept this practice, and important measures have passed through Parliament practically untouched by opposition suggestions.   Inherent in the nature of the British system is a willingness to oppose and to be opposed. In South Africa, as long as the United Party was in power the Nationalists were willing to oppose; but in office they have shown a distaste for criticism that is perhaps partially explicable as the result of a traditional persecution complex.   They resent opposition either in or out of Parliament.   In a radio address delivered on October 7, 1960, Verwoerd declared that he looked forward hopefully to the emergence of a 'co-operative' English-speaking Conservative Party, the leaders of which he could even include in a reshuffled cabinet: 'In that way we can fight jointly for the preservation of white authority.'   He seemed eager for English-speaking co-operation in a 'joint state', but only on Nationalist terms.   The only response to the suggestion was critical, and, on November 23, the Prime Minister, obviously impatient with the unco-operativeness of the English-speaking community, reminded the opposition 'pertinently of what I named as the most preferable method in my appeal for their support . . . namely, that they join the Nationalist Party'.[6]   There are even indications that the Nationalists would prefer to eliminate political parties as such.   However, it is still too early to draw conclusions about what the ultimate structure of their government will be; quite possibly, they themselves do not know.

Nor is the government's dislike of criticism confined to party politics. By the Post Office Act, the Suppression of Communism Act, and the Criminal Laws Amendment Act, the Anti-Sabotage Act, and other laws enacted during the Nationalist regime, the government is empowered to restrain the expression of opinion.   Already in 1931 a Board of Censors was appointed to screen information entering the Union.   This Board, which is responsible to the Minister of the Interior, operates primarily through the Customs Office.[7] The Board informs the Minister of the Interior of books and films that it considers should be excluded.   Between 1939 and 1956, the Board banned the entrance of some 2,000 books.   Dr B. Beinart, professor of Roman Law at the University of Cape Town, has observed that literature may be excluded if it is deemed 'objectionable on any ground whatsoever'.   He insists that as far as imported literature is concerned (and much of South Africa's reading matter is imported from Britain and America), there is unlimited censorship.[8]

In March, 1960, the Publications and Entertainments Bill was introduced in Parliament, but it was later announced that it would be withdrawn. This Bill would have muzzled the last organs of free expression—the press, which is largely anti-Government, and periodicals, books, and motion pictures produced in the country. The Bill was so sweeping that it would have made it a criminal offense, for example, to print, publish, distribute, display, exhibit, sell, or offer or keep for sale any 'undesirable newspaper'. Books, periodicals, and films were to be censored before publication. Newspapers were not, but the wording of the Bill was such as to necessitate voluntary prepublication censorship.[9] The Bill was based on a study by a Commission of Inquiry into Undesirable Literature appointed in 1954 by the Minister of Interior and chaired by Professor G. Cronje. The wording of the Report of this Commission gives some indication of Nationalist attitudes to freedom of publication:

> As the torch-bearer in the vanguard of Western civilization in South Africa, the European must be and remain the leader, the guiding light, in the spiritual and cultural field, otherwise he will go under. The undesirable book can and must be drastically combated because it is obviously a spiritual poison.

In 1963, a new Publications and Entertainments Bill was introduced in Parliament. This time the criticism was less vocal. Apparently the opposition had resigned itself to the inevitability of the measure.

Properly to understand Nationalist attitudes with respect to government, reference should be made to the *Fundamental Principles of Calvinist Christian Political Science,* published by the Dutch Reformed Church. We must remind ourselves that the British—and American—conception of sovereignty is that it resides with the people: government and government personnel derive their authority from the people to whom they are responsible. To the Afrikaner Calvinist, sovereignty lies with God. The government merely acts for God, and, for this reason, the government has exclusive power over the citizenry. Laws in themselves are thus God-given. 'We are Calvinists,' said one government minister, 'who believe God is sovereign and that sovereignty is delegated to the lawful rulers of the land.'[10]

10   Apartheid: The Unclosable Gap

Know for a certainty that the Lord your God will no more drive out any of these nations from before you; but they shall be snares and traps unto you, and scourges in your sides, and thorns in your eyes. . . .

JOSHUA 23 : 13

WITH THE ACQUISITION of political power, the Afrikaners finally exorcized the British threat. Yet, no sooner had they done so than another menace replaced the British in the Afrikaner estimation. They now believed that the greatest danger came from the Africans. This fear seemed destined to play as prominent a role in the development of Afrikaner nationalism as fear of the Briton had done.

The Nationalists' answer to the challenge of the African has been *apartheid*. It is generally conceded that *apartheid* was originally a campaign slogan; the Nationalists believed the details of the concept could be worked out with time, once they were in office. In any event, the election of 1948 exposed white sensitivity to the African, and revealed popular confidence in the ability of the Nationalists to do something about it. To some extent, the results of the election could be interpreted as a mandate to the Nationalists to seek a solution to the growing 'problem' of the African.

During the campaign, the Nationalists carefully refrained from specifying details of the policy that they dangled before the voters. The election manifesto itself was couched in general terms and the candidates avoided taking definitive stands on territorial segregation, self-government for the Bantu, or the rights of non-whites in white areas.

After the election, the Nationalists could no longer skirt the issue that had helped to bring them victory. Yet when they began to implement *apartheid*, they provoked a storm of resistance. The Nationalists themselves are divided as to how far to go with *apartheid,* and how rapidly. There are those who would like to see the immediate implementation of total territorial separation of the races, and those who are more responsive to practical considerations. But in accepting *apartheid* the Nationalists have embarked upon a policy that allows for no turning back. Total *apartheid*, however, as Bishop Reeves points out, is in the nature of a mirage.[1]

Apartheid has brought the non-Europeans together in a bond of common interest and the world to their side, in sympathy if not in deed. At the same time, it has caused the European political parties in opposition to split along fine lines as to the interpretation and application of *apartheid*. The more the non-Europeans resist, the closer are the whites brought together, an alliance that can result only in the adulteration and dilution of Afrikaner nationalism, but may produce a white South African nationalism that lacks nothing of the Afrikaner bitterness and fervor.

Each new Nationalist Prime Minister has partially retreated from his previous commitment to total *apartheid,* and has bowed to the advice of practical politicians. Yet each has been more extreme than his predecessor and has carried *apartheid* a step further. With each advance, the non-European opposition has reacted more strongly; each reaction has, in turn, motivated the Nationalists to strengthen their control. Thus, tensions continue to increase.

J. G. Strijdom once explained *apartheid* to the writer in these terms: 'Our task in South Africa,' he said, 'is to maintain the identity of the white man,' and, he added cryptically, 'in that task we will die fighting.' Another hard-core Afrikaner leader put it this way: 'The Afrikaner nation was placed in this country by God's hand and is destined to remain as a nation with its own character and its own mission.' In 1955, the South African High Commissioner in London declared: 'We claim the right of survival, not, as is so often charged, as a master race, but as a distinctive race.' The fundamentalist Afrikaners reason that God intended men to be different because He made them different, and that it is His purpose that they remain different, otherwise He would not have made them different in the first place. 'God, the great "Divider" ', said a leading article in *Die Kerbode* (January 11, 1961), 'found it good to establish boundaries between people and groups of people.'

The sheer numerical superiority of the Africans in relation to the Europeans, and the increased contacts between the races that have taken place since the cityward movement of Africans and Afrikaners began have created issues that the Nationalists have been able to exploit politically. In South Africa, Africans outnumber Europeans by nearly four to one and Afrikaners by nearly six to one.

As long as the Africans remained on the farms and in the reserves, they did not pose a threat to the Afrikaner. However, when Afrikaners and Africans alike began moving to the cities, they began to compete with each other economically. As noted above, it was this situation, along with the noticeably denationalizing effect of city life on the Afrikaner, that provided much of the impetus in the drive of the militant Afrikaner leaders to keep the Afrikaner tribe together.

Segregation in varying degrees has always existed in South Africa. African and European cultures differ in many respects, and there is also the language barrier. There are still some—although fewer and fewer—Africans who have little or no experience of contact with Europeans. The main reason, however, for the continuing differences of cultural level, differences that are often offered as 'natural' justification for segregation, is, of course, the position of subjection in which the African has been kept. Today, large numbers of Africans have become more or less completely disassociated from their traditional rural culture and live as urban proletariats. In this sense, the cultural differences between African and European have greatly lessened. As the Africans have moved to the cities, their contacts with their tribal groupings have weakened. With the passage of time, many of them have ceased to be in any real sense Zulu, Pondo, or Xhosa, and have become part of the mass of urban Africans. In like manner, as the Afrikaners moved to the cities, they gradually lost their association with their 'tribal' community and began to take on the ways of the cities where British—or perhaps merely modern—cultural influences were dominant. Natural tendencies toward racial intermixture and the use of English as a convenient *lingua franca* by both Afrikaners and Africans have been checked only by the deliberate imposition of restrictions.

Until relatively recently, the full range of racial segregation in South Africa has not been enforced by law. This was not because Botha, Smuts, and Hertzog were unconscious of the racial problems arising from urbanization. On the contrary, in an address in London on May 22, 1917, Smuts said:

> A practice has grown up in South Africa of giving the Natives their own separate institutions on parallel lines. . . . We have felt more and more that . . . it is useless to try to govern black and white in the same system. . . . Their political institutions should be different, while always proceeding on the basis of self-government. In land ownership, settlement and forms of government, our policy is to keep them apart. . . . Thus in South Africa you will eventually have large areas cultivated by Blacks and governed by Blacks . . . while in the rest of the country you will have Whites who will govern themselves according to accepted European principles.

Smuts seems to have been convinced of the importance of permitting Africans to maintain their own traditions and culture. In 1929, he opined: 'Nothing could be worse for Africa than the application of a policy the object or tendency of which would be to destroy the basis of this African type—to de-Africanize the African.' In 1912, Hertzog, then Minister of Justice in Botha's cabinet, outlined a policy of 'segregation', but little was done to implement it. At that time, however, the cityward movement was still fairly new, and the threat from the Africans still seemed minimal. Moreover, Hertzog was then handicapped by his association with Botha and Smuts, who moved slowly and cautiously in racial matters, because of their dependence on the goodwill of the English-speaking community. When Hertzog took office in 1924, he proceeded to put some of his views into practice, but he was then restrained by his association with Creswell. Similarly, in the Fusion Government of the 1930s, Smuts was again a restraining influence.

But the Rand Revolt of 1922, resulting from attempts of the mine owners to
hire more cheap African labor, clearly demonstrated the reaction of European workers when they once conceived their jobs might be threatened by
African competition, and foreshadowed the shape of things to come.
Between 1910 and 1948, there was not a vast amount of legislation overtly
discriminating against Africans, but there was a gentle nibbling at non-
European rights in Natal and the Cape, and a gradual imposition of new
restrictions on non-Europeans generally. For example, the Mines and
Works Act of 1911 gave Europeans pre-eminent rights to certain jobs in the
mines. The Native Land Act of 1913 set aside some 22,532,000 acres of
land as reserves for Africans and prohibited them from purchasing land
outside the defined reserves. In 1936, the Native Trust and Land Act
authorized the purchase of an additional 15,225,000 acres. The Land Acts
of 1913 and 1936 gave the Bantu permanent rights to certain lands and may
be said to have established a precedent of legalizing geographical separation
of the races. In 1923, the Native Urban Areas Act created 'locations' in
cities, segregating Africans from other residents. In 1926, the Mines and
Works Amendment Act (popularly known as the Color Bar Act) forbade
Africans to hold skilled jobs in industry. The Immorality Act of 1927 made
inter-racial sexual relations illegal. In 1932, European women were enfran-
chised, but not non-European women (even in those areas where non-
European men could vote). The Representation of Natives Act of 1936
removed Africans from the common voting roll in Cape Province; instead,
it established representative councils to act as a channel of communications
between Africans and Europeans.

Until 1948, except for the legislation described above, not much had
been done to provide a legal basis for the consolidation and 'freezing' of
existing institutions and traditions. By then, however, the racial problems
resulting from urbanization and industrialization were beginning to disturb
the whites. It was this concern that the Nationalists were able to exploit.
Thus, the idea of *apartheid* brought the Nationalists political victory in 1948;
they were left with the problem of putting it into practice.

Apartheid theory was developed by the South African Bureau of Race
Relations (*Die Suid Afrikaanse Buro vir Raase Aangeleenthede*), popularly known
as SABRA. SABRA was organized in 1947 to provide the Nationalists with
their own counterpart to the South African Institute of Race Relations, a
liberal body organized in Johannesburg in 1929 and frequently referred to as
the 'English Institute' by the Nationalists.

SABRA tends to reflect the thinking of the 'intellectual nationalism'
of Stellenbosch University, where it is located. The founders of SABRA
included Dr Dönges, Cape Nationalist leader and later Minister of Finance,
Dr Ernest Jansen, formerly Speaker of the lower house of Parliament and
subsequently Minister of Native Affairs and Governor-General, Dr Nicolaas
Diederichs, Professor Werner Eiselen, later Secretary of Native Affairs, Dr
Verwoerd, Colonel Charles F. Stallard, leader of the Dominion Party, and
Professors Andries Cilliers and Bernardus van Eeden.

SABRA has, since its foundation, provided guidance for what might otherwise have developed into a system based purely on political expediency.[2] Yet, in the intervening years, SABRA and the government have tended to drift apart because the latter has found it increasingly difficult to implement the theoretical *apartheid* dictated by the former.

In 1950, SABRA began a campaign to induce the Nationalist government to enforce territorial separation of the races. This policy was endorsed by the Dutch Reformed churches at a meeting in Bloemfontein in 1950. Malan, who was then Prime Minister, rejected the policy as 'impracticable under present circumstances in South Africa where our whole economic structure is to a large extent based on Native labour'. His rejection caused a split among the Nationalists. Verwoerd, who later, as Minister of Native Affairs (with Dr Eiselen as his Secretary of the Department), did so much to shape *apartheid*, repudiated Malan's views. It is interesting to note, however, that when the Tomlinson Report on the position as regards *apartheid* was being discussed in Parliament in 1956, Verwoerd, then Minister of Native Affairs, was much more temperate than he had been before taking office. When his ministerial views were challenged by the Stellenbosch purists, he resigned from SABRA.

SABRA's present position cannot properly be interpreted as a manifestation of open opposition to the government or, indeed, to liberalism. It is simply a question of practical considerations hampering the fulfillment of theoretical requirements. The government has not been able to follow the course that SABRA has mapped out for it. SABRA advocates in the most literal sense 'separate development' of the races. Its theorists maintain that only through territorial segregation can the various racial groups distinguish themselves, and that racial separation will permit each race to develop to its fullest capabilities. Over the years, SABRA has not been satisfied with the efforts of the government in carrying *apartheid* to its logical conclusion. SABRA wants to see more than 'token physical separation between the races of a few miles or yards or inches'.[3] SABRA is interested in total racial separation as the answer to 'a major problem'.[4]

Apartheid has been translated into practical terms only slowly, because of the great expense it involves and the strong opposition it has aroused. The way it has evolved has been influenced by various forces, and that evolution has not necessarily been to the liking of its creators. The government that has sponsored it has been torn between the forces demanding its fullest implementation and those either opposing it entirely or seeking its modification.

The Tomlinson Report, named for the chairman of the ten-man Commission on the Socio-economic Development of the Bantu areas that produced it, constitutes a detailed blueprint for total *apartheid*. It represents the Nationalist ideal. The Commission was appointed by the government in 1950 to 'devise a scheme for the rehabilitation of the native areas with a view to developing within them a social structure in keeping with the culture of the native based upon effective socio-economic planning'. The Commission spent five years examining evidence, and investigating all aspects of Bantu life with respect to their development in terms of *apartheid*. By October,

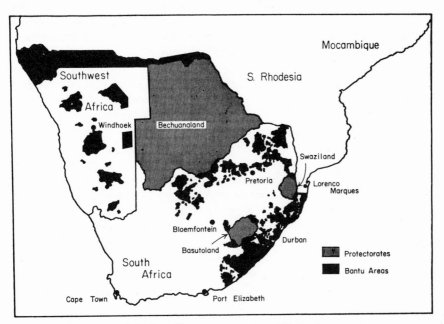

FIGURE 9: Native Reserves as established at present

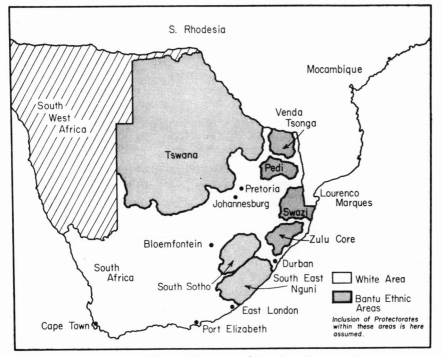

FIGURE 10: Consolidation of Native Reserves as
envisaged in the Tomlinson Commission Report

1954, seventeen volumes of typescript were ready to present to the Minister of Native Affairs, then Dr Verwoerd. The report is an exhaustive survey of the Bantu areas, and represents a prodigious amount of work. It consists of fifty-one chapters, 3,755 pages, 598 tables, and an atlas of sixty-six large-scale maps.[5]

The report recommended the consolidation of the 264 scattered Bantu areas into some seven main divisions or Bantustans. It envisaged the eventual incorporation into them of the three High Commission Territories (Bechuanaland, Swaziland, and Basutoland). The result, in the long run, was planned to be a state composed of separate black and white areas. In its own areas, the theory went, each race would maintain its separate identity and would be permitted to develop to the fullest extent of its abilities and capabilities. The report recommended an extensive program of improving African agriculture, soil conservation, development of secondary and tertiary industry, and establishment of Bantu town sites within the prescribed territories—the whole to be supervised by a development council and a development corporation. The report estimated that the project would cost more than £104 million over a ten-year period.

The report further concluded that, over the next fifty years, the non-white population would increase more rapidly than the white, and that the Africans would therefore need an increasing amount of land. It estimated that in fifty years the present reserves would be able to sustain only half of the African population. Thus, under present trends, an increasing number of Africans will be living in areas now designated for whites.

In 1956, the Tomlinson Report was debated in Parliament. The debates exposed the government's reluctance to accept total *apartheid* with the expense it involved, and made it clear that what it had in mind at the moment was something less than the total separation demanded by *apartheid* theory. In April, 1956, the government issued a White Paper that was in essence a repudiation of the Tomlinson Report.[6] In effect, the government stated that it agreed with the report in accepting the principle that the Bantu areas must be developed as the home of the Bantu people, but that the methods suggested in the report were subject to change. The government declined the suggestion that £104 million should be appropriated for the development of the Bantu areas over a ten-year period on the grounds that it was too difficult to budget that far ahead. Instead, it appropriated £3.5 million for one year. Most of the report was shrugged off on the excuse that it was merely a reaffirmation of the government's own program.

The Tomlinson Report had been long awaited, and government supporters had looked forward to it as a kind of panacea for what was in their view otherwise an apparently insoluble problem. The government's light treatment of the report was a severe blow; it demonstrated the way which *apartheid* was developing in practice as well as the present trends in Afrikaner nationalism. It is safe to conclude that the Tomlinson Report has become more of an ideal to be cherished than a plan to be copied. The preface to the White Paper pays homage to that ideal when it declares:

For the European the Report confirms the views of many in South Africa that the path of racial integration can have only one end, and that it shows the elimination of the European as a separate entity . . .; it also shows that an increasing measure of separate development in the Bantu areas is essential if the European is to hold what he has built up in three centuries of pioneering work on the African continent.

Dr Verwoerd has not, of course, refuted total territorial *apartheid*, and he still insists that it is the 'final logical outcome'. He has told Parliament: 'The policy of *apartheid* moves consistently in the direction of more and more separate development with the ideal of total separation in all spheres.'[7] However, practical exigencies have caused Dr Verwoerd, like his predecessors, to moderate his stand after taking office. On September 15, 1958, he informed Parliament that total territorial *apartheid* is the ideal to aim at, 'but everyone realizes that today that is impracticable. Everyone realizes such a thing cannot be attained within the space of a few years, nor even for a long time to come'.

Verwoerd's answer to those who criticized the delay in implementing *apartheid* was the Promotion of Bantu Self-government Act of 1959, which carried *apartheid* a step further towards its 'logical outcome'. In January, 1962, the government announced its intention to grant 'self-government' to the Bantustans 'as soon as they themselves can and will assume it',[8] and stated that it proposed to grant 'self-government' to the Transkei that year. In 1963, the government let it be known that the African people of the Transkei would receive 'distinct citizenship and will elect their own cabinet with wide executive powers. At the same time all white people living in the Transkei, the land of the Xhosa, will lose their political rights in that area'.[9] It is widely recognized that the 'self-government' granted to the Transkei and promised to other Bantu areas is an official fiction. Self-government can have no real meaning so long as many major functions of government are still exercised by the central administration.

White South African opponents of the government continue to ask: How long will it be before *apartheid* reaches its logical outcome? Indeed, can it ever reach it? Is total *apartheid* really feasible? Could it be fairly applied under existing conditions? Does such policy imply the permanent administration of the Bantu areas by a white aristocracy?

Ideal *apartheid* conceives of absolute economic, political, sexual, cultural, and social separation of the African and European races, physically as well as territorially. Strijdom once advised the Bantu:

> You must learn to govern yourselves in your own areas. You must learn to become your own traders, builders, carpenters, doctors, welfare workers, and so forth. This is a separate development and must be based on your own way of life. In all respects you must learn to make your own communities self-sufficient.

In theory, absolute territorial *apartheid* means that whites would have no more rights in African areas than Africans in white areas. Whites could not own property in African areas, nor Africans in white areas. There would be relatively little movement between the racial areas, which would in some ways resemble contiguous foreign countries. Africans in white areas would be there as nonresidents. The Nationalist government defines *apartheid* as follows:

> The guiding principle behind the policy is that the non-Whites of the country, especially the Blacks, should be guided by the Whites towards self-realization and self-government within their own communities and in their own areas. It is intended that the Blacks in their own sphere should acquire the necessary rights as they become capable of exercising them, and that they should be taught to shoulder the duties and responsibilities which accompany the rights and powers of self-government. The Black man's ambitions must be realized within the bosom of his own people and as he progresses he should not leave the masses of his people in the lurch by seeking to penetrate the White man's society or to participate in the latter's institution of government. The *apartheid* policy aims at providing the Black man with his own institutions, thus offering him ample opportunities to work for the good of his own people. In this way White and Black must each seek their own future in every respect within their respective racial groups. Until the Blacks have developed sufficiently to shoulder the responsibilities and rights of self-government, they will be guided and assisted by the Whites. The *apartheid* policy is based on South Africa's traditional policy of separate development of the races.

In 1947, Strijdom put it this way:

> The Nationalist Party policy is division and *apartheid*. The Native is to live his own life in his own area. The Native must only be allowed to leave his area to come to work in the European areas as a temporary worker. His wife and children must remain behind.[10]

The advocates of *apartheid* maintain that it is theoretically conceivable that in future some type of federation of Bantu and European states might evolve in South Africa. Malan hinted at the prospect of such a federal union in his widely circulated reply to a letter from a Grand Rapids, Michigan, minister. He stated:

> Theoretically the object of the policy of *apartheid* could be fully achieved by dividing the country into two states, with all the Whites in one, all the Blacks in the other. . . . Whether in time to come we shall reach a stage where some such division, say on a federal basis, will be possible, is a matter we must leave to the future.[11]

The government publication, *South African Scope*, stated in its issue for March, 1963, that 'ultimately the policy envisages a number of autonomous Bantu nations alongside and in co-operative association with the white nation —a South African Commonwealth'. In reality, the fact that long-range detailed plans have not been made reflects the unwillingness of the white South African community to face the cost of total *apartheid*.

Theoretical *apartheid* also assumes that the Bantu areas will develop to such a degree that they will sustain their peoples within their own borders. Since the present Bantu territories are, for the most part, extremely poverty-stricken rural areas with no industrial or urban base whatsoever, and since most of their people are only enabled to support life at all by the earnings of the men as migrant workers in the white cities, this prospect seems unlikely in the foreseeable future. It would require investment much more massive than is likely to take place.

But if *apartheid* theory is not being fully implemented, neither is the racial situation being left to take its own course.

More legislation affecting the Africans has been passed since 1948 than in the entire history of South Africa prior to that date. The Afrikaner Nationalists have attempted to legalize a system previously imposed by social custom. As the Reverend J. B. Webb, a South African Methodist leader, observed:

> There has always been this condition in South Africa and the only difference between the state of affairs today and as it existed in the past is that, for the first time, it is being rationalized, regimented, and quite ruthlessly applied by reason of deeply held convictions together with prejudices—and, in some quarters, hatred and fear.

To support their efforts, the Nationalists have gone to great pains to explain and to rationalize the course they have taken.[12]

The more important Nationalist racial legislation includes the Population Registration Act (1950), under which every person in South Africa must be classified as White, Coloured, Native, or Asian. The Immorality Amendment Act (1950) prohibits sexual relations between whites and nonwhites. Previously the Act applied to whites and Bantu only. The Mixed Marriages Act (1949) prohibits marriages between whites and nonwhites. The Bantu Education Amendment Act placed all native education under the Minister of Bantu Education. The Group Areas Act (1950), perhaps the most controversial and certainly the best-known piece of Nationalist legislation, provides for gradual introduction of residential segregation of whites, Indians, Coloureds, and Bantu. Under this act, each city is responsible for demarcating racial areas and seeing that such planning is implemented fully, and persons of one group or classification are not allowed to own or occupy property in the area of another group without a permit. The Bantu Authorities Acts (Urban and Rural) of 1952 extended 'self-rule' to the Bantu communities and gave the government authority over the Africans in the cities. These superseded the 1936 Act and abolished the native representative councils established by the earlier act. The Promotion of Bantu Self-Government Act (1959), referred to above, provided for the gradual development of what were termed self-governing Bantu national units, to be known as Bantustans, and direct consultation between the national government and the various Bantu authorities. Under this and the Bantu Authorities Acts, control over the Africans was given to 'tribal' authorities established by the government, and a complex system of control over Africans outside their territorial authority was set up. In practice, this piece of legislation turned out to be another means of limiting the rights of the vast numbers of Africans not living in the native territories. Thus, an African living in a white area who wished to lodge a complaint would have to do so through his tribal representative in that area, who, in turn, would bring the matter to the attention of the territorial authority; the territorial authority would refer the matter to the Republic commissioner stationed in the native territorial capital, then back to Pretoria to the Department of Bantu Administration. This procedure is supposedly justified by the theory that Africans are aliens in white areas, just as whites are aliens in areas set aside for the Africans. The influx of Africans into white areas from African territories and locations is strictly controlled by the pass laws. All Africans must carry passes which are checked regularly by the police. Africans are frequently imprisoned for pass offences, and the pass laws are one of the most onerous parts of the Nationalist system as far as the non-white population is concerned.

Other laws guarantee separate facilities for the different races in white areas, inasmuch as integrated amenities would reduce the effectiveness of *apartheid*. As it has been described:

> Separate facilities, never equal, for separate races. Separate doors and separate counters in public buildings, separate seats in public buses, separate benches in public parks. Separate laws and laws to separate—residentially, industrially, politically, intellectually, sexually. Separation of white and black, of black and coloured, of white and coloured, of black and black and of white and white.[13]

Absolute *apartheid* conceives of total separation of each racial group in all activities. Mr J. C. van Rooy, former FAK Chairman, has said: 'We want no mixing of languages, no mixing of cultures, no mixing of religions and no mixing of races'. According to SABRA, the policy is a 'formula of peaceful coexistence of the various groups in South Africa'.

Apartheid is the means the Afrikaner Nationalists have conceived for assuring and perpetuating control by the white man—its existence implies the supremacy of the white man in South Africa. The Minister of Transport, J. B. Schoeman, declared on one occasion that 'either the White man goes under or he must keep the Black man in subjection'. J. J. Serfontein, Minister of Education, Arts and Science, has insisted: 'All we are fighting for is the southern point of Africa and to keep it white. Are we wrong? Never. If we are to keep South Africa white, the white man must be and remain master in South Africa.'[14] L. E. Neame, author of *White Man's Africa*, takes a somewhat colder view: 'There can be no common ground unless it is conceded that the Whites themselves form an African-born people occupying their own national home and entitled to mastership in it.'

The Nationalist view is that *apartheid* is necessary to maintain the identity of the Afrikaner nation, and that the implementation of *apartheid*

THE APPLICATION OF APARTHEID IN CITIES WITHIN AREAS DESIGNATED WHITE

Representative Urban Racial Distribution Pattern Before Implementation of the Group Areas Act

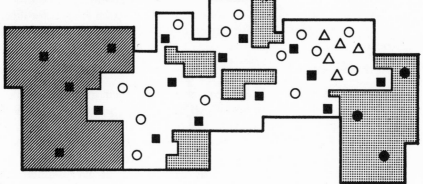

Idealized Urban Racial Arrangement as Envisaged in the Group Areas Act

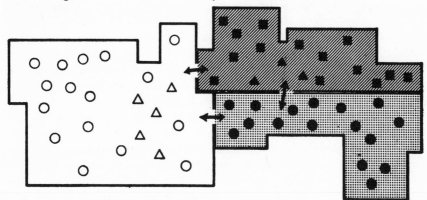

■ Indian Shops
O White Shops
● Bantu Shops
△ White Factories
▲ Indian Factories
□ White Townships
▨ Indian Townships
▦ Bantu Townships

demands the supremacy of the white man and, more especially, the Afrikaner Nationalist, since only he, as history has shown, can be trusted with such a mission. In 1935, P. G. W. Grobler, a member of Hertzog's third cabinet, explained Afrikaner attitudes in these terms:

> Political equality can never exist in South Africa. It is our duty to preserve what is an ordinance of God that there should be separate White and Black entities in the country. . . . There can be no middle course in native policy. You must either have equality or assimilation on the one hand, or, on the other, the golden rule of Calvinism. . . . Indecision can only lead us into an abyss. . . . Ours must be a determined policy that agrees with the traditions of our nation from the days of the Voortrekker.

Strijdom made it even more emphatic:

> Our policy is that the Europeans must stand their ground and must remain *Baas* [Master] in South Africa. If we reject the *Herrenvolk* [master people] idea and the principle that the white man cannot remain *Baas*, if the franchise is to be extended to non-Europeans, and if non-Europeans are developed on the same basis as the Europeans, how can the Europeans remain *Baas*? Our view is that in every sphere the Europeans must retain the right to rule the country and to keep it a white man's country.[15]

Apartheid has been labelled a 'tremendous experiment', but it is a vital experiment for the Nationalists. Obviously, it would be political suicide for the Nationalists to extend the vote to non-Europeans. Their position is in some ways comparable to Kruger's *vis-à-vis* the *Uitlanders*. Kruger's failure to grant the *Uitlanders* the vote resulted in the Boer War. The Nationalists, with their policy of *apartheid*, have sought some alternative to open conflict. *Apartheid* denies Africans the vote on the theoretical grounds that they are aliens in white areas whose rights to participation in government are in the native territories.

The Reverend J. Reyneke, Pastor of *Die Groote Kerk* in Pretoria, once remarked to the writer: 'Total *apartheid* is moral, but partial *apartheid* is immoral.' In the world of practical politics not practising what one preaches sometimes becomes a necessary evil. The promise of 'separate but equal' development under *apartheid* has been the Nationalist answer to African demands for political rights. It has been the excuse for maintaining white political supremacy in South Africa. But, in practice, the theory has never been applied; there are too many obstacles in the way. To understand the course of Afrikaner nationalism it is useful, then, to examine the growing gap between the theory and practice of *apartheid* and the causes for its failure.

The main reason why theoretical *apartheid* cannot be implemented is that industrialization and racial, social, economic, and sexual integration have already advanced too far. It would require too drastic a reversal of institutions, social customs, and ways of life that have developed over many years.

The dependence of South Africa's expanding economy on cheap African labor is a major factor in making full *apartheid* impossible. More than 80 per cent of the labor force in South Africa is African. For example, manual labor in the gold mines is largely done by African workers. And since gold is a primary source of foreign exchange in South Africa, the government could never seriously consider prohibiting the use of African labor in the mines. The small number of Europeans, combined with a rapidly expanding economy, which calls for an increasing supply of skilled labor, militate against the preservation of even the degree of economic racial separation (in the sense of job classification by race) that now obtains; these are factors that make true *apartheid* quite impracticable. The government is establishing new industries near the borders of the native territories to ensure that the Africans shall live in their own areas and yet allow the whites to take advantage of their labor. However, this is a costly and not necessarily an efficient system.

English-speaking South Africans control the major share of capital investment in mining and industry. The English-speaking community likewise controls the newspapers with the largest and most influential circulation, which it employs to voice its opinions. Complete territorial *apartheid* is obviously against the interests of the business community. Nor can the less business-minded Afrikaners ignore economic reality. The financial well-being of the state that the Nationalists control is of the utmost importance to them. Moreover, the numerous and politically influential European farmers, the largest proportion of whom are Afrikaners, also want cheap labor, and an enormous amount of legislation has been passed to ensure the continued supply of African farm workers. The government could scarcely withdraw labor from the mines and industry in the name of *apartheid* without also prejudicing the position of the farmers.

Moreover, as has been pointed out, many whites have come to regard manual labor as the special province of nonwhites, and as something quite beneath them. White South Africans live in a dream world, a country-club fantasy; they might well resent giving up such a life for a less comfortable do-it-yourself existence. In his essay 'Tightening Coils—An Essay on Segregation', Ernest Stubbs described South African society in 1925 in these words: 'The Union of South Africa is, in the economic sense, a slave state, for the body politic is nothing more nor less than a White Aristocracy superimposed on a Black Proletariat.'

In 1955, B. J. Schoeman, the Minister of Transport, warned his countrymen:

> More and more all kinds of manual work are being looked down on as though it were the appropriate labour sphere of Natives. I can hardly imagine anything more dangerous because it is surely an economic law that those who today do the manual work are the rulers of the future. It is, therefore, definitely a danger sign when our younger generation begins to regard manual work as humiliating. The result will simply be that the Native, who is today the assistant, will tomorrow himself

be the artisan.   For who else will do the work if white hands can no longer be found to do it?[16]

P. J. van der Watt put it more bluntly: 'We have one problem—the laziness of the White people.'[17]   Senator Henry Allan Fagan, former Chief Justice of South Africa and chairman of the Commission of Inquiry into Urban African Conditions, states in *Our Responsibility*: 'No sign can be detected of even a commencement of the only process which can bring about the separation of White and Native . . . *viz.*, the mass withdrawal of Bantu labour from European industries.'

When he was Minister of Native Affairs, Verwoerd himself gave some indication of the trends in Bantu cityward migration and their relation to the future of *apartheid*.   In 1958, he confessed that the cityward movement of Africans was increasing and would continue to do so 'for a certain number of years', and that by AD 2000 there would probably be six million non-Europeans in European areas.   After this, he surmised, the process of separation 'would continue further'.   He warned the Europeans that they should 'organize themselves increasingly to manage without Natives'.[18]

Today, more than three million Africans live in or near cities. According to the theory of *apartheid,* they are there temporarily as migrant workers.   In fact, they live there permanently but under increasingly rigid legal restrictions and abnormal conditions, which they are beginning to resist.   Africans living in white areas now have no political rights; and their demands for such rights are becoming louder.   The Europeans possess the media of expression in their parliamentary representatives, in their newspapers, in the public forums—though criticism of the government is increasingly restricted.   But any protest from an African organization results in the banning of the organization.   Thus, outlets for expression become fewer and fewer at the same time that the need for means for protesting becomes greater.   The Africans have been forced to employ work walkouts—even sabotage—as their means of protest, and the government is forced to divert more and more energies to policing the system which it has created.   As *Die Volksblad* commented (November 30, 1962): 'Sabotage is becoming a disturbingly permanent part of our existence.'

Neither in size nor in distribution are the present native territories remotely adequate for the entire African population, or a substantial part of it.   They are inadequate for their present population, and at the moment sixty per cent of the Bantu live outside the territories.   Under the terms of the 1913 and 1936 Acts, 22,532,000 acres are now set aside as native territories, or about thirteen per cent of the total area of the republic.   Setting aside the question of the qualitative inadequacy of the Bantu lands, the quantity is obviously grossly disproportionate to that held by the whites, who constitute only a minority of the population.

Moreover, the present territories consist of 264 scattered and irregularly shaped parcels of land.   The 'separate but equal' states envisaged by the *apartheid* theorists could not possibly be established without drastic changes in the present size, shape, and distribution of the reserves—changes that there is no evidence the government contemplates making.

The Bantu Authorities Act and the Promotion of Bantu Self-government Act returned authority to the tribal chiefs and established an intricate tribalistic hierarchy. For the urbanized African, tribalism belongs to another age, and the tribal hierarchy established by the government is, in any case, far too authoritarian to provide an outlet for his pent-up grievances. The Tomlinson Commission looked hopefully to the establishment in the native territories of a system of representative government. But the actual arrangements made by the government in this respect constitute what is, in effect, a further repudiation of the Tomlinson Report.

Apartheid theory also assumes the absolute territorial separation not only of Africans and whites, but of every other racial group. In South Africa, the Bantu are the largest racial group, and *apartheid* is directed mainly against them. But the population includes 1.5 million Coloureds and 500,000 Indians, who also have to be fitted into the theoretical structure somewhere. If they are not to be given separate territories that they can develop independently, then it must be assumed that they are to be allowed to live (on sufferance) within the white areas. There have been suggestions that a large area in the northern Cape should be set aside for the Coloureds, but the idea has not been enthusiastically received. The government has established a Department of Coloured Affairs to handle problems relating to the Coloureds, and it is considering the establishment of another department for Asians.

In 1927, an attempt was made to get rid of the Indian community entirely by an act for the subsidization of the repatriation of those Indians who volunteered to return to India. This effort met with miserable success, and the present government accepts the fact of the presence of Indians as permanent residents, although grudgingly.[19] J. J. Boshoff, a Nationalist senator, reflected the views of the government when he declared that the South African Indians should wean themselves from India and other countries and behave and live like South Africans within the traditional pattern.[20]

Under the Group Areas Act, non-Europeans other than Africans are being allocated their own areas within European territories. Coloureds and Indians have their own residential locations, schools, colleges, hotels, churches, buses, and restaurants, but few political rights. Even in terms of *apartheid* theory, it is difficult to justify the denial of suffrage to Asians and Coloureds, since there is no prospect of their being settled in 'self-governing' territories outside the white areas. The demands of Coloureds and Asians for the vote are becoming more insistent.

Cape Coloureds are now permitted to vote for seven white members of Parliament. In the 1950s, they were removed from the common voting roll in the manner already described because of their threat to the Nationalist position, and, in October 1960, they were not permitted to vote in the referendum on whether or not a republic should be established, for fear they would vote against it. A number of Nationalists have urged that the Coloureds be given the vote on the common roll and even be permitted to stand for Parliament, but Verwoerd has ignored such recommendations. He has opined that 'integrationists' wanted concessions for the Coloureds as a springboard for the integration of all races, in contrast to Nationalist policy of 'parallel development'.[21]

Even the limited attempts to implement *apartheid* that have taken place have disturbed developing institutions and ways of living, and incited strong resentment. Opposition from within the National Party has been minimal up to now, although the opposition is quick to magnify any squabbles among the Nationalists that take place. Professor B. B. Keet of Stellenbosch University wrote a work entitled *Whither South Africa*, in which he declared: 'The more one examines the case for complete permanent *apartheid*, the less can one avoid the conclusion that its supporters are labouring under a delusion that belongs to a world of make believe.' Nor is he the only prominent Afrikaner to criticize the government. Professor V. L. Pistorius of Pretoria University left the National Party in protest and in 1957 attacked *apartheid* in *No Further Trek*. Professor Ben Marais, also of Pretoria University, had already denounced *apartheid* in his book, *The Colour Crisis and the West* (1953), and, in 1960, eleven Dutch Reformed Church leaders published *Delayed Action* which has been described above. In the same year, J. L. du P. (Japie) Basson, a Nationalist MP from South-west Africa, bolted the NP and founded the National Union Party.

Among English-speaking South Africans, criticism has been widespread. Dr D. Hobart Houghton, Professor of Economics at Rhodes University, has expressed the disappointment of those who had looked upon *apartheid* as a panacea of South Africa's racial problems:

> To the sincere Christians who had placed their faith upon 'apartheid' as a just and equitable solution of the problems of a multiracial society, it has been a severe blow that will necessitate some deep rethinking of the whole position, and to the people of South Africa as a whole it has demonstrated that there is no easy and simple formula for the solution of the nation's economic, social, and moral problem.[22]

The inability and apparent unwillingness of the Nationalists to carry *apartheid* to its logical conclusion—immediately, at any rate—has given grounds for complaint among those who had supported the policy wholeheartedly. Meanwhile, the opposition, anxious to preserve the supremacy of the whites—a position essential to any South African party that hopes to gain office by the vote of a white electorate—but opposed to the methods and some aspects of the philosophy of the Nationalists, has been deeply divided over principle and practice in racial policy. The opposition fears both the growing nonwhite resentment of present policies and the curtailment of the civil liberties of whites in the Afrikaner police state. Nor are these fears illusory. In 1960, the International Commission of Jurists made an investigation of South African racial policy (published as *The Rule of Law in South Africa*), and concluded that 'it is manifestly apparent that the pursuit of the present policy constitutes a serious encroachment upon the freedom of all inhabitants, white and nonwhite alike'.

FIGURE 12: South African Realities   © Punch 1958
(Cartoon by Illingworth from *Punch*, April 16, 1958)

At the same time, hatred of Nationalist policy has brought the non-Europeans strongly together in a bond of common interest; they receive verbal and some material support from the new nations of Asia and Africa as well as from the communist bloc and from liberal and humanitarian elements in the Western democracies. Meanwhile, growing opposition, at home and abroad, is forcing white South Africans together, and causing the emergence of a national, racial consciousness obliterating separatist Afrikaner or English nationalism. The stronger the opposition, the more the white community wants to stand together, and the stronger becomes the consciousness of both Afrikaners and South Africans of British origin of being comrades in a joint venture.

The subtle but profound changes taking place in South African politics and the disappearance of old attitudes are described in an article in the *Star* for December 1, 1962. The writer observes that the old 'Nat-SAP' politics are a thing of the past; 'race politics' between Englishmen and Afrikaners has had its day. Afrikaner nationalism has been diluted in some cases to the vanishing point. In the future 'the varying degrees of liberalism towards nonwhites (from the equal rights for all advocated by the Liberal Party to the position of the National Party, which tries to accommodate nonwhite political aspirations by *apartheid*) will be of paramount importance'.

Thus, in practice, so-called *apartheid* has created a weird checkerboard of separate and segregated areas. Instead of living separately as demanded by *apartheid* theory, the races in South Africa live together with practically all avenues of communication between the different racial groups cut off, and the colored races kept in total subjection. Essentially, *apartheid* was designed to protect the whites from being overwhelmed by the Africans, but as the system has developed it has spread to every racial group. Coloureds are separated from Africans, Africans from whites, Asians from Africans, Coloureds from Asians, Coloureds from whites, and Asians from whites and even whites from whites. The system is inefficient and enormously expensive, both in terms of separate facilities and of the cost of policing it.*

To implement their system, the Nationalists have been obliged to pass an enormous quantity of legislation and to undertake an increasing amount of policing. The more regulations multiply, the greater the prospect of violations; and the greater the number of violations and prosecutions, the greater the resistance of the oppressed, and the greater the demand for new laws to control them. It is a vicious circle. Arthur Keppel-Jones has said:

> Prejudice inspires laws to segregate and discriminate; these laws reduce the possibility of contact between the races; the lack of contact, in turn, gives prejudice free rein. . . . Contact in terms of racial equality has been made almost impossible. . . . What is worse, racial oppression tends to create or perpetuate the very condition that it uses as its excuse. Laws prevent all but a very few Africans from escaping the most degrading poverty and ignorance. Conditions in the cities produce a large class of African criminals.[23]

Or, as Senator H. A. Fagan puts it: 'Closing loopholes without inserting safety-valves will not eliminate the explosive material but will only

---

* But it ensures the economic advantage of cheap black labor for the dominant whites.

put the lid on and keep the White electorate ignorant of its force unless and until there is an explosion'.[24]

The unitary structure of the government has assisted the Nationalists in implementing their program. Cabinet government, the dominance of Parliament, and a franchise restricted to Europeans give the Nationalists unfettered political supremacy. The administrators of the four provinces and Southwest Africa are appointed by the President of the Republic and responsible to him.* In each province, and in Southwest Africa, there is an elected Provincial Council. With the exception of that in Natal, all are Nationalist-controlled. The responsibilities of local government are minor: they include such matters as elementary and secondary education of Europeans, with the exception of special schools; hospitals, with the exception of those for mental and contagious diseases; and roads, with the exception of national highways. The police force is administered nationally, and is under the control of the Minister of Justice. One branch of the police force is the Criminal Investigation Department, an investigatory and enforcing agency similar to the FBI. Political offenses are the province of the Special Branch, a subdivision of the CID. The entire police force is well equipped to move swiftly to any area of the country where trouble occurs. Telephone tapping and a network of informers keep the police alert to any disturbances, and the right of the police to search persons and property widens the area of government control.

All defense force personnel are European, and all important positions in the defense force, as in all government departments, are held by Afrikaners. There has been some talk of combining the police and defense forces for greater efficiency, a step that would further centralize control.[26]

Communications are also closely controlled. The South African Broadcasting Corporation (SABC) is a government-sponsored organization, supervised by the Minister of Posts and Telegraphs, Dr Albert Hertzog, and headed by P. J. Meyer, who is believed to be chairman of the Afrikaner Broederbond. Dr Hertzog has thus far refused to allow television broadcasting on the grounds that it would be a disruptive element. Recently, he has decided to convert AM transmissions to FM, apparently to prevent the reception of 'disruptive' broadcasts from Radio Moscow, Radio Cairo, Radio Accra, and Radio Peking.

The Board of Censors screens imported books and films, and there are good indications the Post Office censors the mails. The government controls the exit and entrance of individuals, and has found a growing number of excuses to refuse passports to South Africans desiring to travel abroad; similarly, many intending visitors have been denied visas. Diplomatic relations with communist states have been broken, and are maintained with very few countries in Africa.

Everyone must carry a card to identify his race, and all names and classifications are registered. Africans are required to carry passes, a require-

---

* It is probable that the Nationalists would like to incorporate Southwest Africa as a fifth province.[25]

ment that is not new, but that has been made much more onerous by a mass of complex new legislation increasing the possibility of violations. Passes are used to control the movements of Africans and especially their influx into towns. Indians must have special permits to leave their provinces or enter others.

One of the most repressive pieces of Nationalist legislation is the Suppression of Communism Act, which defines communism so broadly as, in effect, to make anyone who criticizes the government a 'statutory' communist and subject to penalties. The Riotous Assembly Act, the Public Safety Act, the Criminal Procedure and Evidence Act, the Sabotage Act, and a whole host of others, arm the government with the essential power for absolute control of the state. As one African has observed:

> There can be little doubt that the primary function of the police is ceasing to be the protection of the rights of the people of South Africa and is becoming the defence of the interests and ideas of the Nationalist Party of South Africa.[27]

In the economic sphere, the government controls imports and exports, and, of course, the power to tax extends its influence over industry and commerce; and there has even been talk of nationalization of the mines.

The extensive policing required by the system that the Nationalists have established is expensive in manpower as well as money. In South Africa, the only manpower the Nationalists can trust is European, and, more especially, Afrikaner; with the opportunities for employment in the expanding economy and the relatively slow increase of the European population, the problem of manning the controlling forces is becoming increasingly acute. The maintenance of the *status quo* calls for more police and more jails. The more numerous and stringent the laws, the more violations; the more violations, the more criminals, and the greater the number of persons to be found in jail. The treason trials, to take only one example, dragged on for five years and involved an incredible amount of litigation and expense. Numbers of politically conscious Africans and their sympathizers have taken refuge in other African states and elsewhere; attempts to patrol South Africa's borders so as to prevent the flight of *émigrés* or their return as armed revolutionaries require an expanded defense force. People must be prevented from assembling for meetings; persons, houses, and cars must be searched; publications must be censored—it is an endless task. Certainly, as has been said, 'no one can say what price a person cares to pay for what he wants the most'; but the mounting problems of forcibly administering a system that is loathed by a large majority of the population subjected to it indicate that a reckoning is, sooner or later, inevitable.

11   Republic: Climax of a Destiny

And it shall come to pass when thou shalt have the dominion, that thou shalt break his yoke from off thy neck.

GENESIS 27 : 40

ON KRUGER'S DAY, October 10, 1940, Dr Daniel F. Malan declared: 'First we obtained self-government, later dominion status, but the spirit of Paul Kruger cannot be satisfied with that. The nation will not be satisfied before South Africa has a free, independent republic.'[1] He was stating the ultimate ambition of the Afrikaner extremists. Afrikaner die hards had been struggling to evade or throw off British control from the time it was first imposed; they could not be satisfied while any vestiges of the British connection remained.

By 1914, the establishment of South Africa as an independent republic, free of any ties with Britain, was already an important goal of Afrikaner Nationalist policy. Hertzog worked toward this objective, but in office he was hindered by the necessity of deferring to the views of his partners in coalition governments. While he was Prime Minister, however, South Africa attained effective independence as a dominion through the Balfour Declaration (1926), the Statute of Westminster (1931), and the Status Act (1934); in 1937, the first South African was appointed Governor-General. In the 1948 election campaign, Malan intentionally omitted any reference to a republic, but that this was the Nationalist objective was well known. Malan, in fact, assured the electorate that he would not arbitrarily declare the establishment of a republic; in his view the decision should be made by the people in a plebiscite.

No such plebiscite was held during the Malan administration. Malan knew the time was not ripe. The spirit of Smuts was still a dominant force among many Afrikaners, and the English-speaking community was solidly against any break with the monarchy. Moreover, the Cape Coloureds would undoubtedly have voted with the English-speaking community against a republic.

169

The Nationalists were prepared to watch and wait for the proper moment; in the meanwhile they moved gently in the direction of a final break. In 1927, a national flag to be flown alongside the Union Jack was agreed on following a heated parliamentary debate lasting two sessions. In 1957, another Flag Bill made the national flag the only legal flag of South Africa, and since Van Riebeeck Day (April 6) of that year, it has been flown as the only flag on all government buildings. Also, in 1957, *Die Stem van Suid Africa* became the official national anthem, and, on July 4, 1958, it was played for the first time at the opening of Parliament. In 1958, the initials OHMS (On Her Majesty's Service) were removed from all official envelopes. From 1960, the Queen's head no longer appeared on South African postage stamps. In March, 1960, it was announced that the currency would be changed from the British pound sterling to a new unit to be known as the rand, and that van Riebeeck's picture would replace that of the Queen on the new coins and bills. The Minister of Finance, Dr Dönges, remarked: 'We simply want to make known to the whole world in every possible way that South Africa is a sovereign independent country and that it does not hesitate to publicize this by means of its symbols.'

Die Volksblad (March 7, 1960) added: 'In the republic to be established, the monarch of Britain will no longer be the monarch of South Africa and no reasoned objections can surely be made to the choice of the head of Jan van Riebeeck, as the founder of white civilization in South Africa.'

Nationalist insistence on an independent republic was, of course, partly motivated by the traditional rivalry with Britain. But the desire to retain and extend their control of the country and to impose their racial policies without hindrance has been at least as important in recent years. In order to secure their own position, and that of Afrikanerdom, the Nationalists realized they would need the support of the entire white population, not only the Afrikaners. Division among the Europeans, who comprised only one-fifth of the total population, could in the long run be disastrous to what had become the overriding Nationalist preoccupation— the maintenance of the position of the white man in South Africa. The Afrikaners, so long suspicious of English-speaking South Africans, now needed them as allies. The Nationalists reasoned that division would last as long as the forces contributing to disunity existed, and in their view the British monarchy was a major factor contributing to disunity. In 1955, Dr N. J. J. Olivier, an official of SABRA and Professor of Bantu Studies at Stellenbosch University, and the late Dr Otto du Plessis, former head of the New Order, explained Nationalist thinking on this point to the writer in these terms:

> The question in South Africa today is how to achieve national unity among the European elements. The answer is a republican form of government. Other efforts to achieve unity have failed. A republic would instill a genuine undivided loyalty. Today white loyalties are split between the Union and Britain. For England the Queen is a symbol for unity; for South Africa, disunity.

The Nationalists reasoned that if the political ties with Britain were broken, a genuine South African patriotism could develop. They pointed to the fact that English-speaking South Africans, regardless of how many generations their families had been in South Africa, referred to England as 'home'. As Felix Gross wrote of Cecil Rhodes:

> Like everyone else he had believed that the main task of the colonies consisted in contributing to the wealth and strength of the Motherland, thereby giving her enterprising subjects the opportunity of settling there in their younger years, making enough money, and, in the autumn of their lives, coming 'home' and retiring in one of the Suburbia's charming cottages.[2]

This attitude was naturally resented by the Afrikaners, many generations removed from Europe, who considered South Africa their only home.

By 1960, the stage had been set for a republican majority. In 1949, Europeans in Southwest Africa had been given the vote in the Union. In 1950, Parliament had abolished appeal to the British Privy Council as the court of last resort. And in 1956, the Cape Coloureds had been finally removed from the common voting roll. And the political climate had become much more favorable to the Nationalists. The situation throughout Africa was making the position of the whites seem precarious, while at the same time adding stature (in their eyes) to Dr Verwoerd as their leader. On February 3, 1960, the British Prime Minister, Harold Macmillan, told the South African Parliament that 'the wind of change is blowing through the continent' and that 'there are some aspects of your policies which make it impossible' for Britons to support South Africa 'without being false to our own deep convictions about the political destinies of free men'. Verwoerd replied that whereas Macmillan was defending the black man he was merely asking the same rights for the white man. On March 21, 1960, at Sharpeville, a native location at Vereeniging, sixty-nine Africans were killed and 178 wounded in a clash with the police over pass laws. It was becoming apparent that the coils were tightening. Macmillan had made it quite clear that in the struggle with the Africans that was bound to ensue, South Africa could expect no overt political or military help from Britain.*

If ever there were to be a republic, the time was now. On April 23, 1960, the Prime Minister introduced a bill into Parliament to authorize the holding of a republican referendum, to be limited to white voters and decided by simple majority. Parliament approved the bill on May 2.

Before the referendum, the Nationalists distributed great quantities of propaganda urging the electorate to vote in favor of a republic. (Opposition propaganda urged a 'No' vote.)

On October 5, 1960, the referendum was held; 850,458 Europeans voted 'Yes' and 775,878 'No', a majority of 74,580 in favor of a republic.[3]

On October 15, the FAK sponsored a massive *Republikeinse Dankfees*

---

* South Africa obtains arms from Great Britain, however, and financial interests in London and on the Rand are closely connected.

(literally, Republican Thank Feast) at the Voortrekker amphitheater in Pretoria, which was attended by some 70,000 persons. It was a momentous affair, an impressive ceremony. Dr H. J. C. Snijders gave the invocation:

> Grant, oh God, that we will not be satisfied with the creation of a republic, which is only God-given, something people themselves could never accomplish alone. But You have offered and given it to us. Now we pray that we above all shall seek the establishment of the Kingdom of God and that we Whites of South Africa shall clasp each other's hands to form a unity and to close together and to seek the welfare of this our fatherland and its people. Grant that we shall be as a jewel before the world, a proof of that which a people who become as one are capable.

The solemnity of the occasion was marked by Dr G. J. J. Boshoff:

> So has our Republic come. Come from our God. Our altar was our bulwark. Our belief was our shield. Our history was our conscience. Had it depended only on the ingenuity of our people, then would the ship of our people have sunk in the stormy waters of the Referendum on Wednesday, 5 October, 1960. But the boat has arrived safely. Arrived with its crew! Just as the Ark of Noah arrived on the mountain top. The sun-tinted mountain top of our people's dream of freedom. Of this memorable occasion of the beginning of the Republic, David writes this very afternoon: 'The net has been broken and we have become free.'

He warned, however:

> Compatriots, we have become free, in the first place not to be lax, but to be fast. Freedom without anchors is as grievance mongers without happiness. We must be free in order to be fast.
>
> Fast to our God.
> Fast to each other.
> Fast to our past.
> Fast to our soil.
> Fast to our children.
> Fast to our jobs.
> Fast to our ideals.
> Fast to our fellow Whites.
> Whites who want to be, together with us, free in order to be fast.

Verwoerd then addressed his fellow Afrikaners:

> When we look back at the past to all its beauty, we find something which excels above all else. This is that our people have always been living full of an inextinguishable hope. Writers and poets have sung of this: 'In the people of South Africa there exists an inextinguishable faith that the Republic will one day return.' This inextinguishable faith has proved to be true. That hope today is being fulfilled. . . .

The master of ceremonies declared that 'since 1912 the Judges of our people have, Godlike, sought the ideal. . . '. He quoted the words of Hertzog:

> Our striving is the striving of South Africa: South Africa first! We do not want to be slaves in any sense of the word. . . . We want complete independence in a free republic in South Africa!

And Malan:

> Faith in your God!
> Faith in your people!
> Faith in yourself!

And Strijdom:

> We whites, Afrikaans-speaking and English-speaking, can only continue to exist if we unite together: one faith, one love for one fatherland, South Africa—this we will only get if we become a republic!

And the last words of Kruger:

> With unity of mind and unity of strength can again be built that which now is laid flat.

In December, 1960, the Prime Minister, Dr Verwoerd, finally released the bill that he intended to present to Parliament to establish the Constitution of the Republic. Many people had feared the Nationalists would implement the proposed Republican Constitution of 1940 described above, and it was something of a surprise to discover the bill continued the existing form of government, with only minor changes to meet the needs of an independent state. The only major changes were the substitution of a republic for a monarchy and the replacement of the Governor-General by a State President.

In March, 1961, the Commonwealth Prime Ministers met in London to discuss, *inter alia*, the application of South Africa to remain within the Commonwealth with her new republican status. After lengthy discussions, Verwoerd decided to withdraw the application. His decision was dictated by four considerations: first, as the leader of Afrikanerdom, he did not care to plead for clemency and defend his position before the British and their associates. Second, the fact that a number of Commonwealth prime ministers were non-European leaders of non-European states and that several of them had been outspoken critics of the South African government made relations with them in the Commonwealth Prime Ministers' Conference embarrassing and disagreeable. Third, it had been a policy of the Conference to avoid any reference to the internal affairs of member states, and Dr Verwoerd looked upon discussions about South Africa as deviating from this policy. Fourth, continuing membership in the Commonwealth, even as a republic, would have required accepting the British Queen as the symbol of the association, a practice that began when India became a republic in 1949. For a die-hard Afrikaner, this was a sensitive matter.

Thus, on March 15, Dr Verwoerd left the Conference, but not before

assuring that South Africa would be able to continue the benefits of Commonwealth membership in the form of separate bilateral treaties. He then made
haste for home, to be warmly received by representatives of his *Boerenasie*.

Meanwhile, on March 22, 1961, the British Prime Minister, Harold
Macmillan, carefully explained South Africa's withdrawal to the British
House of Commons:

> All this accentuation and systemization of the policy of *apartheid* is
> something very new. I am not saying that there was no discrimination
> in the days of the great South African leaders like Smuts and Botha, but
> these men had in their minds an inspired vision and had the intention
> and purpose of moving gradually towards it. I still believe that as the
> years go by this ideal will grow in strength in South Africa. . . .

> But the Prime Minister of South Africa, with an honesty which one must
> recognize, made it abundantly clear, beyond all doubt, that he would not
> think it right to relax in any form the extreme rigidity of his dogma,
> either now or in the future, and it is a dogma; to us it is strange, but it is
> a dogma which is held with all the force of one of those old dogmas
> which men fought and struggled for in the past.

On May 31, 1961, exactly fifty-nine years after the signing of the
Treaty of Vereeniging and exactly fifty-one years after the establishment of
the Union, the Republic of South Africa became a reality. Symbolically, the
celebrations were held at Vereeniging. A modernistic statue was erected to
mark the significance of the occasion. It depicts two men, one felled by the
sword, representing Boer defeat, the other, the same man who has extracted
the sword and has risen to brandish it proudly before the world. The
inscription reads *Gewond maar nie oorwonne* (Wounded but not conquered).
For Afrikanerdom, the establishment of the Republic symbolized final
victory in the long struggle for supremacy.

The chairman of the *Afrikaanse Calvinistiese Bond*, D. J. van Rooy,
referred to the establishment of the Republic outside the Commonwealth as a
disposition of God. 'The Afrikaner', he said,

> believes firmly, more strongly than ever now, that the Afrikaner people
> were planted here with a vocation, namely to spread the light of the
> Gospel in Dark Africa. He firmly believes that he must maintain
> himself here in order to be able to pursue his vocation permanently.
> He sees in the hostility of other peoples, White as well as non-White,
> conscious and/or unconscious attacks against what he considers as
> essential for the fulfilment of his calling. Today it is clear that Africa
> to a large extent has become the hunting ground of Islam and the poten-
> tial sphere of influence of Communism. Against these tremendous
> forces of darkness stands the handful of Whites as the bearers of the
> message of Christ, alas also as weak and sinful witnesses. Nevertheless
> they established Christian civilization here and undertook mission work
> zealously. According to current world opinion, they are supposed to
> be the cruel oppressors of all non-Whites. And only because they

FIGURE 13: Brooders
(Cartoon by Bob Connolly from *Rand Daily Mail*)

refuse to be dissolved in the Black masses. As often in its history, the Afrikaans people are going through a process of purification.[4]

The editor of *Die Transvaler*, G. D. Scholtz, alluded to the advent of the Republic as the fulfillment of one of the greatest ideals of the Afrikaner people. He observed that May 31, 1902, was one of Afrikanerdom's saddest dates, but to the enemies of the Afrikaner it was a joyous occasion. He asked whether the work of

we Afrikaners will be of a more permanent nature than that of Chamberlain, Rhodes, Milner, Kitchener and Roberts? Why was the work of these men so brief in duration?... They believed that the Anglo-Saxon or British race was the best in the world and therefore predestined, in the words of Rudyard Kipling, to rule over the 'lesser breeds'.

Scholtz observed that these men did not understand what was going on in the soul of the Afrikaner nor were they in the least concerned with his feelings and attitudes.[5]

The 'period of suffering' has ended for the Afrikaner. The Republic has come, 'the climax of our destinies'.[6] But behind the tumult and the shouting, serious problems faced the new Republic. *Die Oosterlig* opined: 'The joy . . . is not unmixed with concern about tomorrow.'[7] As the guns were proclaiming the Republic's birth, another South African community was turning inward, developing a self-consciousness and self-realization, and struggling to rise, to challenge the hegemony of the Afrikaners. Only a few short months before, the Africans—for how long, in the white view, merely the 'Native question'—had made their voices heard clearly enough at Sharpeville, less than a mile from where the celebrations were held at Vereeniging. The Afrikaners had overcome their frustrations, but South Africa still has its persecuted community, struggling to acquire the strength to overthrow its oppressors.

12   Conclusion

'This then was the lot of the tribe . . .'

JOSHUA 15 : 1

THE ESTABLISHMENT OF THE Republic and the departure of South Africa from the Commonwealth climaxed the development of Afrikaner nationalism as an organized political force. Originally mainly a response to British policy, by 1961, Afrikaner nationalism had grown to gigantic proportions, and had developed an ethic of racial exclusiveness that it imposed on the whole of South Africa.

The Nationalist government had indicated three major policy objectives: *apartheid*, Afrikaner dominance, and a republic. All have been achieved, although practical *apartheid* turns out to be very different from the theoretical variety and to be somewhat hard to distinguish from the simple concept of *baaskaap*. The three are closely interrelated, and on the success or failure of one depend them all. *Apartheid* was designed to preserve white supremacy in South Africa, and to maintain the identity of the white community. The establishment of a republic was intended to unify the European community in South Africa, finally to cut the British connection, and to prevent any future involvement in Britain's wars. These two policies could not be carried out unless control remained in the hands of the Afrikaners, who, as experience had shown, were the only ones who could be trusted to pursue the program undeviatingly.

Afrikaner nationalism has been moving from strength to strength, and success has its own allure. The Afrikaners have displayed an unusual enthusiasm and self-assurance, an impressive will to resist, and a stubborn determination to achieve the goals that they have set for themselves. They have lifted themselves out of the mire of defeat and social and economic backwardness and have attained their ultimate political aims. The pride and self-consciousness of the Afrikaner people has been efficiently developed by the numerous organizations created for that purpose.* To whites in an

* It is worthy of note that in 1918 the Dutch Reformed Church was the only Afrikaner organization of any significance; today *volk* organizations are concerned with every field of activity, to the extent that there have even been serious suggestions for the creation of a separate Afrikaner stock exchange.

Africa seething with black nationalisms, Afrikaner accomplishments have an undeniable attraction. A minority naturally tends to try to avoid isolation, and post-Republic elections indicate that English-speaking South Africans are beginning to drift into the Nationalist camp. With the establishment of the Republic, there has been a general shifting of loyalties among the white population from ethnic groups to South Africa. Verwoerd, like Hertzog, has expressed the view that Briton and Boer must become one, and has stated 'there must be one South Africanism for all. The Afrikaans and English languages must be for all'.[1]

In its rise to power, Afrikanerdom has had the advantage of strong unifying factors that have provided it with a solid base: a unique language, common race and religion, common culture, common experiences, even common occupations. An extremely able, dedicated, and energetic extremist leadership with pronounced organizational abilities has played upon such denominators in welding the *Boerenasie* into a force capable of overcoming its own depressed status and dominating the formerly dominant British element.

Yet, despite its elements of strength, an examination of the ledger reveals that Afrikaner nationalism's liabilities exceed its assets. Urbanization has made the Afrikaner part of South Africa's vast and expanding industrial complex, and its natural tendency is to hasten the process of integration of all groups within the population. It was to counter this tendency that the Nationalists decided on the policy of *apartheid*, and it is precisely that policy that is proving their weakest point.

The inculcation of a strongly nationalist group consciousness permitted the Afrikaner to achieve power, and *apartheid* was designed to perpetuate Afrikaner dominance.

But the Nationalists have discovered that real *apartheid* is impractical, and, that while partial *apartheid* may serve their purpose of preserving the white community in its present position, it is a poor substitute for the fine-sounding Nationalist promises of political equality in separate territories, let alone for political and economic justice, as far as the nonwhites are concerned. European dependence on African labor means that Africans, who in theory reside only on a temporary basis in areas reserved for whites, in reality do so permanently. Their demands for political rights and better living conditions have been voiced by the African National Congress (ANC) and the Pan-African Congress (PAC) (both now banned), by other non-European organizations, and, to a certain extent, by the predominantly English-language press, and by European political parties in opposition to the government. The Africans have learned that the white *baas* is economically vulnerable, and that the strike is a valuable weapon. The strike has become for the Africans what the Great Trek and the 1914 Rebellion were to the Boers—a means of political protest, for which all other outlets have been closed. For the African, however, the period of struggle is just beginning. Nor are African leaders unaware of the lessons to be learned from Afrikaner history. The Bantu publication *The World* (November 16, 1957) declared: 'Let us learn from the Afrikaner. As long as he ignored his nationalism, he played second-fiddle and was even scorned. But when he developed his nationalism, he not only became a power to be reckoned with, but also enjoyed the full rights and freedoms of the citizens of this country.'

Moreover, Afrikaner policy and practice are bringing all the various non-European ethnic groups together in a bond of common opposition and they are receiving support from abroad. The Afro-Asian bloc sympathizes with the non-Europeans of South Africa from racial and anticolonial fellow feeling; communist states see them as victims of capitalist oppression and are not averse to the prospect of further discord in a 'western' country; and the governments of Great Britain and the United States are conscious of the force of liberal opinion in their own countries and anxious to disassociate themselves politically from a régime so obviously repressive. Internationally, in short, South Africa's only friends are Southern Rhodesia and Portugal (although it has important economic links with Great Britain and the USA).

As in the days of Kruger's republic, Afrikanerdom—indeed the whole of white South Africa—is again being 'hemmed in a kraal'; and compelled once again to *laager* defensively. The Afrikaner is becoming painfully conscious of these new threats. *Die Kerkblad*, organ of the Dutch Reformed Church, has observed:

> In this dangerous world we are almost totally isolated. . . . While more and more doors are being slammed in our faces in Africa; the nearly two million Afrikaners stand alone against the world population of about 3,000 million. It is to be expected that as the threats approach us like savage monsters, more will have to be expended on police and defence. . . . There is not one of the peoples which, if it suits it, will not simply sacrifice us. If it comes to that, we can be smashed from Cape Canaveral as well as Moscow.

Kruger and his Afrikaner farmers could reasonably expect to be able to maintain an existence isolated from the rest of the world. Today, isolation is not so easy. Modern communications and economic interdependence with other countries no longer permit South Africa the luxury of isolation.

Nationalist policy, now designed above all to ensure the maintenance of white supremacy, is caught in a vicious circle: to assure that their policy continues to be carried out, the Nationalists must prevent the other ethnic groups in South Africa from sharing the government of the state—the *Boerenasie* is forced to rule with an 'iron fist', but this very dominance makes it, to say the least, difficult for the Nationalists to compel allegiance, even from other whites. This problem remains, although its effects are being modified by the growing unity among the whites.

One solution to the Nationalists' problems would be a substantial increase in the size of the European community. This would provide more manpower to police the system, and more labor for the expanding economy. Despite intensive efforts on the part of the government, immigrants have not so far come to South Africa in sufficient numbers even to offset the difference between the natural rates of increase of Europeans and non-Europeans. The decline of Afrikaner nationalism seems inevitable. And while the wooing and drifting of English-speaking South Africans to the Afrikaner fold is broadening the base of Afrikanerdom, it is also destroying an important element of strength—the fiercely exclusive self-consciousness of the *volk*. 'History', declared *The World* (July 29, 1961),

> teaches that nations come and go. They reach their highest point of development and then decline into extinction. . . . Now the Afrikaner nation has completed its climb . . . and with the inevitable decline of the Afrikaner, the African nation will rise. . . . History will repeat itself in South Africa, as it has repeated itself throughout the world, right through the ages.

Without necessarily agreeing that history always repeats itself, one may find good reason to believe that this comment on the course of Afrikaner nationalism is substantially correct. As Jacques Maritain has said: 'Worlds which have arisen in heroism lie down in fatigue, for new sufferings come in their turn and bring the dawn of another day.'

Notes

Introduction

1. According to the report of the South African Bureau of Census and Statistics, the population in 1960 was 15,841,128, of which 3,067,638 were classified as whites, 10,807,809 as Africans, 477,414 as Asians, and 1,488,267 as Coloureds. Approximately 60 per cent of the whites are Afrikaners. The mandated territory of Southwest Africa had in 1959 a population of 554,000, which included 69,000 whites, 464,000 Africans, and 21,000 Coloureds. Of the whites, 15,000 are German-speaking.

Chapter 1

1. M. K. Gandhi, *Satyagraha in South Africa*, trans. by V. G. Desai (Stanford: Stanford University Press, 1954), p. 14. For an analysis of the development of racial attitudes in South Africa, see I. D. MacCrone, *Race Attitudes in South Africa: Historical, Experimental, and Psychological Studies* (London: Oxford University Press, 1937).

2. Felix Gross, *Rhodes of Africa* (New York: Frederick A. Praeger, 1957), p. 56.

3. M. H. K. Lichtenstein, *Travels in Southern Africa in the Years 1803, 1804, 1805, 1806*, trans. from the German by Anne Plumtre (London: Henry Colburn, 1812). This book has been reprinted by the van Riebeeck Society in Cape Town. The author was the tutor of the son of General Janssens, the last Dutch governor of the Cape.

4. Early population estimates vary. These figures were taken from L. E. Neame, *White Man's Africa: The Problem of a White Nation in a Black Continent* (Cape Town: Stewart, 1952).

5. In 1828 the Reverend John Philip published his two-volume *Researches in South Africa* (London: James Duncan, 1828) to publicize his contention that the Africans were being cruelly oppressed by both the Boers and the Colonial Government.

6. S. G. Millin, *Cecil Rhodes* (London: Chatto and Windus, 1952), p. 38.

7. John Bond, *They Were South Africans* (Cape Town: Oxford University Press, 1956), p. 121.

8. On the Great Trek, see Eric A. Walker, *The Great Trek* (London:

A. and C. Black, 1934). P. J. van der Merwe in *Die Noordwaartse Beweging van die Boere voor die Groot Trek* (The Hague: W. P. van Stockum, 1937) shows the importance of land hunger in providing the impetus for the Great Trek.

9. As quoted in Eric A. Walker, *A History of Southern Africa* (London: Longmans, Green, 1957), p. 198.

10. *Grahamstown Journal*, April 27, 1837.

11. On Covenant Day (the day commemorating Blood River), 1960, Dr Albert Hertzog, Minister of Posts and Telegraphs, declared: 'We stand alone and abandoned. But we have stood alone before. . . . Courage and strength carried us through in the time of the Voortrekkers and they will do so again.' For an account of the massacres, see *The Diary of Francis Owen*, ed. by Sir George Cory (Cape Town: van Riebeeck Society, 1926). Owen was an eyewitness.

12. Sir Harry Smith, *Correspondence with the Trek Boers*, 1848.

13. Sir James Bryce, *Impressions of South Africa* (New York: Century, 1900).

14. For a penetrating account of the emergence of Afrikaner nationalism, see F. A. van Jaarsveld, *The Awakening of Afrikaner Nationalism, 1868–1881* (Cape Town: Human and Rousseau, 1961).

15. C. W. de Kiewiet, *A History of South Africa, Social and Economic* (London: Oxford University Press, 1941), p. 91.

16. Quoted in *ibid.*, p. 90.

17. Gross, *op. cit.*, p. 264.

18. During the diamond-field controversy a Diggers Republic was proclaimed at Klipdrift with one Stafford Parker as President. This came to an end, however, when the British annexed the area.

19. F. Basil Williams, *Botha, Smuts, and South Africa* (New York: The Macmillan Co., 1948), p. 8.

20. It was Shepstone's policy toward the Africans that forced the Natalers, especially the sugar growers, to import Indians. Shepstone is a controversial figure in South African history, as disturbing to the British as to the Afrikaners, and his dealings with Swaziland and later the Transvaal have become historical conversation pieces. For an account of him, see Cornelis Uys, *In the Era of Shepstone: Being a Study of British Expansion in South Africa, 1842–1877* (Lovedale, South Africa: Lovedale Press, 1933).

21. Quoted in Henry John May, *The South African Constitution* (Cape Town: Juta, 1955), pp. 3–4.

22. *The Transvaal from Within: A Record of Private Affairs* (London: Heinemann, 1899), p. 24.

23. Quoted in van Jaarsveld, *op. cit.*, p. 179.

24. Lionel Forman, *Chapters in the History of the March to Freedom* (Cape Town: Real Printing Company, 1959), p. 27.

25. Walker, *History of Southern Africa*, p. 377.

26. Quoted in Gross, *op. cit.*, pp. 7–8.

27. Quoted in van Jaarsveld, *op. cit.*, p. 17.

28. Walker, *History of Southern Africa*, p. 386.

Chapter 2

1. Letter to the *Express,* March 18, 1886. The *Express* was published in Bloemfontein, 1875–99.

2. S. J. P. Kruger, *The Memoirs of Paul Kruger, Four Times President of the South African Republic, Told by Himself* (New York: Century, 1902), pp. 199–200.

3. Quoted in Colwyn E. Vulliamy, *Outlanders: A Study of Imperial Policy in South Africa, 1877–1902* (London: Jonathan Cape, 1938), p. 310.

4. Quoted in S. G. Millin, *Rhodes* (London: Chatto and Windus, 1936), p. 158.

5. F. S. Crafford, *Jan Smuts: A Biography* (Garden City, N.Y.: Doubleday, Doran, 1944), pp. 22–23, 26–27.

6. Bryce, *op. cit.* Sir James Percy FitzPatrick defended the position of the *Uitlanders* at length in *The Transvaal from Within.* On the *Uitlanders,* see also Vulliamy, *op. cit.*

7. Quoted in Gross, *op. cit.,* p. 134.

8. De Kiewiet, *op. cit.,* p. 121.

9. S. G. Millin, *op. cit.,* p. 243.

10. Walker, *History of Southern Africa,* p. 389.

11. For a copy of the 'Rules and Regulations' of the *Boeren Beschermings Vereniging,* see J. H. Hofmeyr and F. W. Reitz, *The Life of Jan Hendrik Hofmeyr* (Cape Town: Van de Sandt de Villiers Printing Company, 1913), pp. 643–45. See the files of the Dutch press at the Cape at this time, particularly *Di Patriot* (now the Paarl *Post*), *De Zuid Afrikaan, De Volksvriend* (a Dutch newspaper founded in 1862, which Hofmeyr later ran, and which absorbed *De Zuid Afrikaan* in 1871), and *Die Volksblad.*

12. For the 'Rules and Regulations' of July 4, 1879, see *ibid.,* pp. 196–97.

13. *Ibid.,* pp. 193–214.

14. *Ibid.,* p. 198.

15. For a copy of the constitution, see Hofmeyr, *op. cit.,* pp. 649–52.

16. For a copy of this document, see *ibid.,* pp. 652–54.

17. Millin, *op. cit.,* pp. 46–47.

18. Reitz was the brother-in-law of William Philip Schreiner, and of the novelist Olive Schreiner. W. P. Schreiner was a great admirer of Rhodes until the Jameson Raid; he was Prime Minister of the Cape, 1898–1900. Reitz's son, Colonel Deneys Reitz, was a Boer War commander and, later, a member of Smuts' cabinet; he wrote a number of books, among them *Commando* (1929), *Trekking On* (1933), *No Outspan* (1943), and *Afrikander* (1933.)

19. Kruger, *op. cit.,* p. 301.

20. *Ibid.,* p. 290. It is instructive to compare Kruger's *Memoirs* with *The Milner Papers.*

21. De Kiewiet, *op. cit.,* p. 139.

22. See Johannes S. Marais, *The Fall of Kruger's Republic* (Oxford: Clarendon Press, 1961). The author traces the origins of the war to the discovery of gold on the Rand.

23. Kruger, *op. cit.,* p. 45.

Chapter 3

1. Quoted in J. J. McCord, *South African Struggle* (Pretoria: de Bussy, 1952), p. 341. For an excellent treatment of this period, see Leonard M. Thompson, *The Unification of South Africa* (Oxford: Clarendon Press, 1960).

2. Quoted in Williams, *op. cit.,* p. 93.

3. Quoted in Henry John May, *The South African Constitution* (Johannesburg: Juta, 1955), p. 8. For the history of the conference, see Sir Edgar H. Walton, *Inner History of the National Convention of South Africa* (London: Longmans, Green, 1912), and *Die Konvensie Dagboek van sy edelagbare François Stephanus Malan, 1908–1909* (Cape Town: van Riebeeck Society, 1951).

Chapter 4

1. *The Black Sash* (Cape Town), September, 1960, p. 8.

2. *The Star* (Johannesburg), December 8, 1911.

3. *Ibid.,* October 5, 1912.

4. Oswald Pirow, *James Barry Munnik Hertzog* (London: Allen and Unwin, 1958).

5. *The Star,* December 7, 1912.

6. Published by *Het Volk Drukkerij,* Potchefstroom, 1914.

7. Quoted in Pirow, *op. cit.,* p. 69. For a personal narrative of the Rebellion, see Deneys Reitz, *Trekking On* (London: Faber and Faber, 1933).

8. F. S. Crafford, *op. cit.*

9. Pirow, *op. cit.,* p. 84.

10. S. G. Millin, *General Smuts* (Boston: Little, Brown, 1936), Chap. 39.

11. De Kiewiet, *op. cit.*

12. Report of the *Commission of Inquiry into European Occupancy of the Rural Areas* (Pretoria: Government Printer, 1959). For the nonwhites, the cityward movement has been equally significant. In 1904, 90 per cent were rural; in 1936, 75.7 per cent; in 1958, 63 per cent. See also W. M. Macmillan, *Complex South Africa: An Economic Footnote to History* (London: Faber and Faber, 1930).

13. De Kiewiet, *op. cit.*

14. Haskel Sonnabend and Cyril Sofer, *South Africa's Stepchildren: A Study in Miscegenation* (Johannesburg: Society of the Friends of Africa, 1949). S. G. Millin told the writer she believed the figure to be as high as 60 per cent.

15. Carnegie Commission of Investigation on the Poor White Question in South Africa, *Poor White Problem in South Africa,* 5 vols. (Stellenbosch: Dutch Reformed Church of South Africa, 1932).

16. Quoted in L. E. Neame, *General Hertzog: Prime Minister of the Union of South Africa Since 1924* (London: Hurst and Blackett, 1930), p. 234.

17. As quoted in Arthur G. Barlow, *Almost in Confidence* (Johannesburg: Juta, 1952), p. 197. See Chap. 5 of that work for an interesting account of the Flag Bill.

18. Deneys Reitz, *No Outspan* (London: Faber and Faber, 1943).
19. Crafford, *op. cit.,* p. 268.
20. Quoted by Pirow, *op. cit.,* pp. 163–64.
21. Leopold Marquard, *The Peoples and Policies of South Africa* (Cape Town: Oxford University Press, 1960), p. 138.
22. Pirow, *op. cit.,* p. 157.
23. *Ibid.,* p. 160.
24. Jan J. van Rooyen, *Die Nasionale Party: Sy Opkooms en oorwinning—Kaapland se aandeel* (Elsie River, South Africa: Nasionale Handels drukkery, 1956).
25. Pirow, *op. cit.,* p. 182.
26. Van Rooyen, *op. cit.,* p. 137.
27. *Ibid.*

Chapter 5

1. Quoted in Barlow, *op. cit.,* p. 307.
2. As a result, demands were later made to avoid the possibility of a recurrence of such a situation. See *Dagbreek en Sondagnuus* (Johannesburg), February 19, 1961.
3. Arthur G. Barlow, *That We May Tread Safely* (Cape Town: Tafelberg-Uitgewers Beperk, 1960).
4. In 1936, the South African Jewish Board of Deputies initiated publication of *The Press Digest* to expose Nationalist expressions of sympathy for the nazis. Since the defeat of Hitler, the publication has become a balanced summary of South African press and periodical reports.
5. *The Star,* December 17, 1938.
6. *Die Volksblad* (Bloemfontein), July 11, 1939.
7. *Rand Daily Mail* (Johannesburg), January 1, 1941.
8. *Die Suiderstem,* September 16, 1940.
9. See *The Star,* December 1, 1936.
10. *Die Volksblad,* November 2, 1940.
11. *Die Oosterlig* (Port Elizabeth), November 11, 1940.
12. *The Sunday Times* (Johannesburg) had a similar article on October 17, 1937.
13. *Die Vaderland* (Johannesburg), November 8, 1940. For the OB Commandant-General's story, see Hans van Rensburg, *Their Paths Crossed Mine: Memoirs of the Commandant-General of the Ossewa-Brandwag* (Johannesburg: Central News Agency, 1956). See also Michael Roberts and A. E. G. Trollip, *The South African Opposition, 1939–1945* (Cape Town: Longmans Green, 1947). Chap. 4 discusses the relation of the HNP and OB.
14. *Die Suiderstem,* September 25, 1940.
15. *Rand Daily Mail,* November 12, 1940.
16. Barlow, *That We May Tread Safely,* p. 59.
17. *Die Transvaler,* October 14, 1940.
18. *Ibid.,* November 1, 1940.
19. *Ibid.,* January 16, 1941.

20. *Die Burger*, October 7, 1940.

21. See *The Star,* November 16, 1940.

22. A copy of this as well as most of the documents cited can be found at the Hoover Institution, Stanford University, in the Vatcher Collection.

23. *Rand Daily Mail*, January 14, 1941.

24. *Die Transvaler*, January 16, 1941.

25. Pirow, *op. cit.*, p. 254.

26. *Die Vaderland*, January 26, 1942.

27. *The Star,* July 7, 1939.

28. *Die Volkstem*, April 11, 1940.

29. Summaries can be found in the United Party pamphlet, *South African 'Nationalism'* (Johannesburg, 1947).

30. A copy can be found in *The British Africa Monthly*, September, 1948.

31. *The Star*, January 12, 1942, and *Die Transvaler,* January 13, 1942.

32. *Ibid.*

33. *Sunday Times,* January 25, 1942. According to General J. A. Smith, second-in-command of the OB, the draft had been prepared by the OB and was accepted by the National Party.

34. The National Party newspaper, *Die Kruithoring*, published the complete text.

35. *Die Transvaler,* February 7, 1942.

Chapter 6

1. T. C. Visser, *Republican Ideal* (Pretoria: A. H. Koomans, n.d.).

2. Interview with Dr E. G. Malherbe, Principal of Natal University, November 23, 1960. Dr Malherbe worked during the war in Military Intelligence for the Smuts government. See Appendix I for a copy of the speech.

3. See Appendix II.

4. In an interview with the writer, however, Mr Wentzel C. du Plessis, an admitted AB member, disputed the Report's information about the initiation procedure of the AB.

5. Louis J. du Plessis, *Letters of a Farmer* (Krugersdorp: L. J. du Plessis, 1951).

6. See Appendix III.

7. 'Report of the Committee on Current Problems about the Existence, Aim and Object of the Afrikaner Broederbond', Addendum B to *Agenda vir die Twee-en Twintigste Vergadering von di Raad von die Kerke* (*The Transactions of the Twenty-second Council of Churches*) (Bloemfontein, May 16, 1951).

8. Marquard, *op. cit.*, p. 174.

9. See, for example, *Rand Daily Mail*, 'Ruiters Had Orders: Move in on Spot', July 3, 1959, and 'Broederbond Meets', September 29, 1960; *Sunday Times*, 'The Broederbond Shall Govern South Africa', October 12, 1958, 'Broederbond Hospital To Become Old-Age Home', February 28,

1960, 'General Hertzog's Letter of Advice to His Son', May 22, 1960, 'Afrikaners Alarmed by Broederbond's Growing Influence', May 22, 1960, and 'Broederbond Grabs Control of SABC', September 18, 1960; and *Sunday Express*, 'Broederbond Out If Havenga Gets In', November 21, 1954, and 'Broeders Oust Hertzog Aide', December 20, 1959.

    10.   J. W. Patten, 'Background and Analysis', *Journal of Racial Affairs* (Stellenbosch, October, 1961), p. 13.

    11.   *Sunday Times*, May 22, 1960.

    12.   Smithfield Address, 1935 (Appendix I).

    13.   *The Star,* October 12, 1948.

    14.   *Ibid.*

    15.   Alex Hepple, *Trade Unions in Travail* (Johannesburg: Unity Publications, 1954), p. 10.

    16.   Interview with Mr Wentzel C. du Plessis, December, 1960.

    17.   *Die Transvaler,* December 14, 1944.

    18.   Article in *The Reporter,* January 9, 1958, p. 11.

    19.   *Africa Special Report* (Washington, D.C., October, 1957).

    20.   Albert Fick, 'South Africa's Ku Klux Klan', *Maclean's Magazine,* February 1, 1952, p. 13.

    21.   *Die Transvaler,* December 4, 1944.

    22.   *Die Transvaler,* January 3, 1945.

    23.   *The Star,* October 12, 1948.

    24.   *The Star,* October 1, 1951.

    25.   Preface to *Christelik-Nasionale Onderwysbeleid* (Christian National Education Policy), by Professor J. C. van Rooy, Chairman of FAK. See Appendix V.

    26.   *Die Vaderland,* October 4, 1939.

    27.   Hepple, *op. cit.,* p. 25.

    28.   *The Star,* October 2, 1950.

    29.   *Die Transvaler,* December 30, 1944.

    30.   *Ibid.*

    31.   *Ibid.*

    32.   Quoted by Hertzog.

    33.   See Appendix IV.

Chapter 7

    1.   The FAK and associated groups issue reports from time to time. For example, there is the *Report of the Second Economic Congress (Verslag van die Tweede Ekonomiese Volkskongres)* of 1950. The FAK issues programs and reports of its biannual FAK Congresses and the *FAK Annual Report (FAK—jaarverslag).* Useful information is presented in Carter, *op. cit.,* and Hepple, *op. cit.*

    2.   *Die Transvaler,* December 30, 1944.

    3.   *Referate en Verslag FAK Kongres,* July 6 and 7, 1937 (Cape Town: Nasionale Pers Beperk, 1937), p. 5.

    4.   *Ibid.,* p. 122.

    5.   In 1960, the Secretary was T. W. S. Meyer, a graduate of the

Witwatersrand University who had worked as a mining engineer at Boksburg for a few years before taking the position. Meyer is responsible for planning. I. J. Smit was the Administrative Secretary, responsible for general administration. W. S. J. Grobler was the Organizing Secretary for the northern section of the country and at the same time was the chairman of the National Party Jeugbond of the Transvaal. A. C. Pienaar was the Organizing Secretary for the southern part of the country. C. du P. Kuhn was the youth organizer for the FAK, as well as being the Organizing Secretary of the *Afrikaanse Studentebond.* P. J. Meyer was the Secretary of the Economic Institute, which is responsible for the 'economic uplifting of the Afrikaner'. He is also head of the SABC and a member of the FAK Executive Committee, as already noted. These data were obtained from interviews with Messrs. T. W. S. Meyer, I. J. Smit, W. S. J. Grobler, and C. du P. Kuhn.

6. In 1960, the Chairman (*Voorsitter*) of the Executive Committee was Dr H. B. Thom, Rector of the University of Stellenbosch and allegedly former head of the Broederbond. (In 1946, the Chairman was Dr J. C. van Rooy, who was at the same time Chairman of the Broederbond.) Dr Thom was elected by the Congress. In 1960, other officers included the Reverend G. J. J. Boshoff, a DRC minister from Johannesburg, later an Army chaplain, Dr W. E. G. Louw, former professor at Rhodes University and later cultural editor of *Die Burger*, and J. H. Stander, Assistant Director of Education in Natal. In 1960, the ANK elected Ivanhoe Makepeace Lombard, the Vice-Chairman (*Ondervoorsitter*) and first Secretary of the FAK and a prominent member of the Broederbond (who was for some time Secretary of the AB); Dr P. J. Meyer, Chairman of the Board of the South African Broadcasting Corporation (SABC), former Secretary of the FAK, and, it is believed, subsequently the head of the Broederbond, and second only to Dr Verwoerd; and Professor Dr G. G. Cillie, of Stellenbosch University and brother of the editor of *Die Burger*. (Meyer's son, Izan, was born during the period when the Nationalists were flirting with the nazis. His name spelled backwards is 'nazi'.) The Executive Committee also has a few additional members as advisers on specialized fields. Anton Hartman, Director of the Musical Department of SABC, Dr M. S. du Buisson, Secretary of the S. A. *Akademie vir Wetenskap en Kuns* (S. A. Academy of Science and Arts), and Professor A. J. la Grange of Stellenbosch University, a specialist on education, were advisers in 1961.

7. *Die Johannesburgs Skakelkomitee Sekretariele Verslag, November, 1951–October, 1952,* as quoted in Gwendolen M. Carter, *The Politics of Inequality* (New York: Frederick A. Praeger, 1958).

8. *Die Transvaler,* December 30, 1944.

9. Each of these banks publishes an annual report, available on request.

10. Quoted in Carter, *op. cit.,* p. 258.

11. *Ibid.,* p. 259.

12. *Die Toekomsrol van die RDB in ons Ekonomiese Lewe* (*The Future of the RDB in Our Economic Life*), quoted in *loc. cit.*

appointment—particularly when taken in conjunction with the naming of the Nationalist extremist John Vorster as Minister of Justice in the preceding August—did not indicate any moderation of government policy. Vorster's appointment seems to have reflected a shift of the power center of the NP from the Cape to the Transvaal, traditionally the home of hard-core Afrikanerdom. The *Sunday Times* (August 6, 1961) stated that control of the Cabinet now resided in the triumvirate of Verwoerd, Albert Hertzog, and Vorster.

7. See H. Lindsay Smith, *Behind the Press in South Africa* (Cape Town: Stewart, 1947).

8. *The Friend,* August 15, 1957.

9. See *Publications and Entertainment Bill: Memorandum Submitted to the Parliamentary Select Committee by Central News Agency, Ltd., 1960.* Copy available at the Hoover Institution, Stanford University, Vatcher Collection. See also *The Friend,* November 2, 1960, on the Board of Censors.

10. As quoted in C. W. de Kiewiet, *The Anatomy of South African Misery* (London: Oxford University Press, 1956,) p. 24.

Chapter 10

1. Bishop Ambrose Reeves, *South Africa—Yesterday and Tomorrow: A Challenge to Christians* (London: Gollancz, 1962).

2. SABRA holds annual meetings and publishes a *Newsletter* (*Nuusbrief*) and a quarterly *Journal of Racial Affairs* (*Tydskrif vir Raase-Aangeleenthede*), as well as various studies from time to time.

3. Anthony Delius, in *The Reporter,* January 9, 1958, p. 27. For an interesting account of SABRA, see Edwin S. Munger's article in *Africa Special Report* (Washington, D.C.), October, 1957.

4. Malan described his conception of *apartheid* at length in answer to a letter he received from the Reverend John E. Piersma of Grand Rapids, Michigan. Malan's letter, dated February 12, 1954, has been reproduced by the State Information Office of South Africa under the title *Apartheid: South Africa's Answer to a Major Problem.*

5. For a summary of the Report, see D. Hobart Houghton, *The Tomlinson Report: A Summary of the Findings and Recommendations in the Tomlinson Commission Report* (Johannesburg: South African Institute of Race Relations, 1956). The South African State Information Office has published an eighty-page summary of the Report called 'The Pattern of Race Policy in South Africa', in *Fortnightly Digest of South African Affairs,* April 16, 1956.

6. The State Information Office published the White Paper in full, along with the parliamentary debates, in January, 1957, in a pamphlet entitled *Sequel to the Tomlinson Commission Report.* For an assessment of the Report and the White Paper, see D. Hobart Houghton, 'The Significance of the Tomlinson Report', *Africa South,* January, 1957.

7. L. E. Neame, *The History of Apartheid* (London: Pall Mall Press, 1962), p. 157.

8. *Cape Times,* January 1, 1962.

9. *South Africa Scope*, March, 1963, p. 12.

10. *Die Transvaler*, November 7, 1947.

11. See note 4 above.

12. One of the best-argued treatises supporting *apartheid* is L. E. Neame, *White Man's Africa: The Problem of a White Nation in a Black Continent*, cited above. Other apologias for *apartheid* are John E. Holloway (former South African Ambassador to the United States), *The Problem of Race Relations in South Africa*; A. B. du Preez, *Inside the South African Crucible*; S. Pienaar's section of S. Pienaar and Anthony Sampson, *Two Views on Separate Development* (Pienaar is the assistant editor of *Die Burger*); and Eric Louw, *The Case for South Africa*.

13. 'The Grave of the Mind,' *Africa South,* January, 1957, pp. 2–3.

14. *Die Volksblad,* October 14, 1957.

15. Speech quoted in *The Observer* (London), December, 1952.

16. *Rand Daily Mail*, September 27, 1955.

17. *Natal Witness* (Pietermaritzburg), September 29, 1957.

18. *Die Transvaler*, March 3, 1958.

19. *Ibid.,* February 10, 1961.

20. *The Star,* February 8, 1961.

21. *The Natal Daily News*, November 24, 1960.

22. 'The Significance of the Tomlinson Report', *Africa South,* January, 1957, pp. 12–21.

23. 'Blind Alley in Africa', *Saturday Review,* May 14, 1960.

24. *Rand Daily Mail*, May 17, 1962.

25. *Cape Times*, November 2, 1960.

26. *The Star,* December 12, 1960.

27. Duma Nokwe, 'The South African Police Laws and Powers', *Africa South*, January, 1958, p. 25.

Chapter 11

1. *Rand Daily Mail*, October 11, 1940.

2. Gross, *op. cit.*, p. 73.

3. The provincial vote breakdown was:

	For a Republic	Against a Republic
Transvaal	406,632	325,041
Cape	271,418	269,784
Orange Free State	110,171	33,438
Natal	42,299	135,598
Southwest Africa	19,938	12,017

4. *Woord en Daad,* April 21, 1961.

5. *Die Transvaler,* May 16, 1961.

6. *Die Burger.*

7. May 12, 1961.

Chapter 12

1. *Die Transvaler,* April 24, 1961.

Bibliography

Bibliographies

Advertising and Press Annual of all Africa. Johannesburg: National Publishing Company, annual.

The African Press and Advertising Annual. Cape Town: Boston House, annually since 1950.

The Cambridge History of the British Empire. Vol. VIII. Cambridge: The University Press, 1963, pp. 917–1017.

Classified List of South African Annual Publications. Cape Town: South African Public Library Supplement, 1951.

COETZEE, NICO S. *South African Catalogue.* Fifth ed. Johannesburg: Technical Books, 1956. Mimeographed.

CONOVER, HELEN F. *Africa South of the Sahara: A Selected Annotated List of Writings, 1951–1956.* Washington, D.C.: Library of Congress, 1957.

The Index to South African Periodicals. Johannesburg: Public Library, 1940—. Monthly. First annual edition covered period 1900–39.

KITCHEN, HELEN (ed.). *The Press in Africa.* Washington, D.C.: Ruth Sloan Associates, 1956.

Library of Congress, European Affairs Division. *Introduction to Africa: A Selective Guide to Background Reading.* Washington, D.C.: The University Press of Washington, 1952.

LOEWENTHAL, RUDOLF. *Russian Materials on Africa: A Selective Bibliography.* Washington, D.C.: Department of State, 1958.

MARTI, PALAU. 'Bibliographie Africaniste', *Journal de la Société des Africanistes,* Paris, annually.

MENDELSSOHN, SYDNEY. *South African Bibliography.* 2 vols. London: Kegan Paul, 1910.

MOCKFORD, JULIAN (ed.). *Overseas Reference Book of the Union of South Africa.* London: Todd, 1945.

MORRIS, G. R. *A Bibliography of the Indian Question in South Africa.* Cape Town: University of Cape Town, 1946.

MUSIKER, REUBEN. *Guide to South African Reference Books.* Rev. ed. Grahamstown: Rhodes University Library, 1963.

NIENABER, PETRUS J. *Bibliografie van Afrikaanse Boeke.* 4 vols. Johannesburg, 1956–58.

PASK, CHARLES R., and BLOOMAN, PERCY A. (eds.). *Advertising and Press Annual of Africa.* Cape Town: National Publishing Co., annual.

Quarterly Bulletin of the South African Public Library. Cape Town, since 1946.

Republic of South Africa. Office of Census and Statistics. *Official Year Book of the Union and of Basutoland, Bechuanaland Protectorate, and Swaziland.* Pretoria:

Government Printer, annual since 1918. Contains an excellent bibliography including government documents. For bibliography prior to 1930, see *Year Book* of that date or earlier. Subsequent *Year Books* contain works published since 1930.

SAUL, C. DAPHNE. *Handlist of South African Periodicals Current in December 1951.* Cape Town: South African Public Library, 1951.

SCHAPERA, ISAAC. *Select Bibliography of South African Native Life and Problems.* London: Oxford University Press, 1941.

South African Public Library. *A Bibliography of African Bibliographies Covering Territories South of the Sahara.* Cape Town, 1955.

————. *South African National Bibliography.* Pretoria, annual since 1933.

————. *Union List of South African Newspapers, November 1949.* Cape Town, 1950. Lists all newspapers published from 1900 to 1950.

Soviet and East European Research and Translation Service. *Selective Soviet Annotated Bibliographies: Asia, Africa, and Latin America.* New York: Slavic Languages Research Institute, quarterly, since May, 1961.

THEAL, GEORGE M. *Catalogue of Books and Pamphlets Relating to Africa South of the Zambezi.* Cape Town: Maskew Miller, 1912.

Periodicals, Magazines, Journals, Bulletins

Africa. Quarterly, International African Institute, London, since January, 1928.

Africa Digest. Bimonthly, the African Bureau, London, since 1952.

Africa Report. Semimonthly, Institute of African-American Relations, Washington, D.C., since July 5, 1956. (Published originally as *Africa Special Report.*)

Africa South in Exile. Quarterly, London, since December, 1956. (Published originally in Cape Town under title *Africa South.*)

Africa Today. Bimonthly, American Committee on Africa, New York, since 1954.

Africa Weekly. American Committee on Africa, New York.

Africa X-Ray Report: A Special Monthly Intelligence Service on Africa below the Sahara. Investors Intelligence, Johannesburg, 1954–59

African Abstracts: Bulletin Analytique Africaniste. Quarterly, International African Institute, London, since January, 1950. (English and French.)

African Affairs. Quarterly, Royal African Society, London, since October, 1901.

African Jewish Newspaper. Weekly, Dornfontein. (Yiddish; non-Zionist.)

African Studies. Quarterly, Department of Bantu Studies of the University of Witwatersrand, Johannesburg, since 1921.

African Studies Bulletin. Irregular; African Studies Association, New York, since 1958.

African Women. Semiannually, University of London Institute of Education, London, since 1954.

African World. Monthly, London, since 1902.

African World Annual. London, since 1904.

The Africanist. Organ of Pan African Congress until banned in 1960.

Allgemeine Zeitung. Daily except Saturday, Windhoek. (German.)

Archives Yearbook of South African History. Cape Town, since 1938.

Bantu. Monthly, Pretoria, since 1954.

Barkai. Semimonthly, Union of Hebrew Writers of South Africa, Johannesburg. (Hebrew, English and Afrikaans.)

The Black Sash (Die Swart Serp). Monthly, Cape Town, since 1957. (English and Afrikaans.)

The British Africa Monthly. 1947–52. (In 1952 became *The British Africa Review* until it ceased publication.)

Build Congress. Irregular, mimeographed, Durban, since November, 1960.

The Cape Argus. Daily, Argus group, Cape Town, since 1856. (English).

The Cape Standard. Coloured newspaper, Cape Town.

The Cape Times. Daily, Cape Times, Limited, Cape Town, since 1876. (English.)

Commando: The Three Forces on Parade. Monthly, Pretoria, since 1950.

A Commentary on Politics Today. Monthly, United Party, Pretoria. (New series first published in September, 1960.)

Contact. Semimonthly, Liberal Party of South Africa, Cape Town, since 1956. (English).

Counter Attack. Monthly, Congress of Democrats, Johannesburg.

Dagbreek en Sondagnuus. Weekly, Dagbreekpers Beperk, Johannesburg, since 1947. (Afrikaans.)

The Daily Dispatch. Argus group, East London, S.A., since 1872. (English.)

The Daily News. Argus group, Durban, since 1887. (English.)

Di Afrikaanse Patriot. Organ of the Afrikander Bond, Paarl. (First newspaper in Afrikaans and the original organ of the movement for the recognition of Afrikaans. First appeared on January 15, 1876, at Paarl and continued as a weekly until 1904 when it was renamed *Paarl Post*, which is still being published.)

The Diamond Fields Advertiser. Daily, Argus group, Kimberley, since 1877. (English.)

Die Brandwag. Weekly, Die Afrikaanse Pers Beperk, Johannesburg. (Afrikaans.)

Die Burger. Daily, Die Nasionale Pers Beperk, Cape Town, since July 26, 1915. (Afrikaans.)

Die Hervormer. Monthly, organ of Nederduitsch Hervormde Kerk, Krugersdorp. (Afrikaans.)

Die Huisgenoot. Weekly, Die Nasionale Pers Beperk, Cape Town. (Family magazine, in Afrikaans.)

Die Kerkblad. Weekly, organ of Gereformeerde Kerk van Suid-Afrika, Potchefstroom. (Afrikaans.)

Die Kerkbode. Weekly, official organ of the Dutch Reformed Church (NGK), Cape Town. (Afrikaans.)

Die Kruithoring. Monthly, official National Party newspaper, Cape Town. (Afrikaans.)

Die Landbouweekblad. Die Nasionale Pers Beperk, Cape Town. Weekly. (For farmers, in Afrikaans.)

Die Nasionale Partynuus. Semimonthly, organ of the National Party of the Transvaal, Johannesburg. (Afrikaans.)

Die Nataller. Weekly, organ of the Natal National Party, Durban. (Afrikaans.)

Die Oosterlig. Daily, Nasionale Koerante Beperk, Port Elizabeth. (Afrikaans.)

Die Stem. Weekly, Johannesburg. (Afrikaans.)

Die Suidwes-Afrikaner. Semiweekly, official organ of the United National South West Party, Afrikaner Pers Beperk, Windhoek. (Afrikaans.)

Die Suidwester. Semiweekly, Suidwes-Drukkery Beperk, Windhoek, official organ of the Nationalist Party in Southwest Africa. (Afrikaans.)

Die Transvaler. Daily, Die Voortrekkerpers Beperk, Johannesburg, since 1937. (Afrikaans.)

Die Vaderland. Daily, Die Afrikaanse Pers Beperk, Johannesburg, since 1935. (Afrikaans.)

Die Volksblad. Daily, Die Nasionale Pers Beperk, Bloemfontein, since 1910. (Afrikaans.)

Die Volkshandel. Monthly, organ of the Afrikaanse Handelsinstituut, Pretoria. (Afrikaans.)

Die Voorligter. Monthly, organ of the Nederduits Gereformeerde Kerk, Johannesburg. (Afrikaans.)

Dorem Afrike. Monthly, South African Yiddish Cultural Federation, Johannesburg. (A literary journal published in Yiddish.)

Drum. Monthly, Johannesburg, since 1951. (Published also in Ghana and Nigeria.) (English.)

The Eastern Province Herald. Daily, Eastern Province Newspapers, Limited, Port Elizabeth, since 1844. (English.)

The Evening Post. Daily, Eastern Province Newspapers, Limited, Port Elizabeth. (English.)

The Farmers Weekly. Weekly, Argus group, Bloemfontein. (English.)

Fighting Talk: A Journal for Democrats in Southern Africa. Monthly, Springbok Legion, Johannesburg, since 1947.

Flash. Passive Resistance Council of the Natal Indian Congress, since 1946. Mimeographed.

Freedom. Semimonthly, official organ of the Central Committee of the Communist Party of South Africa, Cape Town, until 1952.

The Friend. Daily, Argus group, Bloemfontein, since 1850. (English.)

Fyn Goud. Monthly, Johannesburg. (Afrikaans.)

Government Gazette. Weekly, Pretoria. (English and Afrikaans.)

The Graphic. Weekly, Durban. (English.)

Halt. Irregular, Pretoria, since 1954. Mimeographed. (English and Afrikaans.)

Ilanga Lase Natal. Weekly, Bantu Press, Argus group, Durban. Founded by John L. Dube, first president of the ANC. (English and Zulu.)

Indian Opinion. Weekly, Durban, since 1903.

Inkululeko. Official organ of Communist Party of South Africa, Johannesburg. Previously published as *International* (1915–27); *South African Worker* (1928–30); *Umsebenzl* (Worker) (1930–39); *Inkululeko* (Freedom) (1940–52.)

Inlightingsdines van die Nasionale Party van S.A. Monthly, National Party, Bloemfontein, since July, 1960.

Isizwe (Independent Journal). Published by members of All African Convention. Two issues only, 1959.

Izwi Lase Afrika (*The Voice of Africa*). Official organ of the Cape African Congress, Cape Town, since 1941.

Jeugbonder. Monthly, Nasionale Jeugbond van Transvaal, Johannesburg, since 1950. (Afrikaans.)

Jewish Affairs. Monthly, South African Jewish Board of Deputies, Johannesburg. (English.)

The Jewish Herald. Weekly, Johannesburg. (English; extremely Zionist.)

Journal of African Administration. Quarterly, African Studies Branch of the British Colonial Office, London, since 1949.

Journal of Racial Affairs. Quarterly, South African Bureau of Racial Affairs, Stellenbosch, since 1950. (Afrikaans and English.)

Landstem. Weekly, Die Landstem Pers Beperk, Cape Town, since 1950. (Afrikaans.)

The Leader. Weekly, Durban, since 1940. (English; represents Indian opinion.)

Liberation: A Journal of Democratic Discussion. Monthly, Johannesburg.

Monthly Abstract of Trade Statistics. Department of Customs and Excise, Pretoria.

Monthly Bulletin of Statistics. Bureau of Census and Statistics, Pretoria.

Monthly Newsletter. Dutch Reformed Church, Johannesburg.

The Natal Daily News. Daily, Argus group, Durban. (English.)

The Natal Mercury. Daily, Robison and Company, Durban, since 1852. (English.)

The Natal Witness. Daily, Natal Witness, Limited, Pietermaritzburg, since 1881. (English.) (Established in 1846, it is one of the oldest surviving journals in South Africa.)

National News. Organ of National Party, Elsies River.

Official Gazette. Weekly, Pretoria.

Panorama. Monthly, Department of Information, Pretoria, since 1955.

Press Digest. Weekly, Jewish Board of Deputies, Johannesburg, since 1936. (Until 1945 emphasized pro-Nazi tendencies of Nationalists.)

Press Summary: Treason Trial. Weekly, Johannesburg, since June, 1957. Mimeographed.

The Pretoria News. Daily, Pretoria News Printing Company, Argus group, Pretoria, since 1876. (English.)

Race Relations Journal. Quarterly, South African Institute of Race Relations, Johannesburg, since 1933.

Race Relations News. Monthly, South African Institute of Race Relations, Johannesburg.

The Rand Daily Mail. Daily, South African Associated Newspapers, Johannesburg, since 1902. (English.)

Rooi Rose. Semimonthly, Die Afrikaanse Pers Beperk, Johannesburg. (For women, in Afrikaans.)

Sabra News Letter (Nuusbrief). Monthly, South African Bureau of Racial Affairs, Stellenbosch. (English and Afrikaans.)

Sarie Marais. Weekly, Die Nasionale Pers Beperk, Cape Town. (Woman's illustrated, in Afrikaans.)

South Africa. Weekly, London, since 1888.

South African Digest. Weekly, Department of Information, Pretoria. (English.)

South African Freedom Call. Irregular, South Africa Defense Fund, San Francisco, since 1959. Mimeographed.

South Africa Outlook: A Journal Dealing with Missionary and Racial Affairs. Monthly, Lovedale, Cape Province.

South African Jewish Frontier. Monthly, Johannesburg. (English.)

South African Jewish Observer. Monthly, Mizrachi Organization of South Africa, Johannesburg. (English; very orthodox.)

South African Jewish Times. Weekly, Johannesburg. (English.)

South African Jewish Year Book. Johannesburg, since 1953.

South African Journal of Economics. Quarterly, Johannesburg, since 1933.

The South African Law Journal. Quarterly, Juta, Cape Town, since 1883.

The South African Observer. Monthly, Cape Town, since 1955. (English.)

South African Socialist Review. Cape Town.

The Southern Africa Financial Mail. Weekly, South African Associated Newspapers and the *Investors' Chronicle* of London, Johannesburg, since 1958. (English.)

South West Africa Annual. South West Africa Publications, Windhoek. (English, Afrikaans, and German.)

Spark. Weekly, Cape Town. From 1937 until 1952 published as *The Guardian.*

After being banned was published as *Clarion; Peoples World; Advance; New Age*. *New Age* was banned in 1962 and since has appeared as *Spark*. (English.)

The Star. Daily, Argus group, Johannesburg, since 1887. (English.)

Suidwes-Afrikaner. Semiweekly, Verenigde Pers Beperk, Windhoek. (Afrikaans.)

Sunday Express. Weekly, Sunday Express, Limited, Johannesburg, since 1934. (English.)

The Sunday Times. Weekly, South African Associated Newspapers, Johannesburg, since 1906. (English.)

The Sunday Tribune. Weekly, Argus group, Durban. (English.)

South West Bulletin. Organ of National Union Party, since October 20, 1960. (English, Afrikaans, and German.)

Temple David Review. Monthly, Durban. (English; Reformed Jewish.)

Thought: A Journal of Afrikaans Thinking for English-Speaking. Quarterly, South African Institute of Race Relations, Johannesburg, since 1956. Mimeographed.

UNISA. University of South Africa, Pretoria. Annual.

Werda. Monthly, organ of the National Union Party of South Africa, Johannesburg, since October, 1960. (Afrikaans.)

The Windhoek Advertiser. Daily, Windhoek. (English.)

Woord en Daad. Organ of the Afrikaanse Calvinistiese Bond.

The World. Daily, Johannesburg, since 1932. Originally published as *The Bantu World*. Highest circulation of any Bantu newspaper. (English vernacular; sometimes Afrikaans.)

Zonk. Monthly, Johannesburg, since 1949. A monthly for Africans, patterned after *Drum*. (English.)

Pamphlets, Papers, Reports, Memoranda

Afrikander Bond. *The Birth of the Bond*. Grahamstown: Josiah Slater, 1900.

———. *Constitutie*. Bloemfontein: Orange Free State Newspaper Company, 1885.

———. *Official Documents of the Afrikander Bond and Farmers' Association*. Paarl: D. F. du Toit, 1890.

Afrikander Bond en Boerenvereeniging. *Second Meeting of the Provincial Congress*. Cape Town: Jan Regter, 1884.

ALEXANDER, RAY, and SIMONS, H. J. *Job Reservation and the Trade Unions*. Enterprise: Woodstock, 1959.

All African Convention. *Minutes of the All African Convention, December 1937*. Lovedale: Lovedale Press, 1937.

ALLPORT, G. W. *Prejudice in Modern Perspective*. Johannesburg: South African Institute of Race Relations, 1956.

BALLINGER, WILLIAM GEORGE. *Race and Economics in South Africa*. London: Hogarth Press, 1934.

BARNOUW, ADRIAAN JACOB. *Language and Race Problems in South Africa*. The Hague: M. Nijhoff, 1934.

Basutoland; The Bechuanaland Protectorate and Swaziland: History of Discussions with the Union of South Africa, 1909–1939. London: H.M. Stationery Office, 1952.

Bechuanaland: A General Survey. Johannesburg: South African Institute of Race Relations, 1957.

BERNSTEIN, L. *D-Day for Democracy: Another Crisis Call from the Springbok Legion.* Johannesburg: Springbok Legion, n.d.

BIESHEUVEL, SIMON. *Race, Culture and Personality.* Johannesburg: South African Institute of Race Relations, 1959.

BOSHOFF, FRANZ. *Die Afrikaner en Britse Imperialisme.* Johannesburg: Die Ware Republikein, 1940.

BOUWS, JAN. *Die Afrikaanse Volkslied.* Johannesburg: FAK, 1958.

BRAYSHAW, E. RUSSELL. *The Racial Problems of South Africa.* London: Friends Home Service Committee, 1952.

BROOKES, EDGAR H. *The Bantu in South African Life.* Johannesburg: South African Institute of Race Relations, 1943.

——. *Coming of Age: Studies in South African Citizenship.* Cape Town, 1930.

——. *Things New and Old.* Johannesburg: South African Institute of Race Relations, 1961.

——. *We Come of Age.* Johannesburg: South African Institute of Race Relations, 1950.

BUNTING, BRIAN. *Apartheid—The Road to Poverty.* Cape Town: Real Publishing Company, 1959.

BURGER, J. F. *The Dual-Medium School.* Johannesburg: FAK, 1944.

BUSKES, J. J., JR. *Zuid-Afrika's Apartheidsbeleid: Onaanvaarbaar.* Amsterdam: International Fellowship of Reconciliation, 1956.

Cape of Good Hope. House of Assembly. *Report of the Select Committee on the Afrikander Bond.* Cape Town: Government Printer, 1902.

CARTER, GWENDOLEN M. *South Africa.* New York: Foreign Policy Association, 1955.

CLARK, R. D. *The Native Problem: A Lecture Delivered in the Y.M.C.A. Hall, Maritzburg, 18 May, 1894.* Pietermaritzburg: P. Davis, 1894.

Commonwealth Prime Ministers' Conference. *Official text, March 17, 1961.* New York: British Information Service, 1961.

Communist Party of South Africa. *Die Boer en die Kapitalis.* Johannesburg, n.d.

Congress of the People. *The Freedom Charter adopted by the Congress of the People, Kliptown, South Africa, June 26, 1955.*

COULTER, C. W. A. *Empire Unity, with a Brief Account of the Objects and Work of the Dominion Party of South Africa.* Cape Town, 1944.

Council on African Affairs. *Resistance Against Fascist Enslavement in South Africa.* New York, 1953.

——. *Seeing Is Believing: Here Is the Truth about the Color Bar, Land, Hunger, Poverty and Degradation, Pass System, Labour Exploitation, Racial Oppression in South Africa.* New York, 1947.

DADOO, Y. M. *The Indian People in South Africa: Facts About the Ghetto Act.* Johannesburg: District Committee, 1946.

DAVIS, THOMAS BENJAMIN. *Education and the Interaction of Educational Policies and Race Relations in South Africa.* Johannesburg: South African Institute of Race Relations, 1955.

DE KIEWIET, C. W. *Can Africa Come of Age?* Johannesburg: South African Institute of Race Relations, 1960.

DELIUS, ANTHONY. 'The Afrikaners and the Suffering Majority', *The Reporter,* January 9, 1958.

DE WET NEL, M. D. C. *Industrial Development in Peripheral Areas.* Pretoria: Information Service of the Department of Bantu Administration and Development, 1960.

Die Afrikaner Party. *Program van Beginsels en Konstitusie.* Johannesburg, 1948.

Die Ossewa-Brandwag. *Konstitusie.* Bloemfontein: Die Ossewa-Brandwag, n.d.

Die Suidwes-Party. *Konstitusie.* Windhoek: Windhoek Printing Works, n.d.

Dominion Party of South Africa. *Programme of Principles of the Dominion Party of South Africa.* Cape Town, n.d.

DUNDAS, SIR CHARLES C. F. *South-West Africa: The Factual Background.* Cape Town: South African Institute of International Affairs, 1946.

DU PLESSIS, LOUIS J. *Letters of a Farmer.* Krugersdorp, 1951.

DU PLESSIS, OTTO. *Die Nuwe Suid Afrika.* Bloemfontein: Nationalist Party, 1940.

——. 'The New South Africa.' *The British Africa Monthly*, September, 1948.

DU PLESSIS, WENTZEL C. *Highway to Harmony: A Report on Relationships in South Africa.* New York: Information Service of South Africa, 1958.

——. *Special Report on Economic Trends and Policies.* New York: Information Service of South Africa, 1960.

DURRANT, J. T., AND OTHERS. *The U.P. Speaks.* Johannesburg: U.P. Witwatersrand General Council, 1960.

The Dutch Reformed Churches in South Africa and the Problem of Race Relations. Johannesburg: South African Institute of Race Relations, 1956.

Dutch Reformed Conference of Church Leaders. *Christian Principles in Multi-Racial South Africa: A Report.* Pretoria, 1953.

The Education League. *Blackout: A Commentary on the Education Policy of the Institut vir Christelik-Nasionale Onderwys.* Johannesburg, 1959.

EISELEN, W. W. M. *The Native in the Western Cape.* Stellenbosch: South African Bureau of Racial Affairs, 1955.

Federasie van Afrikaanse Kultuurvereniging. *FAK-jaarverslag, 1 April 1958–31 Maart 1959.* Johannesburg, 1959.

——. *FAK-jaarverslag, Taalfeesjaar 1959–1960 en Program vir 15 de FAK-Kongres, 28 en 29 September 1960, Pretoria.* Johannesburg, 1960.

——. *Program vir die Veertiende Tweejaarlikse Kongres (1958) en Jaarverslag, 1 April 1957 tot 31 Maart 1958.* Johannesburg, 1958.

——. *Referate Gelewer by Geleentheid van die Veertiende Tweejaarlikse Kongres van die FAK, 1–2 October 1958, Bloemfontein.* Johannesburg, 1958.

——. *Republikeinse Dankfees 15 October 1960.* Johannesburg, 1960.

——. *Taalfees Die Wonder van Afrikaans, Voortrekker-Amfiteater, Pretoria, 30 Mei 1959.* Johannesburg, 1959.

——. *Verslag van die Werksaamhede van die FAK 1 April 1956 tot 31 Maart 1957.* Johannesburg, 1957.

FERGUSON-DAVIE, C. J. BISHOP. *The Early History of Indians in Natal.* Johannesburg: South African Institute of Race Relations, 1951.

FICK, ALBERT. 'South Africa's Klu Klux Klan', *MacLean's*, February 1, 1952.

FINDLAY, GEORGE. *Miscegenation.* Pretoria: J. L. van Schaik, 1937.

FIRST, RUTH. *Exposure! The Farm Labour Scandal.* Johannesburg: New Age, 1959.

FORMAN, LIONEL. *Black and White in South African History.* Johannesburg: Real Publishing Company, 1960.

——. *Chapters in the History of the March to Freedom.* Cape Town: Real Printing and Publishing Company, 1959.

FOUCHÉ, LEO (comp.). *Report on the Outbreak of the Rebellion, and the Policy of the Government with Regard to Its Suppression.* Pretoria: Government Printer, 1915.

FRANZ, G. H., AND OTHERS. *Bantu Education—Oppression or Opportunity?* Stellenbosch: South African Bureau of Racial Affairs, 1955.

Freedom of the Press Committee. *Press Freedom Is the Life Blood of Democracy.*
Cape Town: Pioneer Press, 1952.

*God's Kingdom in Multi-Racial South Africa: Report on the Inter-Racial Conference of
Church Leaders.* Johannesburg: South African Institute of Race Relations, 1955.

HARRIS, E. E. *'White' Civilisation.* Johannesburg: South African Institute of
Race Relations, 1952.

HARTSHORME, K. B. *Native Education in the Union of South Africa: A Summary of
the Report of the Commission on Native Education in South Africa.* Johannesburg:
South African Institute of Race Relations, 1953.

HELLMAN, ELLEN. *Racial Laws vs. Economic and Social Forces.* Johannesburg:
South African Institute of Race Relations, 1955.

———. *A Sociological Survey of an African Commercial Labour Force.* Johannesburg: South African Institute of Race Relations, 1953.

HEPPLE, ALEX. *The African Worker in South Africa: A Study in Trade Unionism.*
London: The Africa Bureau, n.d.

———. *Censorship and Press Control in South Africa.* Johannesburg, 1960.

———. *Poverty Wages.* Johannesburg: Wages Committee, 1959.

———. *A Trade Union Guide for South African Workers.* Johannesburg: South
African Congress of Trade Unions, 1957.

———. *Trade Unions in Travail.* Johannesburg: Unity Publications, 1954.

Herenigde Nasionale Party. *Konsep—Grondwet van die Republiek.* Pretoria:
Voortrekkerpers Beperk, 1942.

HOFMEYR, JAN HENDRIK. *Christian Principles and Race Problems.* Johannesburg:
South African Institute of Race Relations, 1945.

HOLLOWAY, JOHN E. 'Africa: Ideology or Realism?' An address given in
November, 1957, to the Oxford University Southern Africa Association.

———. *The Problems of Race Relations in South Africa.* New York: South Africa
Information Office, n.d.

HONEYBALL, GEORGE. *A Brief Autobiography.* Johannesburg: Juta, 1936.

HORRELL, MURIEL. *The Group Areas Act: Its Effect on Human Beings.* Johannesburg: South African Institute of Race Relations, 1956.

———. *Non-European Policies in the Union and the Measure of Their Success: A Survey
of the Conflict Between Economic Trends and Ideological Planning.* Johannesburg:
South African Institute of Race Relations, 1954.

———. *An Outline of the Systems of Government and Political Status of Non-European
People in Africa South of Sahara.* Johannesburg: South African Institute of
Race Relations, 1953.

———. *Political Status of Non-Europeans in Southern Africa.* Johannesburg:
South African Institute of Race Relations, 1953.

———. *Race Classification in South Africa: Its Effect on Human Beings.* ('Fact
Paper', No. 2.) Johannesburg: South African Institute of Race Relations,
1952.

———. *Racialism and the Trade Unions.* Johannesburg: South African Institute
of Race Relations, 1959.

———. *South Africa's Nonwhite Workers.* Johannesburg: South African Institute of Race Relations, 1956.

HOUGHTON, D. HOBART. *Life in the Ciskei.* Johannesburg: South African
Institute of Race Relations, 1955.

———. *The Tomlinson Report: A Summary of the Findings and Recommendations in the
Tomlinson Commission Report.* Johannesburg: South African Institute of Race
Relations, 1956.

HOUSER, GEORGE M. *Non-Violent Revolution in South Africa.* New York: Fellowship Publications, 1953.

HUGH, JOHN. 'South Africa after Fifty Years', *The Christian Science Monitor*, August 20, 1959.

India Information Services. *World Opinion on Apartheid.* New Delhi, 1952.

Indian Life and Labour in Natal: A Survey. Johannesburg: South African Institute of Race Relations, 1952.

International African Institute. *Social Implications of Industrialization and Urbanization in Africa South of Sahara.* Paris: United Nations Educational, Scientific and Cultural Organization, 1956.

International Court of Justice. *International Status of South-West Africa: Advisory Opinion of July 11, 1950.* Leyden: A. W. Sijthoff, 1950.

JABAVU, D. D. T. (ed.). *Minutes of the All African Convention, June 1936.* Lovedale: Lovedale Press, 1936.

JANSEN, ERNEST GEORGE. *Native Policy of the Union of South Africa: Statements Made on 20 April 1950 and 19 May 1950.* Pretoria: State Information Office, 1950.

Joint Passive Resistance Council. *Five Months of Struggle: A Brief Account of the Passive Resistance Struggle from 13 June–13 November 1946.* Durban, 1946.

JONES, J. D. RHEINALLT. *The Administration of South West Africa.* Johannesburg: South African Institute of Race Relations, 1952.

———. *At the Crossroads.* Johannesburg: South African Institute of Race Relations, 1953.

———. *The Future of South West Africa.* Johannesburg: South African Institute of Race Relations, 1946.

———. *The Union's Burden of Poverty.* Johannesburg: South African Institute of Race Relations, 1942.

JOOSTE, C. P. *South Africa: Planned Policy of Chaos.* New York: Union of South Africa State Information Office, 1952.

JUNOD, VIOLAINE I. 'U.S. South and South Africa', *The Christian Century*, February 11, 1959.

KARIS, THOMAS G. 'Treason in South Africa', *Political Science Quarterly*, June, 1961.

KEET, B. B. *The Ethics of Apartheid.* Johannesburg: South African Institute of Race Relations, 1957.

KEPPEL-JONES, ARTHUR. *The Dilemma of South Africa.* Toronto: Canadian Institute of International Affairs, 1950.

———. *Race or Civilisation.* Johannesburg: South African Institute of Race Relations, 1951.

KOTZÉ, J. G. *An Appeal to the Inhabitants of the South Africa Republic by J. G. Kotzé.* Pretoria: John Keith, 1898.

KRUGER, JANNIE. *Kultuur in die Republiek.* Johannesburg: FAK, 1960.

The Law and You! Johannesburg: Real Publishing Company, 1957.

League for the Maintenance of Democracy. *The Communist Bogey.* Johannesburg: W. R. Kilok, n.d.

———. *Suid Afrika se Gevaar.* Johannesburg: Commercial Printing Company, n.d.

LE ROUX, T. H. *Vyftig Jaar Afrikaans.* Johannesburg: FAK, 1955.

LEWIN, JULIUS. 'No Revolution Round the Corner', *Africa South*, October–December, 1958.

LOUW, ERIC H. *Changing Continent: South Africa's Role in Africa.* New York: Information Service of South Africa, 1959.

LUTHULI, CHIEF A. J. *Freedom Is the Apex.* Johannesburg: South African Congress of Democrats, n.d.

MACCRONE, IAN DOUGLAS. *Group Conflicts and Race Prejudices.* Johannesburg: South African Institute of Race Relations, 1947.

MACMILLAN, W. *African Beyond the Union.* Johannesburg: South African Institute of Race Relations, 1949.

MACVICAR, NEIL. *Western Civilization and the Bantu.* Johannesburg: South African Institute of Race Relations, 1947.

MALAN, DANIEL F. *Apartheid: South Africa's Answer to a Major Problem: Letter from Dr D. F. Malan . . . to The Reverend John Piersma . . . Grand Rapids, Michigan.* Pretoria: State Information Office, 1954.

———. *Common Ground for National Unity: Message Delivered by Dr Malan at the Opening of the Congress of the Natal National Party in Durban, September 19, 1955.* Cape Town: National Party, Information Committee, 1955.

———. *The Draft Constitution for a Republic,* 1942.

———. *Foreign Policy of the Union of South Africa.* Pretoria: State Information Office, 1950.

———. 'Why South Africans Want Strict Segregation', *U.S. News and World Report,* April 16, 1954.

MALHERBE, ERNEST GIDEON. *Race Attitudes and Education.* Johannesburg: South African Institute of Race Relations, 1946.

MARQUARD, LEO. *South Africa's Colonial Policy.* Johannesburg: South African Institute of Race Relations, 1957.

———. *South Africa's Internal Boundaries.* Johannesburg: South African Institute of Race Relations, 1958.

MARTIN, A. C. *History in Our Schools: Mutual Respect or Antagonism.* Durban: A. C. Martin, 1953.

MATTHEWS, ZACHARIAH K. 'South Africa: A Land Divided Against Itself', *The Yale Review,* June, 1953.

Memorandum Submitted to the Tenth Delimitation Commission, 1952, on Behalf of the War Veterans' Torch Commando. Johannesburg, 1952. (Known also as the *Suzman Report.*)

MEZERIK, A. G. (ed.). *Apartheid in the Union of South Africa.* New York: International Review Service, 1960.

MILLER, H. (comp.). *What Is Nationalist Party Policy for Eighteen-Year-Olds and Under?* Pretoria: Wallachs, n.d.

MOLTENO, DONALD B. *The Assault on Our Liberties: The State of Civil Rights in South Africa.* Johannesburg: South African Institute of Race Relations, 1959.

———. *The Betrayal of 'Natives' Representation'.* Johannesburg: South African Institute of Race Relations, 1959.

———. *Fifty Years of Union.* Johannesburg: South African Institute of Race Relations, 1960.

MSIMANG, H. SELBY. *The Crisis.* All African Convention, 1936.

The Multi-Racial Conference of South Africa. *South Africa's Multi-Racial Conference—A new approach to Race Relations: Held at University of Witwatersrand 3–5 December 1957.* Johannesburg: The Planning Committee, 1957.

MUNGER, EDWIN S. *Letters and Reports from Africa.* New York: American Universities Field Staff, 1950–60.

NAICKER, G. M. (comp.). *A Historical Synopsis of the Indian Question in South Africa*. Durban: Anti-Segregation Council, 1945.

Natal Education Department. *Natal Education, 1849–1949: Then and Now*. Pietermaritzburg, 1949.

National Coloured-European Conference. *First National Coloured-European Conference: Report of Proceedings, Cape Town, June 26–28, 1933*. Cape Town: Atlas Printing Works, 1933.

National European-Bantu Conference. *Report of the National European-Bantu Conference, Cape Town, February 6–9, 1929*. Lovedale: Lovedale Institution Press, 1929.

National Party of South Africa. *Die Gevaar*. Bloemfontein, n.d.

———. *The Facts: Replies to Slogans and Allegations of the United Party*. Bloemfontein, n.d.

———. *The National Party's Colour Policy*. Cape Town, 1947.

———. *The Social and Economic Policy of the Nationalist Party*. Bloemfontein, 1944.

———. Federal Council. *The Republican Order: Future Policy of the Party as Set Out by Dr Malan*. Bloemfontein, 1941.

———. Information Service. *Advent of the Republic*. Bloemfontein, 1960.

———. *Commonwealth Relations: Membership of South Africa*. Bloemfontein, 1960.

———. *Die feite ant woorde op SAP-Stories*. Bloemfontein, 1956.

———. *Masjinerie en Prosedure by die Volkstemming*. Bloemfontein, 1960.

———. *Separate Development: 'Apartheid'*. Bloemfontein, 1960.

National Party of the Transvaal. *Programme of Principles and Constitution*. Johannesburg, n.d.

National Union Party. *The Aims of the National Union*. Johannesburg, 1960.

National Union of South African Students. *The African in the Universities*. Cape Town, 1951.

———. *The African in the Universities*. Cape Town, 1954.

The Native Laws Amendment Bill: Its Effect on Religious and Other Freedoms. Johannesburg: South African Institute of Race Relations, 1957.

NAUDE, W. C. *South Africa and Western Society*. New York: Information Service of South Africa, 1961.

Nederduits Gereformeerde Kerk. *Fundamental Principles of Calvinist Christian Political Science*. Johannesburg, 1951.

NGCOBO, SELLEY BANGANI. *The Bantu Peoples*. New York: Columbia University Press, 1953.

NGUBANE, JORDON K. *Should the Natives' Representative Council Be Abolished?* Cape Town: African Bookman, 1946.

NICHOLLS, G. HEATON. *Greater South Africa: A Political Survey*. Cowies Hill, 1953.

———. *Native Policy of the Union of South Africa*. New York: Union of South Africa State Information Office, 1945.

NICHOLSON, MARJORIE. *Self Government and the Communal Problem*. London: Fabian Publications, 1948.

Non-European Unity Movement. *The Boycott as Weapon of Struggle*. Cape Town, 1952.

OLIVIER, N. J. J. *Apartheid—A Slogan or a Solution?* Stellenbosch: South African Bureau of Racial Affairs, 1954.

PALMER, MABEL, KUPER, HILDA, AND OTHERS. *The Indian as a South African: A Symposium*. Johannesburg: South African Institute of Race Relations, 1956.

CLOETE, STUART. *The African Giant: The Story of a Journey.* Boston: Houghton Mifflin, 1955.

———. *The Turning Wheels.* Boston: Houghton Mifflin, 1937.

COETZEE, J. ALBERT. *Politieke Groepering in die Wording van die Afrikanernasie, ens.* Johannesburg: Voortrekkerpers, 1941.

COETZEE, J. CHRIS. *Onderwys in Transvaal, 1838–1937.* Pretoria: Van Schaik, 1941.

COHEN, SIR ANDREW. *British Policy in Changing Africa.* London: Routledge and Kegan Paul, 1959. Evanston: Northwestern University Press, 1959.

COHEN, LOUIS. *Reminiscences of Johannesburg and London.* London: Robert Holden, 1924.

COLE, MONICA M. *South Africa.* London: Methuen, 1961. New York: Dutton, 1961.

COLENSO, JOHN WILLIAM. *Ten Weeks in Natal: A Journal of a First Tour of Visitation Among the Colonists and Zulu Kafirs of Natal.* Cambridge: Macmillan, 1855.

COLQUHOUN, ARCHIBALD R. *The Africander Land.* London: J. Murray, 1906.

COLVIN, IAN D. *The Life of Jameson.* London: E. Arnold, 1923.

CONSIDINE, JOHN J. *Africa: World of New Men.* New York: Dodd, Mead, 1954.

COOK, E. T. *Rights and Wrongs of the Transvaal War.* London: Edward Arnold, 1902.

COOK, PETER ALAN WILSON. *The Education of a South African Tribe.* Cape Town: Juta, 1934.

COOKSON, JOHN. *Before the African Storm.* Indianapolis: Bobbs-Merrill, 1954.

COPE, JACK. *The Golden Oriole.* London: Heinemann, 1958.

COPE, R. K. *Comrade Bill: The Life and Times of W. H. Andrews, Workers' Leader.* Cape Town: Stewart, 1944.

CORY, SIR GEORGE E. *The Rise of South Africa: A History of the Origin of South African Colonization and Its Development Toward the East from the Earliest Times to 1857.* 4 vols. London: Longmans, Green, 1910–26.

COTTON, WALTER A. *Racial Segregation in South Africa.* London: Sheldon, 1931.

———. *The Race Problem in South Africa.* London: Student Christian Movement, 1926.

COUPLAND, R. *Zulu Battle Piece: Isandhlwana.* London: Collins, 1948.

COWEN, D. V. *The Foundations of Freedom: With Special Reference to Southern Africa.* Cape Town: Oxford University Press, 1961.

CRAFFORD, F. S. *Jan Smuts: A Biography.* Garden City, N.Y.: Doubleday, Doran, 1944.

CRAIG, DENNIS B. *Lost Opportunity: A History of the Federal Movement in South Africa.* Durban: Central News Agency, n.d.

CRESWICKE, LOUIS. *South Africa and the Transvaal War.* 6 vols. Edinburgh: T. C. and E. C. Jack, 1901–2.

CRIPPS, ARTHUR S. *Africa for Africans: A Plea on Behalf of Territorial Segregation Areas and of Their Freedom in a South African Colony.* London: Longmans, Green, 1923.

CRON, GRETCHEN. *The Roaring Veldt.* New York: Putnam, 1930.

CRONJÉ, G. *Voogdyskap en Apartheid.* Pretoria: J. L. van Schaik, 1948.

CROWE, JOHN HENRY V. *General Smuts Campaign in East Africa.* London: J. Murray, 1918.

CURTIS, LIONEL. *With Milner in South Africa.* Oxford: Blackwell, 1951.

DARMSTAEDTER, PAUL. *Geschichte der Aufteilung und Kolonisation Afrikas seit dem Zeitalter der Entdeckungen.* 2 vols. Vol. I, Berlin: G. J. Goschen, 1913; Vol. II, Berlin, Vereinigung wissenschaftlicher verlegen, 1920.

DAVIDSON, BASIL. *The African Awakening.* London: Jonathan Cape, 1955. New York: Macmillan, 1955.

———. *The Lost Cities of Africa.* Boston: Little Brown, 1959.

———. *Old Africa Rediscovered: The Story of Africa's Forgotten Past.* London: Gollancz, 1960.

———. *Report on Southern Africa.* London: Jonathan Cape, 1952.

DAVIES, HORTON, and SHEPHERD, R. H. W. (comps.). *South African Missions, 1800–1950.* London: Nelson, 1954.

DAVIS, ALEXANDER. *The Native Problem in South Africa.* London: Chapman and Hall, 1903.

DAVIS, GORDON, MELUNSKY, L., and DU RANDT, F. B. *Urban Native Law.* Port Elizabeth: Grotins Publications, 1960.

DAWSON, WILLIAM HARBUTT. *South Africa: Peoples, Places, and Problems.* London: Longmans, Green, 1925.

DE BEER, Z. J. *Multi-Racial South Africa: The Reconciliation of Forces.* London: Oxford University Press, 1961.

DE BLIJ, HARM J. *Africa South.* Evanston: Northwestern University Press, 1962.

DE KIEWIET, CORNELIS W. *The Anatomy of South African Misery.* London: Oxford University Press, 1956.

———. *British Colonial Policy and the South African Republics, 1848–72.* London: Longmans, Green, 1929.

———. *A History of South Africa, Social and Economic.* London: Oxford University Press, 1941.

———. *The Imperial Factor in South Africa.* Cambridge: The University Press, 1937.

DE KOCK, GERHARD. *A History of the South African Reserve Bank (1920–1952).* Pretoria: J. L. van Schaik, 1954.

DE KOCK, M. H. *The Economic Development of South Africa.* London: P. S. King, 1936.

———. *Economic History of South Africa.* Cape Town: Juta, 1924.

DE KOCK, VICTOR. *Ons Erfenis (Our Heritage).* Cape Town: Nasionale Boek-handel Beperk, 1960.

———. *Those in Bondage.* Cape Town: Timmins, 1950.

DE LA CAILLE, N. L. *Journal Historique du Voyage fait au Cap de Bonne-Espérance.* Paris: Guillyn, 1763.

DELIUS, ANTHONY. *The Young Traveller in South Africa.* London: Phoenix House, 1947.

DEPPE, LUDWIG. *Mit Lettow-Vorbeck durch Afrika.* Berlin: August Scherl, 1921.

DE RENS, G. C. KLERK. *Geschichtlicher Ueberblick der administratwen, rechtlichen und finanziellen.* Entwicklung der Niederländisch-Ostindischen Compagnie.

DEVITT, NAPIER. *The Concentration Camps in South Africa.* Pietermaritzburg, Shuter and Shooter, 1941.

———. *People and Places: Sketches from South African History,* Cape Town: Unie-Volkspers, 1944.

DE WET, CHRISTIAN RUDOLF. *Three Years' War.* New York: Scribner's, 1902.

Die Nasionale Jeugbond van Transvaal. *Gedenkalbum oor die eerste tien jaar van bestaan van die Nasionale Jeugbond van Transvaal.* Johannesburg: Voortrek-kerpers Beperk, 1950.

DISON, L. R., and MOHAMED, I. *Group Areas and Their Development.* Durban, 1960.

DOXEY, G. V. *The Industrial Colour Bar in South Africa.* Cape Town: Oxford University Press, 1960.

DOYLE, SIR ARTHUR CONAN. *The Great Boer War.* London: Nelson, 1903.

———. *The War in South Africa: Its Cause and Conduct.* London: Smith, Elder, 1902.

DUNDAS, SIR CHARLES, and ASHTON, HUGH. *Problem Territories of Southern Africa: Basutoland, Bechuanaland Protectorate, Swaziland.* Cape Town: South African Institute of International Affairs, 1952.

DU PLESSIS, IZAK D. *The Cape Malays.* Cape Town: Miller, 1944.

———, and LÜCKHOFF, C. A. *The Malay Quarter and Its People.* Cape Town: A. A. Balkema, 1953.

DU PLESSIS, JOHANNES. *History of Christian Missions in South Africa.* Cape Town: Juta, 1912.

———. *The Life of Andrew Murray of South Africa.* Cape Town: Marshall Brothers, 1919.

DU PREEZ, A. B. *Inside the South African Crucible.* Cape Town: Hollands-Afrikaanse Uitgewers-Maatskappy, 1959.

DU TOIT, P. S. *Onderwys oon die Kaap Onder die Bataafse Republiek, 1803–1806.* Pretoria: Van Schaik, 1944.

DU VAL, CHARLES. *With a Show Through Southern Africa, and Personal Reminiscences of the Transvaal War.* 2 vols. London: Tinsley Brothers, 1882.

DVORIN, EUGENE P. *Racial Separation in South Africa: An Analysis of Apartheid Theory.* Chicago: University of Chicago Press, 1952.

EDWARDS, ISOBEL E. *The 1820 Settlers in South Africa: A Study in British Colonial Policy.* London: Longmans, Green, 1934.

ELLENBERGER, D. F. *History of the Basuto, Ancient and Modern.* London: Caxton, 1912.

EMDEN, PAUL HERMAN. *Randlords.* London: Hodder and Stoughton, 1935.

ENGELBRECHT, S. P. *Thomas François Burgers: A Biography.* Pretoria: de Bussy, 1946.

ENGELENBURG, FRANS V. *General Louis Botha.* London: G. G. Harrap, 1929.

EVANS, IFOR L. *Native Policy in Southern Africa.* New York: Macmillan, 1934.

EVANS, M. S. *Black and White in South East Africa:* A Study in Sociology. London: Longmans, Green, 1916.

EYBERS, GEORGE. *Select Constitutional Documents Illustrating South African History, 1795–1910.* New York: Dutton, 1918.

FAGAN, H. A. *Our Responsibility: A Discussion of South Africa's Racial Problems.* Stellenbosch: Die Universiteits-Uitgewers en Boekhandelaars, 1960.

FAIRBRIDGE, DOROTHEA. *A History of South Africa.* London: Oxford University Press, 1918.

———. *The Pilgrim's Way in South Africa.* London: Oxford University Press, 1928.

FARRELLY, MICHAEL JAMES. *The Settlement after the South African War.* London: Macmillan, 1900.

FARSON, NEGLEY. *Behind God's Back.* New York: Harcourt, Brace, 1941.

———. *Last Chance in Africa.* London: Gollancz, 1953.

FEIT, EDWARD. *South Africa: The Dynamics of the African National Congress.* London: Oxford University Press, 1962.

FERGUSON, JOHN H. *American Diplomacy and the Boer War.* Philadelphia: University of Pennsylvania, 1939.

FFOLLIOTT, PAMELA, and CROFT, E. L. H. *One Titan at a Time: The Story of John Paterson of Port Elizabeth, South Africa, and His Time.* Cape Town: Timmins, 1960.

FILMER, HARRY J., and PARRY, CONSTANCE. *Reefs of Fortune*. Johannesburg: Central News Agency, 1958.

FISCHER, LOUIS. *The Life of Mahatma Gandhi*. New York: Harper, 1950.

FISHER, WILLIAM E. G. *The Transvaal and the Boers: A short history of the South African republic, with a Chapter on the Orange Free State*. London: Chapman and Hall, 1900.

FITZPATRICK, JAMES PERCY. *Jock of the Bushveld*. London: Longmans, Green, 1907.

——. *South African Memories*. London: Cassell, 1932.

——. *The Transvaal from Within: A Private Record of Public Affairs*. London: Heinemann, 1899.

FLAVIN, MARTIN. *Black and White: From the Cape to the Congo*. New York: Harper, 1950.

FORBES, CAPTAIN DAVID. *My Life in South Africa: A Narrative of 70 Years Pioneering in Mid-East Africa*. London: H. F. and G. Witherby, 1938.

FORMAN, LIONEL, and SACHS, EMIL SOLLY. *The South African Treason Trial*. London: John Calder, 1957.

FORT, GEORGE SEYMOUR. *Alfred Beit: A Study of the Man and His Work*. London: I. Nicholson and Watson, 1932.

FORTES, M., and EVANS-PRITCHARD, E. E. *African Political Systems*. London: Oxford University Press, 1940.

FRACK, ISADORE. *A South African Doctor Looks Backwards—and Forwards*. Johannesburg: Central News Agency, 1943.

FRANKEN, J. L. M. *Piet Retief se Lewe in die Kolonie*. Pretoria: de Bussy, 1949.

FRANKLIN, J. S. *This Union: Selected Addresses*. Cape Town: Stewart, 1949.

FRANKLIN, N. N. *Economics in South Africa*. Cape Town: Oxford University Press, 1954.

FRENCH, GERALD. *Lord Chelmsford and the Zulu War*. London: J. Lane, 1939.

FULLER, BASIL. *South Africa—Not Guilty?* London: Jarrolds, 1957.

FULLER, CLAUDE. *Louis Trigardt's Trek across the Drakensberg, 1837–1838*. Cape Town: van Riebeeck Society, 1932.

FYFE, HENRY HAMILTON. *South Africa Today: With an Account of Modern Rhodesia*. London: G. Bell, 1911.

GALE, W. D. *Heritage of Rhodes*. London: Oxford University Press, 1950.

GALTON, FRANCIS. *The Narrative of an Explorer in Tropical South Africa*. London: J. Murray, 1853.

GANDHI, MOHANDUS KARAMCHAND. *Satyagraha in South Africa*. Madras: S. Ganesan, 1928.

GARDINER, CAPTAIN ALLEN F. *Narrative of a Journey to the Zoolu Country in South Africa . . . Undertaken in 1835*. London: William Crofts, 1836.

GARVIN, J. L. *The Life of Joseph Chamberlain*. 4 vols. London: Macmillan, 1932–51.

GATTI, ATTILIO. *Here Is the Veld*. New York: Scribner's, 1948.

GEEN, MAURICE STEADMAN. *The Making of South Africa*. Cape Town: Maskew Miller, 1960.

——. *The Making of the Union of South Africa: A Brief History, 1487–1939*. New York: Longmans, Green, 1946.

GERARD, FRANCIS. *Springbok Rampant*. London: F. Muller, 1951.

GERDENER, GUSTAV B. A. *Recent Developments in the South African Mission Field*. London: Marshall Morgan and Scott, 1958.

——. *Studies in the Evangelisation of South Africa*. London: Longmans, Green, 1911.

GEY VAN PITTUIS, E. F. W. *Staatsopvattings van die Voortrekkers en die Boere.* Pretoria: Van Schaik, 1941.

GEYSER, A. S., AND OTHERS. *Vertraagde aksi.* Pretoria: N. G. Kerkboekhandel, 1960. (Published also in English under the title *Delayed Action.*)

GIBBS, HENRY. *Africa on a Tightrope.* London: Jarrolds, 1954.

———. *Background to Bitterness: The Story of South Africa, 1652–1954.* London: F. Muller, 1954.

———. *Twilight in South Africa.* London: Jarrolds, 1950.

GIBBS, PETER. *Death of the Last Republic: The Story of the Anglo-Boer War.* London: F. Muller, 1957.

GIE, STEFANUS F. N. *Geskiedenis van Suid-Afrika.* 2 vols. Stellenbosch: Pro-Ecclesia, 1942.

GLUCKMAN, MAX. *Custom and Conflict in Africa.* Oxford: Blackwell, 1955.

GODEE-MOLSBERGEN, EVERHARDUS C. *De Stichter van Hollands Zuid Afrika.*

GOLDSWAIN, JEREMIAH. *The Chronicle of Jeremiah Goldswain, Albany Settler of 1820.* 2 vols. Cape Town: van Riebeeck Society, 1946–49.

GOLLOCK, GEORGINA A. *Sons of Africa.* London: Student Christian Movement, 1928.

———. *Lives of Eminent Africans.* Cape Town: Longmans, Green, 1928.

GOODFELLOW, DAVID MARTIN. *A Modern Economic History of South Africa.* London: G. Routledge, 1931.

GOOLD-ADAMS, RICHARD JOHN MORTON. *South Africa Today and Tomorrow.* London: J. Murray, 1936.

GORDON-BROWN, A. (ed.). *Year Book and Guide to Southern Africa.* London: Robert Hale, annual since 1893.

GOULD, VERA BUCHANAN. *Not Without Honour: The Life and Writings of Olive Schreiner.* Cape Town: Hutchinson, 1948.

GRAY, REVEREND CHARLES (ed.). *Life of Robert Gray: Bishop of Cape Town and Metropolitan of Africa.* 2 vols. Oxford: Rivingtons, 1876.

GRAY, JAMES. *Payable Gold: An Intimate Record of the History of the Discovery of the Payable Witwatersrand Gold Fields and of Johannesburg in 1886 and 1887.* Johannesburg: Central News Agency, 1937.

GREAVES, LIONEL B. *The High Commission Territories: Basutoland, the Bechuanaland Protectorate, and Swaziland.* London: Edinburgh House Press, 1954.

GREEN, GEORGE A. L. *An Editor Looks Back: South African and Other Memories, 1883–1946.* Cape Town: Juta, 1947.

GREEN, LAWRENCE G. *The Coast of Treasure.* London: Putnam, 1933.

———. *In the Land of Afternoon.* Cape Town: Timmins, 1949.

———. *Karoo: The Story of the Karoos of South Africa.* Cape Town: Timmins, 1955.

———. *Lords of the Last Frontier: The Story of South West Africa and Its People of All Races.* London: S. Paul, 1953.

———. *Old Africa Untamed.* London, S. Paul, 1940.

———. *So Few Are Free.* Cape Town: Timmins, 1946.

———. *Tavern of the Seas.* Cape Town: Timmins, 1947.

———. *To the River's End.* Cape Town: Timmins, 1948.

———. *Where Men Still Dream.* Cape Town: Timmins, 1945.

GREGORY, SIR THEODORE. *Ernest Oppenheimer and the Economic Development of Southern Africa.* London: Oxford University Press, 1962.

GREY, RIGHT REVEREND ROBERT. *Journals of Two Visitations in 1848 and 1850 by . . . Lord Bishop of Cape Town.* London: Society for Promoting Christian Knowledge, 1852.

GREYLING, E. *Christelike en Nasionale Onderwys*. 2 vols. Cape Town: Nasionale Boekhandel, 1941.

————. *Godsdiensonderwys in die skool*. Bloemfontein: Sondagskooldepot, 1946.

GROSS, FELIX. *Rhodes of Africa*. New York: Frederick A. Praeger, 1957.

GUNTHER, JOHN. *Inside Africa*. New York: Harper, 1955.

————. *Meet South Africa*. New York: Harper, 1958.

GUTHRIE, F. H. *Frontier Magistrate: Reminiscences*. Cape Town: Stewart, 1946.

————. *Little Misadventures*. Cape Town: Stewart, 1949.

HAARHOFF, THEODORE J. *Afrikaans: Its Origin and Development*. Oxford: Clarendon Press, 1936.

HAGGARD, H. RIDER. *The Last Boer War*. London: Kegan Paul, Trench, Trübner, 1899.

HAHLO, H. R., and KAHN, ELLISON. *The Union of South Africa: The Development of Its Laws and Constitution*. London: Stevens, 1960.

HAIGH, SCOTT. *Strangers May Be Present*. London: G. Allen and Unwin, 1951.

HAILEY, LORD WILLIAM MALCOLM. *An African Survey: A Study of Problems Arising in Africa South of Sahara*. London: Oxford University Press, 1954.

HALFORD, SAMUEL JAMES. *The Griquas of Griqualand: A Historical Narrative of the Griqua People: Their Rise, Progress and Decline*. Cape Town: Juta, 1949.

HAMILTON, CHARLES. *Sketches of Life and Sport in South Eastern Africa*. London: Chapman and Hall, 1870.

HANCE, GERTRUDE RACHEL. *The Zulu Yesterday and Today: Twenty-Nine Years in South Africa*. New York: Fleming, *c.* 1916.

HANCOCK, WILLIAM KEITH. *Smuts*. 2 vols. (Vol. I, 'The Sanguine Years, 1870–1919.') New York: Cambridge University Press, 1963.

————. *Survey of British Commonwealth Affairs*. 2 vols. London: Oxford University Press, 1937–42.

HANNA, ALEXANDER J. *The Story of the Rhodesias and Nyasaland*. London: Faber and Faber, 1960.

HARDING, REX. *South African Cinderella: A trek Through ex-German West Africa*. London: H. Jenkins, 1937.

HARMSWORTH, C. B. *Pleasure and Problem in South Africa*. London: J. Lane, 1908.

HARRISON, W. H. *Memoirs of a Socialist in South Africa*. Cape Town, 1947.

HATCH, JOHN C. *The Dilemma of South Africa*. London: Dobson, 1952.

HATTERSLEY, ALAN FREDERICK. *The British Settlement of Natal: A Study in Imperial Migration*. Cambridge: The University Press, 1950.

————. *Later Annals of Natal*. London: Longmans, Green, 1938.

————. *The Natalians: Further Annals of Natal*. Pietermaritzburg: Shuter and Shooter, 1940.

————. *Portrait of a Colony: The Story of Natal*. Cambridge: The University Press, 1940.

————. *South Africa, 1652–1933*. London: Butterworth, 1933.

HAYTHORNTHWAITE, FRANK. *All the Way to Abenab*. London: Faber and Faber, 1956.

HEADLAM, CECIL (ed.). *The Milner Papers: South Africa*. 2 vols. London: Cassell, 1931–3.

HELANDER, GUNNAR. *Big City Zulu*. (Trans. by Margery Osberg.) Rock Island, Illinois: Augustana Press, 1957.

HELLMAN, HELEN (ed.). *Handbook on Race Relations in South Africa*. Cape Town: Oxford University Press, 1949.

HENDERSON, R. H. *An Ulsterman in Africa.* Cape Town: Unie-Volkspers, 1944.

HENOCHSBERG, A. J. *An Old Stager's Memories.* Johannesburg: Central News Agency, 1933.

HENSHILWOOD, N. G. *All These under a Summer Sun.* Cape Town: Koston, 1947.

HERBSTEIN, JOSEPH, AND OTHERS. *The Civil Practice of the Superior Courts in South Africa.* Cape Town: Juta, 1954.

HETTEMA, H. *De Nederlandse Stam in Zuid-Afrika.* Zutphen: W. J. Thieme, 1949.

HIEMSTRA, V. G. *The Group Areas Act.* Cape Town: Juta, 1953.

HILLEGAS, HOWARD CLEMENS. *Oom Paul's People: A Narrative of the British-Boer Troubles in South Africa, with a History of the Boers, the Country, and Its Institutions.* New York: D. Appleton, 1899.

HINTRAGER, OSKAR. *Geschichte von Südafrika.* Munich: R. Oldenbourg, 1952.

———. *Südwestafrika in der Deutschen Zeit.* Munich: R. Oldenbourg, 1955.

HOBMAN, DAISY LUCIE. *Olive Schreiner: Her Friends and Times.* London: Watts, 1955.

HOBSON, JOHN ATKINSON. *The War in South Africa: Its Causes and Effects.* New York: Macmillan, 1900.

HOCKLEY, HAROLD EDWARD. *The Story of the British Settlers of 1820 in South Africa.* Johannesburg: Juta, 1957.

HOERNLE, R. F. ALFRED. *Race and Reason: Being Mainly a Selection of Contributions to the Race Problem in South Africa.* Johannesburg: Witwatersrand University Press, 1945.

———. *South African Native Policy and the Liberal Spirit.* Johannesburg: Witwatersrand University Press, 1945.

HOFMEYR, J. H. *South Africa.* New York: Scribner's, 1931.

———, and REITZ, F. W. *The Life of Jan Hendrik Hofmeyr.* Cape Town: Van de Sandt de Villiers Printing Company, 1913.

HOGUE, WILSON THOMAS. *G. Harry Agnew: A Pioneer Missionary.* Chicago: Free Methodist Publishing House, 1905.

HOLDEN, WILLIAM CLIFFORD. *British Rule in South Africa.* London: Wesleyan Conference Office, n.d.

HOLE, HUGH MARSHALL. *Lobengula.* London: P. Allan, 1929.

———. *The Passing of the Black Kings.* London: P. Allan, 1932.

HOLT, BASIL. *Joseph Williams and the Pioneer Mission to South Eastern Bantu.* Lovedale: Lovedale Press, 1954.

HOLT, EDGAR. *The Boer War.* London: Putnam, 1958.

HOOKER, LEROY. *The Afrikanders: A Century of Dutch-English Feud in South Africa.* Chicago: Rand, McNally, 1900.

HOOPER, CHARLES. *Brief Authority.* New York: Simon and Schuster, 1961.

HOUGHTON, D. HOBART. *Economic Development in a Plural Society.* 5 vols. Cape Town: Oxford University Press, 1960.

———, and WALTON, EDITH M. *The Economy of a Native Reserve.* Pietermaritzburg: Shuter and Shooter, 1952.

HUBBARD, MARGARET. *African Gamble.* New York: Putnam, 1937.

HUDDLESTON, TREVOR. *Naught for Your Comfort.* Garden City, N.Y.: Doubleday, 1956.

HUGO, T. G. *Die Afrikaanse Universiteit en Sy Taak in die Volkslewe.* Bloemfontein: Nasionale Pers, 1941.

HUTCHINSON, G. T. *From the Cape to the Zambezi.* London: J. Murray, 1905.

INNES, JAMES ROSE. *Autobiography.* Cape Town: Oxford University Press, 1949.

International Commission of Jurists. *South Africa and the Rule of Law.* Geneva, 1960.

JABAVU, DAVIDSON DON TENGO. *The Black Problem: Papers and Addresses on Various Native Problems.* Lovedale: Lovedale Institution Press, 1921.

——. *The Life of John Tengo Jabavu, Editor of 'Imvo Zabantsundu,' 1884–1921.* Lovedale: Lovedale Institution Press, 1922.

——. *The Segregation Fallacy and Other Papers: A Native View of Some South African Interracial Problems.* Lovedale: Lovedale Institution Press, 1928.

JABAVU, NONI. *Drawn in Colour: African Contrasts.* London: J. Murray, 1960. New York: St Martin's, 1960.

JACKMAN, STUART BROOKE. *The Numbered Days.* London: Student Christian Movement, 1954.

JACOBS, ALICE. *South African Heritage: A Biography of H. J. van der Bijl.* Pietermaritzburg: Shuter and Shooter, 1948.

JACOBSON, DAN. *A Dance in the Sun.* New York: Harcourt, Brace, 1956.

JAMES, SELWYN. *South of the Congo.* New York: Random House, 1943.

JANNASCH, HANS. *Unter Buren, Briten, Bantus.* Berlin: Otto Schlegel, n.d.

JOHNSTON, SIR HARRY H. *History of the Colonization of Africa by Alien Races.* London: Cambridge University Press, 1930.

JONES, J. D. RHEINALT, and DOKE, C. M. *Bushmen of the Southern Kalahari.* Johannesburg: University of Witwatersrand, 1947.

JORDI, G. *Settlers in Our Valley.* London: Quality Press, 1946.

JORISSEN, E. J. P. *Transvaalsche Herinneringen, 1876–1896.* Amsterdam: de Bussy, 1897.

JOSHI, P. S. *The Struggle for Equality.* Bombay: Hind Kitabs, 1951.

——. *The Tyranny of Colour: A Study of the Indian Problem in South Africa.* Durban: E. P. and Commercial Printing Company, 1942.

——. *Verdict on South Africa.* Bombay: Thacker, 1945.

JOUBERT, W. A. *Godsdiensonderwys in die Laer Skool.* Cape Town: Nasionale Pers, 1947.

JUNOD, HENRI A. *Life of a South African Tribe.* 2 vols. London: D. Nutt, 1912–13.

JUNOD, HENRI PHILLIPPE. *Bantu Heritage.* Johannesburg: Hortors, 1938.

KANNEMEYER, A. J. *Hugenote Familieboek.* Cape Town: Unie-Volkspers, 1940.

KARRSTROM, E. J. *Achtzehn Jahre in Südafrika Erlebnisse und Abenteuer eines Schweden in Goldlande.* Leipzig: H. W. Dieter, 1899.

KEET, B. B. *Whither South Africa?* Stellenbosch University Publishers, 1956.

KEMP, J. C. G. *Die Pad van die Veroweraar.* Cape Town: Nasionale Pers, 1942.

KEMP, SAMUEL. *Black Frontiers: Pioneer Adventures with Cecil Rhodes in Africa.* New York: Brewer, Warren and Putnam, 1931.

KENNEDY, WILLIAM PAUL McCLURE, and SCHLOSBERG, H. J. *The Law and Customs of the South African Constitution.* London: Oxford University Press, 1935.

KENYON, J. T. *An Address on the General Council Administrative System of the Transkeian Territories, Delivered at the University of Stellenbosch on 12th, 13th, and 14th October, 1932.* Umtata: Territorial News, 1932.

KEPPEL-JONES, ARTHUR. *Friends or Foes? A Point of View and a Programme for Racial Harmony in South Africa.* Pietermaritzburg: Shuter and Shooter, 1950.

——. *Phillips, 1820 Settler: His Letters.* Pietermaritzburg: Shuter and Shooter, 1960.

——. *South Africa: A Short History.* London: Hutchinson, 1961.

——. *When Smuts Goes: A History of South Africa from 1952–2010, First Published in 2015.* Cape Town: African Bookman, 1947.

KIDD, DUDLEY. *The Essential Kafir.* London: A. and C. Black, 1925.

KIDD, DUDLEY. *The Kafir Socialism and the Dawn of Individualism: An Introduction to the Study of the Native Problems.* London: A. and C. Black, 1908.

KIERNAN, REGINALD H. *General Smuts.* London: G. G. Harrap, 1948.

KILPIN, RALPH P. *The Old Cape House: Being Pages from the History of a Legislative Chamber.* Cape Town: T. M. Miller, 1918.

KINGSNORTH, G. W. *Africa South of the Sahara.* New York: Cambridge University Press, 1962.

KIRK, JOHN. *The Economic Aspects of Native Segregation in South Africa.* London: P. S. King, 1929.

KNOWLES, L. C. A. *The Economic Development of the British Overseas Empire.* (Vol. VIII, 'The Union of South Africa.') London: G. Routledge and Sons, 1932.

KOHLER, C. W. H. *The Memoirs of Kohler of the KWV.* (Ed. by A. Joelson.) London: Hurst and Blackett, 1946.

KOTZÉ, SIR JOHN GILBERT. *Memoirs and Reminiscences.* 2 vols. (Ed. by B. A. Tindall.) Cape Town: Maskew Miller, 1949.

KRAUS, RENÉ. *Old Master: The Life of Jan Christian Smuts.* New York: Dutton, 1944.

KREPPS, ROBERT. *Tell It on the Drums.* New York: Macmillan, 1955.

KRIGE, EILEEN JENSEN. *The Social System of the Zulus.* Pietermaritzburg: Shuter and Shooter, 1957.

KRÜGER, D. W. *The Age of the Generals: A Short Political History of the Union of South Africa, 1910–1948.* Johannesburg: Dagbreek Book Store, 1958.

—— (ed.). *South African Parties and Policies, 1910–1960: A Select Source Book.* Cape Town: Human and Rousseau, 1960.

KRUGER, JANNIE. *President C. R. Swart.* Cape Town: Nasionale Boekhandel, 1961.

KRUGER, NELLIE. *Rachel Isabella Steyn, Presidentsvrou.* Cape Town: Nasionale Pers, 1949.

KRUGER, RAYNE. *Good-bye Dolly Gray: The Story of the Boer War.* Philadelphia: Lippincott, 1959.

KRUGER, STEPHANUS JOHANNES PAULUS. *Gedenkskrifte van Paul Kruger.* Pretoria: J. L. van Schaik, 1947.

——. *The Memoirs of Paul Kruger, Four Times President of the South African Republic, Told by Himself.* New York: Century, 1902.

KUIT, ALBERT. *'n Kommandoprediker: Een en Onder uit die Lewe van die Weleerwaarde Heer James Murray Lowe, ens.* Pretoria: de Bussy, 1948.

——. *Transvaalse Gister.* Pretoria: J. L. van Schaik, 1942.

——. *Transvaalse Verskeidenheid.* Pretoria: J. L. van Schaik, 1940.

KUPER, HILDA. *An African Aristocracy: Rank Among the Swazi of Bechuanaland.* New York: International African Institute, 1947.

——. *Indian People of Natal.* Durban: Natal University Press, 1960.

——. *Uniform of Colour: A Study of White-Black Relationships in Swaziland.* Johannesburg: Witwatersrand University Press, 1947.

——, HUGHES, A. J. B., and VAN VELSEN, J. *The Shona and Ndebele of Southern Rhodesia.* London: International African Institute, 1954.

KUPER, LEO. *Passive Resistance in South Africa.* New Haven: Yale University Press, 1957.

LANHAM, PETER. *Blanket Boy.* New York: Crowell, 1953.

——. *The Road Awaits.* London: Collins, 1955.

LATROBE, REVEREND C. I. *Journal of a Visit to South Africa in 1815 and 1816:*

With Some Account of the Missionary Settlements of the United Brethren, Near the Cape of Good Hope. London: L. B. Seeley and R. Ackerman, 1818.

LAURENCE, SIR PERCIVAL MAITLAND. *The Life of John Xavier Merriman.* London: Constable, 1930.

LE GRANGE, ISAK. *Uit Chaos—Na Orde: Die Wording van 'n Nasionaal-sosialis.* Cape Town: Die Skrywer, 1944.

LEHMANN, OLGA. *Look Beyond the Wind.* Cape Town: Timmins, 1955.

LEIPOLDT, CHRISTIAAN LOUIS. *Bushveld Doctor.* London: Jonathan Cape, 1938.

——. *Jan van Riebeeck: A Biographical Study.* London: Longmans, Green, 1936.

LESSING, C. *Ek, Ellendige Mens.* Johannesburg: Afrikaanse Pers-boekhandel, 1947.

LETTOW-VORBECK, PAUL EMIL VON. *East African Campaign.* New York: R. Speller, 1957.

LEWIN, JULIUS. *Politics and Law in South Africa: Essays on Race Relations.* New York: Monthly Review Press, 1963.

——. *Studies in African Native Law.* Cape Town: A. A. Balkema, 1947.

LEYDS, W. J. *The First Annexation of the Transvaal.* London: T. F. Unwin, 1906.

——. *The Transvaal Surrounded.* New York: Dutton, 1914.

LEYLAND, J. *Adventures in the Far Interior of South Africa: Including a Journey to Lake Ngami.* London: G. Routledge, 1866.

LICHTENSTEIN, M. H. K. *Travels in Southern Africa in the Years 1803, 1804, 1805, 1806.* (Trans. from the original German by Anne Plumtre.) London: Henry Colburn, 1812.

LINDER, C. B. *Christelikheid en Nasionalisme in die Opvoeding.* Johannesburg: Afrikaanse Pers-boekhandel, 1946.

LINDLEY, CAPTAIN AUGUSTUS F. *Adamantia: The Truth About the South African Diamond Fields. Or, Vindication of the Right of the Orange Free State to the Territory.* London: Collingridge, 1873.

LISTER, GEORGINA. *Reminiscences.* Johannesburg: Africana Museum, 1960.

LIVINGSTONE, DAVID. *Missionary Travels and Researches in South Africa.* New York: Harper, 1858.

LOCKHART, J. G., and WOODHOUSE, C. M. *Cecil Rhodes: The Colossus of Southern Africa.* New York: Macmillan, 1963.

LONG, BASIL K. *In Smuts Camp.* London: Oxford University Press, 1945.

LONGMORE, LAURA. *The Dispossessed: A Study of the Sex-Life of Bantu Women In and Around Johannesburg.* London: Jonathan Cape, 1959.

LORAM, CHARLES TEMPLEMAN. *The Education of the South African Native.* London: Longmans, Green, 1917.

LOUW, ERIC, AND OTHERS. *South Africa in the African Continent.* Stellenbosch: South African Bureau of Racial Affairs, 1960.

LOVELL, REGINALD I. *The Struggle for South Africa, 1875–1899: A Study in Economic Imperialism.* New York: Macmillan, 1934.

LOWENSTEIN, ALLARD K. *Brutal Mandate: A Journey to South West Africa.* New York: Macmillan, 1962.

LUCAS, THOMAS J. *Camp Life and Sport in South Africa: Experiences of Kaffir Warfare with the Cape Mounted Rifles.* London: Chapman and Hall, 1878.

LUTHULI, ALBERT. *Let My People Go.* London: Collins, 1962. New York: McGraw-Hill, 1962.

LYTTON, DAVID. *The Goddam White Man.* New York: Avon, 1960.

MAC, J. *Little Indabas: Stories of Kaffir, Boer and Natal Life.* London: Fisher Unwin, 1900.

MacCrone, Ian Douglas. *Race Attitudes in South Africa: Historical, Experimental and Psychological Studies.* London: Oxford University Press, 1937.

Macdonald, Tom. *Jan Hofmeyr: Heir to Smuts.* London: Hurst and Blackett, 1948.

———. *Ouma Smuts: The First Lady of South Africa.* London: Hurst and Blackett, 1946.

Maclean, Joan C. (ed.). *Africa: The Racial Issue.* New York: Wilson, 1954.

Macmillan, William Miller. *Africa Emergent: A Survey of Social, Political, and Economic Trends in British Africa.* London: Faber and Faber, 1938.

———. *Bantu, Boer and Briton: The Making of the South African Native Problem.* London: Oxford University Press, 1963.

———. *The Cape Colour Question: A Historical Survey.* London: Faber and Gwyer, 1927.

———. *Complex South Africa: An Economic Footnote to History.* London: Faber and Faber, 1930.

———. *The South African Agrarian Problem and Its Historical Development.* Johannesburg: Central News Agency, 1919.

Magnus, Philip Montefiore. *Kitchener: Portrait of an Imperialist.* New York: Dutton, 1959.

Mahan, Alfred Thayer. *The War in South Africa: A Narrative of the War in South Africa from the Beginning of Hostilities to the Conclusion of the Peace.* New York: F. F. Collier, 1902.

Malan, Daniel François. *Afrikaner-volkseenheid en my ervarings op die pad daarheen.* Cape Town: Nasionale Boekhandel Beperk, 1959.

Malan, François S. *Die Konvensie-Dagboek.* Cape Town: van Riebeeck Society, 1951.

Malan, J. H. *Die opkoms van 'n republiek: ar Die geskiedenis van die Oranje-Vrystaat tot die jaar 1863.* Bloemfontein: Nasionale Pers Beperk, 1929.

Malherbe, Ernest Gideon. *The Bilingual School: A Study of Bilingualism in South Africa.* London: Longmans, Green, 1946.

———. *Education in South Africa, 1652–1922.* Cape Town: Juta, 1925.

———. *Handbook on Education and Social Work in South Africa.* Pretoria: The New Education Fellowship, 1934.

Malherbe, Janie A. *Complex Country.* London: Longmans, Green, 1944.

Malinowski, Bronislaw. *The Dynamics of Culture Change: An inquiry into Race Relations in Africa.* (Ed. by Phyllis M. Kaberry.) New Haven: Yale University Press, 1945.

Mansergh, Nicholas. *The Commonwealth and the Nations: Studies in British Commonwealth Relations.* London: Oxford University Press, 1952.

———. *Documents and Speeches on British Commonwealth Affairs, 1931–1952.* New York: Oxford University Press, 1953.

———. *South Africa, 1906–1961: The Price of Magnanimity.* London: G. Allen and Unwin, 1962. New York: Frederick A. Praeger, 1962.

———. *Survey of British Commonwealth Affairs: Problems of External Policy, 1931–1939.* London: Oxford University Press, 1952.

Marais, Ben J. *Colour: Unsolved Problem of the West.* Cape Town: Timmins, 1952.

Marais, Johannes S. *The Cape Coloured People, 1652–1937.* Johannesburg: Witwatersrand University Press, 1957.

———. *The Fall of Kruger's Republic.* Oxford: Clarendon Press, 1961.

———. *Maynier and the First Boer Republic.* Cape Town: Maskew Miller, 1944.

MARQUARD, LEO. *Native in South Africa.* Johannesburg: Witwatersrand University Press, 1944.

———. *The Peoples and Policies of South Africa.* Cape Town: Oxford University Press, 1962.

———. *The Story of South Africa.* London: Faber and Faber, 1950.

———, and STANDING, T. G. *The Southern Bantu.* New York: Oxford University Press, 1939.

MARSH, JOHN H. *No Pathway Here.* Cape Town: Timmins, 1948.

———. *Skeleton Coast.* Cape Town: Hodder and Stoughton, 1945.

MARTIN, A. C. *The Concentration Camps 1900–1902: Facts, Figures and Fables.* Cape Town: Timmins, 1957.

MARTIN, A. D. *Doctor van der Kemp.* London: The Livingstone Press, n.d.

MASON, PHILIP. *The Birth of a Dilemma: The Conquest and Settlement of Rhodesia.* London: Oxford University Press, 1958.

———. *An Essay on Racial Tension.* London: Royal Institute of International Affairs, 1954.

MASON, R. *Prehistory of the Transvaal: A Record of Human Activity.* Johannesburg: Witwatersrand University Press, 1962.

MASSON, MADELEINE. *Birds of Passage.* Cape Town: Timmins, 1950.

———. *Lady Anne Barnard.* London: G. Allen and Unwin, 1948.

MAUD, JOHN P. R. *City Government: The Johannesburg Experiment.* Clarendon: Oxford University Press, 1938.

MAUROIS, ANDRÉ. *Cecil Rhodes.* (Trans. by Rohan Wadham.) New York: Macmillan, 1953.

MAY, HENRY JOHN. *Red Wine of Youth.* Cape Town: Cassell, 1946.

———. *The South African Constitution.* Johannesburg: Juta, 1955.

MAYER, PHILIP. *Townsmen or Tribesmen: Urbanisation in a Divided Society.* London: Oxford University Press, 1961.

McCORD, JAMES B., and DOUGLAS, JOHN SCOTT. *My Patients Were Zulus.* New York: Rinehart, 1951.

McCORD, CAPTAIN J. J. *South African Struggle.* Pretoria: de Bussy, 1952.

McKERRON, MARGARETHA EMMA MARTINIUS. *A History of Education in South Africa, 1652–1932.* Pretoria: J. L. van Schaik, 1934.

McNEILL, JOHN T. *The History and Character of Calvinism.* New York: Oxford University Press, 1957.

MEIHUIZEN, J. *Dat Vrije Volk.* Amsterdam: Strengholt, 1948.

METHUEN, HENRY H. *Life in the Wilderness: Or, Wanderings in South Africa.* London: Richard Bentley, 1846.

MEYER, P. J. *Die Afrikaner.* Bloemfontein: Nasionale Pers Beperk, 1940.

———. *Moedertaal en Tweetaligheid.* Stellenbosch: Pro-Ecclesia, 1945.

MILLIN, SARAH GERTRUDE. *Cecil Rhodes.* London: Chatto and Windus, 1936.

———. *General Smuts.* 2 vols. Boston: Little, Brown, 1936.

———. *People of South Africa.* London: Constable, 1951.

———. *The South Africans.* London: Constable, 1937.

MOCKFORD, JULIAN. *The Golden Land: A Background to South Africa.* London: A. and C. Black, 1951.

———. *Here Are South Africans.* London: A. and C. Black, 1944.

MOFFAT, ROBERT. *Missionary Labours and Scenes in Southern Africa.* New York: Robert Carter, 1843.

MOLTENO, SIR JAMES TENNANT. *The Dominion of Afrikanerdom: Recollections Pleasant and Otherwise.* London: Methuen, 1923.

MOLTENO, SIR JAMES TENNANT. *Further South African Recollections.* London: Methuen, 1926.

MOODIE, D. C. F. *The History of the Battles and Adventures of the British, the Boers, and the Zulus . . . in Southern Africa . . . to 1880, with Copious Chronology.* 2 vols. Cape Town: Murray and St. Leger, 1888.

MORRIS, H. H. *The First Forty Years: Being the Memoirs of H. H. Morris, K.C.* Cape Town: Juta, 1948.

MORRIS, JAMES. *South African Winter.* New York: Pantheon, 1958.

MORTON, HENRY C. V. *In Search of South Africa.* London: Methuen, 1948.

MULLER, C. F. J. *Die Britse Owerheid en die Groot Trek.* Cape Town: Juta, 1948.

MULLER, H. P. N. *Oude Tyden in der Oranje Vrystaat-Naar Mr H. A. L. Hamelberg's Nagelaten Papieren Beschreven.* Leiden: E. J. Brill, 1907.

MUNNIK, G. G. *Kronieke van Noordelike Transvaal.* Pretoria: Suid Afrikaanse Boekwinkel, n.d.

———. *Memoirs Covering Eighty Years of Thrilling South African History, Politics, and War.* Cape Town: Maskew Miller, n.d.

MURDOCK, GEORGE PETER. *Africa: Its Peoples and Their Cultural History.* New York: McGraw-Hill, 1959.

MURRAY, MARISCHAL. *Union-Castle Chronicle, 1853–1953.* London: Longmans, Green, 1953.

MURRAY, R. W. (ed.). *South Africa from Arab Domination to British Rule.* London: Edward Stanford, 1891.

———. *South African Reminiscences: A Series of Sketches of Prominent Public Events . . . in South Africa . . . (1854–1894) and of the Public Men, Official and Unofficial, Who Have Taken Part in Them.* Cape Town: Juta, 1894.

NATHAN, MANFRED. *The Huguenots in South Africa.* Johannesburg: Central News Agency, 1939.

———. *Paul Kruger: His Life and Times.* Durban: Knox, 1941.

———. *South Africa from Within.* London: J. Murray, 1926.

———. *The South African Commonwealth.* Johannesburg: Specialty Press, 1919.

NEAME, LAWRENCE E. *City Built on Gold.* Johannesburg: Central News Agency, 1960.

———. *General Hertzog: Prime Minister of the Union of South Africa since 1924.* London: Hurst and Blackett, 1930.

———. *The History of Apartheid.* London: Pall Mall Press, 1962.

———. *Some South African Politicians.* Cape Town: Maskew Miller, 1929.

———. *White Man's Africa: The Problem of a White Nation in a Black Continent.* Cape Town: Stewart, 1952.

NEUMARK, SOLOMON DANIEL. *Economic Influences on the South African Frontier, 1652–1836.* Stanford: Stanford University Press, 1957.

NEWTON, A. P. (ed.). *Select Documents Relating to the Unification of South Africa.* 2 vols. London: Longmans, Green, 1924.

———. BENIANS, E. A., and WALKER, ERIC A. (eds.). *The Cambridge History of the British Empire.* (Vol. VIII; *South Africa, the Rhodesias and the Protectorates.*) Cambridge: The University Press, 1936.

NGUBANE, JORDAN K. *An African Explains Apartheid.* New York: Frederick A. Praeger, 1963.

NIELSEN, PETER. *The Black Man's Place in South Africa.* Cape Town: Juta, 1922.

———. *The Colour Bar.* Johannesburg: Juta, 1937.

NIENABER, P. J. *Dr J. D. Kestell, Vader van die Reddingsdaad.* Bloemfontein: Nasionale Pers, 1946.

NOBBS, DOUGLAS. *Theocracy and Toleration: A Study of the Disputes in Dutch Calvinism from 1600–1650.* Cambridge: The University Press, 1938.

OLDHAM, JOSEPH H. *Christianity and the Race Problem.* New York: George H. Doran, 1924.

———. *New Hope in Africa.* London: Longmans, Green, 1955.

———. *White and Black in Africa: A Critical Examination of the Rhodes Lectures of General Smuts.* London: Longmans, Green, 1930.

OLIVER, RONALD, and FAGE, J. D. *A Short History of Africa.* Baltimore: Penguin, 1962.

OLIVIER, LORD SYDNEY. *Anatomy of African Misery.* London: Woolf, 1937.

———. *White Capital and Coloured Labour.* London: Woolf, 1929.

The Open Universities of South Africa. Johannesburg: Witwatersrand University Press, 1957.

PAKENHAM, ELIZABETH. *Jameson's Raid.* London: Weidenfeld and Nicolson, 1960.

PALGRAVE, W. COATES. *Report of W. Coates Palgrave, Esquire, Special Commissioner to the Tribes North of the Orange River, of His Mission to Damaraland and Great Namaqualand in 1876.* Cape Town: Saul Solomon, 1877.

PALMER, MABEL, AND OTHERS. *The Indian as a South African: A Symposium.* Johannesburg: South African Institute of Race Relations, 1956.

PATERSON, WILLIAM. *A Narrative of Four Journeys into the Country of the Hottentots and Kaffraria in the Years 1777, 1778, and 1779.* London: J. Johnson, 1789.

PATON, ALAN. *Cry, the Beloved Country.* New York: Scribner's, 1948.

———. *Hope for South Africa.* London: Pall Mall Press, 1958. New York: Frederick A. Praeger, 1958.

———. *The Land and People of South Africa.* Philadelphia: Lippincott, 1955.

———. *South Africa and Her People.* London: Butterworth, 1957.

———. *Too Late the Phalarope.* New York: Scribner's, 1953.

PATTERSON, SHEILA. *Colour and Culture in South Africa: A Study of the Status of the Cape Coloured People Within the Social Structure of the Union of South Africa.* London: Routledge and Kegan Paul, 1953. New York: Grove, 1953.

———. *The Last Trek: A Study of the Boer People and the Afrikaner Nation.* London: Routledge and Kegan Paul, 1957.

PEATTIE, RODERICK. *Struggle on the Veld.* New York: Vanguard Press, 1947.

PEGG, H. E. *A History of Southern Africa.* Cape Town: Longmans, Green, 1949.

PELZER, A. N. *Geskiedenis van die Suid Suid-Afrikaanse Republiek.* Cape Town: A. A. Balkema, 1950.

———. *Jan van Riebeeck, 1618–1677.* Pretoria: Unie-Boekhandel, 1944.

PERHAM, MARGERY F., and CURTIS, LIONEL. *The Protectorates of South Africa: The Question of Their Transfer to the Union.* London: Oxford University Press, 1935.

PERHAM, MARGERY F., and SIMMONS, J. *African Discovery: An Anthology of Exploration.* London: Faber and Faber, 1942. Evanston: Northwestern University Press, 1963.

PHILIP, JOHN. *Researches in South Africa.* 2 vols. London: James Duncan, 1828.

PHILLIPS, NORMAN. *The Tragedy of Apartheid: A Journalist's Experiences in the South African Riots.* New York: David McKay, 1960.

PHILLIPS, RAY E. *The Bantu Are Coming: Phases of South Africa's Race Problem.* London: Students Christian Movement Press, 1930.

———. *The Bantu in the City: A Study of Cultural Adjustment on the Witwatersrand.* Lovedale: Lovedale Press, 1938.

PHILLIPS, RAY E. *The Crux of the Race Problem: Are Black People Human Beings?* Stellenbosch: Students Christian Association, 1947.

PHILLIPS, T. *Scenes and Occurrences in Albany and Cafferland, South Africa.* London: William Marsh, 1827.

PIENAAR, E. C. *Die Triomf van Afrikaans.* Cape Town: Nasionale Pers, 1943.

PIENAAR, S., and SAMPSON, ANTHONY. *South Africa: Two Views of Separate Development.* Cape Town: Oxford University Press, 1960.

PIETERSE, H. J. C. *Oorlogsavonture van General Wynand Malan.* Cape Town: Nasionale Pers, 1941.

PIROW, OSWALD. *James Barry Munnik Hertzog.* London: G. Allen and Unwin, 1958.

PISTORIUS, P. V. *No Further Trek.* Johannesburg: Central News Agency, 1957.

PITCHFORD, H. WATKINS. *In God's Good Time: A South African Saga.* Pietermaritzburg: Shuter and Shooter, 1949.

PLAATJE, SOLOMON T. *Native Life in South Africa Before and Since the European War and the Boer Rebellion.* London: P. S. King and Sons, 1916.

PLANT, ROBERT. *The Zulu in Three Tenses: Being a Forecast of the Zulu's Future in the Light of His Past and Present.* Pietermaritzburg: P. Davis, 1905.

PLOMER, WILLIAM. *Cecil Rhodes.* New York: D. Appleton, 1933.

POHL, V. *Adventures of a Boer Family.* London: Faber and Faber, 1944.

PORTER, WILLIAM. *The Porter Speeches: Speeches Delivered by the Hon. William Porter During the Years 1839–1845 Inclusive.* Cape Town: Trustees Estate Saul Solomon, 1886.

POSTMA, F. *Paul Kruger: Die Christen-volksman en-staatsman.* Stellenbosch: Pro-Ecclesia, 1944.

POTGIETER, CAREL, and THEUNISSEN, N. H. *Kommandant-General Hendrik Potgieter.* Johannesburg: Afrikaanse Pers, 1938.

PRELLER, G. S. *Voortrekkermense.* 3 vols. Cape Town: Nasionale Pers, 1918–22.

PRELLER, JOHANN F. (ed.). *Die Konvensie-Dagboek van sy Edelagbare François Stephanus Malan, 1908–1909.* Cape Town: van Riebeeck Society, 1951.

PRESTON, M. *My God en Ek.* Johannesburg: Goeie Hoop Uitgewers, 1949.

PRINGLE, THOMAS. *African Sketches.* London: E. Moxon, 1834.

———. *Narrative of a Residence in South Africa.* London: E. Moxon, 1835.

PYRAH, G. B. *Imperial Policy and South Africa, 1902–1910.* Oxford: Clarendon Press, 1955.

RABIE, JAN. *Die evolusie van nasionalisme: beskouings oor die krisis van nasionalisme in die huidige oor gangstydperk tot 'n wereldstaat.* Cape Town: Mishoring, 1960.

RALLS, ALICE M. *Glory Which Is Yours: Tribute to Pioneer Ancestors.* Pietermaritzburg: Shuter and Shooter, 1949.

RAYMOND, HARRY. *B. I. Barnato: A Memoir.* Cape Town: Juta, 1897.

REED, DOUGLAS. *Somewhere South of Suez.* London: Jonathan Cape, 1950.

REEVES, BISHOP RICHARD AMBROSE. *Shooting at Sharpeville: The Agony of South Africa.* Boston: Houghton Mifflin, 1960.

———. *South Africa, Yesterday and Tomorrow: A Challenge to Christians.* London: Gollancz, 1962.

REICH, HANNS. *Portrait of Southern Africa.* London: Collins, 1956.

REITZ, DENEYS. *Afrikander.* New York: Minton, Balch, 1933.

———. *Commando: A Boer Journal of the Boer War.* New York: C. Boni, 1930.

———. *No Outspan.* London: Faber and Faber, 1943.

———. *Trekking On.* London: Faber and Faber, 1933.

REITZ, H. *The Conversion of a South African Nationalist.* Cape Town: Unie-Volkspers, 1946.

REYNOLDS, REGINALD. *Cairo to Cape Town: A Pilgrimage in Search of Hope.* Garden City, N.Y.: Doubleday, 1955.

RHOODIE, N. J., and VENTER, H. J. *Apartheid: A Socio-historical Exposition of the Origin and Development of the Apartheid Idea.* Cape Town: National Commercial Printers, 1961.

RICHMOND, ANTHONY H. *The Colour Problem: A Study in Racial Relations.* Cape Town: Penguin, 1955.

RINGROSE, H. G. *Trade Unions in Natal.* Cape Town: Oxford University Press, 1951.

RITNER, PETER. *The Death of Africa.* New York: Macmillan, 1960.

RITTER, E. A. *Shaka Zulu: The Rise of the Zulu Empire.* London: Longmans, Green, 1955.

ROBERTS, MICHAEL, and TROLLIP, A. E. G. *The South African Opposition, 1939–1945: An Essay on Contemporary History.* London: Longmans, Green, 1947.

ROBERTSON, HECTOR M. *South Africa: Economic and Political Aspects.* Durham: Duke University Press, 1957.

ROBESON, ESLANDA GOODE. *African Journey.* London: Gollancz, 1946.

ROBINS, ERIC. *This Man Malan.* Cape Town: Scientific Publishing Company, 1953.

ROGERS, HOWARD. *Native Administration in the Union of South Africa: Being a Brief Survey of the Organization, Functions, and Activities of the Department of Native Affairs of the Union of South Africa.* Johannesburg: University of Witwatersrand, 1933.

———. *Native Administration in the Union of South Africa.* 2d ed. Pretoria: Government Printer, 1949.

ROGERS, MIRABEL. *The Black Sash: The Story of the South African Women's Defence of the Constitution League.* Johannesburg: Rotonews, 1956.

ROOSEBOOM, HANS (ed.). *The Romance of the Great Trek: A Collection of Authoritative Articles on the Life and Times of the Voortrekkers.* Pretoria: Central News Agency, 1949.

ROSENTHAL, ERIC (ed. and comp.). *Encyclopedia of Southern Africa.* London: F. Warne, 1961.

———. *General de Wet: A Biography.* Cape Town: Unie-Volkspers, 1946.

———. *Gold Bricks and Mortar: Sixty Years of Johannesburg History.* Johannesburg: Printing House, 1946.

ROSKAM, K. L. *Apartheid and Discrimination.* Leyden: A. W. Sythoff, 1960.

ROUX, EDWARD. *S. P. Bunting: A Political Biography.* Cape Town: African Bookman, 1944.

———. *Time Longer than Rope: A History of the Black Man's Struggle for Freedom in South Africa.* London: Gollancz, 1948.

RUSSELL, ROBERT. *Natal: The Land and Its Story.* Pietermaritzburg: Shuter and Shooter, 1903.

SACHS, BERNARD. *Multitude of Dreams: A Semi-Autobiographical Study.* Johannesburg: Kayor, 1949.

———. *South African Personalities and Places.* Johannesburg: Kayor, 1959.

———. *The Road to Sharpeville.* London: Dobson, 1960.

SACHS, EMIL SOLLY. *The Choice Before South Africa.* New York: Philosophical Library, 1952.

SACHS, WULF. *Black Anger*. New York: Grove, 1947.

ST. JOHN, ROBERT. *Through Malan's Africa*. Garden City, N.Y.: Doubleday, 1954.

SAMPSON, ANTHONY. *Common Sense about Africa*. London: Gollancz, 1960. New York: Macmillan, 1960.

———. *Drum: A Venture into the New Africa*. London: Collins, 1956. Boston: Houghton Mifflin, 1956.

———. *The Treason Cage: The Opposition on Trial in South Africa*. London: Heinemann, 1958.

SARON, GUSTAV, and HOTZ, LOUIS. *The Jews in South Africa: A History*. New York: Oxford University Press, 1955.

SCHAPERA, ISAAC. *Government and Politics in Tribal Societies*. London: Watts, 1956.

———. *The Khoisan Peoples of South Africa, Bushmen and Hottentots*. London: Routledge and Kegan Paul, 1930.

——— (ed.). *Western Civilization and Natives of South Africa: Studies in Culture Contact*. London: Routledge and Kegan Paul, 1934.

SCHMIDT-PRETORIA, WERNER. *Der Kulturanteil des Deutschtums am Aufbau des Burenvolkes*. Hannover: Hahnsche Verlag, 1938.

SCHOLTZ, GERT DANIEL. *Die Konstitusie en die Staatsinstellings van die Oranje-Vrystaat, 1854–1902*. Amsterdam: Swets and Zeitlinger, 1936.

———. *Die Lewensaand van President Kruger*. Johannesburg: Federasie van Afrikaanse Kultuurvereninginge, 1954.

———. *Die oorsake van die tweede Vryheidsoorlog, 1899–1902*. 2 vols. Johannesburg: Voortrekkerpers, 1948.

———. *Die Rebellie, 1914–1915*. Johannesburg: Voortrekkerpers, 1942.

———. *Dr Nicolaas Johannes van der Merwe, 1888–1940*. Johannesburg: Voortrekkerpers Beperk Voorwaarts, 1944.

———. *Europa en die tweede Vryheidsoorlog, 1899–1902*. Johannesburg: Voortrekkerpers Beperk, 1939.

———. *General Christiaan Frederik Beyers, 1869–1914*. Johannesburg: Voortrekkerpers, 1941.

———. *Het die Afrikaanse volk toekoms*. Johannesburg: Voortrekkerpers, 1954.

———. *Hoe die wereld politiek gevoer word*. Johannesburg: Voortrekkerpers, 1952.

———. *President Johannes Henricus Brand, 1823–1888*. Johannesburg: Voortrekkerpers, 1957.

———. *Suid-Afrika en die wereldpolitiek, 1652–1952*. Johannesburg: Voortrekkerpers, 1954.

SCHOLTZ, J. DU P. *Die Afrikaner en sy taal, 1806–1875*. Cape Town: Nasionale Pers Beperk, 1939.

SCHREIBER, A. *Fünf Monate in Südafrika*. Barmen: Verlag des Missions, 1894.

SCHREINER, OLIVE. *Closer Union*. Cape Town: The Constitutional Reform Association, 1908.

———. *From Man to Man*. London: T. F. Unwin, 1926.

———. *The South African Question*. Chicago: Charles H. Sergel, 1899.

———. *Story of an African Farm*. New York: Modern Library, 1927.

———. *Thoughts on South Africa*. London: T. F. Unwin, 1923.

SCHREINER, THEOPHILUS LYNDALL. *The Afrikander Bond and other Causes of the War*. London: Spottiswood, 1901.

SCHUMANN, C. G. W. *Structural Changes and Business Cycles in South Africa, 1806–1936*. London: P. S. King, 1938.

SCHWARZ, E. H. L. *The Kalahari: Or, Thirstland Redemption*. Cape Town: Maskew Miller, 1920.

SCOTT, MICHAEL. *A Time To Speak.* Garden City, N.Y.: Doubleday, 1958.

SEARLE, ERNEST W. *With a Policeman in South Africa.* New York: Abbey Press, 1900.

SEAVER, GEORGE. *David Livingstone: His Life and Letters.* New York: Harper, 1957.

SEGAL, ALBERT. *Johannesburg Friday.* New York: McGraw-Hill, 1954.

SEYMOUR, S. M. *Native Law in South Africa.* Johannesburg: Juta, 1960.

SHAW, REVEREND BARNABAS. *Memorials of South Africa.* London: Mason, Hamilton, Adams, 1841.

SHEPHERD, ROBERT H. W. *Bantu Literature and Life.* Lovedale: The Lovedale Press, 1955.

————. *Children of the Veld.* London: J. Clarke, 1937.

————, and B. G. PAVER. *African Contrasts: The Story of a South African People.* Cape Town: Oxford University Press, 1947.

SIBIYA, CHRISTINA. *Zulu Woman.* New York: Columbia University Press, 1948.

SIEFRIED, ANDRÉ. *African Journey.* (Trans. from the French by Edward Fitzgerald.) London: Jonathan Cape, 1950.

SILBURN, PERCY A. B. *South Africa, White and Black—or Brown?* London: G. Allen and Unwin, 1927.

SILLERY, ANTHONY. *Africa: A Social Geography.* London: Duckworth, 1961.

————. *The Bechuanaland Protectorate.* Cape Town: Oxford University Press, 1952.

SIMMS, KATHARINE L. *Springbok in Sunshine.* London: Hutchinson, 1946.

————. *The Sun-Drenched Veldt.* London: Evans Brothers, 1949.

SIMON, BISHOP JOHN MARIE. *Bishop for the Hottentots: African Memories, 1882–1909.* (Trans. by Angeline Bouchard.) New York: Benziger Brothers, 1959.

SITHOLE, NDABANINGI. *African Nationalism.* Cape Town: Oxford University Press, 1959.

SKOTA, T. MWEL (comp.). *The African Yearly Register: Being an Illustrated National Biographical Dictionary (Who's Who) of Black Folk in Africa.* Johannesburg: R. L. Esson, 1932.

SMITH, EDWIN WILLIAM. *Aggrey of Africa: A Study in Black and White.* Garden City, N.Y.: Doubleday, Doran, 1929.

————. *The Golden Stool: Some Aspects of the Conflict of Cultures in Africa.* London: Holborn, 1926.

————. *Knowing Africa.* London: Butterworth, 1946.

————. *The Life and Times of Daniel Lindley, 1801–1880, Missionary to the Zulus, Pastor of the Voortrekkers.* New York: Library Publishers, 1952.

SMITH, SIR HARRY. *The Autobiography of Lieutenant-General Sir Harry Smith, Baronet of Aliwal on the Stulej, G.C.B.* 2 vols. London: J. Murray, 1901.

————. *Correspondence with the Trek Boers, 1848.* Cape Town: Zuid Afrikaan, 1848.

SMITH, H. LINDSAY. *Behind the Press in South Africa.* Cape Town: Stewart, 1947.

SMITH, R. H. *Labor Resources of Natal.* Cape Town: Oxford University Press, 1950.

SMUTS, JAN CHRISTIAN. *Africa and Some World Problems, Including the Rhodes Memorial Lectures Delivered in Michaelmas Term, 1929, by General J. C. Smuts.* Clarendon: Oxford University Press, 1930.

————. *Greater South Africa: Plans for a Better World.* Johannesburg: The Truth Legion, 1940.

SMUTS, JAN CHRISTIAN. *Toward a Better World*. New York: World Book, 1944.

SMUTS, JAN CHRISTIAN, (JR.). *Jan Christian Smuts*. London: Cassell, 1952.

SOGA, JOHN HENDERSON. *The Ama-Xhosa: Life and Customs*. Lovedale: Lovedale Press, 1932.

———. *The South Eastern Bantu*. Johannesburg: Witwatersrand University Press, 1930.

SOLOMON, W. E. GLADSTONE. *Saul Solomon: The Member for Cape Town*. Cape Town: Oxford University Press, 1948.

South African Churches' Conference. *Christian Responsibility Toward Areas of Rapid Social Change*. Johannesburg, 1960.

South West Africa Annual. Windhoek: South West Africa Publications, since 1956.

SOWDEN, LEWIS. *The Union of South Africa*. Garden City, N.Y.: Doubleday, Doran, 1943.

SPENDER, HAROLD. *General Botha: The Career and the Man*. London: Constable, 1919.

SPIES, F. J. DU TOIT. *Die Dagboek van H. A. L. Hamelberg, 1855–1871*. Cape Town: van Riebeeck Society, 1952.

———. *Hamelberg en die Oranje-Vrystaat*. Amsterdam: Swets and Zeitlinger.

———. *'n Nederlander in Diens van die Oranje-Vrystaat: Uit die Nagelate Papiere van Dr Hendrik P. N. Muller, Oud-Konsul-General van die Oranje Vrystaat*. Amsterdam: Swets and Zeitlinger, 1946.

SPILHAUS, M. W. *The First South Africans*. Cape Town: Juta, 1949.

SPOONER, F. P. *South African Predicament, The Economics of Apartheid*. New York: Frederick A. Praeger, 1960.

SPOTTISWOODE, HILDEGARDE (comp.). *South Africa: The Road Ahead*. Cape Town: Timmins, 1960.

State of the Union: Economic, Financial, and Statistical Year Book for the Union of South Africa. Cape Town: Culemborg, annual.

STICKNEY, ALBERT. *The Transvaal Outlook*. New York: Dodd, Mead, 1900.

STILLMAN, CALVIN W. (ed.). *Africa in the Modern World*. Chicago: University of Chicago Press, 1955.

STOW, GEORGE WILLIAM. *The Native Races of South Africa: A History of the Intrusion of the Hottentots and Bantu into the Hunting Grounds of the Bushman, the Aborigines of the Country*. London: Sonnenschein, 1905.

STRANDBERG, OLLE. *Jambo Means Hello*. (Trans. by Maurice Albert Michael.) Boston: Houghton Mifflin, 1956.

STRANGMAN, EDWARD. *Early French Callers at the Cape*. Cape Town: Juta, 1936.

STUART, JAMES. *A History of the Zulu Rebellion, 1906, and of Dinuzulu's Arrest, Trial and Expatriation*. London: Macmillan, 1913.

SUNDKLER, BENGT G. M. *Bantu Prophets in South Africa*. London: Butterworth, 1948.

SYMONDS, F. ADDINGTON. *The Johannesburg Story*. London: F. Muller, 1953.

TABATA, I. B. *Education for Barbarism in South Africa*. London: Pall Mall Press, 1960.

TABLER, EDWARD C. *The Far Interior: Chronicles of Pioneering in the Matabele and Mashona Countries, 1847–1879*. Cape Town: A. A. Balkema, 1955.

TAIT, BARBARA CAMPBELL. *Cape Cameos: The Story of Cape Town in a New Way*. Cape Town: Stewart, 1948.

TALJAARD, M. S. *A Glimpse of South Africa*. Stellenbosch: University Publishers, 1949.

TANGYE, H. LINCOLN. *In New South Africa: Travels in the Transvaal and Rhodesia.* London: H. Cox, 1896.

TAYLOR, J. V. *Christianity and Politics in Africa.* Harmondsworth: Penguin, 1957.

TAYLOR, REVEREND WILLIAM. *Christian Adventures in South Africa.* New York: Nelson, 1876.

TEENSTRA, M. D. *De Vruchten Mijner Werkzaamheden: Gedurende Mijne Reize over de Kaap de Goede Hoop naar Java.* Groningen: Eekhoff, 1830.

THEAL, GEORGE McCALL. *Documents Relating to the Kaffir War of 1835.* Cape Town: Government Printer, 1912.

——. *Ethnography and Condition of South Africa before A.D. 1505....* London: G. Allen and Unwin, 1919.

——. *History of Africa South of the Zambezi from the Settlement of the Portuguese at Sofala in September 1505 to the Conquest of the Cape Colony by the British in September, 1795.* 3 vols. London: G. Allen and Unwin, 1916–22.

——. *History of the Boers in South Africa.* London: S. Sonnenschein, Lowrey, 1887.

——. *History of South Africa from 1795 to 1872.* 5 vols. London: G. Allen and Unwin, 1915–20.

——. *History of South Africa from 1873 to 1884.* 2 vols. London: G. Allen and Unwin, 1919.

——. *The Portuguese in South Africa, with a Description of the Native Races Between the River Zambezi and the Cape of Good Hope During the Sixteenth Century.* London: T. Fisher Unwin, 1896.

——. *The Yellow and Dark-Skinned People of Africa South of the Zambezi.* London: S. Sonnenschein, 1910.

THOMAS, ELIZABETH M. *The Harmless People.* London: Secker and Warburg, 1959.

THOMPSON, GEORGE. *Travels and Adventures in Southern Africa. . . .* 2 vols. London: Henry Colburn, 1827.

THOMPSON, L. M. *The Unification of South Africa, 1902–1910.* Clarendon: Oxford University Press, 1960.

THUNBERG, C. P. *Voyage en Afrique et en Asie . . . pendant les années 1770–1779.* Paris: Fuchs, 1794.

THWAITE, DANIEL. *Seething African Pot: A Study of Black Nationalism, 1882–1935.* London: Constable, 1936.

TINGSTEN, HERBERT L. S. *The Problem of South Africa.* London: Gollancz, 1955.

TINLEY, JAMES M. *The Native Labor Problem of South Africa.* Chapel Hill: University of North Carolina Press, 1942.

TOEKOMS, JAN. *'When Malan Goes': A Progressive Programme for South Africa.* Johannesburg: Central News Agency, 1953.

TROUP, FREDA. *In Face of Fear: Michael Scott's Challenge to South Africa.* London: Faber and Faber, 1950.

University of Witwatersrand Faculty of Law. *Annual Survey of South African Law.* Johannesburg: Juta, since 1947.

UYS, CORNELIS J. *In the Era of Shepstone: Being a study of British Expansion in South Africa (1842–1877).* Lovedale: Lovedale Press, 1933.

VALENTIJN, FRANÇOIS. *Oud en Nieuw Oost Indien.* 5 vols. Dordrecht: Johannes van Braam, 1724–26.

VAN BILJON, F. J. *State Interference in South Africa.* Westminster: King and Staples, 1939.

VAN BILJON, P. *Grensbakens tussen blank en swart in Suid-Afrika: 'n historiese Ontwikkeling van grensbeleid en beleid van grond toekenning aan die Naturel in Suid-Afrika.* Cape Town: Juta, 1949.

VAN DER HEEVER, C. M. *General Hertzog.* Johannesburg: A.P.B. Bookstore, 1946.

——, and PIENAAR, P. DE V. (eds.). *Kultuurgeskiedenis van die Afrikaner.* 3 vols. Cape Town: Nasionale Pers, 1945–50.

VAN DER HORST, SHEILA. *Native Labour in South Africa.* London: Oxford University Press, 1942.

VAN DER MERWE, N. J. *Marthinus Theunis Steyn.* 2 vols. Bloemfontein: Nasionale Pers, 1921.

VAN DER MERWE, P. J. *Die Noordwaartse Beweging van die Boere voor die Groot Trek, 1770–1842.* Den Haag: W. P. van Stockum, 1937.

——. *Die Trekboer in die geskiedenis van die Kaapkolonie, 1657–1842.* Cape Town: Nasionale Pers, 1938.

——. *Trek-Studies oor die Mobiliteit van die Pionierbevolking aan die Kaap.* Cape Town: Nasionale Pers, 1945.

VAN DER POEL, JEAN. *The Jameson Raid.* Cape Town: Oxford University Press, 1951.

VAN DER POST, LAURENS. *The Dark Eye in Africa.* New York: Morrow, 1955.

——. *The Lost World of the Kalahari.* London: Hogarth Press, 1958. New York: Morrow, 1958.

——. *Venture to the Interior.* New York: Morrow, 1951.

——, AND OTHERS. *Africa's Future.* London: Hogarth Press, 1953.

VAN DER WALT, A. J. H. J. (ed.). *Geskiedenis van Suid Afrika.* 2 vols. Cape Town: Nasionale Boekhandel, 1951.

VAN JAARSVELD, F. A. *Die Ontwaking van die Afrikaanse Nasionale Bewussyn (The Awakening of Afrikaner Nationalism, 1868–1881).* Johannesburg: Voortrekkerpers, 1957.

VAN OORDT, J. W. G. *Slagtersnek.* Amsterdam: de Bussy, 1897.

VAN RENSBURG, HANS. *Their Paths Crossed Mine: Memoirs of the Commandant-General of the Ossewa-Brandwag.* Johannesburg: Central News Agency, 1956.

VAN RENSBURG, PATRICK. *Guilty Land.* London: Jonathan Cape, 1962. New York: Frederick A. Praeger, 1962.

VAN RIEBEECK, JAN. *Journal.* 3 vols. Cape Town: Van Riebeeck Society, 1952–54.

VAN ROOYEN, JAN J. *Die Nasionale Party: Sy Opkoms en Oorwinning—Kaapland se Aandeel.* Elsiesrivier: Nasionale Handelsdrukkery, 1956.

VAN TONDER, I. W. *Oom Izak van Kaapstad Kyk Terug.* Cape Town: Nasionale Pers, 1946.

VAN WINTER, P. J. *Onder Krugers Hollanders: Geschiedenis van de Nederlandsche Zuid Afrikaansche Spoorweg Maatscappij.* 2 vols. Amsterdam: de Bussy, 1937.

VEDDER, HEINRICH. *South West Africa in Early Times: Being the Story of South West Africa Up to the Date of Maharero's Death in 1890.* (Trans. and ed. by Cyril G. Hall.) London: Oxford University Press, 1938.

VENTER, M. J. *Joop Gaan op Kommando.* Johannesburg: Afrikaanse Persboekhandel, 1945.

VULLIAMY, COLWYN EDWARD. *Outlanders: A Study of Imperial Expansion in South Africa, 1877–1902.* London: Jonathan Cape, 1938.

WALKER, ERIC A. *The Cape Native Franchise.* Cape Town: National Conference on the Native Bills, 1936.

WALKER, ERIC A. *The Frontier Tradition in South Africa*. London: Oxford University Press, 1930.

———. *The Great Trek*. London: A. and C. Black, 1934.

———. *A History of South Africa*. London: Longmans, Green, 1957.

———. *Lord de Villiers and His Times: South Africa, 1842–1914*. London: Constable, 1925.

———. *The South African College and the University of Cape Town . . . 1829–1929*. Cape Town: *Cape Times*, 1929.

———. *W. P. Schreiner: A South African*. London: Oxford University Press, 1937.

WALKER, OLIVER. *Sailor Malan: A Biography*. London: Cassell, 1953.

WALLBANK, T. WALTER. *Contemporary Africa: Continent in Transition*. Princeton: D. van Nostrand, 1956.

WALLIS, J. P. R. *Fitz: The Story of Sir Percy FitzPatrick*. London: Macmillan, 1955.

———. *Thomas Baines: Artist and Explorer*. London: Jonathan Cape, 1941.

——— (ed.). *The Northern Goldfield Diaries of Thomas Baines*. 3 vols. London: Chatto and Windus, 1946.

WALTON, SIR EDGAR H. *Inner History of the National Convention of South Africa*. New York: Longmans, Green, 1912.

WANGEMANN, T. *Die Berliner Mission in Zulu-lands mit Bildern*. Berlin: Evang. Missionshaus, 1875.

WARD HARRIET. *The Cape and the Kaffirs: A Diary of Five Years' Residence in Kaffirland*. London: Henry G. Bohn, 1851.

WARREN, SIR CHARLES. *On the Veldt in the Seventies*. London: Isbister, 1902.

WATERHOUSE, GILBERT (ed.). *Simon van der Stel's Journal, 1684–1686*. 1936.

WEEBER, E. J. *Op die Transvaalse Front, 1 Junie 1900 tot 31 Oktober 1900*. Bloemfontein: Nasionale Pers, 1942.

WEILBACH, J. D. and DU PLESSIS, C. N. J. *Geschkeidenis van de Emigranten—Boeren en van den Vrijheidsoorlog*. Cape Town: Saul Solomon, 1882.

WEINBREN, B., and WALKER, IVAN L. *Two Thousand Casualties*. Johannesburg: South African Trade Union Council, 1961.

WELCH, SIDNEY R. *Europe's Discovery of South Africa*. Cape Town: Juta, 1935.

———. *South Africa under John III, 1521–1557*. Cape Town: Juta, 1949.

———. *South Africa under King Manuel, 1495–1521*. Cape Town: Juta, 1946.

———. *South Africa under King Sebastian and the Cardinal, 1557–1580*. Cape Town: Juta, 1949.

WELLINGTON, JOHN H. *Southern Africa: A Geographical Study*. 2 vols. Cambridge: The University Press, 1955.

WELLS, ARTHUR WALTER. *Southern Africa Today and Yesterday*. New York: Dutton, 1956.

WESSELS, J. W. *History of Roman-Dutch Law*. Grahamstown: African Book Company, 1908.

WESTERMANN, DIEDRICH. *Africa and Christianity*. London: Oxford University Press, 1937.

———. *The African Today and Tomorrow*. London: Oxford University Press, 1949.

WETHERELL, V. *The Indian Question in South Africa*. Cape Town: Unie-Volkspers, 1946.

WHEARE, K. C. *The Statute of Westminster and Dominion Status*. London: Oxford University Press, 1953.

WHITE, A. C. *The Call of the Bushveld*. Bloemfontein, 1948.

WHITFIELD, G. M. B. *South African Native Law.* Cape Town: Juta, 1948.

WHITTALL, W. *With Botha and Smuts in Africa.* London: Cassell, 1917.

WHYTE, FREDERIC. *The Life of W. T. Stead.* London: Jonathan Cape, 1925.

WIEDNER, Donald L. *A History of Africa South of Sahara.* New York: Random House, 1962.

WIERINGA, P. A. C. *De Oudste Boeren-Republieken: Graaff-Reinet en Zwellendam van 1775–1806.* The Hague: M. Nijhoff, 1921.

WILDE, RICHARD. *Joseph Chamberlain and the South African Republic, 1895–1899.* Cape Town: Archives Yearbook, 1956.

WILKINSON, MRS. *A Lady's Life and Travels in Zululand and the Transvaal During Cetewayo's Reign.* London: J. T. Hayes, 1882.

WILKINSON, SPENSER. *British Policy in South Africa.* London: S. Low, Marston, 1899.

WILLIAMS, A. F. BASIL. *Botha, Smuts and South Africa.* New York: Macmillan, 1948.

———. *Cecil Rhodes.* London: Constable, 1938.

———. *My Life and Two South African Pioneers.* Cape Town: Unie-Volkspers, 1946.

WILLIAMS, J. GRENFELL. *Moshesh: The Man on the Mountain.* London: Oxford University Press, 1950.

WILLOUGHBY, W. C. *Native Life on the Transvaal Border.* London: Simpkin Marshall, Hamilton, Kent, 1900.

———. *Race Problems in the New Africa: A Study of the Relation of Bantu and Britons in Those Parts of Bantu Africa . . . Under British Control.* Oxford: Clarendon Press, 1923.

WILSON, D. F. *Smuts of South Africa: Soldier and Peacemaker.* London: S.C.M. Press, 1946.

WILSON, G. H. *Gone Down the Years.* Cape Town: Timmins, 1947.

WILSON, HELEN C. *The Two Scapegoats.* Pietermaritzburg: P. Davis, 1914.

WILSON, MONICA (HUNTER). *Reaction to Conquest: Effects of Contact with Europeans on the Pondo of South Africa.* 2nd. ed. London: Oxford University Press, 1960.

———. *Social Structure.* Pietermaritzburg: Shuter and Shooter, 1952.

WILSON, LADY SARAH. *South African Memories: Social, Warlike, and Sporting.* London: Edward Arnold, 1909.

WOLTON, DOUGLAS G. *Whither South Africa?* London: Lawrence and Wishart, 1947.

WOOD, C. T. (ed.). *Where We Stand.* Cape Town: Oxford University Press, 1960.

WOODS, CLEMENT A. *The Indian Community of Natal: Their Economic Position.* Cape Town: Oxford University Press, 1954.

WOON, CAPTAIN HARRY VERNON. *Twenty-Five Years Soldiering in South Africa.* London: Andrew Melrose, 1909.

WORSFOLD, WILLIAM BASIL. *Lord Milner's Work in South Africa from Its Commencement in 1897 to the Peace of Vereeniging in 1902.* London: J. Murray, 1906.

———. *South Africa: A Study in Colonial Administration and Development.* London: Methuen, 1927.

———. *The Union of South Africa.* London: J. Pitman and Sons, 1912.

WRENCH, JOHN EVELYN. *Alfred Lord Milner: The Man of No Illusions, 1854–1925.* London: Eyre and Spottiswoode, 1958.

WRIGHT, CHARLOTTE. *Beneath the Southern Cross: The Story of an American Bishop's Wife in South Africa.* New York: Exposition Press, 1955.

WYMER, NORMAN. *The Man from the Cape.* London: Evans Brothers, 1959.

Young, Francis Bret. *In South Africa.* London: Heinemann, 1952.
Young, Robert. *African Wastes Reclaimed: The Story of the Lovedale Mission.* London: J. M. Dent, 1902.
Ziervogel, C. Brown. *South Africa.* Cape Town: M. Miller, 1938.

Unpublished Materials

African National Congress. 'Constitution of the African National Congress.' (Mimeographed.)
Afrikaanse Studentebond. 'Constitution.' Pretoria, 1958. (Mimeographed.)
———. 'Gedenkblad, 1948–1958.' Pretoria, 1958.
———. 'Notule van Twaalfde Bondskongres, 28 Maart tot 2 April 1960.' Pretoria, 1960. (Mimeographed.)
———. 'Waarvandan? Waarom? Waarheen?' Pretoria, 1959. (Mimeographed.)
The Black Sash. "Constitution of the Black Sash.' October, 1959. (Mimeographed.)
Buskes, J. J. 'South Africa's Apartheid Policy—Unacceptable.' Heidelberg, Transvaal, 1956. (Multigraphed.)
Communist Party of South Africa. 'Constitution of the Communist Party of South Africa.' (Mimeographed.)
———. 'The War and South Africa: A Report given by J. Morkel to a Conference of the Communist Party of South Africa, 23 March 1940.' Johannesburg, 1940. (Mimeographed.)
———. Political Bureau. 'The Communist Party's Policy on the War Now!' Johannesburg, 1940. (Mimeographed.)
Friedman, Bernard. 'Constitutional Policy.' Johannesburg: The Progressive Party, n.d. (Mimeographed.)
Hertzog, General J. B. M. 'Text of Smithfield Address, 7 November 1935, Exposing the Afrikaner Broederbond.' (Mimeographed.) In Afrikaans.
———. 'English text of Smithfield Address, 7 November 1935, Exposing the Afrikaner Broederbond.' (Mimeographed.)
Jonker, A. H. 'The Broederbond and Christian National Education: A Searching Examination.' (Mimeographed.)
Levy, Leon. 'Presidential Address to the Third Annual National Conference of the South African Congress of Trade Unions." Johannesburg: SACTU, 1958. (Mimeographed.)
Luthuli, Albert J. 'Address at Indian Centenary Observance Held at Curries Fountain, Durban, 16 November 1960.' (Mimeographed.)
Maliba, A. M. 'The Conditions of the Venda People.' ('Nkululeko Pamphlet,' No. 1.) Johannesburg: Communist Party District Committee, 1940. (Mimeographed.)
Martin, A. C. 'Speech at Rally, Durban, 14 November 1960. (Mimeographed.)
'Memorandum on the Extension of Passes to African Women Submitted to the Native Commissioner of Durban by the African Women's Anti-Pass Committee, 1960.' (Mimeographed.)
'Memorandum Presented by the South African Indian Congress to Mr Dag Hammarskjold . . . April 1960.' (Mimeographed.)
Naicker, G. M. 'Racial Differentiations: The Colour Bar.' n.p., n.d. (Mimeographed.)

Natal Indian Congress. 'Amended Constitution Adopted by Fifth Provincial Conference, 1951.' (Mimeographed.)

——. 'Twelfth Annual Provincial Conference Held at Durban 9–11 October 1959: Agenda Book.' Durban, 1959. (Mimeographed.)

Nasionale Jeugbond van Transvaal. 'Handleidings Tweede Hersiene Druk, 1959.' Johannesburg, 1959. (Mimeographed.)

National Union of South African Students. 'Correlated Resolutions of NUSAS Policy as of August 1960.' Cape Town, 1960. (Mimeographed.)

——. 'Minutes, 36th Annual Student Assembly, 3–14 July 1960.' Cape Town, 1960. (Mimeographed.)

Progressive Party of South Africa. 'The Constitution Incorporating the Principles of the Party Adopted at Inaugural Congress, 13–14 November 1959.' Johannesburg, 1959. (Mimeographed.)

——. 'Fact Paper.' Johannesburg: Progressive Party, issued from time to time since 21 April 1960. (Mimeographed.)

——. 'Main Principles and Policies Adopted at Inaugural Congress, 13–14 November 1959.' Johannesburg, 1959. (Mimeographed.)

——. 'Motion on Franchise Qualification.' Johannesburg, 1960. (Mimeographed.)

——. 'National Congress 1960, 15–16 November, Duncan Hall, Johannesburg.' Johannesburg, 1960. (Mimeographed.)

'Report of the Tomlinson Commission for the Socio-Economic Development of the Bantu Areas.' 17 vols. Unpublished manuscript in possession of Professor F. R. Tomlinson, Pretoria.

Socialist League of Africa. 'Ten Years of the Stay-at-Home: A Critical Discussion.' 1960. (Mimeographed.)

South African National Party. 'Constitution.' Cape Town, n.d. (Mimeographed.)

South African Bond. 'The South African Bond's Programme of Principles and Policies for Peace, Progress and Prosperity.' Johannesburg, 1960. (Mimeographed.)

South African Congress of Trade Unions. 'Annual report presented to the Third Annual National Conference, 17–18 March 1958.' Johannesburg, 1958. (Mimeographed.)

——. 'Minutes, Fifth Annual National Conference." Johannesburg, 1960. (Mimeographed.)

——. 'Minutes, First Annual National Conference, 1–4 March 1956.' Johannesburg, 1956. (Mimeographed.)

——. 'Minutes, Fourth Annual National Conference, 28–29 March 1959.' Johannesburg, 1959. (Mimeographed.)

——. 'Minutes, Third Annual National Conference, 17–18 March 1958.' Johannesburg, 1958. (Mimeographed.)

——. 'Annual Report and Balance Sheet for the year ended March, 1957. Second Annual National Conference, 12–14 April 1957.' Johannesburg, 1957. (Mimeographed.)

——. "Annual Report and Balance Sheet for the year ended March, 1956. First Annual National Conference, 1–4 March 1956.' Johannesburg, 1956. (Mimeographed.)

——. 'Presidential Address to the Fifth Annual National Conference, October, 1960.' Johannesburg, 1960. (Mimeographed.)

————. 'Presidential Address to the Fourth Annual National Conference, 28–29 March 1959.' Johannesburg, 1959. (Mimeographed.)

South African Congress of Trade Unions. 'Report of the General Secretary Pre-esnted to the Fourth Annual National Conference, 28–29 March 1959.' Johannesburg, 1959. (Mimeographed.)

————. 'Report of the Secretariat Presented to the Fifth Annual National Conference, October, 1960,' Johannesburg, 1960. (Mimeographed.)

————. 'Statement of Policy To Be Submitted to the First Annual Conference of SACTU To Be Held in Cape Town on March 1st, 2nd, and 3rd, 1956.' Johannesburg, 1956. (Mimeographed.)

South African Indian Congress. 'Statements and Addresses.' Durban. (Mimeographed.)

————. 'Twenty-First Conference of the South African Indian Congress Held at Durban, 9–11 July 1954.' (Mimeographed.)

————. 'Twenty-Second Conference of the South African Indian Congress Held at Johannesburg, 19–21 October 1956.' (Mimeographed.)

South African Labour Party. 'Non-European Franchise Policy.' Johannesburg, 1954. (Mimeographed.)

————. 'Non-European Policy.' Johannesburg, 1946. (Mimeographed.)

South West Africa. 'Budget Speech, 1960.' Windhoek: Administrator for SWA, 1960. (Mimeographed.)

————. 'Supplements to the 1960 Budget Speech.' Windhoek: Administrator for SWA, 1960. (Mimeographed.)

Suzman, Arthur. 'Race Classification in South Africa: An Analysis of the Union's Legislative Spectrum.' (Unpublished manuscript.)

Union Defence Forces. Intelligence Division. 'The Afrikaner Broederbond.' Pretoria, 29 March 1944. (Mimeographed.)

Union of South Africa. Government Information Office. 'Crown Outlines Treason Allegations.' New York, 1957. (Mimeographed.)

————. Government Information Office. 'Notes on the Judicial Procedures Applicable in Connection with the Treason Preparatory Examination at Present Being Conducted in Johannesburg.' New York, 1957. Mimeographed.)

————. Information Service of South Africa. 'South Africa and the Commonwealth.' New York, 1961. (Mimeographed.)

United Party. 'South African "Nationalism—Its Black Record in the 1939–1945 War." ' Johannesburg, n.d.

————. Division of Information and Research. 'A Review of the United Party Contribution to the 1959 Session of Parliament.' Johannesburg, 1959. (Mimeographed.)

————. Division of Information and Research. 'Notes for speeches.' Johannesburg, 1959. (Mimeographed.)

————. Division of Information and Research. 'Speakers' Notes—Addendum: Special Note on Defection of Certain Members of the Party After Union Congress, 1959.' Johannesburg, 1959. (Mimeographed.)

————. Division of Information and Research. 'Transvaal Provincial Elections, 1959; Notes on Provincial Matters.' Johannesburg, 1959. (Mimeographed.)

————. Division of Information and Research. 'United Party Policy Statements.' Johannesburg, 1957. (Mimeographed.)

United Party. Division of Organization. 'The United Party Union Congress.'
Johannesburg: J. D. Opperman, 1959. (Mimeographed.)

University College of Zululand. 'Information for Students, 1959–1960.'
(Mimeographed.)

'Wie Regeer Suid-Afrika? Die volk teen Die Broederbond.' (Mimeographed.)

World Council of Churches Consultation. 'Statements.' Johannesburg, 7–14
December 1960. (Mimeographed.)

Appendices

APPENDIX I. GENERAL J. B. M. HERTZOG'S SMITHFIELD ADDRESS, NOVEMBER 7, 1935, EXPOSING THE AFRIKANER BROEDERBOND

In answering the question, who is responsible for the present discord among our people?, you must permit me to go back briefly to 1913-14 when the old Nationalist Party was formed; for the first time, the Afrikaans-speaking portion of our population was torn into two. As you will all still remember, leading men in the Church and the congregation pleaded strongly with us against the breaking away and the separation. Congresses were even held to try and persuade us against breaking away from the South African Party, and to go back.

The answer will also still be fresh in the memory of all of you, namely, that as soon as we had realized the three great ideals which we had gone out to strive for: namely, national freedom, language equality, and acknowledgement of the motto, South Africa First, we would again take the hand of those whom we had left behind and would again work with them in a spirit of national unity.

We went from platform to platform in all the Provinces—Natal no less than the Free State—and everywhere we invited and encouraged the population—English-speaking no less than the Dutch-speaking—to come and help us to realize our ideals, and each time we also gave them the assurance that when we had succeeded in gaining our ideals, we would see to the restoration of the unity of the Afrikaner nation, English-speaking as well as Dutch-speaking.

Our struggle was extraordinarily successful. By November, 1926, we had already achieved our three fixed ideals to such an extent that Dr Malan, in a press interview with the *Volksblad* of November 24, 1926, when speaking about the Declaration of our Freedom by the Imperial Conference, had to exclaim with passionate enthusiasm:

> I look upon this as the most important step which has ever yet been taken in the actual and enduring conciliation of the two races. . . . By this the walls of division between English- and Dutch-speaking Afrikaners will fall away completely, and any feeling of grievance against England which might still exist, would disappear, and on the foundation of a general S.A. patriotism, a great united South African nation will be built up.

That this was not just an emotional outburst of a timely nature by Dr Malan, but actually his decided conviction, appears from his opening speech of October 7, 1927, before the Nationalist Party Congress at Robertson which, as reported in the Minutes of the Congress, reads as follows:

> Continuing, Dr Malan pointed out that in the past there had been striven for the restoration of the unity of our people but that the reconciliation movement . . . had failed because the Nationalist Party strove for unity with independence. The last-mentioned has now been obtained, and it is therefore clear that the restoration of the national unity is today an obvious matter.

Even in February of last year (1934) the following report of a press interview by Dr Malan with the *Vaderland*, was approved by him when in the proof.

> Dr Malan declared himself enthusiastically in favour of a united Afrikanerdom by which was meant an Afrikanerdom of English-speaking as well as Afrikaans-speaking people, on the foundation of South African nationality. It would be a happening of tremendous significance to the Afrikanerdom of the future and to our country, if we could unite all national feeling Afrikaners in united strength, on the forward path, and so eradicate the unfortunate division and quarrelling which has during the past twenty-two years existed between Afrikaner and Afrikaner.

Quite a number of other extracts from speeches by Dr Malan since November, 1926, could be made which would show to what extent Dr Malan was convinced that with the obtaining of our national freedom the time had also arrived for a united Afrikanerdom of English- as well as Afrikaans-speaking people: but after what I have already quoted it will be unnecessary for you to be still further convinced of Dr Malan's feelings during that period about the necessity of bringing into being a South African national unity, in which all Afrikaners, English-speaking as well as Dutch-speaking, would be included.

Within four months, however, after his enthusiastic declaration of February 27, just quoted by me, pleading for national unity between all Afrikaners as something which would be of tremendously great significance for our country, we find Dr Malan at a Conference of the Nationalist Party in Pretoria, where, in co-operation with Dr N. J. v. d. Merwe, exerting all his strength to destroy national unity at that Conference, we see him call his followers together to separate themselves and establish a separate party of 'purified Nationalists'. Instead of continuing with his pleading for a united Afrikanerdom, Dr Malan suddenly swerved and became the champion of division and quarrelling among the Afrikaner people.

A sudden swinging round of this kind, such as carried out by Dr Malan tearing the Afrikaner people right to the depths, must have had a very serious reason as its prime cause. I will come back later to the answer as to what that reason might be. Meanwhile, I must remind you how that, ever since Coalition, I constantly requested Dr Malan as well as Dr van der Merwe, with their Cape and Free State schismatic followers, to tell us: 'What was the object and what did they think to gain by division and quarrelling, which could not equally well have been obtained by national unity and co-operation?' To this question they have constantly failed to give a satisfactory answer.

It was clear to me from the beginning that they could not give an honest satisfactory answer; and just because I was convinced of it, that they were busy driving after something, by means of national disunity, of such a nature that they did not dare to make it public. It was clear to me that racial feeling, ill-feeling toward the English section of the Afrikaans population was influencing their conduct. I had also, on various occasions, persisted that Dr Malan and other purified Nationalist leaders did not want to work with the United Party, mainly for the reason that they were cherishing a strong racial feeling against the English-speaking people amongst us, and because they wanted to domineer over them and to accept no equality in co-operation with them.

This was strongly censured as a gross insult by Dr Malan and his purified Nationalist fellow leaders that I should have laid such a thing as a charge against them.

I do not wish to deal Dr Malan any injustice and therefore, when I this evening repeat the statement that he was led by racial feeling in 1933 when he refused to take part in Coalition; and that, when in 1934, he refused to support Fusion, and went over to the establishing of a new party, by means of which purposeful national division was caused, he was led by racial feeling and the desire to rule and to domineer over the English-speaking portion of our fellow Afrikaners, it is a statement which I am now prepared to prove out of documents about the genuineness of which there is no doubt whatsoever.

Before I start to give you the proof of what I have just said, you must allow me to make a disclosure to you of a discovery which fell to my lot recently. It concerns a secret society called 'The Afrikaner Broederbond' and the relation in which Dr Malan and other prominent leaders of the purified Nationalist Party stand to it.

The Afrikaner Broederbond is a secret society founded in 1918. According to its original destiny and object it was entrusted with the praise-worthy object of caring for and watching over the cultural needs of the Dutch-speaking Afrikanerdom, with a clear stipulation in its Constitution: party politics are excluded from the Bond. There can therefore be no objection made to the Broederbond's membership being confined to the Dutch-speaking people, and, as a purely cultural association, I will accept it that the Bond also did good work.

As far as the Bond was of a purely cultural nature with purely cultural objects, no particular objection could either be made to its having come into being as a secret society, except that out of the nature of the case with secret societies they may be misused for other ends than those destined for them and also cause great danger.

Unfortunately THIS is exactly what happened also with the Bond. Party politics could not for always be kept out of it; and according to the measure that the influence and political views of a certain section in our public life increased in the Bond, the Bond recreated from a cultural to a party-political association, as will appear from what I am further going to tell you.

Already in August 1932 this Broederbond had advanced so far on the road of a political association that the Chairman of the Executive Council, which is the highest authority of the Bond, could declare as Chairman of the Bond Congress, with the general approval of the Congress:

> We, the Afrikaner Broederbond, may not withdraw its hand from the cultural work because so many wide-awake maintainers have come to the front. But yet, for the time being, provision has been made in that first actually national need.
>
> In accordance with this new situation we find that the AB is slowly handing over the cultural work itself to our so much bigger son, the FAK, and I think that we shall be wise to follow the same course also with this Bond Council.
>
> I consider that national culture and the welfare of the nation will not be able to flourish to the fullest extent if the people of South Africa do not politically break all foreign bonds.
>
> After the cultural and economic needs, the AB will have to dedicate its attention to the political needs of our people. And with this the aim must be a completely independent real Afrikaans Government for South Africa. A Government which by its embodiment in our own personal Head of the State, bone of our bone, and flesh of our flesh, who will inspire us and bind us together to irresistible unity and power (*sic*).

Yet the Bond had quickly to go much further on the party-political road. On January 16, 1934, a circular letter was sent out by the highest executive authority of the Bond, namely the Executive Council, signed by the Chairman, Professor J. C. van Rooy, and the Chief Secretary, Mr I. M. Lombard. This letter, which was addressed to all members of the AB, read as follows:

> Our test of Brotherhood and Afrikanerhood is not a party-political direction but . . . persons who strive for the ideal of the everlasting existence of a separate Afrikaans nation with its own culture. Above all at the former Bond Council it was clearly expressed that one expected from such persons that they would have as their object Afrikanizing of South Africa in all its spheres of life. Brothers, your Executive Council cannot say to you: 'Further party-political Fusion or Union or Reunion; or fight against it . . . but we can however make a call on every Brother to choose in the sphere of party politics what, according to his fixed conviction, is the most profitable for the object of the Bond and the Bond's ideal, as recorded above and as known to all of us. Let us keep the eye fixed on this that the main object is . . . that the Afrikanerdom shall reach its ultimate destiny of domination in South Africa.' . . . Brothers, our solution for South Africa's troubles is not that this or that

party shall gain the upper hand, but that the Afrikaner Broederbond shall rule South Africa.

In order to realize the real tendency and the meaning of the words just quoted by me from the Chairman's speech of Professor du Plessis and the Circular from the Executive Committee of the Bond, one must take note here that to become a member of the Broederbond a person must comply with the following demands:

1. He must be Afrikaans-speaking.
2. His home language must be Afrikaans.
3. He must strive after the ideal of the everlasting existence of a separate Afrikaans nation with its own culture.

As has been declared on certain occasions by Mr du Plessis, Professor van Rooy, and others, in the Broederbond circles, under the designation Afrikaner only the Dutch Afrikanerdom is understood, which also is made abundantly clear in the Constitution and other articles by the Bond.

When one considers now that when the two Potchefstroom teachers use the words Afrikaner and Afrikanerdom, they mean only the Dutch-speaking Afrikaner and Dutch-speaking Afrikanerdom, and when one further takes into consideration, that the membership of the Afrikaner Broederbond is strictly limited to the Dutch-speaking persons, the words of Mr du Plessis as little as those of Professor van Rooy, leave any doubt as to what is meant here.

The high ideal and the striving of the Afrikaner Broederbond is, according to what they communicate to us, to let the Dutch-speaking Afrikanerdom gain domination in South Africa, and to bring about that the Dutch-speaking Broederbond shall rule South Africa!

Very nice, is it not? Flattering to the soul of the Dutch-speaking Afrikaner, like you and I! Only it suffers from a great defect—the defect that must necessarily lead to the downfall of Dutch-speaking Afrikanerdom itself, if there is any continuation of perseverance in this kind of Afrikaner-jingo self-glorification; it is being forgotten, for instance, that there are also English-speaking Afrikaners in South Africa, who also are entitled to a place in the South African sun. When will this mad, fatal idea cease to exist with some people of thinking that they are the chosen of the gods to rule over others? The English-speaking tried it and did not manage it over the Afrikaans-speaking. The Afrikaans-speaking also tried it and did not succeed over the English-speaking people. Neither the one nor the other will ever succeed in dominating the other; and when Potchefstroom fanaticism is out once more to try and incite Dutch-speaking Afrikanerdom to a repetition of the past, then I would ask the Dutch-speaking Afrikanerdom—my nation—has South Africa not yet suffered enough in the past from Afrikaner quarrelling and disagreement? Is our language, our freedom, of so little value to us and so little significance, that we must once again gamble with it all purely on account of racialism and fanaticism?

When I called out a little while ago, 'Very nice, is it not? Flattering to the soul of the Dutch-speaking Afrikaner like you and I!' I unfortunately forgot one thing. Out of the dictates and stipulations of the Broederbond, even as from the Circular letter of the Executive Committee and Professor van Rooy, it appears quite clear, unfortunately, that when there is any talk by them about the Afrikaner or the Afrikanerdom which must dominate South Africa, you and I, not being Brothers, are not included in it! You and I will just have to comfort ourselves, that we shall never have the privilege of sharing in the Broederbond domination in South Africa! We are not Afrikaners!

Yet, what is more, even all the Broers do not count as Afrikaners, or are accounted worthy of having a share in that privilege of domination! According to the test put forward by the Executive Council and Professor van Rooy, as to the true Afrikanerhood, it is only people who have as their aim the Afrikanizing of South Africa, in all its spheres of life. Since this means an Afrikanizing with the exclusion of the English language and the English Afrikaner, so also a fusion brother, like you and I, and everyone who is a supporter of national unity, is immediately excepted from the privileged circle of real Afrikaners, predestined by Professor van Rooy and his Executive Council to domination in South Africa!

With the opening speech of Mr du Plessis quoted by me, and the Circular letter of the Executive Council, signed by Professor van Rooy, the Afrikaner Broederbond is deprived of its cultural mask, and has entered the political arena with no undecided call to arms! As will appear much more clearly just now: the Broederbond has been translated into a secret purified Nationalist Party which busies itself with secret propaganda work for the advantage of the interests of the purified Broeders and of the purified Nationalist Party.

As can be expected, since 1932, the Bond has been placed more and more at the disposal of the purified Nationalist Party, and its doors have been set wide open for everyone who can go through as leaders and prominent members of the purified Nationalists. The wider the doors are opened to the purified Party, the tighter they are closed to the United Party, so that while, since that time, not a single foremost political person, active in the politics and belonging to the United-minded or the United Party, has been admitted to the Bond, the Broederbond's membership list has been added to by nearly all the promient bearers of arms and propagandists of the purified Nationalist Party.

The Broederbond has also, since that time, fallen almost exclusively into the hands of the purified Nationalists, with the pushing aside as far as possible of all Brothers who do not belong to the purified Party. It is also to the Purified Nationalist Brothers that we must impute the fact that the Bond, since that time, has been misued for the purposes and objects for which it was never intended, and which so badly shocked the feeling of right and honesty among the Brothers who did not belong to the purified Nationalist Party, and that some of them were obliged to take refuge in actual protest.

I have just said that since 1932 the Bond has been more and more placed at the disposal of the purified Nationalist Party and its purposes. To the question how that this can be possible without the knowledge of the Fusion-Brothers in the Bond, the answer is quite simple.   The nonpurified, who are known as unsympathetic with the purified politics, or as active Fusionists, are simply ignored and avoided as apostate Brothers, and are left as far as possible in the dark with regard to what is going on.   As regards matters of interest to the purified Nationalist Party, they are not consulted, and thus remain in ignorance of what is being done.

How easy it is for a section to intrigue to their hearts' content, as pointed out here, is understandable when I say that it is an order to every member of the Bond that every member must be well acquainted with every other member of his division.   Everyone knows therefore, for instance, who is a Fusionist or not and who must be avoided as an apostate.

Whatever therefore may have been the cultural aim and striving of the Afrikaner Broederbond in the past, in the light of what has been laid before me, there can be no doubt that we have today in the Broederbond to deal with a secret political association accessible only to and consisting only of Afrikaans-speaking members, the leading political spirits of whom are determined to rule South Africa over the heads of the English-speaking among us; and who are striving to raise Dutch-speaking Afrikanerdom to domination in South Africa, with the neglect of the rights and claims of the English-speaking portion of our population.

This is the declared striving of the Bond as a secret political association, as we have now heard, as well out of the words of the Potchefstroom professor, du Plessis, speaking as the Chairman of the Broederbond Congress, and also out of the Circular of the Executive Council itself, specially circulated for information to all members of the Bond.

Of this secret Broederbond, which places as its ideal, dissension and disunity among the Afrikaner nation by the exclusion of the English portion from the government of the country, Dr Malan, since Coalition, has become a member.

It is quite clear at present to everyone why Dr Malan changed so suddenly from a supporter to an opponent of Afrikaner national unity. His joining of this secret anti-English Afrikaner movement must have obliged him inevitably to discard the policy of national unity with the inclusion of the English-speaking Afrikaner; and he was also further obliged by his connection with the Broederbond to enter the road of national disunity and disagreement.

Out of what has been communicated by me three perfectly clear theorems follow:

1. That membership of this secret association is completely incompatible with co-operation for the realization of a united Afrikanerdom of English- and Afrikaans-speaking.
2. That Dr Malan, by becoming a member of this secret association, necessarily had to become untrue to his former doctrine of a united nation and necessarily had to refuse co-operation with the United Party as was done by him.

3. That when Dr Malan denies that, with his refusal to work together with the United Party for national unity, he was influenced and is still being influenced by racial feeling and the desire to domineer over the English portion of our population, he is making himself guilty of falsehood.

The question with which I began my speech to you this evening has been answered now. We know now quite definitely who and what is responsible for the national division and disagreement amongst us. What a miserable figure is cut by Dr Malan in this pitiful episode of our national history.

Yet what I have said here this evening about Dr Malan concerns to no lesser degree his chief lieutenants, Dr van der Merwe, Adv. Swart, Dr C. W. du Toit, Adv. J. G. Strydom, Messrs Werth, Haywood, Martins, etc., all of them members of the Broederbond, and thus all of them, together with Dr Malan, obliged not to support any national unity in co-operation with the English portion of our fellow-citizens.

Even as Dr Malan, they have taken an oath secretly to permit no co-operation from the English side with an eye to national unity, and in this way they stand in direct racial conflict with our English fellow-Afrikaners, striving by means of an Afrikaans-speaking domination to place the foot on the neck of English-speaking South Africa.

We also see now in what a close relation the Afrikaner Broederbond stands to the purified Nationalist Party. The leaders and the leading spirits of the one are the leaders and leading spirits of the other. If we take the Transvaal we find: Adv. Strydom, Mr L. J. du Plessis, and others as members of both. If we take the Cape, we find: Dr Malan, Rev. C. W. du Toit, Mr Stephen le Roux, and others. When we come to the Free State, we have: Dr van der Merwe, Adv. Swart, Messrs Werth, Haywood, Hiemstra, Dr van Rhyn, etc. There is no doubt that the secret Broederbond is nothing else but the purified Nationalist Party, secretly busy underground, and that the purified Nationalist Party is, as the secret Afrikaner Broederbond, carrying on its activities above ground. Between the two the unity of Afrikanerdom is exchanged for a Republican-Calvinistic Bond!

By leaving the territory of pure national culture and mixing itself with politics, the Afrikaner Broederbond abandoned its youthful innocence, and suddenly became a most threatening danger, as well to the rest and peace of our citizen society, as to the pure irreproachableness of our public life and of our civil administration—even when it moves in the economic-cultural sphere.

To realize the nature and extent of the danger with which we are being threatened at present by the secret interference and activities of the Broederbond, it is necessary for me to communicate to you something from the secret documents of the Bond about its organization, members, and various other particulars.

How densely secret the Bond is in all its goings out and comings in, becomes evident immediately from the extremely small number of persons outside its ranks which even knows about its existence, although it has been in existence for seventeen years already, and there are but a few towns or villages in the Free State in which it has not got its organization doing active work.

The members of the Bond are not many—at the utmost about 2,000. The strength of the Bond does not lie in its membership, but in its secret organization, which, for instance, is spread over the whole of the Free State like a network, destined for active propaganda, where through each cell or nest, any kind of information useful to the purified Nationalist Party, whether true or false, can be gathered up and spread still further. The kind of propaganda which goes out from these nests is of the same nature as what is found again daily in *Die Volksblad* or *Die Burger*. Here, in this network of secret propaganda, the strength and influence of the Bond mainly lies. Yet not only here. The Broederbond stands in secrecy in the closest relationship with a whole number of other institutions, which are being exploited by interested politicians and semipoliticians, who intentionally use them secretly as instruments for the furtherance of secret aims. The FAK, the Handhawersbond, the Helpmekaar, the Voortrekkers, the Republican Bond, the Calvinistic Bond, however useful and necessary some of them might also be for the Dutch-speaking Afrikaner nation and their interests, are all being systematically used and misused by means of the Bond. Under a very solemn promise every member is bound to the most stringent secrecy. Nothing concerning the Bond, its existence, its members, its activities or organization dares to be made known.

The Bond is organized in local divisions or branches of at least five members, each with its own directorate and its own by-laws. For the rest, each division stands by itself and does what its directorate pleases as a separate independent unit, if need be without knowledge of the rest—a secret circle or little circle within a secret organization. At the head of the Bond stands the Executive Council of nine members, chosen annually at the Bond Council or Congress, and embued with unlimited powers of control over the affairs of the Bond.

To become a member the person concerned has to go through a very severe and secret test, on the mould of the Freemasons. First the person must be proposed by two members, and even without his knowledge; and before this proposal can take place, proof must first be given that he satisfies certain stringent qualifications. Then, secondly, he must, again without his knowledge, be approved of, and this must be done by the members of all the divisions. Three adverse votes can reject him. Thirdly, he must be approached in a careful manner to find out whether he would like to be a member, and fourthly, if he agrees, he must be introduced, under oath, by the laying down of the most solemn promise of silence, fidelity, etc. Up to the very end the Executive Council retains the right to reject him as a member. The Broederbond is thus a closed circle of Brothers bound together by oath, compelled to keep the uttermost measure of secrecy.

In the secret Manual, printed for the use of the members of the Bond, it is laid down that Brothers must try to support the interests of Brothers, and that Brothers must, as far as possible, support each other's undertakings. This spirit of giving preference by a Brother to a Brother and his interests, appears throughout the rule of the Bond, and controls the relations between Brother and Brother. So much is this the case that in the Domestic Regulations of certain Divisions of the Bond, which have received the approbation of the Executive Council of the Bond, among others the following is definitely stipulated: 'Furtherance of each other's interests in social life . . . will be the duty of the Bond. . . . Brothers will, where possible, support each other's business with word and deed, and be intercessor one for the other when the opportunity offers.'

Even if the Broederbond had never deviated into a political organization and had continued to go forward as a purely cultural association, there would still, necessarily, have been gross injustice happening on various occasions, along a secret way, to further the interests of a fellow-Brother to the disadvantage of a non-Brother, who had an equally great or greater right of address. Since the Bond was a secret body, with the most stringent obligation on every member to the uttermost secrecy about everything that took place, and that it was therefore quite impossible what was happening behind the curtain, there was also no protection for this non-Brother against the secret supporters of the Brother; and there was nothing in general for the Bond to be misused as an instrument of organized injustice against non-Brothers, yes, even to organized action in conflict with the best interests of the state and the civil service.

As a sample of how the Broederbond misuses its power as in a secret political association, I must remind you what happened a while ago when the so-called Le Roux motion came before Parliament. While the discussion on this was proceeding, the Broederbond set to work secretly, and secretly, in an organized manner, propaganda was made by the Brothers in the country districts in support of the motion. The Brothers, encouraged by purified Nationalists in Parliament, succeeded in managing to have numbers of telegrams sent to practically every Member of Parliament from the country districts, with the object of bringing pressure to bear on them to force them to vote for the motion. By its secret actions the Bond wanted to give the impression that the Members had to do with a spontaneous expression of feeling by the people in the district concerned.

The Bond here deliberately took part in a game of deceit, in which it hoped to influence the free vote of members of Parliament in favour of the purified Nationalists in Parliament. The Broederbond, a secret association, made use deliberately of its secret character to mislead the representatives of the people of the Union in the fulfilling of their national task!

Another sample of secret interference and secret misuse of the Broederbond is found in the following: The purified Brothers in Parliament some time ago in Cape Town, found themselves inconvenienced by the want of co-operation among the Brothers who, according to their wish, should have voted against the Government. To improve this condition of affairs, the purified Brothers without the knowledge of other Brothers, agreed to make use of the secret existence of the Bond with its secret authority and influence. Suddenly one fine day, the Brothers in Parliament received a notice that a certain gentleman from Potchefstroom had been appointed, or was going to be appointed, as Political Commissioner of the Bond at the Parliament, and that the task would be laid upon him to be present at all meetings of Parliament, from somewhere in the Gallery, with power from time to time, from his exalted seat, to issue orders to the Parliamentary Brothers, ordering them how they were to vote, etc.

This was a little too much for the Brothers in Parliament, who were not ready to be placed under a Bond dictator as voting cattle. Mutiny and rebellion were the result from the side of the Fusion Brothers, and the Broederbond had to put its Political Commissioner back into its pocket and get away.

The Fusion Brothers in Parliament deserve our compliments! But I cannot help warning them that he who eats with the Devil needs to provide himself with a long spoon!

Once again it appears from this to what extent the Bond and the purified Nationalist Party are one and the same body, functioning in two different compartments—the one above, the other under the ground.

What is there to prevent the Brothers seeking to further each other's interests in appointments and promotions in the civil service to the detriment of non-Brothers better entitled to it? Has it not already happened more than once without its even having been known?

I am putting the question to you tonight! What protection have you and I and our children, who are not members of the Broederbond, against the misuse of secret influences by Brothers by which we shall be prevented from enjoying what rightly belongs to us?

Well do I know that responsible officials of the state, members of the Broederbond, have requests made to them by fellow-Brothers on the acknowledgement of preference of the interests of Brothers above those of non-Brothers. If I understand it well, the request is sometimes extended to such an extent as to state that Brothers in the service should allow the orders of the Broederbond to supersede even the lawful regulations of the civil service.

Fortunately these efforts fail, and for the reason of the opposition which such presumptuous demands immediately experience from the officials concerned.

If the orders of the secret Manual to which I have referred, or of the Domestic Regulations of the Division quoted by me, had to be strictly followed, then, where a Brother had a shop, his fellow-Brothers would have to buy from him for that would be Bond duty, as expressed by the rule quoted. Where there is an opening in the service, whether for appointment or for promotion, then a Brother would have to exert himself to see a fellow-Brother competitor appointed or promoted to that post, for in terms of the regulation that would be Bond duty. As far as the Broederbond and the Brothers are concerned, it would matter very little what our claims might be for the support of our shops; or what claim you or I might have to an appointment or a promotion.　We are not Brothers and therefore we simply do not count.

Meanwhile we are denied the opportunity of acting in an honourable, open way for the protection of our threatened interests.　Everything against us happens in a secret way underground, where you and I can impossibly know what is being done, or what secret methods are being employed there to deprive us of what belongs to us.

In connection with the Broederbond, I have this evening to direct a very serious word to the teaching class.　When I was at Oudtshoorn lately, at a Circle Conference of the United Party, and the Conference had gone in to Committee, there were unexpected complaints by a number of persons about the excessive participation of teachers in politics, and finally a very serious appeal was made to me by a prominent woman delegate.

These were her words: 'In God's name, General, we mothers make a call on you to do everything in your power to prevent our children in school being so put up against their parents.　You have no idea how bad it is.'

This charge of improper influence exercised by teachers on children on the school benches, had already come to my ears more than once here in the Free State.　What was the truth about it?　If it were true I could not picture to myself a grosser and more serious misuse of position and office.

I do not know if it is true.　Yet what I really know is that the number of teachers in the Broederbond form more than one-third of the Bond's membership.　I know also that there are few towns and villages in the Free State where the Bond has not made a little nest for itself of five or more Brothers, which must serve as a centre for Bond propaganda; and I know that there is pretty well not a single one of these nests where one or more teachers are not sitting hatching.　When it is accepted that there are on an average at least two teachers in the Free State for each of these hatching nests—indeed a too low estimate—then one can form a fair idea of what the underground activities and interferences carried out by teachers behind the curtains of the school benches must be.　When to the number of these underground purified teacher Nationalists is added, as ought to be done, the above ground purified teacher Nationalists, then I can well see that the parents of children from nonpurified houses have something to complain about.

Is this a state of affairs which should be permitted by the state?

We have seen that the Broederbond is a secret political association, which has placed before itself as an aim, the dominance of the Dutch-speaking portion of the population over the English-speaking portion, by which the nation is being torn asunder to dissension and bitter disagreements.

Should it be allowed that teachers, who are being paid by the state to educate the children of the nation, should misuse the opportunity given them of coming into contact with the children, for the peace-political propaganda? Is it right that it should be permitted to teachers through membership of the Broederbond, to declare their inimical frame of mind to the English-speaking section of the parents of the children which they have under their care, and who, equally with the Afrikaans-speaking parents, pay their salaries?

The common participation in public by some teachers in ordinary party politics, has already been for the parent and for the educated public in general such a tremendous clashing against what was considered becoming and proper, that opposition had to be registered against it, which led to a certain measure of control. Now, seeing that the impression had arisen by the parent of a secret devotion to the ignoble task of bringing the youthful childish mind secretly in rebellion against that of the parent, it might well lead to very sad damage to what still remains cherished by the public of respect and goodwill to the teachers as a class.

Membership of a secret association must necessarily bring the person concerned under suspicion by his fellow-men, and let him decline in the same proportion in the trust if not in the respect of his environment. When this suspicion manifests itself in the direction of parental fear of the corruption of the youthful minds of their children, that suspicion will not neglect, no matter in what degree, to cause a feeling to arise of hatred and contempt.

The great misfortune of contempt or hatred of this kind is that it does not confine itself to the guilty individual, but spreads itself and very soon embraces the whole of the class to which that individual belongs. That this is going to be the result for teachers as a class, which will arise through the relationship of some of them to the Broederbond, is to be expected. The teacher where he sits in secrecy today, must come out into the open. There is nothing which needs the bright daylight more to remain sound than does our education.

The teacher class has never received anything from me but the greatest and most upright affection and respect, and as long as they are faithful to the charge of the welfare and education of the youth of South Africa, they will enjoy that respect and good feeling from me. But as has again been shown by what I have just said this evening, it cannot be expected from me that I shall remain silent about individual pedagogic misuses and evil deeds on account of my kindly feeling toward teachers as a class.

That on various occasions, when I have drawn attention to misuses and misdeeds, carried out by individual teachers, a cry has arisen, such as happened recently again at the Free State Teachers' Congress, cannot frighten me from doing my duty toward my people. Whether I was justified in speaking as I did at the Congress at Bloemfontein two months ago, and this evening repeated and did again here, I am willing to leave to the judgment of men and women who still possess a feeling of what is honourable and fitting. I only wish this evening to offer a little communication to the Executive of the Orange Free State Teachers' Association, which I think will interest them!

In August last year they were good enough to send me, unasked for, through their Secretary, the assurance that they:

As a Teachers' Association, have never taken any part in party politics, and that they [we] do not approve of this active participating by teachers in public, and further that they [we] are not aware that an active part has been taken by teachers in the Orange Free State,

an assurance which was accepted by me. Now, however, I have come into possession of better information, and I want to communicate to them that they would not have given me that assurance had they not been deceived and kept in the dark by their fellow teachers, who are members of the Broederbond!

The Executive Committee will forgive me if I tell them that I have just had in my hands the minutes of a Broederbond Congress with an agenda no less comprehensive of all possible political and party political points for discussion than that of any other party political congress and that this Congress was attended by not less than twenty-one teachers among the more or less 100 delegates, among them six teachers from the Free State.

What I have laid down before you this evening displays a state of affairs which might well cause the question to arise of 'Whither are we going?' by everyone who loves South Africa and has a feeling of responsibility.

Has the Afrikaner nation sunk to such a hopeless degree that it must seek for its salvation in a secret conspiracy for the advancement of racial hatred, of national dissension and of fraternal dissension? Is there for the Afrikaner son and daughter no higher striving, no nobler duty assigned than that of racial hatred and division? Does there remain no higher ideal for our children to reach than that of racial domination and of racial domineering?

APPENDIX II. MILITARY INTELLIGENCE REPORT ON THE AFRIKANER BROEDERBOND, MARCH 29, 1944

The Afrikaner Broederbond

I.   GENERAL

In November, 1935, the late General Hertzog, at the time Prime Minister of the Union of South Africa, made public a series of remarkable revelations about a sinister secret association, the Afrikaner Broederbond (hereinafter to be referred to as the AB), about which very few people at the time had even the remotest inkling.

The immediate result of this denunciation was that the organization submerged completely, and apparently disappeared from the scene.

This was not so.   It had merely become more secretive than ever before, but also more active and more dangerous.

In the period since 1935 it has grown enormously in power and has succeeded in establishing concerns and contacts in every sphere of public life in the Union.   The framework for achieving its ultimate object, Afrikaner domination of the Union, has been well and truly laid.   With its intricate network of branches and cells, it can 'manufacture' public opinion at will in spite of Government victories at the polls.

How successful it is in this respect, and how widespread its tentacles, can best be judged by the reaction, out of all proportion to the numerical strength of its participants, to the Government's bilingual medium policy.

Secret and reliable investigation since 1935 has proved that General Hertzog's revelations were true in every detail, but represented only part of the truth about the Afrikaner Broederbond.

It is proposed, therefore, to give a brief but comprehensive account of the Afrikaner Broederbond's origin and development, with particular stress on developments since 1935, when the organization entered upon its most dangerous phase.

It is recommended that the attached summary of General Hertzog's 1935 Broederbond speech be read in order to obtain a clear picture of the background of this formidable secret society.

II.   FOUNDATION AND AIMS

The AB, which is 'accountable only to God' for its actions, was founded in 1918 'on the Rock of Jesus' with the broad aim of bringing about

South Africa's 'God-given destiny', a Christian-National Calvinistic Afrikaner Republic.

In 1934 Professor van Rooy of the Potchefstroom University College, then Chairman of the AB, and Mr I. M. Lombard of Johannesburg (Chief Secretary of the movement since its inception) expressed themselves as follows in a secret circular:

> Let us bear in mind the fact that the main point is for Afrikanerdom to reach its ultimate goal of dominance in South Africa. Brothers, our solution for South Africa's troubles is that the Afrikaner Broederbond must rule South Africa.

As General Hertzog so significantly pointed out, 'Afrikanerdom' in the AB sense of the word, refers only to the Afrikaners who believe in Afrikaner domination of South Africa. All English-speaking South Africans are excluded, as well as Afrikaners who support the United Party as it exists today.

Any form of co-operation with the English-speaking section is frowned upon by the AB, and many prominent members have been ruthlessly blacklisted for being guilty of furthering and approving such co-operation.

A clerk who was associated with the AB for a period of three years said: 'Their real aim is to enrol as members officials in key positions in the service, and at an opportune moment to overthrow the Government and form a republic'.

Had the neutrality motion not been outvoted in September, 1939, the AB would have come very near to proclaiming its republic. The so-called 'spontaneous' gathering of thousands of people at Monumentkoppie in that first week of that eventful month, when Dr Malan and General Hertzog gave each other their hands 'never to let go again', was carefully organized by the AB for weeks before the time for this very purpose, which was fortunately wrecked by General Smuts' prompt and deft handling of the situation.

Like the proverbial cat, the AB, however, always comes back again, and is now patiently preparing for, and awaiting its next opportunity.

In the meantime, to use the words of one of the leading *Broers* at one of the organization's annual conferences,

> The AB must gain control of everything it can lay its hands on in every walk of life in South Africa. Members must help each other to gain promotion in the civil service or any other field of activity in which they work, with a view to working themselves up into important administrative positions.

A careful watch on the HNP press will invariably betray which candidate for a vacancy is AB by the preliminary boosting, and post-reproachful recriminations or approbation (depending on success or otherwise) attendant on the filling of the post.

In order to help realize their aims, members are instructed:

(i) to seek close acquaintances with each other, and to help themselves and each other.

(ii) to act individually, and in whatever capacity most suitable for the cause in cases where the organization as a whole cannot exert influence.

As a matter of fact, part of the oath taken on initiation solemnly binds each member 'to further the interests and undertakings of fellow *Broers*'. This is considered to be one of the many types of *Bondsplig* (Bond duty) than which there is nothing more holy and binding!

III.   CONDITIONS OF MEMBERSHIP AND INITIATION

It must be stressed that the AB does not aim at quantity, but at quality. Prospective candidates, who must not be under twenty-five years of age, are secretly watched and tested for years.   They must be men of standing and influence, and members of as many concerns as possible.   As one of the AB leaders stressed at one of the secret conferences:

Each new member must be a new power to the division to which he will belong.   He must, in other words, belong to a profession or circle in which that division has as yet no link.   He must be vitally alive and active; a man who still has the courage and enthusiasm to jump into the breach on behalf of any cause of *volksbelang*.

Prospective members must:

1. Be proposed by two members, without knowledge of the person concerned.
2. The proposers must satisfy themselves that the member-elect satisfies the basic requirements as set out above.
3. The prospective member must, once more without his knowledge, be approved by all the divisions.   Three counter votes blackball him.
4. He must then circumspectly be approached and sounded as to his desire to become a member.
5. If he is agreeable, he is then formally inducted.

The Initiation

The organization of the Bond is Masonic down to the smallest detail. There are the usual three degrees with an elaborate ritual of initiation, secret signs of recognition, grips and passwords for every degree.   The mystic symbol of the order is *die Lig van Majuba* (The Light of Majuba), hence the frequent references to '*Voor op die wapad brand 'n lig*' ('Before us on the trail of the wagon a light is burning'), whenever some intensive campaign is in progress.

The members speak in confidence '*Onder die Vierkleur*' ('under the four colours'), like Masons do 'on the square'.   To those of the second degree it is explained: '*Onder die beskerming van die Vierkleur van Transvaal sal Afrikanerdom altyd seevier*' ('Under the shield of the four colours of the Transvaal Afrikanerdom will prevail').   Hysterical homage is paid to it at the initiation.

The third degree worships an image of *Geliefde Suid Afrika* (Loved South Africa).

The initiation is rather gruesome. In complete darkness a corpse-like body lies on a bier, wrapped in a black winding sheet on which is embroidered in letters of blood: *Verraad* (Treason). A bloody dagger is thrust to the hilt in the body of the 'corpse'. A torch throws brief flashes of light on the scene, while the chaplain intones:

> He who betrays the Bond will be destroyed by the Bond. The Bond never forgives and never forgets. Its vengeance is swift and sure. Never yet has a traitor escaped his just punishment.

In cases of serious betrayal, the storm-troop section of the Ossewa-Brandwag is detailed to mete out punishment. The OB is secretly controlled by the AB.

Although the outward forms of Masonry are slavishly imitated, its fundamental creed, that all men are brothers, and its absolute prohibition of politics, are conspicuously rejected.

The AB is ostentatiously religious. There is much psalm singing and bible kissing throughout its ritual; but in the eyes of this esoteric fraternity, the Great Architect of the Universe has hitherto designed only one model—the *Ware Afrikaner*.

Precautions of Secrecy

1. No notices, instructions, etc., are ever conveyed through the post. They are delivered verbally or personally.

2. Members attending meetings must present membership credentials to the chief secretary, Mr I. M. Lombard.

3. At each subsequent session, each member must scrutinize the credentials of his neighbour before proceedings continue.

4. Members are constantly warned not to leave any evidence, e.g., scraps of paper, notes, etc., when then leave.

5. Meetings are always convened under a bogus name, e.g., the Vissersaal, Normal College, Bloemfontein, the venue of a recent AB Conference, was booked under the pretext of a SCA (Students Christian Association) Conference.

6. In addition, whenever one of the AB's subsidiary organizations (FAK, Reddingsdaadbond, etc.) holds a conference, it is an automatic signal that proceedings will be preceded by an AB meeting, since all AB members are members of these other organizations.

7. Secret code letters are used. These are changed from time to time to suit various circumstances and occasions. At the time of the Voortrekker Centenary celebrations, which were organized and controlled by the AB, the code letter was 'V'!

IV.   THE SET-UP OF THE AFRIKANER BROEDERBOND

1. *The 'Trinity':* This is the inmost nucleus of the AB, and consists of

the supreme, secret chief, supported by two assessors, who are members of the *Uitvoerende Raad* (Executive Council)—hereafter to be referred to as the UR.

2. *The Uitvoerende Raad:* The UR consists of twelve members, known as the Twelve Apostles. The UR meets annually, and whenever additional need may arise.

3. *The Algamene Raad:* The *Algamene Raad* consists of the twelve 'Apostles', and numerous 'Disciples' drawn from the various divisions or cells (one representative for each). It meets annually, but an emergency meeting may be called if the occasion warrants it.

4. *Local Branches or Cells:* A cell has five to ten members, and a division consists of two or more cells. A division must have a maximum of forty members. Each independent cell or division is directly responsible to the UR, and is simply a small secret circle within a large secret circle.

5. *Vigilance Committees:* Vigilance committees, directly responsible to the UR. This is the AB's Gestapo system. Such committees are appointed at various strategic points to guard over and report on AB-sponsored interests; e.g., the Afrikaans Medical Faculty at Pretoria, the Engineering Faculty at Stellenbosch, SA Railways, etc.

V. THE DEVELOPMENT OF THE AFRIKANER BROEDERBOND

The Afrikaner Broederbond was formed on May 24, 1918, by the foundation *Broers* H. W. van der Merwe (of Kroonstad), H. J. Klopper, MP (Vredefort), the Rev. Bertie Naude' (Roodepoort), and D. A. C. du Plessis (Secr.). The original membership amounted to fourteen, and has grown since then to 2,528.

The movement was in the first instance called *Jong Suid Afrika*, but at its Conference on June 18, 1918, it was changed to Afrikaner Broederbond. Rev. Bertie Naude' was its first President.

In 1921, the AB decided to take up the sword on behalf of Afrikaanse medium schools, and to make propaganda by this means, directly and indirectly, for achieving the Bond's aims.

Henceforth it became a standing instruction for members 'to fight secretly but with all your might for unilingual medium schools'.

In the same year it was decided to observe absolute secrecy, and to avoid postal communications.

The first dissension in the AB occurred in 1924 as a result of Nationalist amalgamation with Labour. When it was seen, however, that more power could be obtained by strong representation in Parliament, a reconciliation was effected.

In 1927 the AB decided to take an active part in the life of the community at large, 'leaving no avenue neglected'.

In order to carry out this policy without risk of detection, the AB called into being the *Federasie van Afrikaanse Kultuurvereniging* (FAK). By this means it was planned to extend the AB's sphere of influence into every town and village in South Africa.

By 1931 the movement had extended into the OFS and the Cape Province.

In 1933 the second crisis occurred in the AB as a result of the fusion of the parties of General Smuts and General Hertzog. As a result the *Herenigde Nasionale Party* was formed, which has since become completely identified with the Broederbond. Dr Malan now became a member.

The direct result of this was the establishment, in 1934, of the AB's first economic venture, *Die Volkskas* (People's Bank).

A major crisis occurred in 1935 when General Hertzog openly attacked the AB and much heartburning was caused as to which member or members were responsible for the leakage of information. Hertzog supporters now resigned *en masse*, and the concern became purified Nationalists in the literal sense of the word.

A special meeting was called, and undying vengeance sworn against General Hertzog.

By contriving to have the Voortrekker Centenary celebrations put into charge of the *Afrikaanse Taal en Kultuurvereniging* (AKT), a subsidiary of the FAK under chairmanship of AB foundation member H. J. Klopper of the SAR, the Broederbond was able to pull strings and control the whole affair at will. This accounts for the violent and unreasonable anti-British outbursts which disgraced the celebrations both at Pretoria and Blood River, and for the fact that no Voortrekker descendant, no matter how distinguished and respected, was allowed to participate in a leading role if he or she happened to be a United Party supporter.

The AB also scored a most satisfying triumph in managing to have General Hertzog debarred from participating in the ceremonies concerned, whereas Dr Malan was allowed to be one of the chief speakers at Blood River.

The Ossewa-Brandwag, whose origin was inspired by the commemoration trek of the ox-wagons, and which was started by Colonel Laas as a purely cultural association, became a menace to the AB's rival concern the FAK. A skilful whisper campaign, based ironically enough on the rumour that Colonel Laas was a Freemason, caused the Colonel to be ejected, and *Broer* Dr Hansie van Rensburg successfully installed.

In the meantime the AB, ever since the arrival, *circa* 1933, of the first nazi agents camouflaged as scientists, educationists, etc., had become immensely interested in the nazi system.

Broers Dr N. Diederichs and Dr van Rensburg both visited Germany to study the nazi system at first hand, and became ardent admirers and adherents of National Socialism.

Through Broederbond intervention the *Afrikaanse Nasionale Studentebond* (ANS) was formed with Hans van Rensburg as honorary president, as an antidote to the liberally inclined NUSAS, and conducted tours of Afrikaans students were arranged to nazi Germany; this became a regular procedure.

A nazi student (*gerlach*) was even imported to convert and organize

South African students *in loco*. As he was not much of a success due to his mechanical nazi robotlike methods, Dr Diederichs and a specially selected Stellenbosch student were sent over to study National Socialism. Both of them qualified as quislings in the nazis' Anti-Komitern training school.

Holm of Zoesen, also a *Broer,* is the AB's direct link with nazi Germany.

The war crisis of September, 1939, brought about the AB's fourth crisis, and also additional strength.

In spite of the apparent reconciliation between Malan and Hertzog, the latter was still on the AB blacklist, and vengeance was merely postponed. From the very inception of this new coalition, diabolically clever tactics were used to make things so impossible for General Hertzog, that he would be forced to resign, leaving the field clear for *Broer* Dr Malan. This plan was consummated in 1940, when General Hertzog was not elected Chairman of the HNP Congress at Bloemfontein, and after equal rights for English, Afrikaans-speaking South Africans had been made an issue, walked out in disgust!

The Broederbond's vengeance was as sweet as it was complete. General Hertzog, erstwhile hero of the OFS, was henceforth spurned and cold-shouldered by the majority of opposition Afrikaners, including the constituency of Smithfield, which he had represented for more than thirty years. He died, brokenhearted, two years later. One of the AB's most important types of *Bondsplig* had been successfully accomplished.

Part of the AB's scheme of vengeance recoiled on its own head when the split occurred in 1941 between Malan and Pirow, leading to rupture with the OB as well, and precipitating the AB into its most serious crisis. There was also a strained atmosphere in the *Uitvoerende Raad* as well, since some of the members sided with Malan, and some with Pirow and van Rensburg.

The first breach between Malan and van Rensburg occurred early in 1941 when van Rensburg prematurely published the Broederbond's *Konsepgrondwet* for the intended republic.

The so-called *Eenheidefront* (United Front) which tried so hard but so unsuccessfully to reunite the warring opposition factions, was the Broederbond's attempt to retrieve the damage that had been done. The *Eenheidefront* functioned under the leadership of Professor L. J. du Plessis of Potchefstroom, member of the UR of the AB, and the *Beleid-Studiehoof* (Policy Planning Chief) of the OB. It was this failure that led one of the AB's leaders to exclaim dejectedly at the last annual conference that politically the Bond had not been as successful as it hoped to be.

VI. TWENTY-FIVE YEARS OF GROWTH AND POWER IN THE AFRIKANER BROEDERBOND

Although the AB has not been very successful in its attempts in the political sphere to keep all opposition Afrikaners welded into one united group, it has nevertheless been spectacularly successful in other fields.

The AB's tremendous influence must be attributed to the fact that its policy is based on two fundamental principles, namely to control the minds of Afrikanerdom through control of its educational institutions, and to control its actions by gaining a tight grip on its purse-strings. In other words, the Afrikaner Broederbond has, octopuslike, spread its tentacles into the economic, as well as the educational and cultural fields in South Africa. In addition, it has representatives in key positions throughout the civil service.

1. The Economic Sphere

The *Reddingsdaadbond* (Rescue Action Society), under present leadership of *Broer* Dr N. Diederichs, was originally started by the late Dr Kestell with the noble object of regenerating the poor whites. On his return from Germany, Dr Diederichs was quick to see the possibilities of the Reddingsdaadbond, which, like the OB, was unobtrusively taken over by the AB. Henceforth, it became the South African equivalent of the *Winterhilfe* organization of the nazi system. Like the *Winterhilfe* it professes to assist the poor, where it is in actual fact a purely capitalistic and highly lucrative concern which unscrupulously exploits the needy and the gullible for the benefit of a select and powerful few. Some of these men figure on every single board of directors of the most powerful of the innumerable economic concerns which are wholly or completely controlled by the AB.

Among these undertakings we find banks, factories (clothing, furniture, tobacco, etc., etc.), wholesale and retail concerns (butchers, drapers, shoe stores, etc., etc.), as well as maternity homes, hospitals, funeral arrangements (AVBOB), etc. Everything the Afrikaner might need from the cradle to the grave, is provided for.

Among the concerns completely controlled by the Broederbond, are *Volkskas, Unie-Winkels, Economiese Instituut, Sashbank,* and *Asokor* (Cold Storage Company). *Volkskas* was started in 1934 in a borrowed office, with a handful of voluntary helpers, and with a first annual turnover of £700. It is now housed in a palatial four-storeyed building in Pretoria, owned by the Broederbond, employs over 300 people, and handled over £4 million in its last financial year!

Dr Diederichs, Professor du Plessis, and their associates have involved the Reddingsdaadbond in a complicated financial maze. A terrific fiddling with paper assets is carried on by means of ticket subscriptions, wrung from the poorest of the poor through monthly extortions of more than 370 branches of the RDB.

There is every probability that a thorough investigation by impartial auditors will reveal the gravest irregularities and exploitation.

Professor du Plessis, present Chairman of the AB, is in one way and another connected personally with over twenty economic concerns controlled by the RDB. He is also Chairman of *Volkskas*.

All the members of the UR of the AB have, as a matter of fact, through a pretty system of interlocking directorates, absolute control over some thirty commercial organizations, with a membership of nearly 300,000 persons.

A specimen letterhead of one of these directorates claims to represent twenty different branches of sixteen different bodies, totalling 26,000 members. These are all bodies controlled by the AB, but its own name, as always, is significantly absent. Thus is the public bluffed!

The Reddingsdaadbond's activities are supplemented by a very efficient system of advertising, through its 300 branches, every single vacancy or opportunity for a doctor, dentist, attorney, or any other professional opportunity in any centre where a branch or cell of the AB exists. The prospects are explained, and details of existing opposition—English, Jewish, or Hanekakie—together with addresses of local *Broers* are supplied. Approved candidates thus get the immediate support of the local representatives and all their contacts, which, in the shape of individuals as well as school hostels, youth organizations, etc., is usually considerable. Thus an effective boycott of 'alien' competitors is achieved.

The strength of the AB in the DR churches can best be judged from the fact that those churches were successfully persuaded (without the knowledge of the rank and file of the members) to withdraw their considerable funds from the banks in which they had been vested since their inception, and transfer them to the AB bank, *Volkskas*. It is understood that *Volkskas* has successfully applied to the Department of Finance to be raised to the status of a bank.

2.   The Educational and Cultural Sphere

Fifteen years ago the Afrikaner Broederbond succeeded in amalgamating all Afrikaans cultural organizations (some twenty or more) into one solid bloc, under the name of *Die Federasie van Afrikaanse Kultuurvereniginge* —the FAK.

This body is entirely controlled by I. M. Lombard of Johannesburg, Chief Secretary of the Broederbond.

The FAK functions very effectively through its numerous subsidiaries, chief of which are the following:

The NIOO
This body handles all educational matters for the FAK, and has recently been nominated by the AB as the 'action committee' to handle the anti-bilingual medium agitation.

The *Kultuurrade*
These are established in the larger centres to watch over the cultural interests of the AB. In addition, there are the *Skakelkomitees*, which are liaison committees to represent the FAK in smaller centres or communities.

The above two have innumerable links with church and educational institutions, since 40 per cent of the 2,528 members of the AB are either teachers in schools, normal colleges, and universities, or predikants and others, who are members of bodies controlling schools and colleges. A list is available of at least 500 teachers in the Union who have become members in the last two years! All teaching posts are secretly canvassed by AB members, and in areas where they have the say in the various school bodies, nobody not approved by the AB vigilance committees has a ghost of a chance of appointment or promotion.

This is further made possible by the fact that the AB has managed to gain considerable influence in the Education departments of the Transvaal, OFS, and the Cape. Their Natal representative in the Department, while he was still there, could not do much, since he had no backing from those below him, and furthermore on account of the Natal system of teacher appointment, which is not controlled by local bodies.

The OFS

The whole of the Department of Education of the OFS is controlled by the Afrikaner Broederbond, and from the Director downward, all controlling positions are held by members of the AB or by persons controlled by such members. To judge by the pathetic appeals in *Die Vrystater* (December 14, 1943, and January 4, 1944), a reign of terror seems to exist as far as Government-supporting teaching personnel are concerned.

That this is in no way an exaggeration of the state of affairs, can be determined by what General Hertzog said nearly ten years ago:

> I know of few towns and villages in the Free State where the Broederbond has not established for itself a nest of five, six, or more *Broers* to serve as a focal point for Bond propaganda, and I also know that there is hardly a single nest on which there isn't at least one teacher sitting as hatcher. . . .
>
> Thus we can form a fair idea of the underground activities and meddling, carried out by teachers behind the curtains of the school desks.

Investigation since 1935 has shown that matters have become increasingly serious in the OFS.

Apart from the Department of Education itself, we find leading professors of the UCOFS, the Rector and teaching personnel of the normal college, the majority of inspectors and teachers to be members of the AB.

The Transvaal and the Cape Province

The same situation is to be found in a less intensified degree, but to quite a dangerous extent, in the educational spheres of the Transvaal and the Cape.

The Transvaal Department is ruled almost Gestapo fashion by its Broederbond secretary, supported by numerous inspectors and principals, as well as the rank and file of the teachers. The TOV is entirely under Broederbond influence, as well as the normal colleges of Pretoria and

Potchefstroom. The few English-speaking officials in the Transvaal Department have either left, or have been sidetracked.

The Cape Education Department is strongly suspect, chiefly because of the type of man who gets promotion. If anything, the position of the Cape Department is more dangerous than in the Transvaal, since the AB members here (in the CP) work very circumspectly, giving an impression of genuine desire to find the best solution for, say, the bilingual medium question. So, for instance, a very senior official of this Department, who commonly is considered to support the Government's policy, used all his powers of persuasion in order to try to prove to the Director of the Natal Department that it would be unwise for Natal to go through with its bilingual medium policy at the present juncture.

The most recent move by the AB to sabotage the carrying out of the Government's bilingual medium policy is a circular sent out by the NIOO to their members and branches instructing them to do everything in their power to get their representatives in Parliament and in the provincial councils to demand that the Government appoint a committee of experts to go into the whole question before embarking upon the bilingual medium policy. By this dodge it is hoped to get the governmental machinery to stall the adoption of the bilingual medium in the schools.

Experience has shown that no matter what the findings of such a committee may be, the NIOO will see to it that a certain proportion of the members will be against bilingual medium. That will be to them sufficient justification still to remain 'against the Government's policy'. The fact, for example, that the Transvaal Education Committee in 1939, under the chairmanship of Rev. Nicol, reported in favour of the bilingual school, did not in the least discourage them in their attack on bilingual medium; simply because there was a minority report against it.

In areas where English-speaking children attend the same schools as the Afrikaans-speaking majority, these Broederbond-influenced teachers frequently discriminate against them, but mostly in such a way that it is almost impossible to get the required evidence. Even where such evidence is procurable, the children and parents concerned are afraid to speak out, for fear of further ultimate discrimination of perhaps a harsher nature. No wonder General Hertzog said:

> Is it right that teachers should be allowed, through their membership in the Broederbond, to declare their hostility toward the English-speaking section of the parents whose children are entrusted to their care, and who help pay their salaries just as well as the Afrikaans children's parents do?

General Hertzog was speaking from actual facts in his possession, and these facts have been established over and over since then.

After the split in the ranks of the *Ware Afrikaners* in 1942, the *Eenheidsfront* (which is nothing more or less than the *Uitvoerende Raad* of the AB), under leadership of Professor L. J. du Plessis, chose the education medium issue as the most hopeful means of reuniting the opposition factions.

Elaborate secret preparations for a great agitation on this question were set afoot. Special monographs were written, sets of lectures were drawn up by 'experts', and circulated to the branches. Thus was ammunition gathered for the fight.

In spite of all this, the AB's political representative, the HNP, promptly accused the Government of dragging the language question into the political arena, when it was decided to take up the challenge as the issue at stake in the provincial elections of 1943. Since then this 'Big Lie' policy has been consistently openly applied by the HNP, assisted by the FAK, and the DR churches.

If the AB is left alone for another few years to complete its white-anting of our schools, the Bond will have gained its primary object, which was outlined by a Free State inspector of schools at one of the AB conferences as follows:

> Giving the assurance that the school teachers would see to it that every effort by the Government to introduce bilingual medium was sabotaged, he said:

> 'The Afrikaans teachers will demonstrate to Afrikanerdom what a power they possess in their teachers organizations for building up the youth of the future republic.

> I know of no more powerful instrument. They handle the children for five or more hours daily for five days in each week; while at hostels and *kosekole* the contact is continuous for long periods.

> A nation is made through its youth being taught and influenced at school in the tradition, customs, habits, and ultimate destination of its *volk*.

> Whatever happens in any of the other provinces of the Union, the OFS will openly fight the Government to the bitter end and will then give continual lead to the other provinces to carry on constant agitation.'

The nazi poison which is being instilled into the young minds is well exemplified in the 'request' solemnly presented to the FAK's *Taal-Kongres* at Bloemfontein on December 14, 1943, by local school children, the concluding sentence of which reads:

> *Ons bid die Kongres Gods ryke en onmisbare seen op my verrigtinge toe mat die varige hoop dat ons vyand nou so'n teragslag sal kry, dat by dit nooit weer sal waag om hierdie skans van die Afrikaner aan to val nie. Ons sal handhaaf, ons sal bou!*

The unilingual normal colleges are, of course, one of the AB's super triumphs. As long as teachers are produced of whom the majority have a very low standard of bilingualism, so long will it be possible to prevent the carrying out of the Government's bilingual medium policy, due to 'staffing difficulties'.

Apart from the unilingual Afrikaans medium schools—those breeding grounds for propagating the AB principles in perpetuity, and for turning out voting robots for the HNP—the AB has provided for the preschool period by starting *unilingual nursery schools*, and for the postschool period by deciding to engulf the *Trekmaats* organization, which caters for the age group seventeen to twenty-five.

In addition, leisure time is skilfully accounted for through the Voortrekkers, a movement which is almost wholly controlled by the AB. The evil tendencies which have penetrated this organization, were the reason for the resignation of Professor Ben Taute as leader of the movement for the Cape Province. How the AB must also have laughed up its sleeve with glee when one of its most influential members, Dr C. F. Visser, was appointed as Director of the Youth Land Organization by the Government, thus completing the AB's control of the youth of this country. Already, complaints are being heard in the OFS because the members of this organization go in teams to work on the farms of well-to-do farmers, not one of whom is government supporting!

3. The Civil Service in General:

As General Hertzog pointed out in 1935:

> Well do I know that claims are made on responsible state officials, members of the Broederbond, by fellow *Broers*, for priority to be given to the interests of *Broers* above those of non-*Broers*. . . .
> It is even claimed that with *Broers* in the service the instructions of the Broederbond should take priority even before the legitimate regulations of the service.

There are prominent positions throughout the civil service which are held by Broederbonders, and the fact that some of these are vitally connected with the war effort is a cause for the gravest concern, since a clever man can always obstruct in such a way that he keeps his activities 'within the law'.

The Department of Agriculture, especially its Extension Section, is almost completely controlled by Broederbonders, and the fact that so many of the personnel of the Control Boards consists of these gentry may account to an interesting extent for the innumerable 'unavoidable' blunders which are doing more to make the Government unpopular with the masses than any other single factor.

The Department of Railways and Harbours was a veritable paradise of jobs for pals for the AB, until the present Minister took over (1944). The extent to which he has penetrated and forestalled their carefully laid plans can best be judged by the vehement outcry by parliamentary Broederbonders during the last two sessions about promotions in this Department.

Not even the Department of Justice is exempt, and at least one judge, as well as several magistrates, are members of the AB.

The police force is one of the special preserves of the Bond, and it was an ironical circumstance that led to members of the Broederbond figuring on the commissions of inquiry appointed to report on the Rand and Potchefstroom riots, both of which were precipitated by the AB's unruly child, the

OB. One of these men has, however, since broken with the Bond, and now appears on their blacklist.

Firm and prompt action by the authorities eliminated most of the AB's representatives from the army at an early stage, but there is no reason to think that this elimination was complete.

Initially, the Board of Directors of the SABC was also infected by the AB virus, but the clean-up there was also pretty thorough.

The AB was not very successful in getting a toehold in the Department of Mines and Industries, so it has tried to make up for this deficiency by establishing a special department under Dr Albert Hertzog, Professor J. C. van Rooy, and others to foment unrest and encourage strikes in mines and industries.

Special funds are provided for this sinister purpose by the Reddings-daadbond's subsidiary, the *Nasionale Raad van Trustees*.

The same group, under Dr Albert Hertzog, also arranged for the white-anting of town councils in the various centres. The prematurely disclosed *Pretoria Redemta* is an example of the kind of subterranean activity indulged in. In the Bloemfontein municipal elections they worked more circumspectly and, as a result, the Broederbond candidates swept the board.

4. The Dutch Reformed Churches

The AB has complete control of the *Nederduits Hervormde* or *Gereformeerde Kerk* (the *Verenigde Kerk*), and the *Gereformeerde Kerk* (the 'Dopper' Church), as far as their political activity is concerned. Although many ministers of the *Hervormde Kerk* are members, the controlling bodies are still more or less free, as evidenced by the fact that the synod of this church has refused to identify itself with the resolutions passed by the Broederbond's FAK *Taalkongres*.

The position in the *Verenigde* and Dopper churches is, however, tremendously serious, especially since these churches have such a predominating influence in the selection of personnel for the Afrikaans medium schools. In addition, these churches are now also penetrating the industrial sphere, and the agitation in the Germiston clothing factory was fomented by their personal interference in the matter.

5. Propaganda and Publicity

This is cared for by innumerable publications and leaflets, of which there is an apparently limitless supply!

In addition, all activities sponsored by the AB are given full publicity and reporting in the many papers of the Nasionale Pers Bep., as well as in *Die Transvaler*, which is also HNP, but which is published by Die Voortrekkerpers Bep., owned by the Broederbond. The manager of the Voortrekkerpers is the treasurer of the Broederbond. In addition *Die Vaderland* has, since General Hertzog's death, come strongly under the influence of his son, Dr Albert Hertzog, and is also for the first time giving prominence to

Broederbond activities (of course, the name Broederbond is never mentioned under any circumstances). Recently, this paper actually had a leader in defence of Dr Malan's cable to Eire!

The Afrikaners where to buy, *Die Afrikaner in Plaaslike Besture*, gives directions for gaining control of municipal affairs through subsidiaries like the OB, the RDB, the *Vrou-Federasie*, Voters' Associations (*cf.* in Pretoria *Die Federasie van Belastingbetalersverenigings* and *Pretoria Redempta*), etc.

'Inspan', mouthpiece of the FAK, is another valuable medium of contact with the whole country, as well as the HNP's own special effort *Die Kruithoring*, and innumerable students' publications.

6. Future Schemes

The most immediate plan is to restore opposition unity under the single banner of the HNP, and the AB's most fervent prayer at present is to be left undisturbed and unexposed in its plans for the language medium agitation, since it is hoped that this will provide the plank to bridge the gulf of differences created by RNP versus OB and New Order friction since 1942.

The result of the Soutpansberg election shows that those plans are not going too badly, and the newly elected *Groot Raad* of the OB consists entirely of members of the AB.

The *Eenheidsfront*, which strove so desperately to ward off and heal the breach in the opposition ranks in 1942, has now girded its loins once more. A new scheme of liaison officers has been devised to keep the closest contact between the Afrikaner Party, the OB, and the New Order. The change of front of the Afrikaner Party organ, *Die Vaderland*, has already been indicated, and another significant event is the acceptance by Mr Klassie Havenga, Afrikaner Party Leader, of a directorship on the Broederbond's huge Cold Storage Concern, *Asokor Bep.*

7. Various Achievements

The AB has been directly responsible for the following:

(a) The establishment of the *Volksmonumente-kommissie*.

(b) Broadcasting agitations. (How they roared through camouflaged mouths when *Broeder* Botha was deprived of the Chairmanship!)

(c) The translation of the Bible into Afrikaans.

(d) The recognition of the *Stem van Suid Afrika* as national anthem for South Africa.

(e) Repatriation of the Argentine Boers.

(f) Laying down and controlling the Government's Social Welfare Policy (or so it claims!).

(g) Engineering of the UCOFS (Bloemfontein) language crisis.

(h) Fomenting of the agitation in connection with the Afrikaans Medical Faculty, Pretoria University.

(i) The sponsoring of extensive bursary schemes at the various

Afrikaans universities and colleges, in order to get a hold on those institutions.

(j) The engineering of the breach in the W.P. Rugby Union and in the Transvaal Rugby Union, by which it is hoped still further to separate Afrikaans- and English-speaking South Africans into two incompatible groups.

(k) The agitation against Witwatersrand University for admitting non-Europeans to some of its courses, resulting in the Broederbond-controlled University of Pretoria breaking off all relations with Wits.

(l) The 'reform' movement within the Mine Workers Union organized by Dr Albert Hertzog.

8. Details

In separate appendices, there are available lists of Broederbond-controlled organizations, and concerns, with names of directors, etc.

A list is also attached of prominent persons known to be members of the AB.

In order, however, to preserve absolute secrecy of identity, prominent officials of the service are generally treated as *los Broers*, i.e., not attached to any branch or cell. This makes it very difficult to obtain names, and those on the attached list are only a few that have been caught up accidentally.

The list, impressive though it may seem, is therefore not exhaustive or even comprehensive. From it will be seen that the AB has its representatives in the Union's legations, in the Department of Economic Development and Demobilization, in the Treasury, Departments of Social Welfare and Education, in the SAR and H (which numbers two of the AB's foundation members among its senior officials), in Posts and Telegraphs, in Agriculture, and in Justice, etc.

A chart is also attached to give a bird's eye view of the Broederbond's incredible ramifications.

9. The Language Medium Agitation

The membership of the two large interlocked groups, the Reddingsdaadbond and the FAK, runs into thousands of men, women, and children. In the hands of the Broederbond they have become a political weapon of immense power.

It is accordingly very simple for Diederichs and Lombard to 'manufacture' public opinion. The flood of hysterical emotion at the time of the Trek Centenary celebrations in 1938, was a typical example.

A present case in point is the language medium controversy.

The result of the provincial council elections, which were fought on the question of bilingual medium, proved conclusively that the vast majority of South African voters favoured bilingual medium and coeducation of both sections of the white population.

In spite of this the AB was able, through its 'so much bigger son the

FAK', to organize the *Moedertaalkongres* at Bloemfontein in December, 1943, and create the impression of nationwide protest by hundreds of delegates and thousands of telegrams, cleverly assembled through 'cell' representatives of the Broederbond's innumerable ramifications throughout the country, e.g., charitable organizations, church councils, school committees and boards, youth organizations, etc., etc.

This is nothing new to the Broederbond. General Hertzog gives a striking example of how the AB, in connection with a certain measure before Parliament, tried to influence parliamentary policy by secretly instructing every cell, and every organization controlled or influenced by these cells, to shower MP's with telegrams, thus artificially creating the impression of spontaneous and countrywide public feeling on the matter. '*Die Broederbond, 'n geheime vereniging, het sig opsetlik bedien van sy geheime karakter om die verteenwoordigers van die volk van die Unie te mislei by die vervulling van hul volkstaak.*'

There was not a single organizer of the *Moedertaalkongres* (more aptly termed the *Leuenkongres*), who was not also a member of the HNP. Quite obviously, the organization counted on the fact that the public at large had long since forgotten how convincingly General Hertzog had proved that the HNP and the Afrikaner Broederbond were one and the same thing.

> *Van hierdie geheime Broederbond wat eig as ideaal stel tweedrag on onenigheid onder die Afrikanervolk dour uitsluiting van die Engelse deel uit die regering van die land, is Dr Malan sedert Koalisie medelid en Broer geword. . . .*
>
> *Dit ly geen twyfel dus, dat dit geheime Broederbond niks anders is as die Gesuiwerde Nasionale Party beheimelik besig onder die grond, en dat die Gesuiwerde Nasionale Party niks anders is as die geheime AB, sy bedrywighede voorsittende bo die grond.*

Before the *Taalkongres* was due to take place, the Broederbond-controlled *Afrikaanse Kultuurraad* of Pretoria had been secretly asked to draw up a detailed plan of action for the FAK for opposing the introduction of bilingual medium into the schools. This plan fell into the hands of Government supporters, and its premature exposure effectively cracked up the whole plan. To show the lines on which the Broederbond is prepared to act, it is produced here:

Die FAK nader en beweeg:

1. Die Moderature van die drie Afrikaanse Kerke in al vier provinsies om in die pers 'n beleidsverklaring te publiseer waarin hulle enderneem om by al die Ringe aan te beveel on Afrikaanse ouers te beweeg om te weier om hul kinders na skole te stuur waar die beleid van die regering ingevoer word. Die Ringe kom bymekaar om dieselfde te doen. Waar 'n predikant omstimpatiek is, moet 'n sterk persoonlikheid in sy Kerkraad of gemeente die voortou neem.
2. Die skoolkommissies (Beh. Ligg.) wat sterk en simpatieke persons kam ko-opteer, die ouers onder hulle verdeel (se elkeen is vir 10 ouers en of kinders verantwoordelik), hulle bewerk en laat staak of die gegewe comblik. Simpatieke hoofde en onderwysers kan in stilte saamwerk.
3. Verder nader die FAK alle simpatiele skoolraade of indiwidueke skool-readslede en provinsiale raadslede. Persons van alle groepe word dringend versoek om op hierde punt hul geledere te aluit on saam te werk.
4. Die FAK nader alle bevriende boereverenigings, kunsenkiltuurliggame,

die voortrekkerbeweging, ens. ens. om 'n landawye propagandadiens in die lewe te roep met die oog op staking.

5. Die FAK stel 'n perzveldtog in om die regering te intimideer; hy moet ook waar moontlik, die Engelse pers gebruid.

6. Die FAK nader die Afrikaanse universiteite en kolleges en normaalskole deur die S.V.R. om die studente te laat staak.

7. Die organisasie moet so wees dat 'n betroubare persoon persoonlik verantwoordelik sal wees vir die staking se van elke 10 leerlinge of studente. Die staking moet lang genoeg duur om die regering tot sy sinne to bring.

The AB submerged in characteristic fashion when this plan was publicly exposed and the Broederbond openly mentioned in connection with it. The only opposition paper that mentioned the matter, studiously avoided mention of the word Broederbond, and feebly tried to make out that not a single delegate knew about such a plan.

They had to change their plans as a result of the exposure, and consequently decided to leave the policy of 'action' in the hands of the FAK subsidiary, the NIOO, trusting that the public would not find out that both these were AB-controlled.

At present the NIOO is very busy organizing (in the same way as indicated above) for telegrams to be 'rained' from all over South Africa on the Prime Minister, on the administrators, and the members of Parliament, urging for the appointment of a committee of 'educational experts' to investigate the question of bilingualism.

Since the only educational experts (e.g., Dr Malherbe, Inspector Logie, Professor Rayburn, Dr Cook, etc.) who have ever made an *ad hoc* scientific investigation into the matter, are rejected by the unilingualists, it is obvious that the proposal is simply a clever means of stalling the practical application of the bilingual medium policy, and still further assisting the impression the HNP has assiduously been instilling into the minds of the voters that the present Government is incapable of redeeming its promises, and of taking determined action in any controversial matter.

In the meantime Natal has evaded the AB net, so a plan is under consideration to turn the OB farm Majuba into an Afrikaans Training College for OB sons and daughters. Schools and hostels are to be built with £250,000 which the OB is said to have available. When complete reconciliation has been effected between the HNP and the OB, it is hoped to entice all opposition Afrikaans children from Natal to be educated in this unilingual medium *Christelik-Nasionale* institution.

VII.   CONCLUSION

The Ossewa-Brandwag waxed with the rise of nazi power, and waned proportionately with its decline.

The Afrikaner Broederbond will, however, unless checked, outlive both, since its policy is far more patient and insidiously clever.

Knowing the full circumstances of this dangerous growth in the life of the South African State, General Hertzog warned passionately:

Owing to the secret nature of the AB, it is impossible to ascertain what is going on behind the scenes, and there is accordingly no protection for the non-*Broer* against the secret supporters of the *Broer*.

Generally speaking, there is nothing to prevent the Bond from being misused as an instrument for organized action in conflict with the best interests of the state and the civil service.

Demobilization: In proportion as this policy of Afrikaner dominance creeps into the various spheres of employment and particularly into the higher professional and state services, those who are English-speaking and also those Afrikaans-speaking men who are not of that particular brand of *ware Afrikaner* required by the AB, will be more and more pushed into the background to posts of secondary importance.   Professional men and particularly teachers who are now in the army and who have thrown in their lot with the Government will thus have but scant chance of future advancement.   It is already beginning to worry them, though most are not yet aware of the power that is operating against them.   It works so cleverly behind the scenes and is nearly always just within the regulations.

What chance, may we well ask, has the Government, under such conditions, of effectively carrying out its demobilization plans insofar as they impinge on spheres impregnated with Broederbond influence?   Also where Broederbond officials are present (and a prominent one figures in demobilization), there are innumerable ways of subtle obstruction calculated to create annoying delays with subsequent disillusionment, which is so detrimental to the Government, and so valuable for the opposition.

The Broederbonders themselves have nothing to fear, since their powerful and wealthy organization cares well for those who get into trouble for services rendered.

Broederbond candidates for Parliament or the provincial councils, for example, are not afraid of throwing up a Government post, because if they should be unsuccessful, the AB guarantees them a good job.   There are numerous instances of such cases.

In 1935, in full peace time, and with a powerful Coalition Government, General Hertzog judged it necessary to try to destroy the Afrikaner Broederbond by dragging all their unsavoury doings into the open.   No action was taken, however.   This was possibly due to the fact that the Coalition Government considered itself strong enough to ignore such a despicable mushroom growth.

Today, with the bitter experience of the Broederbond's evil influence on the war effort, and its stronghold on South African public life, the need for action is much more urgent.   If we are to dwell together in peace and amity in South Africa, the Broederbond must be destroyed.

General Hertzog was quite right when, in warning against the machinations of the secret Broederbond, he said that:

The future more than the present and the past depends on that co-operation between English and Dutch Afrikaners based on a realization of national unity.   Our happy position today (1935) of being able to

275

prevent our people from going under, is chiefly due to the fortunate and hearty co-operation between city and platteland; between our industrial, and our farming population.

Without that benign, well-disposed relationship between English and Dutch Afrikaners, we shall not have co-operation and rehabilitation, but conflict, disunity, and downfall.

The Ossewa-Brandwag was robbed of its menace and power when all its activities were mercilessly revealed to the public gaze, and Government servants were warned to resign as members. When this warning was subsequently followed up by stern measures against those who were still involved, the organization finally lost its immediate dangerous aspect.

If the Afrikaner Broederbond is not similarly immediately exposed and its stranglehold eradicated root and branch—in particular its insidious hold on education— it will, at its present rate of growth, within a few years destroy South Africa.

Thus did the nazi system, also starting with a small but powerful underground group, gain ultimate control, dragging the whole world into the most devastating war of all time.

The potentialities, in the case of South Africa, are more dangerous. Germany's Nemesis was disguised in the form of a humble and poorly educated housepainter. South Africa's equivalent is a university professor!

APPENDIX III

In reply to Smuts' attacks on the Afrikaner Broederbond, Professor J. C. van Rooy, Broederbond Chairman, and Mr I. M. Lombard, Secretary, issued a series of five articles explaining the aims and objects of their organization. This was made public December, 14, 21, 28, 1944, and January 4, 1945. Below are summaries of these reports printed in the English-language newspaper, *The Friend*, published in Bloemfontein. The complete texts may be found in Afrikaans in *Die Transvaler*.

DECEMBER 14, 1944

'The Afrikaner Broederbond was born out of the deep conviction that the Afrikaner nation was planted in this country by the hand of God and is destined to continue to exist as a nation with its own character and own calling,' says a statement issued by Professor J. C. van Rooy and Mr I. Lombard, Chairman and Secretary, respectively, of the Broederbond.

'The aim of the Broederbond, taken literally from the constitution,' the statement continues, is:

(a) 'The establishment of a healthy and progressive unanimity among all Afrikaners who strive for the welfare of the Afrikaner nation.

(b) 'The awakening of national self-assurance among Afrikaners and the inspiration of love for the language, religion, traditions, country and people.

(c) 'The promotion of all the interests of the Afrikaner people.

'The language of the Bond is Afrikaans. Party politics is excluded from the Bond. Only those can be members who are Afrikaans-speaking, of Protestant belief, of clean character, who are firm in the principle of maintaining their Afrikanderhood and who accept South Africa as their only fatherland. From every member it is expected that he will live and act in the firm belief that the destiny of nations is guided by the hand of God and that he at all times by his behaviour will hold high the honour, dignity, and good name of the Afrikaner Broederbond.

'Hitherto the Afrikaner Broederbond has never defended itself in public against the frequent absurd, uninformed, and also shamelessly false accusations. Its members have become members with the definite understanding that they will get absolutely nothing for themselves from their membership—not even fame or honour for service that may be rendered to the Afrikaner nation.

'Their powers and talents must be dedicated entirely and unselfishly to the interests of their nation in accordance with the demands of a Christian conscience and an unimpeachable character.

'Now that the Prime Minister, General J. C. Smuts, in his ignorance or driven by those of his followers imbued with a spirit of persecution, has found himself called upon, together with them, to try to stone the Bond, the interests of the Afrikaner nation demand that the history, objects, nature, aims, methods, and activities of this servant of Afrikanerdom be so revealed to the latter that it will cling with both hands to that weapon to help itself in its national struggle and will not allow an injustice to be done to its (the Broederbond's) members or injury to be done to the value and extent of its work.

'The Afrikaner Broederbond is giving its evidence in full belief in the God of its fathers before the court of its people in whose judgment and in whose conscience it has the fullest confidence.

'The Bond appeals to the people to judge whether its life and work deserve abuse and suppression instead of appreciation, and whether those who have faithfully served their fatherland in a legal way and in observance of all the obligations to which an honourable person and a professed Christian is subject, deserve martyrdom in any form.

'The people have the power not only to judge what is right, but to demand that the Government let justice prevail, and if this does not happen, then to throw in its forces in the struggle which in such an event must necessarily follow.

'Since this official statement and appeal to the people as the highest court of justice in the land, as well as the series of statements the Secretary has been instructed to prepare, give the facts for which the hostile press and persons apparently have been yearning, we challenge them to publish this and the other statements fully. Then their readers and audiences, too, can judge what is probable and correct.

'If this demand—because after all the slander against the Bond it has, like a victim whom they already want to lead to the gallows, a right to a final demand—is not fulfilled, but the revelation of facts and the defence are again concealed from Government supporters, as happened when a member of the Bond replied to Mr H. G. Lawrence conclusively, then we declare now that such assailants, who only stab in the back and run away, are hypocritical cowards. They have chosen to spread the basest accusations and the most flagrant untruths about the Bond; they are now in duty bound to publish the other side in the form in which the defenders are compelled to defend themselves.

'While it is not possible, within the scope of this statement to give many details, a promise is made here to do full justice to the various other matters of interest, one by one, in further statements. But we wish to take this opportunity to emphasise the following matters most strongly:

(1) 'It is not true that the Broederbond is a subversive organization which incites sabotage or will tolerate it from members in any form. It is absolutely untrue that the Bond has ever encouraged the giving away by its

members of state secrets or tolerated it. On the contrary, the Bond takes the attitude that complete loyalty to their duties and official oath is a necessary guarantee that members will comply with the desired high religious and moral demands in their lawful work for the benefit of Afrikanerdom in the cultural, economic, social, and political sphere. On behalf of the Bond we challenge the Government, or the Public Service Commission, or any other legal body or any person to prove the contrary.

(2) 'It is not true, as General Smuts alleges, that members consist "mostly of teachers and civil servants", and that "the rest are mostly party-political persons". Of the total membership of 2,672, at the most 8.4 per cent are civil servants and at the outside 33.3 per cent teachers. These figures include civil servants and teachers who have already retired on pension or who, after joining the Bond, have left the service and are now carrying on other callings. The rest are mostly farmers.

'No more true is General Smuts' allegation that membership is limited to influential persons in key positions. In point of fact the standard used is the zeal and readiness of persons to work for popular causes, and to make sacrifices regularly, monetary or otherwise, without any expectation of reward, and the tendency is rather to give preference to zealous young men so that they may have the opportunity to learn to perform useful national service. Older persons in key positions already have that opportunity.

(3) 'It is not true that the Broederbond is undemocratic or Fascist. On the contrary the Broederbond is pre-eminently organized on democratic lines. Every executive is elected by its members annually. The highest Executive Council and the Chairman are elected every two years by secret ballot by chosen delegates to a congress. Even in the admittance of new members these democratic principles apply, because every member has the fullest say on the question of who is to be admitted. In contrast with the allegation that members may not know one another, actually any member may have the fullest information about every other member.

'Further, it is an indisputable fact that the Bond accepts a system of democracy in accordance with the traditions of the Afrikaner people as carried out by its model republics. It is absolutely denied here in public that the Bond at any time declared itself in favour of a National-Socialist system for South Africa or that it has ever had, or sought, any connection with the nazi rulers of Germany.

'The Bond denies as a barefaced lie the allegation made in the *Sunday Times* that the Zeesen broadcaster Holm is a member, or ever was a member of the Bond, as well as the other efforts made in this connection to throw suspicion of traitorous deeds or alliances on the Broederbond.

'Space does not allow any further details. Therefore, they will be supplied later. Also in the coming session of Parliament its members are free to put the Broederbond's case. In all fairness, however, now that this evidence has been laid before the people it can be expected that no rash or hasty action will be taken by the Government.

'No self-respecting person and no body with a sense of honour can submit to injustice and oppression. The Afrikaner people have had to endure much during this war. To begin with, no ordinary citizen was trusted with the possession of a firearm for his own protection. Then followed attacks on Afrikaans schools, the Church and almost all Afrikaans organizations, even *volkspele* [folk dances] and *jukskei*. It has now come to this that an association with high ideals, whose only sin was not to advertise its work for the benefit of its people, must suffer under venomous misrepresentations and be threatened with further demonstrations of hate, as well as persecution, by the authorities.

'If it is conceded that the Government, through ignorance perhaps, fears that the Broederbond is taking measures similar to those which it (the Government) possibly knows friendly disposed secret associations such as Freemasons, the Sons of England and the Jewish patriotic association take, or might take, against the interest of nationalist-inclined Afrikanerdom, then it (the Government) should realize now that it has to deal with an organization concerning whose work and aims it is entirely misinformed.

'While, thus, it is expected that the Government will not obstinately anticipate the verdict of the people, the members of the Bond, too, will take up a waiting attitude.'

DECEMBER 21, 1944

The Broederbond, in the first of the series of promised statements on its activities, deals with two matters—the secrecy maintained in regard to deliberations, and the rule that no member of the Broederbond may disclose the membership of any other person.

A statement issued by the Secretary of the Broederbond and published in *Die Transvaler* says: 'The fact that the Broederbond is confidential in nature has led to the basest accusations of deceit, subversion, and so on. Yet there is nothing strange about this—that is to say, nothing that is not in accordance with what is happening throughout society.

'By this I do not mean that in the case of the Broederbond one is dealing with the mysterious secrecy of the Freemasons. It has nothing to do with the secret promotion of the interests of a group, as in the case of Jewish societies.

'Here one is not dealing with secret intrigue, as is sometimes found in connection with the deliberations of money magnates and even in the political sphere.

'One is not dealing here with the secret promotion in South Africa of the interests of a foreign country or the quiet pushing ahead in state appointments of one section of the people, as the Sons of England does.

'No. The confidential character of the Broederbond is comparable with what one finds at a Cabinet meeting, at a meeting of directors of a decent business undertaking, or at an executive meeting of a church or cultural organization before it comes to a decision which can be conveyed to its members.

'When the Smuts Cabinet deliberates on matters of policy—not only in connection with the prosecution of the war—it does not broadcast everything immediately! More especially does it not do so when it has not yet reached clarity or agreement in regard to policy of methods of action. Does such a procedure make a Cabinet a crafty machine that wants to undermine the interests of the people? Of course not.

'Why, then, must the Broederbond be so branded while it is only a deliberation body, where members discuss privately what they consider to be best for the Afrikaner people?

'When members have thus arrived at a conclusion on any matter, for instance in regard to economic, social, or cultural life, their attitude has always been submitted fully and publicly to the judgment of the people.

'On a subsequent occasion I shall develop this thought further, when I show how the Bond works, and I shall give examples of how the results of members' deliberations have always been laid openly before the people.'

Dealing with the question of secrecy in regard to who are members of the Bond, the statement says it is a strict demand which applies even to those who resign, that members undertake not to reveal one another's membership.

'The reason for this is obvious,' the statement says. 'Those who regard the progress of Afrikanerdom with the greatest jealousy, and who try to prevent it in every way, do so in very cunning ways. If there is someone in their employ who, they know, devotes his talents and spare time in an entirely lawful way to the Afrikaner people, then they withhold promotion or make his life intolerable in other ways.

'During a century of injustice the Afrikaner has learnt that his greatest sin in the eyes of his enemies is that he wants to be loyal to his nation.

'Therefore the crafty fighting methods employed by those who want to deny Afrikanerdom its place under the sun are the reason why those who can be persecuted in this way have the right to conceal the fact that they, as sons of the fatherland, are doing good but always lawful work for their people.

'The present persecution shows how a measure which was found necessary in the earlier days of the Bond, and which meanwhile had been largely tradition, is really justified today.'

DECEMBER 28, 1944

The membership of the Broederbond and the size of groups to discuss various plans were dealt with in a second statement issued by Mr I. M. Lombard, Secretary of the Broederbond, last night.

The Bond, he said, had been built up by ordinary people who wanted to consider how the national life of the Afrikaner could be enriced. They had organized themselves into small groups and each member was free to take part in discussions.

Not only was it necessary to make groups small, but they had also to be representative of the various professions. If a number of doctors, or teachers, or mineworkers or highly placed officials only formed such a group they could only talk and think about things which concerned their limited sphere of work, and they would not know how the lives of other sections of the people were affected.

The view was adopted that every group must contain a small number of members who could easily meet to discuss various matters and who were representative of as many different sections of the people as possible. If there were one or two teachers in a section, no more teachers would be appointed to it, even though there were other outstanding teachers in the vicinity.

The exclusion of many good Afrikaners from the Bond had resulted from this attempt to keep groups small from the point of view of efficiency and from the attempt to obtain representatives from different sections of the Afrikaner people.

The statement said that every member of the Bond had the right to propose new members and to vote on their acceptance. If members of a local division considered that a person could not co-operate with them in their small discussion circle they had the right not to accept him. The Prime Minister had the right not to accept certain members of his Party in his Cabinet.

Every association had its own rules and customs, and those of the Bond were certainly less objectionable (*aanstootlik*) than those of the exclusive clubs of which the Britisher was so proud.

The Bond did not ask for the right to prescribe how the Toc H, the BESL or the SOE should choose their members. They, in turn, had no authority over the Broederbond's enrolments.

It was absolutely untrue to say that all sorts of good Afrikaners were excluded from the Bond because there were objections to their work or characters.

DECEMBER 30, 1944

Mr I. M. Lombard, Secretary of the Broederbond, in the third of his series of statements about the activities of the Bond, describes the procedure adopted in connection with research by the Broederbond into various problems affecting Afrikaners.

He gives two examples—the language and culture of Afrikaners and their economic status—and describes how, after the fullest investigation into the matter, the FAK (Federation of Afrikaans Cultural Associations) and the *Volkskas* were established.

Mr Lombard states that he hopes that these two examples will help to show the Broederbond, through intensive study and serious deliberation, has often been able to help in the establishment of institutions and organizations of great value to Afrikaners, which function openly and which are public property.

The Broederbond also made certain monetary demands on its members to raise funds for good Afrikaans causes. The Broederbond contributed £1,000 toward the repatriation of the Argentine Boers, £500 towards the Daisyfield Orphanage School in Rhodesia, £3,000 for study loans for students at the Afrikaans Medical Faculty at the Pretoria University, and £3,000 for study loans for students at the Afrikaans Engineering Faculty at the Stellenbosch University.

'All the work of the Broederbond can be measured by these examples,' Mr Lombard says. 'Dare anyone with an honest conscience say that it is not noble, unselfish work and born out of love of the nation?'

JANUARY 4, 1945

In the fourth of his series of statements on the activities of the Broederbond, Mr I. M. Lombard, Secretary of the Bond, deals with whether or not the Broederbond is a political or a subversive organization.

'In our first statement, Article 6 of the constitution was quoted that party politics is debarred from the Broederbond,' the statement says. 'I wish, however, to quote more fully what the rules and regulations have to say on this subject. They read as follows: "In connection with the activities of general district meetings, the meetings may discuss any national problem or historic point with a view to ascertaining, in an impartial manner, what is the best for the moral, intellectual, social, and political progress of our nation.

' "No speaker may, however, act as a propagandist for any existing political party or for party politics as such.

' "On the other hand, the Bond desires that all brothers should strive for the following seven ideals in their political activities:

' "(1) The removal of everything that is in conflict with the full international independence of South Africa; (2) putting an end to the inferiority of the Afrikaans-speaking section and their language in state organizations; (3) the separation of the Coloured races in South Africa, while allowing them independent development under the guardianship of the European; (4) putting a stop to the exploitation of the resources and population of South Africa by foreigners, including more intensified industrial development; (5) the rehabilitation of the farming community and the guarantee of a civilized existence by employment for all European citizens; (6) the nationalization of finance (*geldhandel*), and the systematic co-ordination of political economy; (7) the Afrikanerizing of public life and our education and teaching in the Christian-National sense, leaving free the internal development of all sections of the community who do not constitute a danger to the state."

'I quote this part of the constitution fully purposely, because it has already been misrepresented by the Government press.

'It is unthinkable that in any country the Government should expect that there should be people who have no opinion about fundamental principles. Even the public servant in Britain is not forbidden to take a personal or philosophical view of national problems.

'The English Church in South Africa, for example, adopts a policy in regard to the treatment of natives, politically. In connection with such political questions as participation in and membership of the British Empire it makes itself heard. Anyone who reads the newspapers knows to what extent the English Church intervenes in political questions. Yet the Government never dreams of banning membership of the English Church to public servants.

'The Government, as such, even encourages public servants to be active propagandists and collectors for participation in the war—something which is in the midst of the political conflict in South Africa.

'The Government does not object to membership of the Sons of England. This body has, however, repeatedly interfered in the active political struggle and has openly clashed with the Government of the day—the flag question, to quote one example.

'While the Broederbond may not believe in an independent South Africa as a principle without being judged, Sons of England members may make one of their aims the strengthening of the British connection and even the watering down of the constitution and the constitutional freedom laid down in the Statute of Westminster.'

The statement says that while the Broederbond is branded as a political organization to which public servants may not belong, membership of the Unity Truth Legion—a secret organization in the true sense of the word and one which spies on fellow citizens—is encouraged.

The form of address *jy* or *u* is optional in this form. (Both *jy* and *u* mean 'you', the latter being used to denote respect, usually to an older person.)

1. The preparation: Song (optional). As soon as the aspirant is ready for initiation, a suitable song, such as Psalm 130 : 3 can be sung.

Prayer: By the initiation master or by someone with whom previous arrangements will have been made.

Scripture reading: The initiation master reads a short, suitable portion of Scripture.

2. The initiation master reads the full name of the aspirant and says:

'You appear here because you have indicated a desire to join the ranks of the *Ruiterwag*. Before you are told what is intended and what demands will be made on you as a *Ruiter,* you must in true good faith and sincerely undertake:

First, to maintain the strictest secrecy about all matters concerning the *Ruiterwag* that may come into your possession;
Second, never to join or be associated with any other secret movement without the permission of the *Hoofwag*;
Third, to submit yourself to instant explusion if the executive decides you have failed in this binding undertaking in any way.'

3. *Initiation master*: If, after what you have heard, you have doubt in your mind, you now get the chance to go in peace. No one will hold it against you.

A few moments of silence.

4. *Initiation master*: By not leaving us, you have indicated that you remain firm in your intentions. It can now be told to you that the *Ruiterwag* was born out of the urge to help further freedom and self-determination of the Afrikaner nation in all spheres of life.

Because the youth of a nation is the power source of its existence and development, the *Ruiterwag* wishes, with firm bonds of mutual trust and love of nation, to weld together a hard core of picked young men who are prepared unconditionally to pledge their service to the people and to the honour of God.

You, therefore, do not come here to ask for recognition of actions or achievements in the past, but to offer yourself in unselfish service to the nation and to become a *Ruiter* on the Road of South Africa. There will be no turning out of this road for you. The song of the progress of the *Ruiterwag* will always echo in your ears and out of the people's past will come the call: Be prepared. Be faithful.

For this you must know that the only man who can become a *Ruiter* is one who measures up to the following demands:

5. (Assistant initiation masters who stand behind the aspirant then intone):

Speaker A: To pay homage to the Protestant faith and hold it in honour;

Speaker B: To accept his own nationhood and to maintain it as a task laid down by God;

Speaker A: Firm in principle and strong character;

Speaker B: Comradeship, a spirit of sacrifice, faithfulness and self-discipline;

Speaker A: To be able to give responsible leadership and also to be able to subject himself to intelligent leadership.

6. *Initiation master*: Are you prepared to carry out these principles and to base faithfully all your actions on them? Call the aspirant's name out in full and say: What is your answer?

Aspirant: Yes.

7. *Initiation master*: Because very strict demands are made on members of the *Ruiterwag*, it is necessary that you should carefully consider what is expected of a *Ruiter*.

8. *Speaker A* (behind the aspirant): The *Ruiterwag* wants you always to remain honest and true to the highest Afrikaner traditions;

Speaker B: The *Ruiterwag* wants you always to strive for unity among all right-thinking young Afrikaners;

Speaker A: The *Ruiterwag* wants you to be faithful in the smallest things and in your labours to seek only your wage;

Speaker B: The *Ruiterwag* expects you faithfully to attend every meeting of your *Wagpos* and to work in active co-operation with other *Ruiters* in a spirit of genuine unity and comradeship;

Speaker A: The *Ruiterwag* expects that you will submit yourself to such censure and discipline as the executive might have to exercise under the standing orders.

9. *Initiation master*: You now know the significance of the choice which you must make and you get another chance to consider these high demands. If you cannot face this call and this task, then you had better go in peace.

A few moments of silence.

10. *Initiation master*: Now that you have had plenty of time to consider your decision, you are asked to give the following undertakings:

To serve God and your people faithfully to the death without expecting honour or reward;

To maintain the greatest, strictest secrecy about all *Ruiter* matters;

Never to join or to co-operate with other secret organizations without the permission of the *Hoofwag*;

Always to carry out the instructions of those set above you and to work honestly, faithfully, and heartily with all other *Ruiters*;

To regard all your promises binding to the death, no matter what punishment is meted out to you and even if you are deprived of your membership.

11. *Initiation master*: Do you solemnly and unconditionally promise this in the full realization of the seriousness of your promises?

The initiation master then calls out the full name of aspirant and asks: 'What is your answer?'

Aspirant: Yes.

12. The initiation master then intones:

'The struggle that our fathers began,

'Will rage till we have died or won.

'That is the oath of Young South Africa.'

The initiation master then goes forward and gives the new *Ruiter* a warm and hearty handshake: 'With this handshake I declare you a member of the *Ruiterwag*.'

13. *Initiation master*: After all those present have welcomed you with a handshake, you will be led out to ratify the promises that you made here with your signature.

All those present then give the *Ruiter* a hearty handshake and he is led out.

APPENDIX V. CHRISTIAN-NATIONAL EDUCATION POLICY AS OUTLINED BY THE INSTITUTE FOR CNE OF THE FAK, 1948, WITH A PREFACE BY J. C. VAN ROOY

Preface

It is with great pleasure that I comply with the request of the Institute of Christian-National Education of the Federation of Afrikaans Cultural Societies to write a preface for our Christian-National Education policy, which is now published as a formulated directive; and so I would like to take this opportunity of congratulating the member of the CNE Institute in the success they have achieved in the formulation of this policy, so that this document can be circulated as a guiding principle in our cultural struggle, which is now also definitely a struggle in the schools.

The ideal of the CNE is no novelty among us. A great fight has already been fought for it, and the struggle will still be long and hard, but we are progressing all the time, and we firmly believe that our point of view will in the end prove victorious.

After the second Boer War the well-known CNE schools were established in the Northern Province in order to counteract the intentional Anglicizing of our children in the British state schools. It is in these schools that the soul of our nation lived on in the younger generation. The CNE schools were indeed a tremendous financial burden for people impoverished by war; but the struggle was kept up long enough, because, when the CNE schools were at last handed over to the state in 1907, there was already a second front already occupied in the struggle for the preservation of our nation's identity. This was the second language movement. The struggle on this front was for the official recognition of our language. This struggle was carried on with the unyielding perseverance and conviction, with the result that we began to reap the first fruits of our efforts when Afrikaans was recognized as a school subject in 1914. Further victories followed. About 1920 Afrikaans was recognized as a medium of instruction at school, and in 1925 our language was put on an equal footing with the English as one of the official languages of the country. After that we were able to experience a decade of peace, of steady growth and extension in the domain of language. Afrikaans literature made tremendous strides, and Afrikaans medium schools arose everywhere. It can be said with truth that quite a few generations of children passed our mother-language schools without interference. They are a source of strength in our present language struggle. In 1937 and 1948, however, signs began to appear heralding a new struggle. The worn-out idea of double-medium schools was seized upon once again in a fresh effort that came too late to Anglicize our children by the means of the medium of instruction.

The FAK, however, faithful to its aim of roping in the Afrikaners in the maintenance and further development of our language, and in the protection and spread of our own Afrikaans culture based on the foundation and traditions of our nation, did not allow these signs to pass unnoticed. Following on the usual FAK Congress, a CNE Congress was arranged and held by the FAK at Bloemfontein on July 5, 6, and 7 in 1939. At this Congress our CNE ideal was again clearly stated and elucidated, and one of the decisions of the Congress was that the FAK should found an institute for the continuous propagation and furtherance of the now historically established ideal of Christian and National instruction and education, and to ensure that the general lines of policy laid down by the Congress should be systematically pursued. An institute of this type was immediately established by the FAK and is known today as the ICNE. Those who were responsible for the activities of this institute soon became aware that it was a pre-requisite of their task to arrive at a more or less complete formulation of our CNE policy. This task was taken in hand and now after almost ten years of working in private, this directive can be published. Various drafts of this policy were considered by the whole Institute, by the managing committees of the FAK, and the bodies and institutions represented in the ICNE and the FAK—that means all the Afrikaans bodies and institutions which are in any way interested in education.

The brochure in its present form had therefore been approved by the whole of Afrikanerdom in so far as it is represented by its organized branches in the FAK. Truly we have made progress.

There will doubtless still be a few people, or groups of people, who are not entirely satisfied with everything, but of course complete agreement on all points of policy can never be achieved. That is, however, no reason why our struggle should not be just as unanimous and full of enthusiasm in the future as it has been in the past. There is too much at stake to allow of any slackening in the struggle. The recognition of our language as a medium of instruction does not mean that we have achieved everything. On the contrary, we have achieved very little. Afrikaans as a medium of instruction in a school atmosphere which is naturally foreign to our nation is like 'a sounding brass or a tinkling cymbal'. The real cultural 'stuff' is still not there. Our culture must be brought into the schools, and this cannot be done merely by using our language as a medium of instruction. More is necessary. Our Afrikaans schools must not be merely mother-language schools; they must be in the true sense of the word Christian and National schools; they must be places where our children are soaked and nourished in the Christian-National spiritual cultural 'stuff' of our nation. The double-medium struggle has opened the eyes of our people, and helped them to appreciate still further this ideal; it is for the realization of this ideal that the struggle is coming. We will have nothing to do with a mixture of languages, of culture, of religion, or of race. We are winning the language-medium struggle. The struggle for the Christian-National school still lies ahead, and it is really for this struggle that a policy has been now laid down, a policy which can claim to be based on the greatest possible agreement of our people.

Let everyone, therefore, accept this policy, every parent, every teacher, and pupil, and in the light of this policy let us continue our tasks in the interests of the education of our children, and to the glory of God, and to the salvation and blessing of our people and the fatherland.

Introduction

The following explanation of the CNE policy falls into two parts. In the first part, consisting of nine articles, the policy for primary and secondary instruction and education is rather fully laid down. In the second part, consisting of six articles, this policy is described in relation to infant schools, higher education and vocational training, adult education, etc.

This is done in the second part in less detail because the principles of all CNE instruction are clearly stated in the first part, and can be applied to the second part with the necessary change.

PART I: PRIMARY AND SECONDARY INSTRUCTION AND EDUCATION
Article 1: Foundation

We believe that the instruction and education of the children of European parents must be carried out on a basis of their parents' attitude to life and to the world. For Afrikaans-speaking children this means that they must be reared on the basis of the CNE attitude to life and to the world as held by our nation. In this attitude C. and N. principles are of basic significance and its object is the propagation, protection, and development of the essentially C. and N. character of our nation. The Christian foundation of this attitude is based on the Holy Scripture and expressed in the Articles of Faith of our three Afrikaans churches. By national principle we love everything that is our own, with special reference to our country, our language, our history, and our culture. We believe that both these principles must be developed to the full in the instruction and education of our children in such a way that these two principles are characteristic of the whole school as regards its spirit, aim, curriculum, method, discipline, staff, organization and its activities. Corresponding to the basic structure of our C.N. attitude to life and to the world, the National principle must always be under the guidance of the Christian principle, the national must sprout from the Christian.

Article 2: Christian Instruction and Education

By Christian instruction and education for Afrikaans-speaking children we mean instruction and education given in the light of God's revelation in the Bible expressed in the Articles of Faith in the three Afrikaans churches. In order to have the whole school filled with the light of God's revelation as contained in Holy Scripture, we believe that religious instruction according to the Bible and our Articles of Faith must be the key subject at school. It should shape the spirit and direction of all other subjects, and of the whole school in such a way that the whole instruction carried out at school is based on the Christian foundation of our nation's attitude to life and to the world. It must not be merely an information subject.

Article 3: National Instruction and Education

By national instruction and education we mean instruction and education in which adequate expression is given to the whole content of instruction and in all the activities of the school to the national principle of love for one's own based on and with the terms of the Christian principle, so that the child is introduced thoroughly and with pride to the spiritual-cultural inheritance, the spiritual-cultural wealth of the nation, and becomes a worthy bearer of that cultural wealth. The school should not be separate from, but should stand in the centre of, our national life, and must derive strength and inspiration from the soil of its culture and all its activities.

Article 4: The Child and C. and N. Instruction and Education

We believe that (a) God created man originally pure and good, and in His image, i.e., in true righteousness and holiness without sin, so that he could really know and glorify God, his Creator; (b) that man through his own choice fell into sin, with the result that the image of God in him has been so obscured that he has kept nothing else of it except only insignificant remnants which are enough to deprive man of any excuse; that owing to the Fall, sin has penetrated through each successive generation by inheritance; and that the child, for that reason, as object of instruction and education is a sinful, and not a sinless being; (c) that God of His own free mercy has established His Covenant in Jesus Christ with the believing generations, and in regeneration plants the seed of the new Christian life in the child; that His Covenant of mercy moves among the generations and for that reason a child professing Christian parents must be treated as a believing Christian and not a heathen; (d) that God has implanted in man at the Creation a living, immortal, active, self-responsible, self-conscious, purposeful principle, which is called simply the spirit or soul of man, which distinguishes him from all other living creatures, and which furnishes him with possibility of development; (e) that the possibility of and necessity for all instruction and education lies in the child's condition of immaturity, of dependence, of ability to learn by experience, of docility and imperfection; (f) that apart from the joint characteristics which every child has in common with all children of all parents, there are also national characteristics which must be respected.

Article 5: The Aim of Instruction and Education

We believe that all instruction and education is the essentially dominating guidance and formation of a child's development into an adult in subjection to the word of God in all things; and that the highest aim of all instruction and education is the moulding of people in God's image so that they become fully equipped for every good work. We consider the essentials of the process of education to lie in this—that the younger generation is introduced to all that is good and beautiful and noble in the cultural wealth of the nation in such a way that the younger generation takes over this wealth in accordance with its own aptitude and needs, and develops and extends this further according to the nation's attitude to life and the world. We believe that only in this way is the individual, as well as the nation, enabled to know God, to glorify Him through their various roles in the cultural tasks of humanity, namely, to subdue the earth and rule over it, to achieve in all sections of life in subjection to the Creator's will. We believe that this process can only be carried out and this aim only achieved in schools which are Christian and National.

Article 6: Content of Instruction and Education
1. Introduction

We believe that in order to achieve the aim of Christian and National instruction, namely, the moulding of Godly people entirely equipped for every good deed, the content of instruction and education should not be limited to a few subjects. We are meant to learn from the whole of God's creation as expressed in the laws of Nature and the labour of man. We believe, moreover, that the spirit and trend of instruction in all subjects must correspond with the Christian and National attitude to life and to the world, i.e., that every subject must be taught in the light of the word of God, namely, on the basis of the applicable principles of Scripture; and in no subject may anti-Christian or anti-National propaganda be conducted, nor yet propaganda which is not in accordance with the Christian and National view of life. We believe that religious knowledge and subjects like the mother language (as medium and as subject), civics, geography, and history are subjects which from their nature, if properly taught, inculcate a Christian and National view of life.

2. Religious Instruction

By religious instruction we mean chiefly instruction in Bible history and subjects related to this, and instruction in the Christian doctrine of faith. Instruction in Bible history must not be merely the communication of facts, and instruction in the Christian doctrine of faith must not be colourless and hermetically cut off from the other school activities; but must form, together with other activities, an organic whole and both must be supported by and in accordance with the religious convictions of the parents of the school-going children as these are expressed in the Articles of Faith of our three Afrikaans churches. Not only must religious instruction itself be of high standard, but it must occupy such a central place in the teaching that it determines the spirit and trend of all subjects of the whole school. We believe that religious instruction as here advocated must be given in the primary and in the secondary schools, and the recognized church music of the Afrikaans churches must also be properly provided for.

3. Mother Language

We believe that the mother language is the basis of all instruction and education and that the mother language is the most important secular subject taught at school. It must be the only medium of instruction in all other subjects, except in the case of other modern languages. Bilingualism cannot be made the aim of teaching, and the learning of the other official language can only then be begun after the child has had a thorough grounding in the mother language and has acquired a basic knowledge of how to express himself in it.

4. Civics

We believe that every scholar must be moulded into a Christian and National citizen of our country. We believe that every citizen has his rights, responsibilities, and duties toward family, church, community, and state. We believe that instruction in the subject 'civics' must be such that it will produce Christian and National citizens, so that each one in his turn by the proper exercise of his rights and the carrying out of his responsibilities and duties shall respect, preserve, and perpetuate the Christian and National character of the family, the church, the community, and the state.

5. Geography

We believe that every people and nation is attached to its own native soil allotted to it by the Creator. We believe that this knowledge must be imparted to the scholar in such a way that he develops a love for our native land as such also as compared in contra-distinction to the other countries. We believe that this feeling of being rooted in, and this attachment to our own soil must induce him, if necessary, to defend his own native soil, to preserve it from impoverishment, to cultivate it, and to improve it for the next generation.

6. History Teaching

We believe that history must be taught in the light of God's revelation and must be viewed as a fulfilment of God's decreed plan for the world and for the human race, more definitely as the fulfilment of the task enjoined upon man by God, the Creator, namely, to multiply and to subject the earth and to rule over it. We believe that the great facts of the Creation—the Fall and the breaking of the Covenant; the human birth, suffering, death, resurrection, and ascension of Christ; the regeneration in Jesus Christ; and the Day of Judgment—are of world historical importance and that Jesus Christ is the great turning point in the history of the world. We believe that the great antithesis between the kingdom of God in Jesus Christ and the kingdom of darkness permeates everything, and must be traced in history. While fully maintaining the essential unity of history, we believe that God, in the accomplishment of the great task He has laid down upon men, willed separate nations and peoples; that He gave each separate nation and people its special vocation, task, and gifts; that each nation and people, in accomplishing its vocation and task, is a builder of culture by controlling and moulding the character with which it is endowed, its structure, and condition and only then can fulfil its vocation and task to the glory of God for all things. We believe that the youth can only then faithfully take over the task and vocation of the older generation and carry them to fruition if it ' obtains in history instruction a real vision of the nation's origin, of its cultural inheritance, and of the content of the proper trend in that inheritance. We believe that alongside of the mother language, national history is the chief means of fostering love of one's own.

Article 7: Methodology and Discipline

We believe that the method of instruction and education must be based on a thorough knowledge of the child and on the education practice, historically developed and tested, which is linked up with the aforementioned knowledge of the child. We believe that the teacher, acting deliberately and according to a fixed plan, to achieve the object of teaching, must be free to use the means that will enable him to achieve that object in accordance with our Christian and National attitude to life and to the world.

We believe that the notion of discipline may be described as all the internal and external actions and influences that work together to ensure such conduct on the part of everyone in the school as shall make the achievement of the purpose of teaching and education most effective. We believe that all authority in the school is God-given authority, and that it imposes great responsibility, duties, and rights not only on the Christian teacher, but also on the child. We believe that the object of all discipline must be the preservation and moulding of the child, the well-being of the community, and above all the glory of God.

Article 8: Control of Instruction

1. No Mixed Schools

We believe that there must be at least two types of schools for primary and secondary education, one for the children of Afrikaans-speaking parents, with their social creed and language, with Afrikaans only as a medium, and one for children of English-speaking parents with English as a medium. We believe that in both types of schools there must be the right relation between the family, the school, the church, and the state, so far as concerns the spirit and trend, the establishment, maintenance control, and supervision of the schools.

2. Home, School, and Church

We believe that the home, school, and church are the three places in which our nation is trained and constitute, therefore, a cord with three strands in teaching and education, and that they should supplement one another so that each receives its rightful share in the moulding of the young child.

3. The Home

We believe that the teaching and education of the child is the duty and right of the parents, that they in co-operation with the church and the state must, therefore, decide as to the spirit and trend of education in the schools, in accordance with their attitude to life and to the world; maintain and control them; that they must appoint teachers in the schools for their children and exercise supervision over their teaching. The parents collectively, and not as individuals, must determine the spirit and trend; in co-operation with the church and the state they must establish, maintain, and control schools.

4. The Church

We believe that the church as the community of believers (adults and children) has a great interest in the schools; that it must exercise supervision over the spirit and trend of education, and, therefore, of education in the schools also; that it must see that there are Christian and National schools for the education of its young members; that it must exercise disciplinary measures when the need arises; with reference to the doctrinal opinions and lives of the teachers as members of the church.

We believe also that the church must exercise supervision through the agency of the parent; that it must stimulate the parent to establish, maintain, and control Christian schools, and it must afford the necessary support to needy parents so that they may adequately perform the task of educating their children. We believe that in ordinary circumstances the church does not establish schools but that it is obliged to establish schools for the sake of the faith, and in extraordinary circumstances if (a) the existing schools do not conform to the Christian and National principles and (b) in the heathen world.

5. The State

We believe that the state as an institution for the maintenance of law in human society, being the bearer of authority and power, must see to it that a proper standard of popular education is continually maintained; that the principle of equity is enforced and maintained in educational institutions, and that the state, therefore, has an interest and right in the organization of education.

But we believe also that the state has not the right to decide on matters affecting the spirit and trend of the school provided that in accordance with the standard of God's law they do not tend to harm and destroy the state. We believe also that the state must see to it that the instruction which is given is of good scientific standards; that the moulding of the child which takes place at school is also the moulding of a moral nature; and that all the essential virtues are fostered. We believe that in cases where the parents as natural guardians neglect their duty in relation to the school education of their children, the state, as the supreme guardian of all children, is entitled to take the initiative in the establishment of schools and retain it until such time as the parents decide to exercise their rights themselves.

6. The School

We believe that the schools receive the right and authority to give instruction and education from the parents, and that the schools, therefore, are bound to educate the children in accordance with the attitude to life and to the world of the parents as a community and as a national group. But we believe that the school must be in a position to carry out its function independently. While the home and the church decide on the spirit and trend of school education and the state determines the standard of such education and regulates the maintenance of equity in the schools, the school must at the same time be sovereign in its own sphere, and particularly in relation to the method of teaching and education; that is to say, it must take independent decisions with reference to the organization of the curriculum, the method of teaching, discipline, etc. We believe in the ideal of a Christian-National school.

7. Organization of the School System

We believe in the ideal of a system of Christian-National schools. In conformity with this, we reject in principle the domination of the school by the home, the church, or the state, and, therefore, also a system of parents' schools, or church schools or state schools. The school must be free to work in a spirit of self-determination and independence within the limits assigned to it. But freedom must not be conceived in a revolutionary sense; it must be freedom under authority. The establishment of schools must in the first place emanate from the community of parents in co-operation with the church and the state. The maintenance of schools must be a joint undertaking of the home, the church, and the state, and moreover in the following relation: the parents must contribute to the defraying of expenditure on schools; the church must lend financial aid to needy parents to perform tasks of educating their children; the state, being the authority to obtain financial means lawfully, must assume the main share in defraying expenditure on schools. The control of a school must, in the first instance, be vested in the parents. The church may exercise the necessary control only through the agency of the parents; but the state must see to it that the lawful division of rights is maintained between the parents, the church, and the state. Therefore, we believe that the school committees for individual schools have a right to exist. In the higher tribunals of schools control the community of parents must have its rightful place. In the school boards, representatives of the school committees (parents' councils) and of the state must have seats, but representatives of the teaching profession must also hold office on these boards. In the highest tribunals, namely the council for education for each province, the school boards, the state, and the teaching profession must be represented, but also educationists and other specialists. We believe that our ideal is and remains the Christian-National school, but we realize also that our task for the present at any rate is directly leavening the ordinary public schools through the medium of our Christian-National spirit and trend.

Article 9: The Teacher

1. We believe that the teacher acts for the parent in a representative capacity, and thereby we acknowledge the honourable status of the teacher. He must do the work of the parent, as the parent would have done it himself, if he were capable of doing it. The highest demand we make of the teacher, therefore, is that he must be a man with a Christian attitude to life and to the world without which he for us is nothing less than a most terrible danger. Next to this highest demand we stipulate that the teacher must be a personality, who can in all things take our place at school and who in all things serves as an example to our children. Therefore, we expect that the right men and women are also to be fully equipped for their life work.

2. We believe that our deputies should be properly trained for their task. In the institutions for training our teachers attention must be paid to the following demands: the young men and women must receive in the above-mentioned institutions a Christian attitude to life and to the world, based on science and systematized accordingly; they must be instructed in all the necessary sciences, but most particularly in educational science. We believe that their training can and will succeed only if, after proper selection, they are placed under the guidance of men and women who themselves, by conviction, have a Christian-National attitude to life, and have been trained on those lines. We, therefore, wish to see the institutions for the training of our teachers functioning as Christian and National institutions.

PART 2: OTHER TEACHING AND EDUCATION

Article 10: Infant Schools

We believe that it is the duty in the first place of the parent to bring up the preschool child in the Christian home and that he is not entitled to look to others to shoulder his responsibility and duty; but we accept the position that owing to the living conditions of many parents, especially of the underprivileged in the cities, they are forced to send their children to infant schools. We believe that the Christian and National attitude to life applies just as much to the infant schools as it does in the primary and secondary schools. We believe that religious instruction in accordance with the child's comprehension should form the most important part in the curriculum of the infant school. We believe that the medium of instruction in the infant school should be the mother tongue exclusively, and that in no circumstances may a foreign tongue be employed. We believe that teachers should be specially well trained and moulded people with a healthy Christian and National attitude to life and to the world. We believe that a managing body, elected by the parents, should be responsible for the appointment and supervision of the teachers concerned. We believe that the state is largely responsible for the financial burden.

Article 11: Higher Education

1. We believe that our higher education should have the same found-

ations as our primary and secondary education: the Christian-National attitude to life and to the world, and the moulding of God's people, fully equipped for every good work.

2. We believe that the content of our higher education must be scientific, but that it must be established on the basis of the Christian faith. Side by side with the ordinary secular sciences, therefore, we require that in our institutions for higher education, Christian doctrine shall also be taught and practised, and especially Christian philosophy. But we require still more; the teaching and practice of the secular sciences must start from the Christian attitude to life and to the world; the light of God's truth must not be absent from any single science. We believe that above all our university teaching should be thetic rather than antithetic; never purely eclectic. Nor must any attempt at reconciliation be made. Christian institutions must expound Christian science positively, contrast it with non-Christian science, but never give unco-ordinated instruction, merely choosing here and there, and they are not entitled to try to reconcile the fundamental opposites, or indeed to neutralize them; Creator and creation, man and animal, individual and society, authority and freedom remain in principle insoluble in one another. Even more than is the case in other spheres we believe that our university education can be fully adequate only if the right men and women are present at the head of our affairs. Professors and lecturers make the institution; their thought determines its spirit and trend. Therefore, we believe that university councils have no more important task than to appoint the right men and women for lecturers; the professors and lecturers must be convinced Christian and National scientists. For we believe finally in the existence and practice of the type of science which looks to Christian and National ideas for its guidance.

3. We believe that the control of our university institutions for higher education must be of such a nature that the Christian and National attitude to life and to the world shall have justice done to it in this sphere of education as well.

Article 12: Technical and Other Specialized Education

1. We believe that the Christian-National attitude to life and to the world is applicable in technical colleges, reform schools, high schools for domestic science, and schools for specialist instruction in the case of the deaf and the blind, and schools for physical and mental defectives, etc.

2. We believe that the aim of teaching in the technical and special schools is not merely to give knowledge and skill in technical subjects, and specialized instruction to the underprivileged, but also to convey the Christian and National cultural wealth of the nation in broader significance.

3. We believe that the mother tongue should be the medium of instruction in all the abovementioned schools, and that, therefore, there ought to be separate schools for those who speak Afrikaans and those who speak English.

4. We believe that these schools should not only be opened and/or closed with a religious service, but that religious teaching should form an

important part of their activities; and that adequate time and attention should be devoted to it, in order in this way to determine the Christian spirit and trend of all the activities.

5. We believe that the further content of the instruction must be adapted to the condition of our country and national needs.

6. We believe that there ought to be proper integration between the fields of activities of these schools and colleges and those of the ordinary secondary schools and university institutions.

7. We believe that the teachers should be Protestant Christians and bilingual South Africans.

8. We believe that the full period of training of pupils at industrial schools, reform schools, and technical high schools ought to secure recognition from trades unions in respect of apprenticeship.

9. Owing to the fact that the parents of children in industrial schools, reform schools, technical high schools, and high schools for domestic training for the most part are not in a position to elect a majority of the representatives for the control of these schools, we believe that a complete controlling body should be elected from and by the local community, wherever schools of this type may exist; from and by the Afrikaan community, a controlling body for an Afrikaans-medium school: from and by the English-speaking community for the English-medium school. We believe that the controlling body of the technical colleges should consist for a large part of parent representatives irrespective of other representatives in accordance with the statutory rights of the various colleges. We believe that the abovementioned controlling bodies should be invested not only with advisory powers, but also with such powers as are granted to school committees in terms of Article 8 of this directive.

Article 13: Instruction and Education of Adults

We believe that instruction and education constitute a continuous process and that there is a need for instruction and education of persons who have already left the existing teaching institutions. As far as Europeans are concerned, we believe that such instruction should be given with due observance of the principle of cultural *apartheid*, and that so far as Afrikaans-speaking citizens are concerned, it should be given on the basis of the Christian-National attitude to life and to the world of the Boer nation. We believe that the initiative with regard to the imparting of instruction to adults should be taken by the adults themselves, more particularly by their organized cultural groups; and that it is not the task and function of the state to have such instruction given by its Government authorities and forcibly to compel people to accept definite views and to imbue them with a definite spirit and trend. In agreement with the principles already expressed in Article 8(5) of this directive, we believe that it is indeed the task of the state to stimulate the education of adults, and in a large measure to make available the Government must also see to it that instruction given to adults in accordance with the criterion of God's law is not calculated to harm the state or endanger it.

Article 14: Instruction and Education of Coloureds

We believe that the instruction of Coloured people should be regarded as a subdivision of the vocation and task of the Afrikaner to Christianize the non-European races of our country. We accept the principle of trustee-ship of the non-European by the European, and particularly by the Afrikaners. This trusteeship imposes on the Afrikaner the solemn duty of seeing that the Coloured people are educated in accordance with Christian and National principles. So far as Christian-National principles are concerned the same remarks as were made earlier in this connection are, *mutatis mutandis*, applicable. We believe that the Coloured man can and only be truly happy when he has been Christianized and that he will be proof against his own heathen ideology and all sorts of foreign ideologies which promise him pseudo-happiness, but leave him in the long run dissatisfied and unhappy. In regard to the National principle we believe that the previous remarks made in this connection can and should be applied, *mutatis mutandis*, to the Coloured people. We believe that he can be made race-conscious if the principle of *apartheid* is strictly applied in teaching just as it is in his church life. Further we believe that it is essential to stress the principle of the mother tongue as a medium of teaching in the case of the Coloured people. We believe that the welfare and happiness of the Coloured man rests upon his realizing that he belongs to a separate racial group, that he will be proud of it, and that he will be educated on Christian and National lines in accordance with this conception. The financing of Coloured education must be placed on such a basis that it is not provided at the cost of European education.

Article 15: The Teaching and Education of Natives

We believe that the education and task of white South Africa with respect to the native is to Christianize him and to help him on culturally, and this vocation and task has found its immediate application and task in the principles of trusteeship, no placing of the native on the level of the white, and in segregation. For this reason we believe that any system of teaching and educating natives should be based on these principles. In accordance with these principles we believe that the teaching and education of the native must be based on the European's attitude to life and to the world, more particularly that the Boer nation is the senior European trustee of the native; and that the native should be led, *mutatis mutandis*, to an acceptance of the Christian and National principles in education as these principles are more fully described in Articles 1, 2, and 3, provided it is an independent acceptance. We believe also that the mother tongue is the basis for instruction and education, but that the two official languages of the country should be learned as subjects because they are official languages of the country and constitute for the native the keys for that adoption of culture which is necessary for his own cultural advancement. Because of the cultural immaturity of the native, we believe that it is the duty and task of the state in co-operation with the Christian Protestant churches to provide and superintend education for natives. We believe, however, that the actual teaching and education of natives and the training of native teachers should be undertaken by the natives themselves as soon as possible and under the control and guidance of the state; with the proviso that the financing of native education be placed on such a basis that it is not provided at the cost of European education. Finally, we believe that instruction and education for natives must lead to the development of a native community on Christian-National lines which is self-supporting and provides for itself in all ways.

Index

Act of Union, 37, 137, 142

Afrikaans: establishment of, *see* Language; newspapers in, 24, 98–9, 111, 178–80

Afrikaanse Taal, 81, 90, 262

Afrikaans Nasionale Kultuurraad (ANK), 91

Afrikaner Bond (1879), 24–7, 29, 35–6

Afrikaner Broederbond (AB), 76–87; aims and objects of, 70, 78, 83, 118, 128, 135, 257–9, 277–84; chain of influence, 84, 251; establishment of, 40, 46–7; Hertzog's Smithfield address on, 44, 77, 243–56; initiation into, 259–60, 285–7; membership and leaders, 109, 126, 167, 259; Military Intelligence report on, 79–80, 257–76; organizations controlled by, 128–9, 264–5, 272; propaganda, 270–1; secret Manual, 251–3; structure of, 82–3, 251, 260–1

Afrikaner Front, 128–9

Afrikaner Party, 60, 67, 75, 82, 135–9

Afrikaner Rebellion (1914), 40, 44–7, 76, 114, 118, 178

Anglo-Boer War, *see* Boer War

Apartheid, 149–68; AB's aim, 78, 299; books on, 164; Church's opinion on, 115–16, 152; in practice, 166, 177; legislation on, 151, 157, 163, 166; Nationalists' programme of, 60, 75, 136, 140, 149, 156, 158; practical difficulties, 159–63, 178; resistance to, 149, 155, 162; theory of, 151, 155–7

Argentina, 87, 271, 282

Asians: legislation on, 163, 166

Bailey, Sir Abe, 35

Balfour, Lord, 34

Balfour Declaration, 44, 51–2, 54, 56

Bamangwato tribe, 23

Bantu Authorities Acts, 157–8, 163

Bantu Education Act, 104, 157

Bantustans, 154–5, 157

Barlow, Arthur, 53n.

Basson, Japie, 141, 164

Basutoland, Basutos, 9n., 12, 38, 52, 154

Basuto War, 15, 16

Batavian Republic, 6

Bechuanaland, 23, 38, 52, 154

Beinart, B.. 146

Berg River Valley, 4

Beyers, Gen. C. F., 45–6

Blackout, 105

Black Shirts, 63, 65

Bloemfontein, 38; CNE conference at, 100; Convention (1854), 10–11; DRC meeting, 152; Economic Congress, 85, 93; municipal elections, 270; National Party conferences, 44, 47–8, 59, 81–2, 135, 255, 268; NP offices, 123, 125; newspaper, 98–9; Smuts speaks on AB at, 77; student organization, 107

Blood River, 9, 97, 262

Bloukrans, 9, 93

Boerenasie, 42, 86, 174, 178–9

Boer Rebellion, *see* Afrikaner Rebellion

Boer War, 5, 7, 9, 11, 16, 20–1, 25–9, 33–7, 39, 40, 45–6, 49, 76, 98, 114, 118, 160

Boshoff, J. J., 163, 172

Botha, Gen. Louis, 26, 29, 35–6, 38, 40–8, 54, 76, 98, 117, 144, 150, 174

Brand, J. H., 12, 13, 21, 25–6, 29

Brebner, 60

British: arrival of, in S. Africa, 3–6, 11;

efforts to anglicize Boers, 7, 11, 35, 39–41

British Kaffraria, 9, 14n.

British S. Africa Co., 23

Broadcasting Corp. (SABC), 88, 96, 167, 270

Brown Shirts, 63, 65

Bryce, Sir J., 12, 20

Burger, Die, 47, 61, 98–100, 110, 251

Burgers, T. F., 15, 25

Bushmen, 3, 5

Bywoners (squatters), 49–50

Cairo, 18, 23

Calvinism, 3, 5, 10, 100, 110–12, 147

Campbell-Bannerman, Sir Henry, 34

Cape Colony: British settlers, 4–15, 21, 49; Church established (NGK), 113; coloured governor of, 116; Dutch arrive in, 3–4, 23–8; self-government of, 23, 33, 35

Cape Coloureds, 7–8, 138, 141–3, 157, 163–4, 169, 171

Cape Province: African voters, 144; Church in, 114; education, 267; Nationalists gain power in, 55–7

Cape Times, 64, 66

Cape Town, 4, 10, 38, 96, 98, 123, 252; university, 104, 109, 146

Carnarvon, Lord, 14, 15, 23–4, 29

Carnegi Commission, 93

Carter, Gwendolen M., 78

Censorship, 146–7, 167

Chamberlain, Joseph, 18, 27, 175

Charter of Justice (1828), 7

Chinese workers, 33–6

Christian-National Education (CNE), 42, 84–6, 95–6, 100–9, 127–8, 140; Institute's outline of, 288–301

Cilliers, Andries, 151

Civil Service, 269–70

Coetzee, Chris, 105, 108

Color Bar Act, 151

Commonwealth Prime Ministers' Conference (1961), 173–4

Communism, 167–8, 174

Crafford, F. S., 19, 46, 61

Creswell, F. H. P., 34–5, 40, 45, 47–51, 53

Creswell Memorandum, 51

Cronje, G., 147

Cultural organizations, 90–2

Davie, T. B., 109

de Kiewiet, Cornelius W., 7, 21, 27, 39

de Klerk, Jan, 95

Delagoa Bay, 19, 21, 26

de la Rey, Gen. J. H., 45–6

Delayed Action, 116, 141, 164

Delius, Anthony, 78, 83

de Villiers, Sir Henry, 37

de Wet, General, 44, 46

De Wildt, 44, 85

Diamonds, 11–13, 17–18, 23

Diederichs, Nicolaas, 81, 93–5, 107, 126, 128, 151, 262–4, 272

Dingaan, Chief, 9

Disraeli, Benjamin, 15, 18

Dominion Party, 54, 57, 135

Dönges, Theophilus E., 60, 90, 93, 125, 151

Draft Constitution, 34, 69–73, 75

Duncan, Sir Patrick, 52–3, 59

du Plessis, D. A. C., 80, 261

du Plessis, Louis J., 77–80, 82, 85, 93, 128, 247–50, 264, 267

du Plessis, Otto, 68–70, 75, 170

du Plessis, Wentzel C., 82

Durban, 10, 37, 99, 123

Dutch East India Co., 4–5, 7, 28, 40, 49

Dutch Reformed Church (DRC), 110–16; in education, 42, 100, 295; Jews attacked by, 61, 63; organization of, 113; reports on AB, 77, 80, 86; segregation upheld, 115–16, 152; support for Afrikanerdom, 128, 135, 179; three groups of, 12, 90, 105

du Toit, Rev. C. W., 250

du Toit, Daniel François, 25–6, 28, 35, 57, 117

du Toit, Jacob Daniel, 133n.

du Toit, Rev. Stephanus, 15–16, 24

du Toit, Rev. W. J., 41–2

East London, 10

Economic Conference, 93–4

Economic Institute, 92–5, 97, 110, 128, 135

Education, 36, 38–9, 41–2, 80, 100–6, 127; Act of 1960, 103; for Africans, 103–4, 157, 300–1; for Asians, 103; for Coloureds, 103, 300; influence of AB on, 254–6, 265–9, 288–301; Roman Catholic schools, 101, 104

Eiselen, Werner, 151–2
Erasmus, Rev. D. F., 128

Fagan, Henry Allan, 162, 166
Farmers' Defence Soc., 24–5
Farrar, Sir George, 35
Federation of Afrikaner Cultural Organizations (FAK), 80–2, 85, 87–100, 102, 105, 107–9, 123, 128–9, 135, 158, 171, 246, 262, 265, 270–4, 282, 289; branches of, 90–2; main activities, 96–8; organization of, 91
Fick, Albert, 78
First Boer War, 16–17, 25
First World War, 45–6, 48–9, 58, 114, 118, 133
Fish River, 6, 7
Fitzpatrick, Sir James, 14, 35
Flag Bill, 53, 170
Fort Hare, 104
Fourie, Japie, 46
Fraser, Sir John, 35, 38
Freemasonry, 79, 82, 260, 280
Frere, Sir Bartle, 14n.
Fusion Government, 51–7, 60, 117, 150

Gandhi, Mahatma, 4
George VI, King, 133
Germans in Africa, 9, 17, 23, 64–5, 82
Germany, 41, 45, 58, 81 (see also Nazism)
Germiston, 43, 270
Geyser, A. S., 116
Gladstone, E. W., 16
Gladstone, Viscount, 38
Gold-mining, 12–13, 17–18, 20, 23, 26, 29, 34, 94, 134, 161
Graaf, Sir de Villiers, 26, 110
Grahamstown, 6
Grand Rapids (Mich.), 156
Great Depression, 118
Great Trek, 5–11, 28–9, 178
Grey, Sir George, 11
Griqualand West, 13, 23
Griquas, 9, 12, 13
Gross, Felix, 5, 13, 171
Greybe, Mr, 80
Grey Shirts, 63–5
Grobler, P. G. W., 160
Grobler, W. S. J., 98, 123
Groot Schuur, 63

Group Areas Act, 157, 163

Hartman, Anton, 96
Havenga, Nicolaas C., 53, 60, 67, 75, 82, 115, 125, 129, 135–6, 138–9, 271
Heidelberg College, 108
Hepple, Alex, 78, 85–6, 93, 95
Herenigde Nasionale Volksparty (HNP), 35–6, 59, 65, 67, 70, 80, 82, 109, 135, 262–3, 268, 270–4
Hertzog, Dr Albert, 79, 88, 93, 95, 126, 167, 270, 272
Hertzog, Gen. J. B. M.: advocates equal language rights, 42–3; advocates neutrality in 1939 war, 58; alliance with Smuts, 51–7; attitude to the AB, 77–9, 81–4, 87, 109, 243–58, 262–3, 266–9, 273–6; becomes Prime Minister, 38, 51, 57, 169; develops National Party, 40–61; favours republic; 46, 51; hon. member of Afrikaner Party, 67; joins HNP, 59; leader of Orange Union, 35–6; spheres of influence, 98–100; split with Botha, 43–5
Hertzog Act, 42
Hertzog-Creswell Pact, 45, 47–51, 53, 80, 117, 138, 150
Hicks Beach, Sir Michael, 15
Hitler, Adolf, 60, 63, 67–9, 75, 118, 126, 128
Hofmeyr, Jan Hendrik, 16, 24–7, 29, 35–6, 41, 53, 57, 98, 117
Holm (broadcaster), 263, 279
Hottentots, 3–5, 7–8, 50
Houghton, D. Hobart, 164
Huddleston, Trevor, 100

Immigration policy (S.A.), 11
Immorality Acts, 151, 157
Indians, 10, 50, 73, 92, 157, 163, 168
International Committee of Jurists, 164
Inene (town), 80

James, William, 126
Jameson, Dr L. S., 27, 36, 38, 86
Jameson Raid, 27
Jansen, Ernest, 151
Jews, 60–6, 111, 280
Johannesburg, 20, 23, 37, 46, 63, 79–80, 90–4, 98–9, 115, 123, 151

Jonker, A. H., 105
Joubert, Petris J., 15, 16

Kaffirland, 9
Kaffir Wars, 7, 11
Keet, Prof. B. B., 164
Kellogg-Briand Pact, 56
Kemp, Gen. Jan, 46
Keppel-Jones, Arthur, 166
Kestell, Rev. J. D., 93, 264
Khama, Chief, 23
Kimberley, 12n., 13
Kimberley, Lord, 14
Kipling, Rudyard, 175
Kitchener of Khartoum, Earl, 175
Klopper, H. J., 80–1, 261–2
Kok, Adam, 9, 12
Kosi Bay, 21
Kotze, J. G., 27
Kruger, Rev. J. D., 128
Kruger, J. J., 88
Kruger, 'Oom' Paul: character and habits, 18–21; fights for Afrikaner nationalism, 15–17, 23, 25–9, 35, 117, 160, 179; last words, 173; statue of, 97–8
Kruger, Siena, 19
Kuhn, C., 108

Laas, Col. J. C. C., 65–6, 81, 262
Labor Party (S.A.), 34–5, 45, 47–51, 53–5, 78, 135, 138
Language: theories and restrictions, 24–5, 28–9, 34–5, 38, 42, 57, 76, 82, 85, 96, 102–4, 140, 268, 288–9, 293; present controversy, 272–4
Lawrence, Harry G., 65, 278
League of Nations, 47, 56, 58, 133
Leibbrandt, Robey, 64
le Roux, Stephen, 250, 252
Liberal Party, 141, 144, 166
Lichtenstein, M. H. K., 5
Livingstone, David, 23
Lloyd George, David, 47
Lombard, Ivanhoe Makepiece, 77, 79–80, 83–4, 86–7, 89, 91, 96, 98, 128, 246, 258, 265, 272, 277, 281–3
Louw, Eric, 61
Louw, M. S., 94, 139

Macmillan, Harold, 171, 174
Madely, W. B., 135

Majuba Hill, 16, 96
Malan, Dr Daniel F., accepts Afrikaner Front Declaration, 128–9; career of, 110; *Draft for a Republic*, 70–1, 73; introduced flag Bill, 53; joins Havenga, 75; National Party of, 40, 44–5, 51, 114–15, 117, 119, 135–6, 138–9; policy and aims, 26, 43, 46–7, 54–68, 98, 107, 126, 144, 169, 173; Prime Minister, 38, 125–6, 138–9, 142, 152; relations with Hertzog, 82, 243–5, 249–50; supports the AB, 81
Malan, M. P. A., 125
Malherbe, E. G., 42
Marais, Prof. Ben, 164
Maree, W., 125
Maritain, Jacques, 180
Maritz, General, 46
Marquard, Leo, 54, 77–8, 102, 107, 111, 113
Matabele, 9
Merriman, John X., 20, 36, 144
Meyer, P. J., 88, 91, 107, 167
Millin, J., 64
Millin, Sarah Gertrude, 6, 26, 56
Milner, Sir Alfred (afterwards Lord), 7, 20, 27, 33–6, 39–42, 100, 102, 175
Mines and Works Act, 49, 151
Mineworkers' Union, 86, 95, 272
Missionaries, 6, 9, 23, 110–11
Mixed Marriages Act, 157
Molteno, John C., 14
Mombasa, 115
Mosesh, 9, 12
Mozambique, 21
Munger, Edwin S., 114
Music Committee, 96
Mussolini, Benito, 69, 73

Natal: church in, 113; early days, 9–10, 13–15, 21, 26; education, 101, 103, 106, 266; elections, 37–9, 55; flag, compromise over, 53; Indians in, 50; National Convention (1908), 37; pro-British attitude, 34, 36, 101, 144; Provincial Council, 167; university, 42, 104
Natalia, republic of, 8
National anthem, 170
National Conservative Party, 141
National Party, 117–29; Malan's 'puri-

fied', see Purified Nationalists; merges with Afrikaner Party, 138–40; new laws, 146; organization of, 118–26; parliamentary evolution of, 141–5; pledge, 126; Programme of Principles, 126–7; publications, 68–75; relations with church, 114–15; steering committee, 124–5; three major objectives, 177

National Union Party, 141, 164

Native Land Acts, 151

Native reserves, 153 (maps)

Naude, Rev. Bertie, 80, 261

Nazism, 58–75, 81, 114, 133, 262–3, 276, 279

Neame, L. E., 158

Netherlands Reformed Church (NGK), 111–16

New Order, 43, 63, 66–70, 75, 118, 128–9, 135, 170, 271

Nicol, Rev. William, 80

North, Lord, 60

Nylstroom, 43

Olivier, N. J. J., 170

Oosthuizen, A. J. G., 115

Orange, Prince of, 6

Orange Free State: Church in, 113–14; early days of, 8, 10–13, 15–16, 21, 26, 47; education, 41–2, 103, 255–6, 266, 268; Nationalists, 54–5, 57, 125; university, 104, 106

Orange River, 8, 9, 13

Orange River Colony, 33–5, 37, 43

Orange River Sovereignty, 9–10

Orange Union, 35–6

Ossewa-Brandwag (OB), 63, 65–9, 75, 81–2, 97, 107, 118–19, 128–9, 135, 139, 260, 262, 271, 274, 276

Ossewa Trek, 97

Oudtshoorn, 254

Paarl, 24, 108

Pact Government, see Hertzog-Creswell pact

Pan-African Congress, 178

Pannevis, Arnoldus, 24

Pass laws, 158, 167–8, 171

Passports, 167

Pauw, Samuel, 105

People's Party, see Herenigde Nasionale Volksparty

Philadelphia, 37, 39

Philip, John, 6

Pietermaritzburg, 8

Pirow, Oswald, 43, 46, 55–6, 66–8, 75, 82, 135

Pistorius, V. L., 164

Police force, 167–8, 269

Pondo tribe, 9, 150

'Poor whites', 49–50, 93

Population Registration Act, 157

Port Elizabeth, 6, 10, 99

Portugal, Portuguese, 17, 19, 23, 179

Potchefstroom, 46; university, 79, 100, 104–6, 108, 114, 247, 258

Potgieter, Andries Hendrik, 9

Press, 98–100; censorship of, 146–7; on AB activities, 78

Pretoria: annexed by Shepstone, 14; capital city, 19, 38; cathedral, 113, 160; conferences and meetings, 16, 57, 65, 96, 115, 122–3, 158, 244; coup d'état fails, 45–6; university, 87, 108, 114, 164, 271–2, 283; Voortrekker centenary celebrations, q.v.

Pretoria, Bishop of, 6

Pretorius, Andries, 9

Pretorius, Marthinus, 16

Progressive Party, 36, 39, 141, 144

Promotion of Bantu Self-government Act, 163

Publications and Entertainments Bill, 146–7

'Purified' Nationalists, 40, 45–6, 51, 117, 138, 244, 248, 250–3, 262

Rand Daily Mail, 70, 88, 140

Rand Revolt, 49, 151 (see also Witwatersrand)

Reddingsdaadbond (RDB); Rescue Action Assoc.), 80, 85, 87, 92–5, 97, 110, 128–9, 135, 264–5

Reeves, Bishop, 149

Reitz, Deneys, 53

Reitz, Francis W., 26–7

Representation of Natives Act, 151

Republican Order, 70

Republican Thanksgiving Feast, 97, 172

Retief, Piet, 8, 9, 97–8

Reyneke, Rev. J., 113, 160

Rhodes, Cecil, 15, 18–19, 21, 23, 26–7, 86, 144, 171, 175

Rhodesia, 18, 37–8
Rhodes university, 104, 164
Roberts, Earl, 175
Robertson, NP Congress at, 244
Roos, T. J. de Villiers, 47, 53–4
Rousseau, J.-J., 111
Roux, General, 114
Ruiterwag, 88; initiation ceremony, 285–7

Sabotage Act, 168
Sampson, H. W., 35
Sand River Convention, 10, 11
Sanlam Corporation, 94
Schoeman, B. J., 95, 158, 161
Scholtz, G. D., 99, 175–6
Schreiner, W. P., 27, 144
Second World War, 44, 58, 81–2, 114, 118, 126, 129, 133
Selborne, Lord, 34, 36
Senate Act, 142–3
Serfontein, J. J., 125, 158
Sharpeville, 171, 176
Shepstone, Theophilus, 14–15
Simonstown, 25
Slagtersnek Rebellion, 8
Slavery, abolition of, 6, 7
Smartt, Sir Thomas, 45
Smith, Sir Harry, 9–10
Smithfield, 263; Hertzog's address at, 77, 243–56
Smuts, Jan Christian, 37–41, 44–50, 53–61, 64, 75–7; allied with Botha, 26, 29, 35, 40; allied with Hertzog, 53–8, 81, 109, 262; denounces the AB, 77, 277–8; in opposition to Hertzog, 47–8, 59; 1st world war, 47, 133–5; 2nd world war, 64, 82, 87, 98, 258; moderate policy of, 29, 46, 150, 169, 174; Prime Minister, 38, 47–9, 117, 144; death of, 125
Snijders, H. J. C., 172
Social and Economic Policy, 69, 73–4
Society of True Afrikaners, 24
Solomon, E. P., 35
Solomon, Harry, 35
Somerset, Lord Charles, 7
Somerset West, 57
Sons of England, 79, 82, 280
Sothos, 104
South Africa: Constitution (1910),

37–9; Constitution (1960), 173; internal difficulties, 178; Prime Ministers, 38, 40; union of, 29, 33, 36–40, 174; university, 105; republic declared, 97, 169–76; world criticism, 179
South Africa Act, 14, 38, 142–3
South African Bureau of Race Relations (SABRA), 151–2, 158, 170
South African League, 26
South African Republic (Transvaal), 8, 10–11, 16, 18, 47
South Africa Party (SAP), 36, 39, 43–8, 50–1, 53–5, 57, 109, 117
Southwest Africa, 17, 23, 46–7, 64, 94, 118, 123, 134, 139, 141, 167, 171
Spengler, Oswald, 68
Stallard, Col. Charles F., 54, 57, 135, 151
Status of the Union Act, 52, 56–7, 169
Steenkamp, Anna, 8
Stellenbosch, 4, 96; university, 61, 87, 104–5, 114, 151–2, 164, 170, 263, 283
Steyn, Fritz, 92–3
Steyn, Marthinus, 20, 27, 29, 44–7, 64
Strauss, 26
Strijdom, J. G., 26, 38, 44, 46, 57, 86, 95, 98, 100, 106, 115, 117, 125–6, 138–9, 144, 173, 250; on apartheid, 149, 155–6, 160
Strikes, 48, 178, 270
Stubbs, Ernest, 161
Student organizations, 63, 81, 90, 107–9, 262
Suiderstem, Die, 66
Sunday Times, 70, 86, 88, 99, 279
Supremacy of Parliament Act, 142
Suzman, Arthur, 137
Swart, Charles Robbert, 57, 59, 60, 64, 125, 133, 136, 139, 142n., 250
Swaziland, 21, 38, 52, 154

Taute, Professor Ben, 269
Thom, H. B., 87, 105
Tomlinson Report, 152–5, 163
Torch Commando, 67, 137
Trade Unions, 78, 95–6
Transkei, 155
Transvaal: as Boer republic, 8–29, 50; church in, 113–14, 116; crown colony, 33–5, 37, 47; education, 41–2, 103–4, 266–7; mines, 13, 20, 23; Nationalists of, 55, 57, 118–25, 127;

political parties organized, 35; Progressive Assoc., 35
Transvaler, Die, 61, 64, 70, 77, 85, 88, 98–100, 127–8, 175, 280
Trek Festival (1938), 93
Truth Legion, 82, 284
'Two-stream' policy, 42–3, 109, 141

Uitlanders, 13, 19–21, 26–7, 29, 35–6, 69, 160
Uitvoerende Raad (UR), 82–3
Union Flag Bill, 53–4
United Nations Assoc., 133–4
United South Africa National Party, 51, 54, 57, 60, 133–9, 138; new offshoots of (1959), 141
Universities, 104–8 (*see also* Education)

Vaal River, 8–10, 13, 20
Vaderland, Die, 95, 98–100, 244, 270–1
van der Merwe, N. J., 80, 89, 244, 250, 261
van der Stel, Simon, 116
van der Spuy, Rev. J. P., 128
van der Wath, J. G., 125
van der Watt, P. J., 162
van Eeden, Bernardus, 151
van Rensburg, J. F. J. (Hans), 63, 65–8, 81–2, 107, 128, 139, 262
van Rhyn, A. J., 92–3, 250
van Riebeeck, Jan, 41, 97–8, 112, 116, 170
van Rooy, D. J., 174
van Rooy, Prof. J. C., 78, 87, 100, 158, 246–8, 258, 270, 277, 288
Venter, C. N., 112
Vereeniging: celebrations at, 174, 176; Treaty of, 29, 34, 38, 41–3, 46–7, 171, 174
Versailles, Treaty of, 47
Verwoerd, Dr Hendrik F.: and the AB, 88; on *apartheid*, 106, 151–2, 154–5, 162, 164; attempt on life, 110, 112;

declares republic, 73, 172–4; National Party of, 93, 117, 125–6, 138–9, 144; Nazi sympathies, 64; newspapers of, 99–100; policies of, 26, 46, 98; Prime Minister, 38, 95, 171; on unity of Boer and British, 146, 178
Victoria East, 9
Visser, C. F., 269
Visser, T. C., 73, 76
Volksblad, Die, 68, 98–100, 162, 170, 243, 251
Volkskas, 87, 92, 95, 262, 264–5, 282
Voortrekkers, 4–5, 8–12, 23, 28, 68, 98, 109, 269; centenary, 60, 65, 81–97, 260, 262; monument to, 97, 172
Vorster, Rev. J. D., 63, 65, 109, 114
Vredefort, 80

Walker, Eric A., 136
Waterboer, Andries, 9, 13
Waterboer, Nicholas, 13
Webb, Rev. J. B., 157
Weichardt, L. T., 64
Wellington training college, 108
Westminster, Statute of, 44, 52, 54, 56–7, 169
White Workers' Protection Assoc., 85–6, 95
Windhoek, 64, 123, 141
Witwatersrand (The Rand), 20, 27, 48–9, 65, 95, 122–3; university, 104, 272
Wonderfontein, 16
World, The, 178, 180
World Council of Churches, 115–16

Xhosa, 104, 150, 155

Young Turks, 44–5, 55
Youth organizations, 64, 90, 109, 120, 122–3, 269

Zululand, Zulus, 9, 17, 104, 150
Zulu Rebellion (1906), 36
Zulu War (1877), 15, 97